Reco izing the ... nce
... S, ...

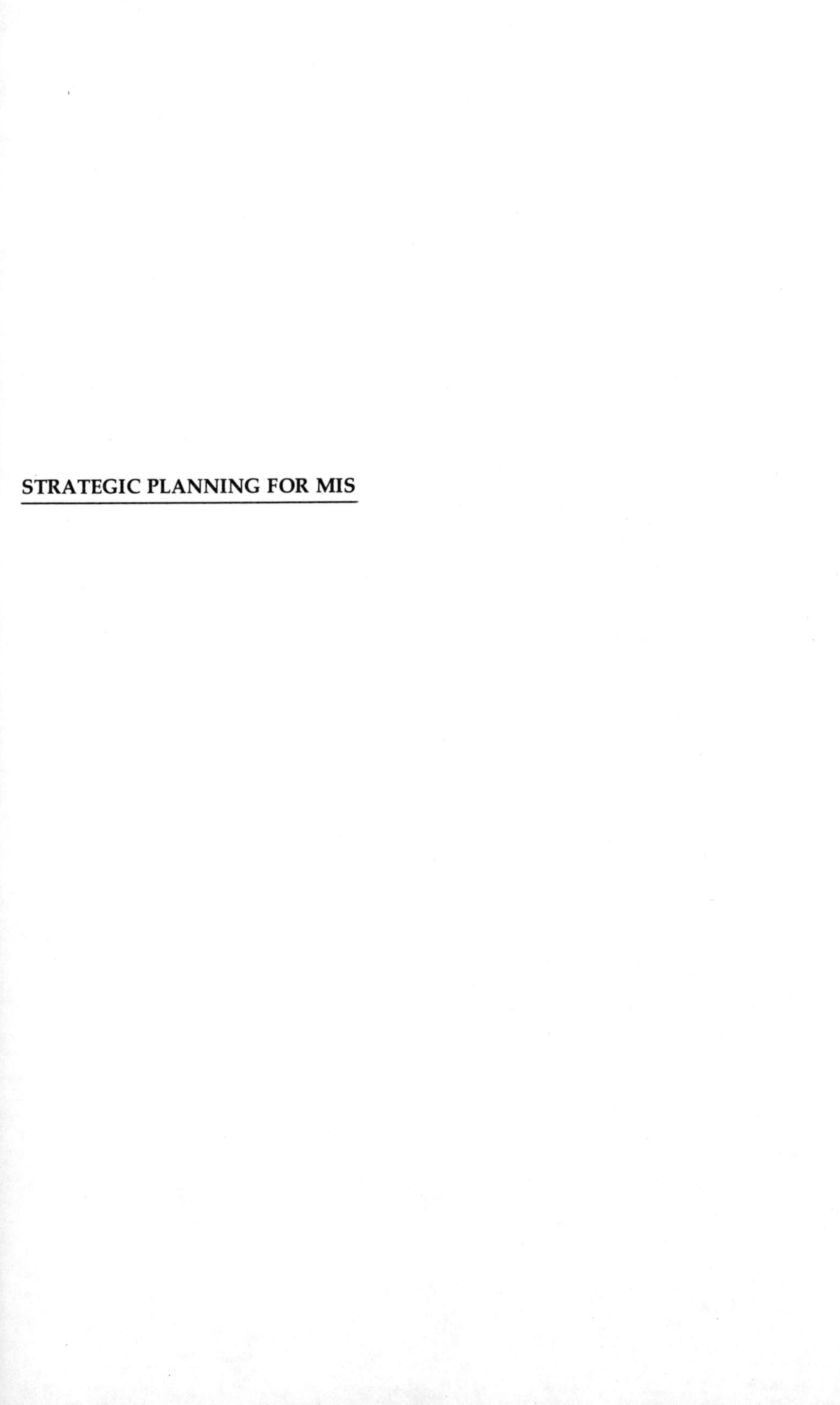

STRATEGIC PLANNING FOR MIS

Strategic Planning for MIS

EPHRAIM R. McLEAN

University of California, Los Angeles

JOHN V. SODEN

McKinsey & Company, Inc.

With a Special Contribution by George A. Steiner

A WILEY-INTERSCIENCE PUBLICATION

JOHN WILEY & SONS, New York • London • Sydney • Toronto

This publication is designed to provide accurate and authoritative information in regard to the subject matter covered. It is sold with the understanding that the publisher is not engaged in rendering legal, accounting, or other professional service. If legal advice or other expert assistance is required, the services of a competent professional person should be sought.
From a Declaration of Principles jointly adopted by a Committee of the American Bar Association and a Committee of Publishers.

Library of Congress Cataloging in Publication Data:

Main entry under title:

Strategic planning for MIS.

Papers of a conference held at the University of California, Los Angeles, in 1974 and sponsored by McKinsey & Company and the UCLA Graduate School of Management.
"A Wiley Interscience publication."
Includes bibliographical references and index.
1. Management information systems—Congresses.
I. McLean, Ephraim R. II. Soden, John V.
III. McKinsey and Company. IV. California. University. University at Los Angeles. Graduate School of Management.

T58.6.S76 658.4'03 76-58483
ISBN 0-471-58562-9

Printed in the United States of America

10 9 8 7 6 5 4 3 2

Foreword

This is a much needed state-of-the-art book on long-range planning for computer-based information services. Although a few other books and articles have dealt with long-range planning for information services, this one is unique in its accumulation of actual operating experience.

The introduction of computer-based information systems in organizations has developed with astonishing speed during the past decade and a half. During this period there have been several fundamental conceptual and operational changes in these systems. A decade ago, for instance, some misguided zealots were searching for a single integrated management information system (MIS). They failed, of course. Now, conceptually and operationally, we see different interrelated information systems throughout organizations, especially the larger ones.

Years ago computer-based information systems were considered to be new tools or techniques for managerial decision making. Today it is recognized that they are interwoven into the entire process of management.

Coinciding with these fundamental trends have been others more directly connected with planning. First, managers and staffs of information services departments and groups have recognized a pressing need for long-range planning of their activities. Second, they have seen the importance of interrelating these plans with comprehensive corporate planning systems. The two developments have paralleled each other.

The evolution of these planning systems has not been smooth. We have learned the hard way that corporate planning systems must be tailored to the unique characteristics of each organization. As a consequence, there is no one best way to set up a long-range corporate planning system. Furthermore, any system, no matter how satisfactory it is considered to be, will inevitably change as circumstances change. Thus long-range information services planning, too, must be matched with the circumstances existing in each organization and must alter with evolving conditions.

We are still learning how to do better corporate long-range and information services planning. Nevertheless, we know today many of the processes which are most likely to produce effective plans. We also know much more about what not to do, if effective plans are to be achieved. This book is a rich mine of information for those who want such knowledge.

This book fills a gap in the literature about lessons of experience and current practice in making effective long-range information services plans. Thus it should be examined and studied by top managers who guide and direct such planning; management information managers and staff experts who should be deeply involved in long-range planning; staffs in other functional areas such as planning, finance, and marketing; professional consultants in the field; and academic scholars interested in the subject.

Those who read this book carefully and profit from the experience it contains will avoid "snarking" their information systems, to use a word coined by Lewis Carroll in "The Hunting of The Snark":

> This was charming, no doubt: but they
> shortly found out
> That the Captain they trusted so well
> Had only one notion for crossing the
> ocean,
> And that was to tingle his bell.
> He was thoughtful and grave—but the
> orders he gave
> Were enough to bewilder a crew.
> When he cried 'Steer to starboard, but
> keep her head larboard!'
> What on earth was the helmsman to do?
> Then the bowsprit got mixed with the
> rudder sometimes:
> A thing, as the Bellman remarked,
> That frequently happens in tropical climes,
> When a vessel is, so to speak, "snarked."

But the principal failing occurred in
the sailing,
And the Bellman perplexed and distressed,
Said he had hoped, at least, when the
wind blew due East
That the ship would not travel due West!

GEORGE A. STEINER

Los Angeles, California
July 1976

Acknowledgments

We would like to express our considerable thanks to the management consulting firm of McKinsey & Company, Inc., and in particular to Jack O. Vance, managing director of the firm's Los Angeles office, for providing the motivation and financial support that made possible the conference on long-range planning for information systems and thus this book. Also we wish to thank the UCLA Graduate School of Management and the GSM Office of Executive Education for acting as host for the conference, and we appreciate the efforts of Miss Maddie Contreras as conference program assistant.

In planning for the conference and in assisting in its deliberations, Prof. George A. Steiner, of the Graduate School of Management, was of immense help, with able participation by Prof. Richard O. Mason. Similarly, Charles C. Tucker and George M. Crandell, associates in the Los Angeles office of McKinsey & Company, played major roles in the conference, particularly with regard to the preparation and evaluation of the survey in which the conferees participated. And, of course, the conference itself would not have been possible without the interest and active participation on the part of the MIS executives who gave freely of their time and energies to attend the conference and to prepare the papers that appear in Parts II through IV.

As our efforts shifted from the conduct of the conference to the preparation of this book, Mrs. Del Sims and her colleagues in the Los Angeles office of McKinsey proved to be our mainstay. Her patience with our scribbled notes, her many hours of transcribing our ideas into typescript, and her general quiet competence were everywhere evident.

Finally, we must thank our respective families, who accepted our long absences with forebearance and who welcomed us home with surprising good cheer.

EPHRAIM R. McLEAN
JOHN V. SODEN

Los Angeles, California
New York, New York
July 1976

Contents

Conference Participants Planning for Information Services

April 10–11, 1974

Graduate School of Management
University of California, Los Angeles

Mr. Roger W. Barbey, Manager
Information Development
Pacific Gas and Electric Company
245 Market Street
San Francisco, California 94106

Morris F. Collen, M.D., Director
Medical Methods Research
The Permanente Medical Group
3779 Piedmont Avenue
Oakland, California 94611

Mr. Anthony J. Craine, Director
Management Services
CIBA–GEIGY Corporation
Ardsley, New York 10502

Mr. John R. Frey, Director
Computer Services
Consumers Power Company
212 West Michigan Avenue
Jackson, Michigan 49201

Mr. Jack B. Gearhart, Vice President and Director,
Management Systems
TRW Systems Group
One Space Park
Redondo Beach, California 90278

Mr. Alan H. Gepfert, Manager
Management Sciences Programs Department
Mobil Oil Corporation
150 East 42nd Street
New York, New York 10017

Mr. John C. Gilbert, Director
Management Information Systems
Headquarters, U. S. Army Material Command
Department of the Army
5001 Eisenhower Avenue
Alexandria, Virginia 22304

Mr. F. A. Gitzendanner, Manage
Information Systems Development
Information Services Management
Management Sciences Department
Standard Oil Company (Indiana)
P. O. Box 5910 A
200 East Randolph Drive
Chicago, Illinois 60680

Mr. George Glaser, President
American Federation of Information
Processing Societies
225 Warren Road
San Mateo, California 94402

Mr. Kent H. Gould, Chief
EDP Control and Development
Department of Finance
State of California
1025 P. Street, Room 199
Sacramento, California 95814

Mr. Charles L. Hampton, Director
Division of Data Processing
Board of Governors of the Federal Reserve
System
20th Street and Constitutional Avenue
Washington, D. C. 20551

Dr. Richard O. Mason
Associate Professor of Information Systems
Assistant Dean, Professional Masters
Program
Graduate School of Management
University of California
Los Angeles, California 90024

Dr. Ephraim R. McLean
Associate Professor of Information Systems
Director, Center for Information Studies
Graduate School of Management
University of California
Los Angeles, California 90024

Mr. Eldon G. Nicholson, Director
Systems and Data Services Planning and
Control
Trans World Airlines, Inc.
Administrative Center
Kansas City, Missouri 64153

Dr. Thomas E. Reece, Assistant
Superintendent
Management Information Division
Los Angeles Unified School District
G Building, Room 370
450 North Grand Avenue
Los Angeles, California 90012

Mr. Carl H. Reynolds, Director
Computing and Data Processing
Hughes Aircraft Company
1901 West Malbern
Fullerton, California 92634

Dr. Ward C. Sangren
Coordinator of Computer Activities
University of California
Room 11A, University Hall
2200 University Avenue
Berkeley, California 94720

Mr. John J. Shea, Vice President
Systems Planning
Fireman's Fund Insurance Company
P. O. Box 3395
San Francisco, California 94119

Dr. John V. Soden, Partner
McKinsey & Company, Inc.
245 Park Avenue
New York, New York 10017

Dr. George A. Steiner
Professor of Management and Public Policy
Director, Center for Research and Dialogue
on Business in Society
Graduate School of Mangement
University of California
Los Angeles, California 90024

Mr. Donald E. Stiling, Manager
System Services
The Procter & Gamble Company
P. O. Box 599
Cincinnati, Ohio 45201

Mr. Francis A. Stroble, Director
Management Information and Systems
Monsanto Company
800 North Lindbergh Boulevard
St. Louis, Missouri 63166

Mr. Charles C. Tucker, Associate
McKinsey & Company, Inc.
611 West Sixth Street
Los Angleles, California 90017

Mr. Robert E. Umbaugh
Manager of Data Processing
Southern California Edison Company
P. O. Box 410
100 Long Beach Boulevard
Long Beach, California 90801

Mr. P. Duane Walker
Manager of Business Systems
IBM Corporation
133 Westchester Avenue
White Plains, New York 10604

Mr. Laurence S. Weinstein
Corporate Systems Controller
Xerox Corporation
High Ridge Park
Stamford, Connecticut 06904

STRATEGIC PLANNING FOR MIS

I
Introduction

1

The Planning Challenge for MIS

Mark Twain's remark about the weather might well be applied to planning: "Everyone talks about it, but nobody does anything about it." The importance of planning for improved managerial effectiveness is widely endorsed by practitioners and academics alike. In fact, given the accelerating pace of change in almost every aspect of the economy, planning is frequently touted as the key to success, if not to survival. But as our paraphrase implies, the gap between interest and achievement in the planning area is great. Faced with the pressing problems of day-to-day operations, many executives have neither the time nor the inclination to invest in planning for the longer term. However a number of major organizations in the United States *are* doing something about planning—in particular, about planning for management information services. This book is about their efforts.

The term "MIS," standing for either management information *systems* or management information *services,* is being used increasingly throughout the world to refer to the cluster of activities that surround the computer and its supporting personnel. However it is more than the data processing department alone, for it includes the planning, analysis, and design activities, as well as the operational functions, which are necessary for effective computer-based information systems to serve corporate needs. For this reason, many MIS groups go under the broader title of "management services," incorporating not only the computer department but also, for example, operations research and management science staff specialists.

In addressing the topic of planning for this group of activities, it is important to establish a proper perspective. Planning can be examined both from its time horizon and from its focus. The former refers to whether it is short term (one to two years), medium term (two to five years), or long term (five years or more); the other dimension relates to whether its principal concerns are strategic, managerial, or operational. This book concentrates on the strategic and longer term planning issues.

The reason for this choice is simple. As the MIS function assumes a more central role within organizations, proper planning becomes vital to ensure that the role played by MIS will be congruent with that of the overall organization. No longer is it feasible—if it ever was—to have systems for their own sake. This is a luxury no organization can afford. And if MIS is to be made responsive to larger corporate objectives, strategic planning is essential. In recognition of the importance of this issue, a conference on the theme was held in 1974. Bringing together a wide cross section of thoughtful practitioners, this gathering produced a number of findings, as well as 16 formal papers. These papers comprise the latter part of the book. The balance of this chapter describes the conference in some detail and briefly reviews the literature on planning for information systems. Finally, these ideas are synthesized into a framework for MIS planning, and the structure of the remainder of the book is discussed.

THE McKINSEY–UCLA CONFERENCE

In the spring of 1974 an invitational conference was held at the University of California, Los Angeles (UCLA), sponsored by McKinsey & Company, Inc., the management consulting firm, and the UCLA Graduate School of Management. This working conference was chaired by the editors of this book, assisted by Prof. George A. Steiner of UCLA. Some 20 top electronic data processing (EDP) executives from the public and private sectors participated in a preconference survey to determine the objectives, development process, and end products of their respective long-range planning efforts. These executives also participated in two days of discussions of various aspects of their planning experience. The results of the survey and subsequent discussions are included in Chapter 3. In addition, the executives prepared summaries of their long-range planning activities and perspectives, and these appear as individual chapters in Parts II, III, and IV.

The conference dealt with those aspects of planning that had to do with the central issues of the information services organization itself, as opposed to the planning for individual information systems projects. There were two reasons for this focus. First, we wanted the conference to have a broad managerial orientation rather than a technical one. We believed that such an orientation would be of interest not only to MIS managers and practitioners but to corporate executives as well. Because of the increasingly large share of corporate resources being devoted to information systems, and because these systems are becoming more closely woven into the main organizational fabric, top executives are paying much more attention to these efforts than they have in the past. Not surprisingly, this interest on the part of top management has induced MIS and information services managers to devote more of their time and attention to the subject. Thus by focusing on questions of strategy, policy, and long-term planning, we felt we could serve both audiences.

The second reason for our choice was the relatively virgin nature of the MIS planning field. Had we chosen to look at the planning problems associated with the design and installation of specific information systems, we would have been addressing an area in which much work has already been done, with articles and books on project and systems management in abundance. However as the next section indicates, the literature on strategic and long-range planning for information services is fairly sparse.

To obtain a good cross section of various approaches to planning, the conference participants were chosen to represent industries such as aerospace, airline, business equipment, chemicals, consumer goods, insurance, medical services, petroleum, and utilities, as well as government and education enterprises at the local, state, and federal levels. The following organizations were represented.

CIBA–GEIGY Corporation
Consumers Power Company
Department of the Army
Federal Reserve System
Fireman's Fund Insurance Company
Hughes Aircraft Company
International Business Machines Corporation
Kaiser-Permanente Medical Group
Los Angeles City Unified School District
Mobil Oil Corporation
Monsanto Company

Pacific Gas and Electric Company
The Procter & Gamble Company
Southern California Edison Company
Standard Oil Company (Indiana)
State of California
TRW Systems Group
Trans World Airlines, Inc.
University of California
Xerox Corporation

The "average" participant represented an organization that had annual revenues or total budget expenses greater than $1 billion, had an annual MIS budget of over $15 million, and had been carrying out a formal MIS planning effort for more than three years. A number were multinational in scope and had MIS expenditures in excess of $100 million annually. These participants, therefore, represented relatively large, mature MIS organizations, experienced in planning for the information services effort.

The following major findings were brought to light or reconfirmed during the conference discussions.

1. There is a growing need for more formal long-range information systems planning as systems become more complex; require longer to develop; utilize common data bases; involve multiple functions, departments, operating companies, and/or countries of the world; cost more money; and have greater competitive impact.
2. The benefits from long-range planning—improved short-term decision making, enhanced communication, and a firmer commitment of resources—generally outweigh the costs of the undertaking.
3. Formal planning approaches range from the "controlled reaction" tactics of formally evaluating and ranking known project ideas, to the strategic "top-down" scanning for high-potential application opportunities within the context of the overall organization's strategic plan.
4. The selection of a particular planning approach requires a careful balancing of such factors as the role of the MIS organization, its degree of maturity, and the sophistication of the overall company and individual "user" executives.
5. Success in planning for information systems hinges on three factors:
   A. Previous credibility of the MIS group in managing new project development and ongoing computer operations.
   B. Maturity of the overall organization's management processes, such as methods for conducting business planning and making capital allocation decisions.

C. Choice of an approprate MIS planning approach that suits the needs and constraints of the organization.
6. In those organizations most advanced in their planning, the MIS planners have become an integral part of the management team of the organization; and in these companies MIS strategies have a major impact on, and a corresponding interrelationship with, the longer term business plans of the enterprise.
7. Good formal planning must complement, but cannot replace, the political sensitivity, entrepreneurship, conceptual contribution, and basic business leadership required of the successful MIS executive.

As mentioned earlier, these findings are further detailed in Chapter 3.

STRATEGIC AND LONG–RANGE PLANNING

With our choice of the title for the conference—Long-Range Planning for Information Systems—we had hoped to indicate the breadth and high-level focus of the meeting. We also wanted to avoid any impression that it was merely another gathering to discuss improved techniques for MIS project management. However we found that this was easier said than done.

Because of the multiyear planning horizon of most computer-related projects, it is easy to equate long-range planning with any planning effort that has a horizon greater than one year. Thus fundamental questions such as "Where is the information services organization going?" and "How is it contributing to the overall success of the enterprise?" became confused with "What project should be started next?" and "How can the continued development of existing projects be more effectively coordinated?"

Unfortunately, the term "long-range planning" does little to sharpen this distinction. For some conference participants it meant focusing on the former questions; for others, concentration on the latter ones. This dual interpretation became evident from the conference discussion and from the papers the participants prepared. It can be argued, of course, that the two uses of the term are equally valid and equally important for the success of the information services organization. Certainly if the ongoing operations and project development is not effectively planned and managed, it does little good to speculate on where the organization will be five to seven years in the future. More than likely, it will be an organization with a new cast of characters!

As discussed earlier, however, we wanted the conference—and this book—to focus on the central issues of setting organizational objectives and deciding on appropriate strategies and policies. Thus we now recognize that "strategic planning" would have been a more appropriate title than "long-range planning." As defined by Robert Anthony in his book *Planning and Control Systems: A Framework for Analysis,*

> *Strategic planning* is the process of deciding on objectives of the organization, on changes in these objectives, on the resources used to attain these objectives, and on the policies that are to govern the acquisition, use, and disposition of these resources. Strategic planning . . . is a process having to do with the formulation of long-range, strategic plans and policies that determine or change the character or direction of the organization.[1]

To describe strategic planning, and to show how it differs from long-range, medium-range, and short-range planning, Chapter 2 of this book discusses these terms in detail, using the point of view of the general business enterprise, not just the MIS function. The chapter is entitled "Comprehensive Managerial Planning," a term the author, Prof. Steiner, uses to describe the whole spectrum of planning activities. This chapter, originally published in 1972 as a pamphlet by The Planning Executives Institute, is probably the most concise, yet comprehensive treatment of the subject available. For readers who are not familiar with the general literature of planning, this chapter should prove to be a valuable aid.

LITERATURE ON PLANNING FOR INFORMATION SERVICES

With Chapter 2 providing a coverage of general planning topics, this section examines the literature on planning specifically for information services. We have selected materials that we believe to be relevant to this subject, listing the references at the end of the chapter. The following paragraphs briefly summarize each reference; quotations are included to provide examples of the thoughts of these authors regarding the objectives, end products, processes, and philosophy of planning for MIS. Our summary is organized in alphabetical order by authors' names, since there appears to be little relationship among the conceptual models of these authors, with the possible exception of the foundation-setting work of Blumenthal and Kriebel. This section, therefore, is not intended to be a conceptual synthesis but merely to serve as

[1]Robert N. Anthony, *Planning and Control Systems: A Framework for Analysis,* Boston: Graduate School of Business Administration, Harvard University, 1965, p. 24.

an annotated bibliography, designed to furnish the reader with an overview of the field and to aid him if he wishes to pursue a particular aspect of information systems planning in more detail.

Leon Albrecht's *Organization and Management of Information Processing Systems* (1973) is an excellent and thorough treatment of the wide range of activities involved in the managing of an information services organization, complete with sample forms and procedures. The subject of long-range planning is given extensive coverage. A categorization of planning levels, presented in his introductory material, includes the following:

1. *Overall plans.* These plans express in general terms how and why the company will operate and outline a systems philosophy, that is, the logical structure that systems within the organization should follow.
2. *Specific plans.* These plans concern the specific projects being planned—hopefully within an overall scheme—to meet the current short-range company requirements, indicating how these plans are translated into resource requirements.
3. *Individual project plans.* These plans are very specific and relate to the stages of the systems creation cycle.

In addition, Albrecht discusses the related subject of the executive MIS steering committee in some detail. An appendix furnishes a detailed example of its objectives and makeup for a hypothetical company.

Albrecht pragmatically notes that the single most important aspect of an MIS divisional plan is a clear statement of what results are being planned, how these results will be achieved, the quantity and quality of resources needed to execute the plan, and how resources will be allocated. He includes examples of action programs and discusses the development of a streamlined, bare-bones division budget forecast. Interestingly, he cautions against revealing the long-range system design architecture to top management because of the risk that it will be considered either irrelevant or too time-consuming to implement. This perspective of the system design architecture as a working statement of intent—not of commitment—is reinforced in a later chapter that spells out the means for developing the system design plan itself.

Sherman Blumenthal's *Management Information Systems: A Framework for Planning and Development* (1969) synthesizes a comprehensive, integrated system plan for the corporate enterprise. A classic in information systems planning, this book is sprinkled with many common-sense guidelines regarding the practical, economic use of information systems technology in the firm. In the first chapter Blumenthal portrays systems planning as being similar to general business planning:

1. A systems plan constrains the behavior of that portion of the organization charged with the design and implementation of these systems specified in the plan.
2. Systems planning is a form of strategic planning wherein objectives are formulated in terms of proposed systems authorized for development, resources assigned to authorized systems projects, and policies formulated to guide the manner in which these resources will be used. . . .
3. Selections have to be made among proposed systems competing for the use of limited resources. . . .
4. A systems plan is not merely the enunciation of a set of operating goals in terms of systems, but contains a prescription of how the goals are to be achieved by means of a scheduled series of projects and subprojects.
5. There are relationships between factors in a systems plan, although these are not always explicitly set forth. These are what should be called rules of thumb. . . .
6. A systems plan is finally a precedent, although a flexible one, more often honored in the breach than not. Few systems plans remain unchanged for long.[2]

In addition, he proposes the following objectives for systems planning:

1. To avoid overlapping development of major systems elements which are widely applicable across organizational lines, when there is no compelling technical or functional reason for difference.
2. To help ensure a uniform basis for determining sequence of development in terms of payoff potential, natural precedence, and probability of success.
3. To minimize the cost of integrating related systems with each other.
4. To reduce the total number of small, isolated systems to be developed, maintained, and operated.
5. To provide adaptability of systems to business change and growth within periodic major overhaul.
6. To provide a foundation for coordinated development of consistent, comprehensive, corporate-wide, and interorganizational information systems.
7. To provide guidelines for and direction to continuing, system-development studies and projects.[3]

He labels the various methods for classifying systems as the organization chart, the data collection, the management survey (or "top-down"),

[2]Sherman C. Blumenthal, *Management Information Systems: A Framework for Planning and Development*, Englewood Cliffs, N.J.: Prentice-Hall, 1969, p. 10. Reprinted by permission of Prentice-Hall, Inc.
[3]*Ibid.*, p. 13.

the data bank, the integrate-later, and the integrate-now (or "total systems") approach, and amplifies each one.

Blumenthal states that development priorities in a company should be determined by four primary factors: technical precedence, payoff, available technology, and management objectives. He particularly discounts the alleged indispensability of a "total, integrated management information system" as the target of systems planning and development efforts. He notes that a good systems plan should have the following characteristics:

1. The plan should embody moving forward on many fronts at the same time. . . . This minimizes risk by distributing it. . . .
2. The plan should allow for escalating slowing to larger and larger systems aggregations. . . .
3. In establishing priorities, it is vitally necessary to begin with the urgent, but achievable. This may mean that those projects with the largest payoff are not necessarily first. . . .
4. The plan must provide for measuring achievement—has what was promised been delivered? . . .
5. The role of the feasibility study or feasibility project prior to establishing a project is vital for defining precise goals. . . .
6. Where goals must be changed, the plan must be updated and a new "model" created. . . .[4]

A later section of the book spells out a number of procedures for system development, including those related to management steering committee decisions on development priorities.

Richard Canning, editor and publisher of the monthly *EDP Analyzer,* recently devoted two issues to topics of particular relevance here. In "Are We Doing the Right Things" (May 1975), he deals with the selection of data processing projects and the setting of priorities for those projects. Canning portrays the steering committee approaches being used in some half-dozen companies and provides several guidelines for consideration in establishing similar bodies. In "Do We Have the Right Resources?" (July 1975), he profiles the corporate systems planning approach at Pacific Mutual Life Insurance Company and gives his own ideas regarding the content of a long-range plan.

Robert Curtice's monograph "Planning For Data Base Systems" (1976) is one of a series of thought pieces on data base management published by Q.E.D. Information Sciences, Inc. Curtice first discusses in practical terms the meaning of systems planning and the benefits of planning, particularly as they relate to, or are affected by, data base considera-

[4]*Ibid.*, pp. 90–91.

tions. He then portrays the information systems planning process as starting with a plan for the plan. This is launched by a review of the overall corporate plans, interviews with operating and top management, a study of specific operating departments, a review of existing MIS systems, and finally, visits with other organizations. Curtice next suggests the preparation and approval of planning objectives. The subsequent development of two types of plan—an application system plan and an EDP environment plan—is discussed with particular focus on the data base section of the plan. In particular, Curtice deals with the need to define the evolving data base, as well as the various development strategies for moving toward the data base environment. These include the building of special input and/or output data bases and the development of bridge programs to extend the life of existing programs until they are replaced with new data base programs.

John Dearden, Warren McFarlan, and William Zani's *Managing Computer-Based Information Systems* (1971) contains an article on "Long-Range Planning for Computer-Based Information Systems" by McFarlan, Cole, and Rieger, as well as several case writeups on long-range information systems planning at McDonnell Douglas Corporation. The article notes four major reasons for planning the development of computer-based information systems:

1. To provide a framework for making tradeoffs between projects.
2. To assure the compatibility of portions of interrelated systems developed at different time.
3. To achieve thorough communication between the different elements of an organization.
4. To provide a framework within which the information systems development can be molded to ensure that the systems will be responsive to and coordinated with the firm's long-run strategy and plans.

The article discusses limitations on planning; presents a conceptual framework for portraying the role of top management, the computer organization, and computer users in the long-range planning effort; and defines in more precise terms the roles of each. The case material presents the information systems plan of the Douglas Aircraft Company and gives examples of information and data flow diagrams for the financial area of the company.

Freiser's "Developing an ADP Plan" (1975) tells briefly why a data processing plan is important, what constitutes a good plan, why plans often fail, and what the steps in a planning process should be. The following planning steps are advocated: (1) the design of a target system architecture, (2) the making of decisions regarding the organization and staffing of the function, (3) the development of an implementation schedule, and (4) the definition of the related costs and benefits of the plan.

Louis Fried, in "Long-Range Planning for EDP" (1974), takes the position that "it is impossible to develop a long-range plan for DP unless there is a specific long-range plan with stated goals and objectives for the corporation as a whole and for the individual user divisions."[5] He also stresses the need for the establishment of a consistent data processing chargeback system prior to undertaking a planning effort, since in his mind such a system is the keystone for proposed system economic feasibility studies. In addition, he views the establishment and use of an applications steering committee as an integral step in the data processing planning process. Finally, he strongly recommends the inclusion of a "controls" section in the data processing long-range plan. This controls section consists of the policies, procedures, and techniques necessary to control and monitor the performance of the data processing organization as it seeks to implement the plan.

IBM's *Business Systems Planning: Information Systems Planning Guide* (1975) presents a two-phase approach—a combination of top down and bottom up—to the development of an information system plan that grew out of the corporation's own internal information systems planning efforts. The need to perform a top-down analysis of business objectives, management processes, and organizational relationships, as well as defining a target systems network and data architecture before laying out a bottom-up implementation schedule, is stressed. In particular, an initial *identification of requirements* phase is prescribed to determine the relationships among, and relative values of, subsystems in an information systems network. This phase is followed by the *definition* phase to document a long-range plan for the design, development, and implementation of a network of decision-oriented management information and control systems using integrated data bases. The document contains several chapters detailing this methodology, with numerous interview guidelines, project schedules, end-product outlines, and examples of analysis techniques used in various industries. There are also a number of examples of the benefits that result from this planning, from developing information systems networks, and from using more formalized management processes for the information systems function itself.

[5]Louis Fried, "Long-Range Planning for EDP," *Auerbach Data Processing Management Reports,* 1974, p. 2.

Charles Kriebel points out the dichotomy between a computer *strategy* and a computer system *plan* in an early paper entitled "The Strategic Dimension of Computer Systems Planning" (1968). He states that

> Formulation of a computer strategy involves decision making [by top management] in three areas: establishing computer planning objectives on the basis of corporate goals; determining corporate policy for growth, resource commitment, and the management organization for computer systems; and appraising the company's current position computer systems development.[6]

He provides several examples of computer strategies employed by American businesses and conceptually portrays the computer strategy of a typical company in diagrammatic form (Figure 1).

Warren McFarlan, Richard Nolan, and David Norton's *Information Systems Administration* (1973) is a practical text that discusses a conceptual framework for information systems management, presenting more than 20 cases and a dozen or more selected readings on related management topics. In the early chapters of the book the authors propose a top-down framework to guide the development of an organization's information system (Figure 2). They also suggest a planning-programming-budgeting system for allocating resources to information systems, and they present criteria useful in identifying existing systems where a new design would promise significant payoffs to the overall organization.

A reprint of Richard Nolan's "Systems Analysis for Computer-Based Information Systems Design" (1971) also appears in the book. This article is a tutorial treatment, complete with extensive literature references, of the top-down, bottom-up, and total systems approaches to designing computer-based information systems. Of particular interest is the description of the formal MIS long-range planning effort of Genesco (prepared by Profs. William Rotch and Brandt Allen of the Graduate School of Business Administration, University of Virginia). The material summarizes the history of Genesco's first formal planning effort and explains in some detail each of the 25 steps in their formal MIS planning process (Figure 3). In addition, criteria for identifying areas with potential for the development of information systems are listed in the Genesco case material.

Information Systems Administration also includes a reprint of Warren McFarlan's "Problems in Planning the Information System" (1971), which points out the important factors in planning for computer-based information systems and discusses the approaches to planning chosen

[6]Charles H. Kriebel, "The Strategic Dimension of Computer Systems Planning," *Long Range Planning*, September 1968, p. 12.

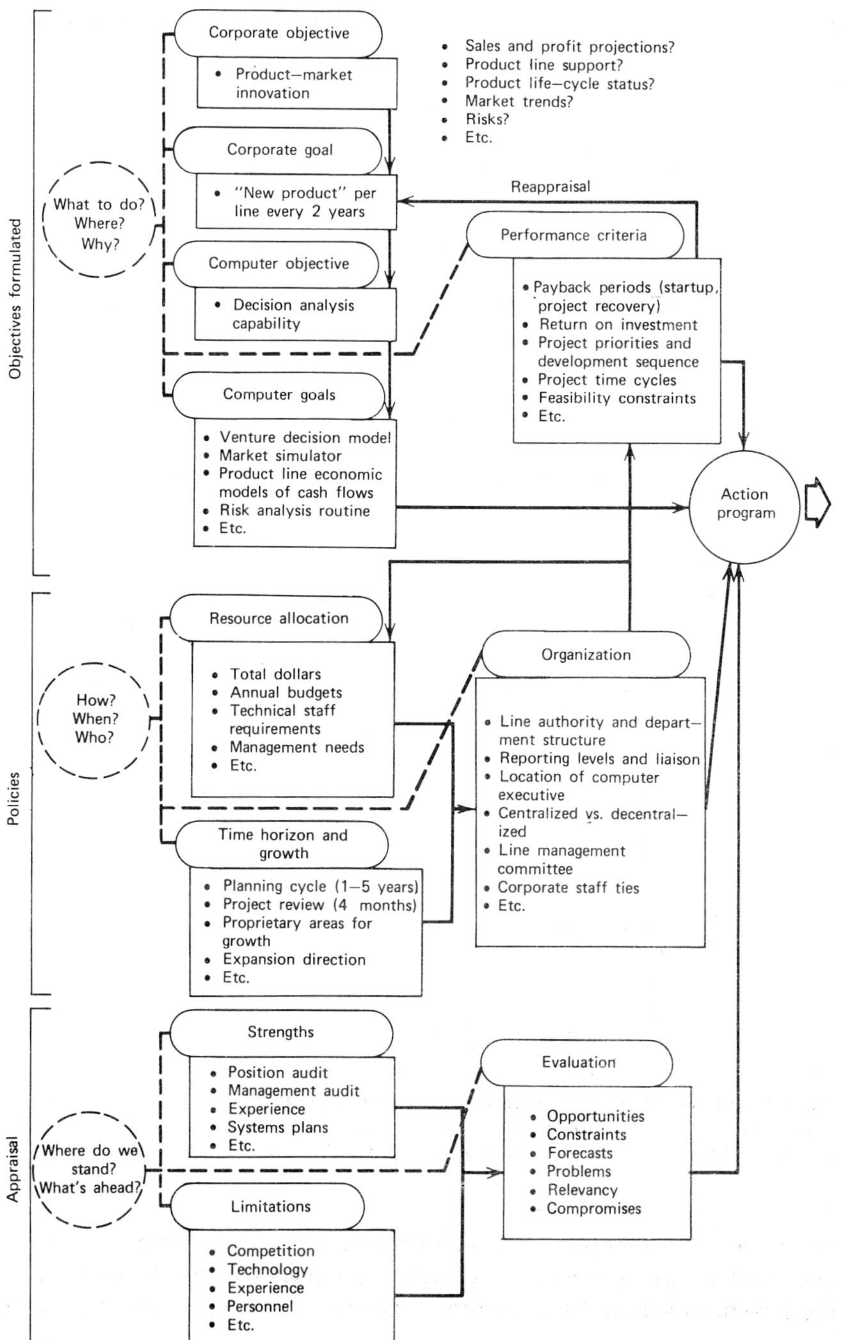

Figure 1 Sample profile of a company computer strategy. *Source.* Charles H. Kriebel, "The Strategic Dimension of Computer Systems Planning," *Long-Range Planning,* September 1968, p. 11.

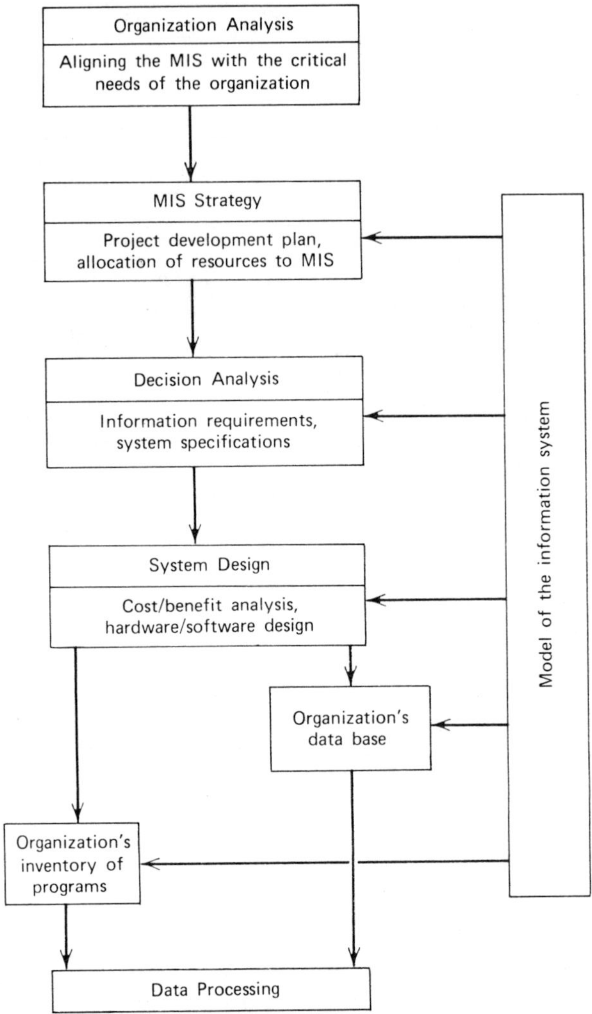

Figure 2 Framework for information systems development. *Source.* F. W. McFarlan, R. L. Nolan, and D. P. Norton, *Information Systems Administration,* Holt, Rinehart & Winston, New York, 1973, p. 7. Reprinted by permission of Holt, Rinehart & Winston.

by an aerospace company and an international manufacturer of electrical and mechanical equipment. McFarlan also describes the contents of an ideal computer-based information systems planning document (Table 1).

M. H. Schwartz summarized the planning approach he was experimenting with at the Atomic Energy Commission in "MIS Planning"

Table 1 The Contents of a CBIS Plan

A. Introduction
   1. Summary of major goals, a statement of their consistency with corporate goals, and current state of planning vis-à-vis these goals
   2. Summary of aggregate cost and savings projections
   3. Summary of manpower requirements
   4. Major challenges and problems
   5. Criteria for assigning project priorities

B. Project identification
   1. Maintenance projects, all projects proposed, and development projects
   2. Estimated completion times
   3. Manpower requirements, by time period and job category
   4. Computer capacity needed for system testing and implementation
   5. Economic justification by project—development costs, implementation costs, running costs, out-of-pocket savings, intangible savings
   6. Project control tools
   7. Tie-ins with other systems and master plans

C. Hardware projections (derived from projects)
   1. Manpower needed by month for each category
      a. General—management, administrative, training, and planning personnel
      b. Developmental—application analysts, systems designers, methods and procedures personnel, operating system programmers, and other programmers
      c. Operational—machine operators, key punchers/verifiers, and input/output control clerks
   2. Salary levels, training needs, and estimated turnover

E. Financial projections by time period
   1. Hardware rental, depreciation, maintenance, floor space, air conditioning, and electricity
   2. Manpower—training and fringe benefits
   3. Miscellaneous—building rental, outside service, telecommunications, and the like

Source. F. Warren, McFarlan, "Problems in Planning the Information Systems," *Harvard Business Review,* (March–April, 1971), p. 82. Reprinted by permission.

(1970), expressing the opinion that an MIS should be visualized as a federation of systems; it should be planned, designed, and implemented in an evolutionary manner, with the planning methodology itself also being evolutionary. He presents a 12-step "ideal" planning approach as a starting point, to be shaped to fit the realities of a particular situation.

1. Working closely with management, line, and staff people of the organization at large, identify—in terms of management and user needs and

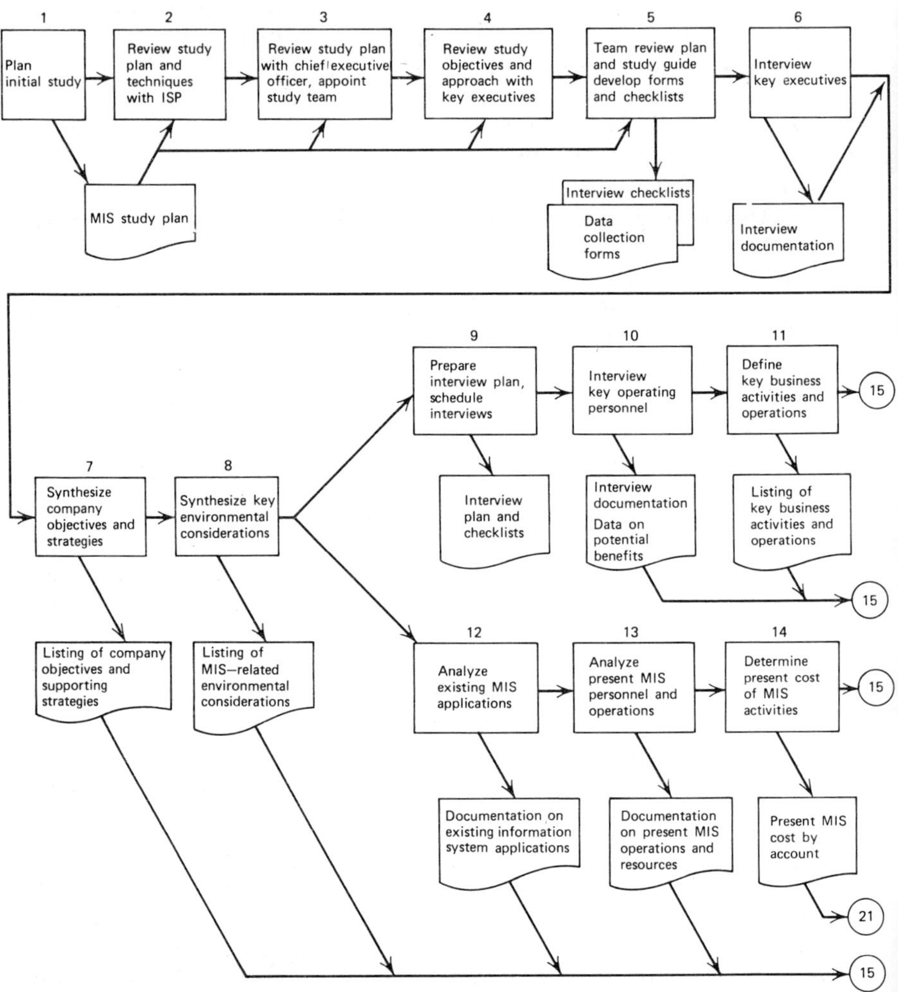

Figure 3 Genesco MIS planning procedures. *Source.* F. W. McFarlan, R. L. Nolan, and D. P. Norton, *Information Systems Administration*, Holt, Rinehart & Winston, New York, 1973, pp. 174–175. Reprinted by permission of Holt, Rinehart & Winston. Reproduced from the Genesco Case authorized by Professors Brandt Allen and William Rotch with permission of the University of Virginia Colgate Darden Graduate Business School Sponsors.

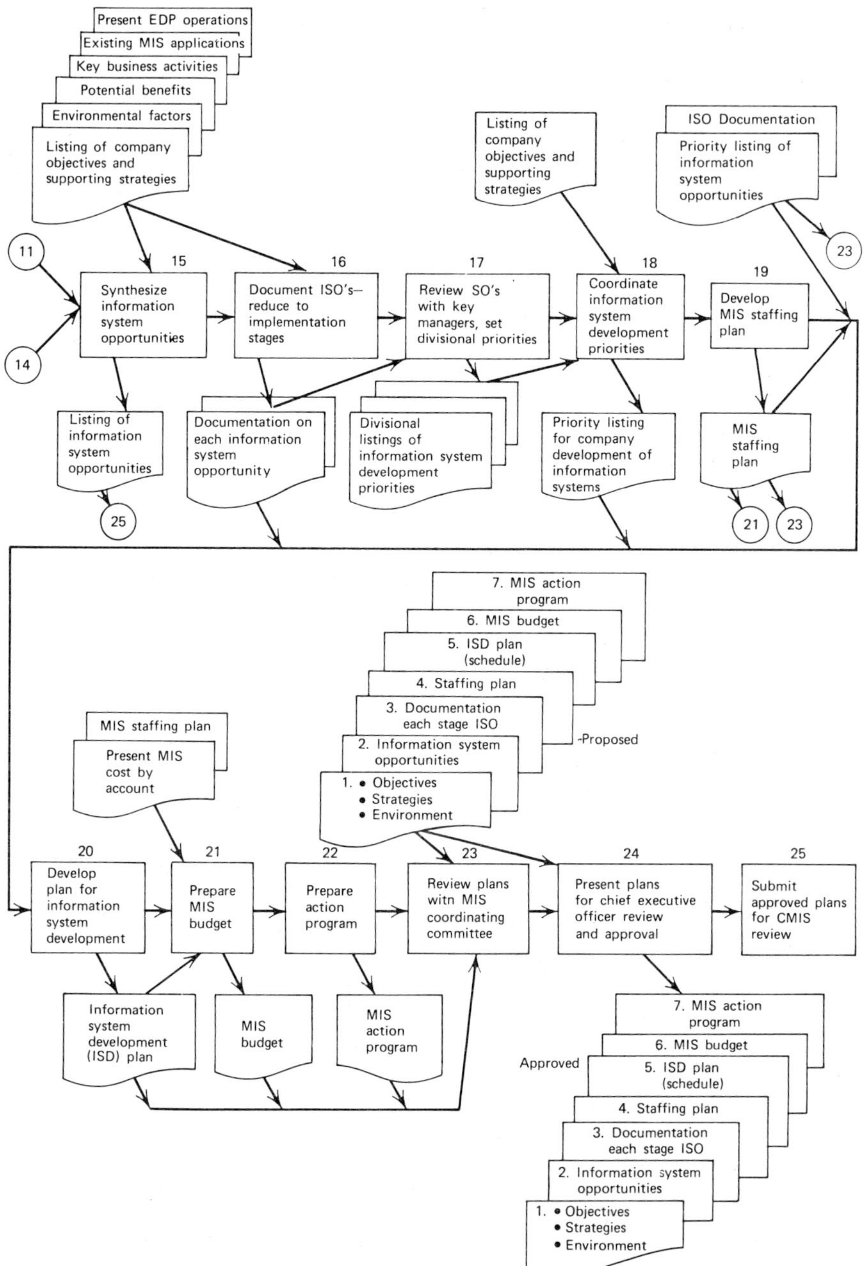

Figure 3 *(Continued)*

aspirations—the broad missions of MIS effort and the specific objectives whose achievement will fulfill the missions.

2. Map the framework structure of *(a)* the external systems that affect and are affected by the organization, and *(b)* the internal systems—present and potential—that comprise the organization.
3. Delineate as fully as possible the purposes, structures, contents, and interrelationships of the management information systems, distinguishing between present and potential systems.
4. Identify those current systems and applications that are working reasonably well. . . .
5. Identify those *current* systems and applications for which highly preliminary priority considerations suggest that either thoroughly revised implementation or substantially improved implementation is desirable.
6. Identify those *potential* systems and applications for which highly preliminary priority considerations suggest that initial implementation is desirable.
7. Consider alternative approaches to developing, and alternative ways of operating, the various identified opportunities for current and potential systems and applications.
8. Perform a critical priority analysis of the set of grossly screened possible projects in order that we may be as sensible as we can in deciding what to do, how to do it, and when to do it.
   A. Process of analysis:
      (1) Describe the expected direct and indirect benefits of each alternative.
      (2) State the grounds for the expectations.
      (3) Evaluate the merits of each alternative.
      (4) Estimate the resources needed for development, conversion, and operation of each alternative. . . .
      (5) State the grounds for the estimates.
      (6) Measure the costs of the resources.
      (7) Allow for the influence of undesirable side effects on the merits of each alternative.
      (8) Choose the alternatives that appear to yield the greatest net value from the investment of resources.
   B. Criteria for evaluating the merits of alternative projects:
      (1) Explicit dollar estimates of the (discounted) value of returns where feasible. . . .
      (2) Qualitative factors. . . .
      (3) Institutional factors. . . .
      (4) Systems management factors. . . .
      (5) Systems technical factors. . . .
9. Prepare a five-year proposed implementation and operating plan.
   A. Show for each priority project:
      (1) The purposes to be served and the implications of implementation —and of delay in implementation.
      (2) The justification revealed by the priority analysis.

(3) Broad plans for development conversion and operation, including resource requirements and schedules.

B. Specify and justify nonproject resource requirements
  (1) Management and administration
  (2) Planning
  (3) Resource development
  (4) Standards
  (5) Production operations

10. Present the proposed plan to management for approval, in the context of missions, objectives, and the framework of systems.
11. Continuously review, test, and refresh the statement of missions and objectives of the MIS effort, and the contents of the priority analysis.
12. Each year recycle,
    A. Mapping of the framework structure of systems.
    B. Delineating possible management information systems.
    C. Identifying desirable tasks and procedures.
    D. Performing a priority analysis.
    E. Improving upon and extending the five-year plan another year.
    F. Presenting the five-year plan to management.[7]

Paul Siegel, in *Strategic Planning of Management Information Systems* (1975), divides management information systems into six levels: data administration, computing, modeling, forecasting, controlling, and planning. He names three types of planning:

1. *Strategic*—setting objectives and defining methods for achieving them.
2. *Resource development*—planning development of resources for long-range growth.
3. *Operational*—allocating resources and scheduling of short-range operations.

He defines a strategic MIS plan as consisting of MIS objectives, a system development plan, and a system control plan. He proposes the following major strategic MIS objectives:

1. Integrate the six levels of MIS.
2. Support strategic organizational objectives.
3. Maintain primacy of management decisions over machine decisions.
4. Automate repetitive control functions.

[7]M. H. Schwartz, "MIS Planning," *Datamation*, September 1970, pp. 30–31. Reprinted with permission of *Datamation*. Copyright 1970 by Technical Publishing Company, Greenwich, Connecticut 06830.

5. Streamline adaptability process.
6. Keep MIS adaptable.
7. Keep MIS effective.

Siegel visualizes the major strategic MIS planning efforts as being focused on six studies:

1. Qualitative modeling of the organization's management system.
2. Defining a system of measurements for the management system.
3. Setting standards for working relationships between man and machine and between man and man via machine, which support the measurement system.
4. Defining related data standards.
5. Producing a time-phased system development plan.
6. Translating MIS objectives into MIS measures of performance.

Last, he describes MIS strategic planning as an art and points out that there are no hard and fast rules that are always applicable.

John Soden and George Crandell's paper, "Practical Guidelines for Long-Range Planning" (1975), is an early version of the concepts presented in the next section of this chapter and in Chapter 4.

Richard Young's article, "Systems and Data Processing Departments Need Long-Range Planning" (1967) explores the factors that make planning particularly important: long lead times for most EDP projects, uncertainty due to rapid technological change, growing pains of many data processing departments, high costs, lack of clear authority and responsibility, need to set a good example, and self-protection. He also outlines the benefits of planning and discounts a number of typical reasons offered for lack of planning in the EDP function.

Out of all these studies, a few major ideas emerge. First, it is essential to recognize that there is not *a* plan but a hierarchy of plans, running the gamut from a single strategic statement, which is quite conceptual, to detailed operational plans for individual projects. And each type of planning must be approached in a different way. In the case of Genesco and the Atomic Energy Commission, detailed step-by-step procedures were given. Other authors referred to the relative merits of top-down, bottom-up, and other competing planning approaches. Most of the authors agreed, however, that it is vital to have a clear statement or plan from the host organization identifying *its* goals and objectives. Without this, it becomes extremely difficult to do effective strategic planning for MIS.

Another critical area is the establishment of priorities. It is not necessarily the purpose of strategic planning to decide what projects should be undertaken. Rather, a procedure must be established whereby priorities can be set in a fair and consistent fashion. Many of the writers felt that an executive or user steering committee was a valuable means of achieving this end. But all recognized that there is no sure-fire guarantee of success and that all planning efforts must be, above all, flexible and adaptable to changing circumstances.

A STRATEGIC PLANNING FRAMEWORK

In light of the preceding discussion, we believe that it is worthwhile to synthesize these views of MIS planning, our findings from the conference, and George Steiner's view of comprehensive managerial planning for the overall enterprise. Figure 4 presents such a framework: the left half of the diagram portrays the tasks needed to arrive at MIS objectives, strategies, and policies; the right half notes the tasks necessary to accomplish the more detailed planning efforts within the long-range, medium-range, and short-range time frames.

As we pointed out previously, there is an important difference between strategic planning and long-range planning. Specifically, we propose the following terms and definitions.

Strategic MIS planning, following Anthony's definition of corporate strategic planning, is the process of deciding on objectives for the MIS organization; on changes in these objectives; on the resources used to obtain these objectives, and on the policies that are to govern the acquisition, use, and disposition of the resources. Strategic MIS planning can occur at infrequent intervals and is often triggered by the need for an enterprise to resolve a particular substantive issue or issues that involves the MIS entity.

Long-range MIS planning deals with meeting the *future* MIS needs of the host organization. It is largely conceptual and can have a horizon of five, six, seven, or more years. It does not deal with specific projects or even groups of projects, but with emergint types of user needs and services that might be useful in addressing these needs. It must also plan for the MIS organization of the future and for the skills and capabilities that will be needed in developing and managing the systems of the future.

Medium-range MIS planning is what many organizations call their long-range plan. It is the planning that is necessary to meet the host organization's *present* MIS needs, projected two to five years into the future. It is, on one hand, a portfolio of projects, ranked by importance,

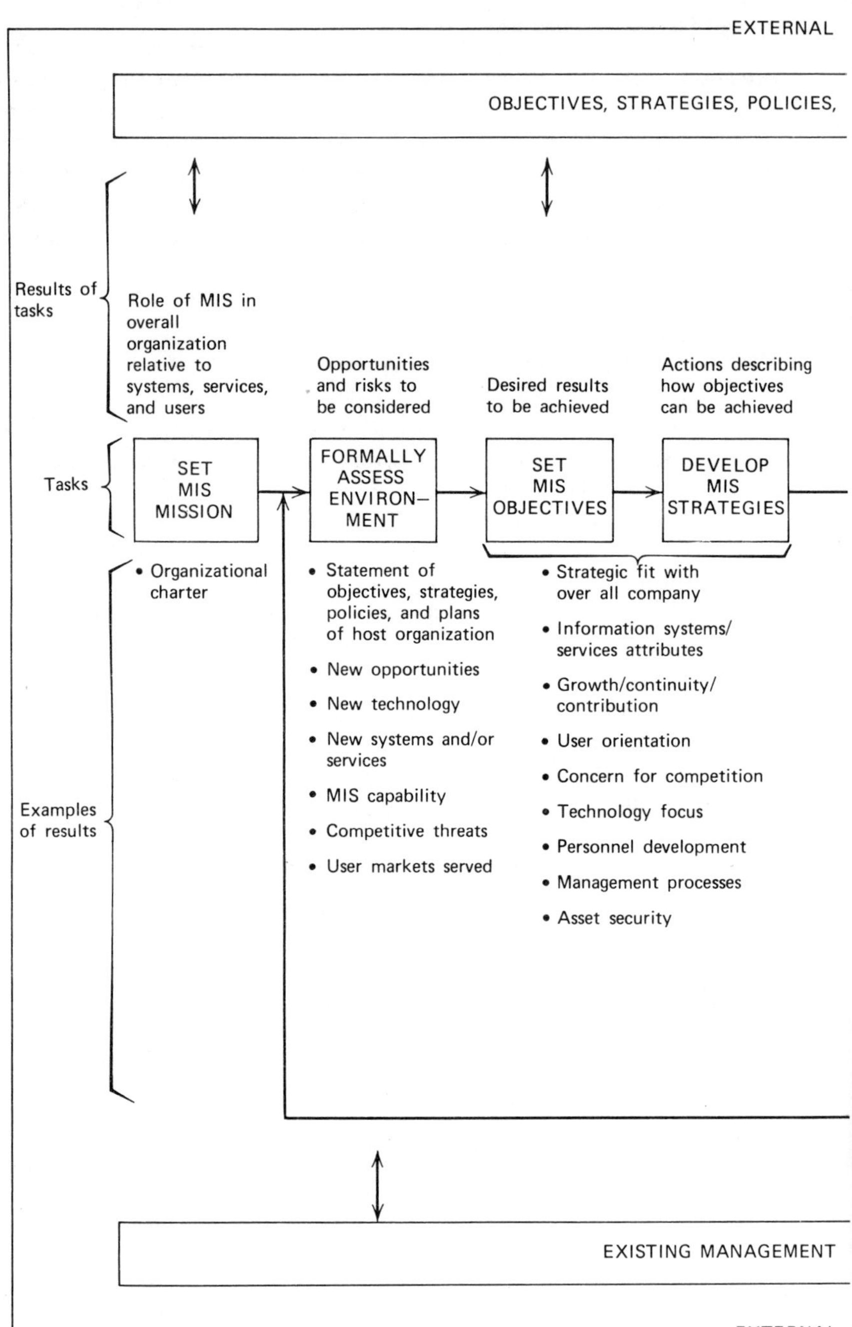

Figure 4 MIS strategic planning framework

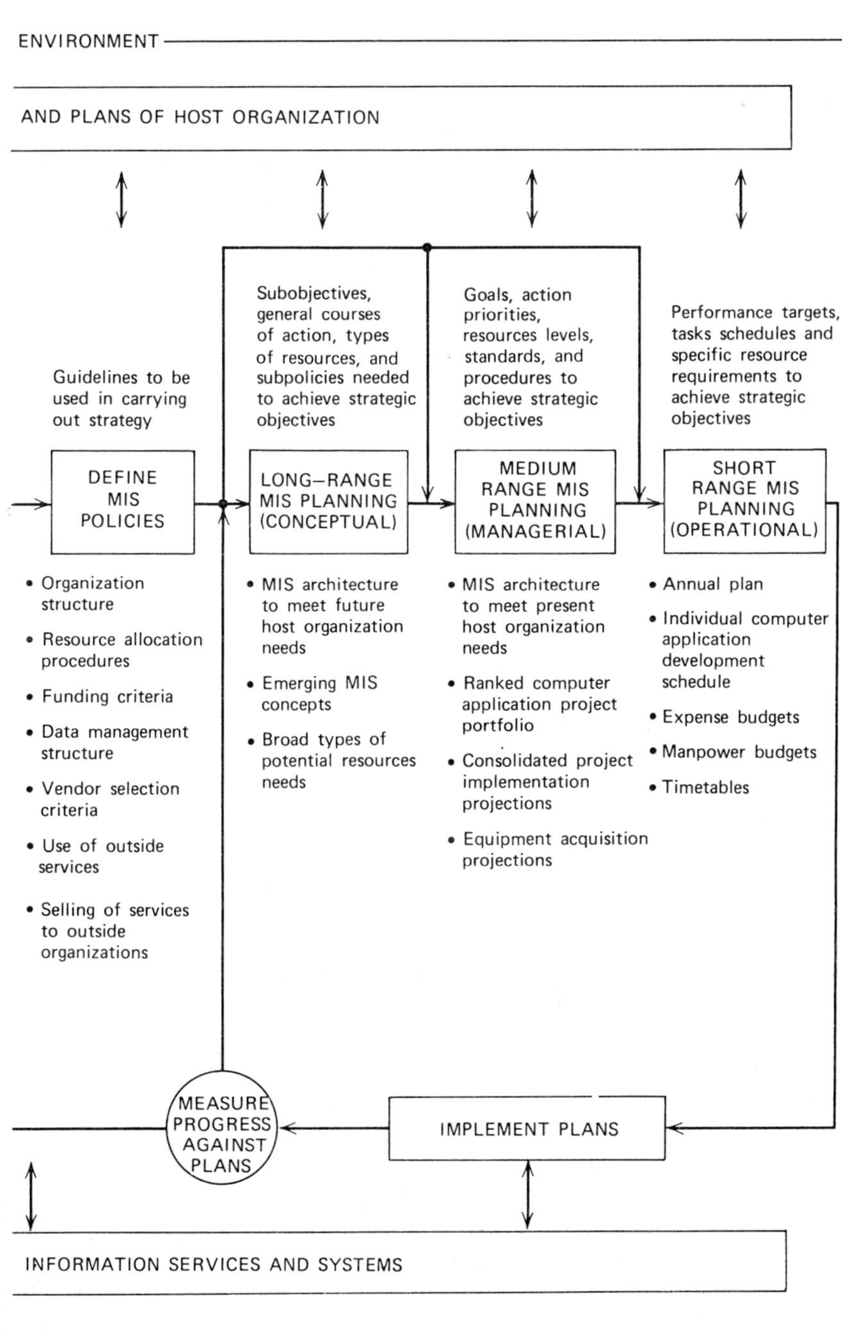

Figure 4 *(Continued)*

coupled with projections for their implementation. It also involves the technical planning for systems and data base network architecture, for hardware and software acquisitions and conversions, and for the staffing of multiyear projects and developmental activities.

Short-range MIS planning is generally equivalent to the MIS annual plan. It involves detailed budget preparation, manpower scheduling, and the creative of timetables for individual projects. It also often includes quantitative statements regarding performance targets for the MIS group. It is relatively operational.

The choice of approach or set of approaches to MIS planning, *assuming that the strategic planning has been properly done,* is particularly important. Many organizations falter because they attempt to carry out all three types of MIS planning simultaneously, before mastering the intricacies of the short-term plans necessary for the effective management of present activities.

Planning Tasks

The first task appearing in the framework (Figure 4) is to set the MIS mission; that is, to define the charter of the information services organization. Naturally this broad definition of organizational role must be done within the mission and purpose of the organization of which MIS is a part. The MIS organization may receive this mission as a given; or it may be arrived at through discussion with top management. Following this, the next task in MIS strategic planning is to assess the environment—to consider the opportunities and risks that are present now and that might arise in the future. This would include consideration of such matters as the following:

1. The objectives, strategies, policies, and plans of the host organization.
2. The competitive position of the overall organization.
3. The user groups within the organization—their own management systems needs, the current share of MIS resources they use, and the fit of information services with their own plans.
4. The present and emerging technology for information processing.
5. The ability of the MIS organization to effect change.

When the MIS mission is established and a thorough appraisal has been made of the environment, it becomes necessary to set the MIS objectives, the desired results to be achieved by the MIS organization. Closely linked with the statement of objectives is the development of the strategies or broad courses of action that will be needed to achieve these objectives. Thus objectives and strategies are intimately interwoven; consideration of one invariably involves consideration of the other. These objectives, and their accompanying strategies, should deal with the following items:

1. The fit of the MIS objectives with the overall organizational objectives.
2. The growth, continuity, and level of contribution of the MIS function within the organization.
3. The classes and types of systems and services to be offered.
4. The role of users in systems development efforts.
5. The types of technology to be employed.
6. The type of management and staff to be developed.
7. The posture of the MIS organization vis-à-vis the user, the host organization, the competitive environment, and the professional milieu.

The final task in the strategic planning phase is the determination of policies. These are the guidelines to be used in carrying out the strategy. They are specific statements covering the organizational structure of the MIS function; the criteria to be used in deciding on overall funding levels and resource allocations; the use of steering committees; the procedures to be used in selecting vendors, buying outside services, and/or selling services to outside users; the standardization of hardware, systems software, applications, and/or data bases; and so forth. Once the foregoing are in place, the planning needed to implement these strategies can be initiated with a better likelihood of success. Implementation planning involves long-range conceptual planning, medium-range managerial planning, and/or short-range operational planning. Each of these planning activities has the goal of translating the MIS objectives and strategies into increasingly more detailed and specific plans. They are discussed in greater detail in Chapter 4.

It is important to recognize that the planning process and resulting decisions are dynamic, not static. As the bottom part of the framework (Figure 4) indicates, there is an important feedback loop, measuring progress against plans and, ultimately, against the objectives and strategies themselves. For nothing should be fixed or "cast in concrete." Many an MIS executives has wailed, "But this isn't the way things were planned last year," forgetting that a plan is not a forecast *of* the future, but a framework for making decisions so as to be better prepared *for* the future. Plans and strategies should be flexible and amenable to modification and change as circumstances dictate.

THE BALANCE OF THE BOOK

Of the remaining chapters in Part I, Chapter 2 is Steiner's in-depth coverage of comprehensive managerial planning. Chapter 3 summarizes the results from the survey that was conducted among the conference participants concerning their MIS planning practices. Chapter 4 continues the discussion of strategic planning for MIS that was introduced in the preceding section.

Parts II, III, and IV book contain the papers contributed by the conference participants, grouped according to sectors of the economy: private, quasi-private or regulated, and public. The following organizations are represented:

Part II: The Private Sector

CIBA–GEIGY Corporation
TRW Systems Group
Hughes Aircraft Company
Mobil Oil Corporation
Standard Oil Company (Indiana)
International Business Machines Corporation
Xerox Corporation

Part III: The Regulated or Quasi-Private Sector

Consumers Power Company
Pacific Gas and Electric Company
Trans World Airlines, Inc.
Kaiser-Permanente Medical Group

Part IV: The Public Sector

Board of Governors, Federal Reserve System
U.S. Army Materiel Command
Los Angeles City Unified School District
State of California
University of California

We originally anticipated that these groupings would bring to light certain commonalities among the three groups; that is, that the private sector companies would be quite alike as a group, yet different from the regulated or public enterprises. This did not prove to be the case. The *intra*group differences are at least as great as the *inter*group differences. Such factors as the status of the long-range plan of the parent organization and the relative effectiveness of existing MIS applications are far more important in determining the ability to undertake comprehensive long-range planning than whether an organization is in the public or private sector. However we have retained these groupings for the convenience of the reader, allowing individuals interested in, say, the public sector to find organizations with similar characteristics (although not necessarily similar planning practices) appearing in the same section.

Although the papers were all written in early 1974, thus describing planning activities that are earlier still, the reader should not be misled into thinking that the material is outdated. Some of the examples the authors use are now three or more years old, but the insights the papers contain and the planning approaches and techniques they discuss are as fresh and timely today as they were when first written.

Biographical sketches of the contributors appear at the end of the book. Also, the planning documents, procedures, and forms of several of the participating organizations are reproduced as appendices. These materials are not offered as ideal models; but they are detailed examples of the MIS planning efforts of a number of large organizations whose planning experience is relatively mature.

REFERENCES

Albrecht, Leon K. *Organization and Management of Information and Management of Information Processing Systems*. New York: Macmillan, 1973.

Anthony, Robert N. *Planning and Control Systems: A Framework for Analysis*. Boston: Graduate School of Business Administration, Harvard University, 1965.

Blumenthal, Sherman C. *Management Information Systems: A Framework for Planning and Development*, Englewood Cliffs, N.J.: Prentice-Hall, 1969.

Canning Richard G. "Are We Doing the Right Things?" *EDP Analyzer*, May 1975, 13 pp.

Canning, Richard G. "Do We Have the Right Resources?" *EDP Analyzer*, July 1975, 12 pp.

Curtice, Robert M. "Planning for Data Base Systems," *Data Base Management Monograph Series*, Wellesley, Mass.: Q.E.D. Information Sciences, 1976, 44 pp.

Dearden, John, F. Warren McFarlan, and William M. Zani. *Managing Computer-Based Information Systems*, Homewood, Ill.: Irwin, 1971.

Freiser, Ted. "Developing an ADP Plan," *Computer Decisions*, January 1975, pp. D2–D4.

Fried, Louis. "Long-Range Planning for EDP," *Auerbach Data Processing Management Reports*, 1974, 16 pp.

IBM Corporation. *Business Systems Planning: Information Systems Planning Guide*, Application Manual GE20-0527-1, August 1975, 92 pp.

Kriebel, Charles H. "The Strategic Dimension of Computer Systems Planning," *Long Range Planning*, September 1968, pp. 7–12.

McFarlan, F. Warren. "Problems in Planning the Information System," *Harvard Business Review,* March–April 1971, pp. 75–89.

McFarlan, F. Warren, Brady M. Cole, and Louis J. Rieger. "Long-Range Planning for Computer-Based Information Systems," in J. Dearden, F. W. McFarlan, and W. M. Zani, *Managing Computer-Based Information Systems,* Homewood, Ill.: Irwin, 1971, pp. 623–630.

McFarlan, F. Warren, Richard L. Nolan, and David P. Norton. *Information Systems Administration.* New York: Holt, Rinehart & Winston, 1973.

Nolan, Richard L. "Systems Analysis for Computer-Based Information Systems Design," *Data Base,* Winter 1971.

Rotch, William, and Brandt R. Allen. "Genesco Case," Graduate School of Business Administration, University of Virginia, 1971. Distributed by the Intercollegiate Case Clearing House, Boston.

Schwartz, M. H., "MIS Planning," *Datamation,* September 1, 1970, pp. 28–31.

Siegal, Paul. *Strategic Planning of Management Information Systems.* New York: Petrocelli Books, 1975.

Soden, John V., and George M. Crandell. "Practical Guidelines for EDP Long-Range Planning," *National Computer Conference Proceedings,* Montvale, N.J.: AFIPS Press, 1975, pp. 675–679.

Steiner, George A. *Comprehensive Managerial Planning,* The Planning Executives Institute, Oxford, Ohio, 1972, 36 pp.

Young, Richard C. "Systems and Data Processing Departments Need Long-Range Planning," *Computers and Automation,* May 1967, pp. 30–33, 45.

2 GEORGE A. STEINER

Comprehensive Managerial Planning[1]

INTUITIVE-ANTICIPATORY VERSUS FORMAL LONG-RANGE PLANNING

Fundamentally, there are two types of comprehensive long-range corporate planning. The first is intuitive-anticipatory planning. While no one really knows the precise mental processes by which it is done it has several discernable major characteristics. Generally it is the work of one person. It may or may not, but often does not, result in a written set of plans. It is based upon past experience, the "gut" feel, the judgment, and the reflective thinking of a manager. It is very important. Many managers have extraordinary capabilities in intuitively devising brilliant strategies and methods to carry them out.[2]

In contrast, the formal planning system is organized and developed on the basis of a set of procedures. It is explicit in the sense that people know what is being done. It is research based, involves the work of many people, and results in a set of written plans.

These two systems of planning often clash. A manager who has been successful with his intuitive judgments is not likely to accept completely the constraints of a formal system. He may be uneasy with some of the new language and methods incorporated by sophisticated staff in a for-

Source. Reprinted, by permission, from George A. Steiner, *Comprehensive Managerial Planning,* The Planning Executives Institute, Oxford, Ohio, 1972.

mal planning system. Or, he may feel a challenge to his authority as those particpating in the system engage in the decision-making process.

There should be no conflict, however, between these two systems. They should complement one another. The formal system should help managers to sharpen their intuitive-anticipatory inputs into the planning process. At the very least, the formal system should give managers more time for reflective thinking.

In a fundamental sense, formal planning is an effort to replicate intuitive planning. But formal planning cannot be really effective unless managers at all levels inject their judgments and intuition into the planning process.

FORMAL COMPREHENSIVE MANAGERIAL PLANNING DEFINED

In its early history the words long-range planning were used to describe the system which is the subject of this chapter. Other names have subsequently been coined. Long ago, for reasons which will be developed in this chapter, I abandoned the use of the words long-range planning to describe the system. I use synonymously these words: comprehensive corporate planning, comprehensive managerial planning, total planning, long-range planning, integrated planning, formal planning, over-all planning, corporate planning, and other combinations of these words.

Corporate long-range planning should be defined in at least four ways, each of which is needed in understanding it. First, long-range planning deals with the futurity of current decisions. This means that long-range planning looks at the chain of cause-and-effect consequences over time of an actual or an intended decision that a manager is going to make. If he does not like what he sees ahead he then will change the decision. Long-range planning also looks at the alternative courses of action what are open in the future and when choices are made they become the basis for making current decisions. The essence of long-range planning is a systematic identification of opportunities and threats that lie in the future which, in combination with other relevant data, provide a basis for a company's making current decisions to exploit the opportunities and avoid the threats.

Second, comprehensive corporate planning is a process. It is a process which begins with the development of objectives, defines strategies and policies to achieve objectives, and develops detailed plans to make sure that the strategies are carried out to achieve the objectives. It is a process of deciding in advance what is to be done, when it is to be done, how it is to be done, and who is going to do it.

Third, it is a philosophy. Many businessmen talk about corporate planning as being a way of life. Executives speak of assuring the proper climate in their enterprise to do the most effective corporate planning. This climate is a function of many forces among which is an attitude of wanting to do effective planning.

Fourth, comprehensive corporate planning may be defined as a structure of plans. It is a structure which integrates strategic with short-range operational plans. In this structure, are integrated, at all levels, major objectives, strategies, policies, and functions of an enterprise.

All these characteristics of corporate planning will be further examined. Before looking at them, however, it is important to make a few comments on what long-range planning is not.

WHAT LONG-RANGE PLANNING IS NOT

Long-range planning does not attempt to make future decisions. Rather, planning involves choosing the more desirable future alternatives open to a company so that better current decisions can be made.

Comprehensive corporate planning is not forecasting. It is not forecasting product sales and then determining what should be done to assure the fulfillment of the forecasts, with respect to such things as material purchases, facilities, manpower, and so on. Corporate planning goes beyond present forecasts of current products and markets and asks such questions as: are we in the right business? What are our basic objectives? When will our present products become obsolete? Are our markets accelerating or eroding? For most companies there is a wide gap between a simple forecast into the future of present sales and profits and what top management would like its sales and profits to be. If so, there is a gap to be filled by comprehensive corporate planning.

Comprehensive long-range planning is not attempting to blueprint the future. It is not the development of a set of plans which are cast in bronze to be used day after day into the far distant future. Indeed, long-range plans are obsolete the very minute they are completed because the environment assumed in their preparation has already changed. On the other hand, long-range planning permits a company to "invent" its future. This means that a company, through the corporate planning process, tries to foresee the future it wants for itself. It then, very often, can fulfill the targets it sets for itself by the development of wise strategies and detailed plans.

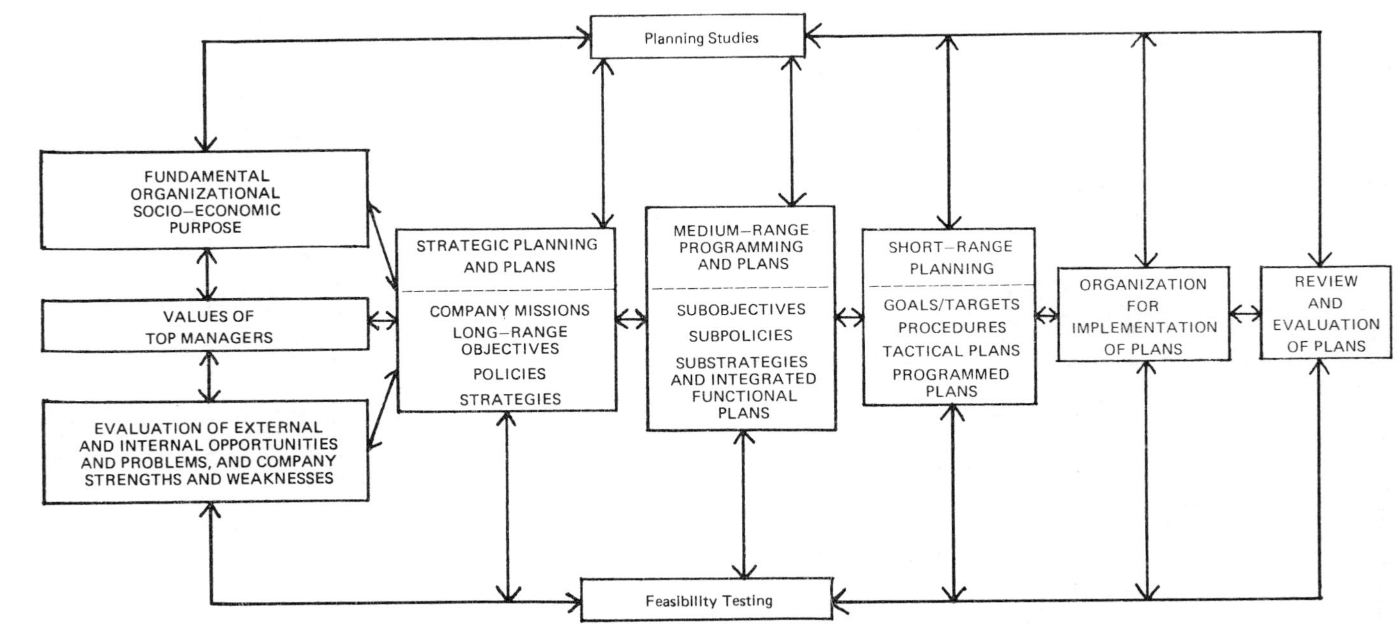

Chart I A structure and process of business planning. *Source.* Adapted from George A. Steiner, *Top Management Planning,* Macmillan, New York, 1969.

CORPORATE PLANNING MODELS

Chart I shows my conceptual model of the structure and process of corporate planning. It further elaborates the meaning of comprehensive planning, particularly strategic planning, and explains how the process can be carried out. Over a number of years I have examined planning systems of many companies and conclude that those that do effective comprehensive planning follow this model explicitly or implicitly. Yet, paradoxically, I have never found an operational system diagramed in precisely the same way as Chart I. Operational flow charts vary depending upon differences among companies but, underneath, the basic elements of Chart I are found in the better systems. If one element of the model in Chart I is missing, either explicitly or implicitly, the system will not operate effectively. Conceptual models of leading authors in the field are quite comparable to this model.[3]

In the following exposition I shall use Chart I to explain the planning process. It should be pointed out, however, that in actual practice the process is iterative and may begin at different points. In practice there is much back-and-forth analysis before decisions are made. For instance, a tentative objective may be established and then strategies are examined to achieve them. Depending upon the analysis of strategies the objectives may be changed and vice versa.

THE STRATEGIC PLANNING PROCESS

The strategic planning process includes the four blocks to the left of the model shown in Chart I and may extend to the blocks to the right of the model, as illustrated in Chart VII. The activity in the block marked "strategic planning and plans" results in a determination of a company's fundamental missions, objectives, policies and strategies that govern the acquisition, use, and disposition of resources to achieve its basic aims. In doing this, of course, the understanding of the socioeconomic purpose of the enterprise is important; the values of top managers must be considered; and facts about future opportunities, threats, and company strengths and weaknesses, are significant data inputs.

Several other characteristics of the strategic planning process should be observed. First, the time spectrum covered ranges from the very short range to infinity. While the general thrust and content of strategic planning is long range a decision can be made in this process to stop producing X product tomorrow or start to build tomorrow a new plant to produce Y product.

Another important characteristic is that while the process may produce a written document on a periodic basis, such as once a year, the process is a continuous activity of top management, as illustrated in Chart IX. Top management cannot, of course, develop a strategic plan once a year and forget strategy in the meantime.

Another important characteristic of strategic planning, as compared with medium-range and short-range planning, is that the results are not usually neatly incorporated in a prescribed form. Medium-range and short-range planning result in numbers for specific functions for a prescribed period of time, as shown in Chart IV. Strategic planning covers any element of the business which is important at the time of analysis and embodies details which are of sufficient scope and depth to provide the necessary basis for implementation. The format for strategic plans generally is much more flexible, and varying in content from time to time, than for other type plans.

Attention in both the business and academic world is moving more and more to the strategic planning process. This is so simply because of the growing significance of this process to business growth and survival. Most of the literature in the field, however, is of recent origin and is growing slowly.[4] The work of scholars has been delayed not alone because of the recent attention to business strategy but also because it involves difficult and messy unstructured problems.

In the following discussion will be presented a few highlights of the nature of each of the major elements in the strategic planning process. This will combine concept, methodology, and operational principles to the extent space permits.

The Socio-Economic Purpose of a Company

Up to a few years ago, in the academic as well as in the business world, a business was said to have but one socio-economic purpose and that was to use the resources at its disposal as efficiently as possible in producing the goods and services that consumers wanted at prices they were willing to pay. Many people in both the educational and business worlds still think this business's only responsibility. But more and more people in and out of business think that the socio-economic purpose of a business is not so narrow. For example, Edward N. Cole, President of General Motors Corporation has written: "The big challenge to American business—as I see it—is to carefully evaluate the constantly changing expressions of public and national goals. Then we must modify our own objectives and programs to meet—as far as possible within the realm of economic and technological feasibility—the new demands of the society we serve."[5] Any large company that begins its long-range planning solely on the basis of the short-range profit maximization principle as its only objective will inevitably wind up in a heap of trouble.

Top Management's Values Systems

The value systems of top managers are basic and fundamental premises in any comprehensive corporate planning system. Sometimes executive values are written but most of the time they are not written nor even articulated. Many of these values cannot be proven or disproven to be correct on the basis of numbers or even logic yet they may determine basic long-range objectives of a company. For instance, a chief executive may say: "I want my company to be the biggest in our industry in ten years." Or, he may say: "I want my company to be the technologically best in the industry." Or, he may say: "My goal is to make my company the biggest and the technically best company in my industry in the next decade." Each of these objectives provides a very different frame of reference for doing corporate planning. Each is to rooted in the value system of the chief executive officer in the company.

Not only do value systems influence objectives but also all sorts of decisions made in the planning process. For instance, one executive may wish to do business with the Mexicans because he likes them. Another in the same industry may prefer not to extend his operations to Mexico. The reasons of both managers may have nothing to do with sales and profits but may be solely determined by the values which each holds.

The Current Position and Future Environment

Chart II, which is a modification of Chart I, illustrates in the two left blocks the range and variety of subject matter involved in assessing the current position of strengths and weaknesses and in identifying future opportunities, threats, and risks. It also shows that operationally and conceptually the planning process can begin with this assessment. A large part of the analytical work of corporate planning staffs is performed in this area. Analysis in this area can be done before, during, or after objectives and strategies are formulated.

The number of environmental factors which may be of importance to a company, either as opportunities or threats, is so great that it is necessary to determine those which are most significant and to spend as much time and effort as possible in studying them. Consumer disposable income is very important to an automobile company but not to an

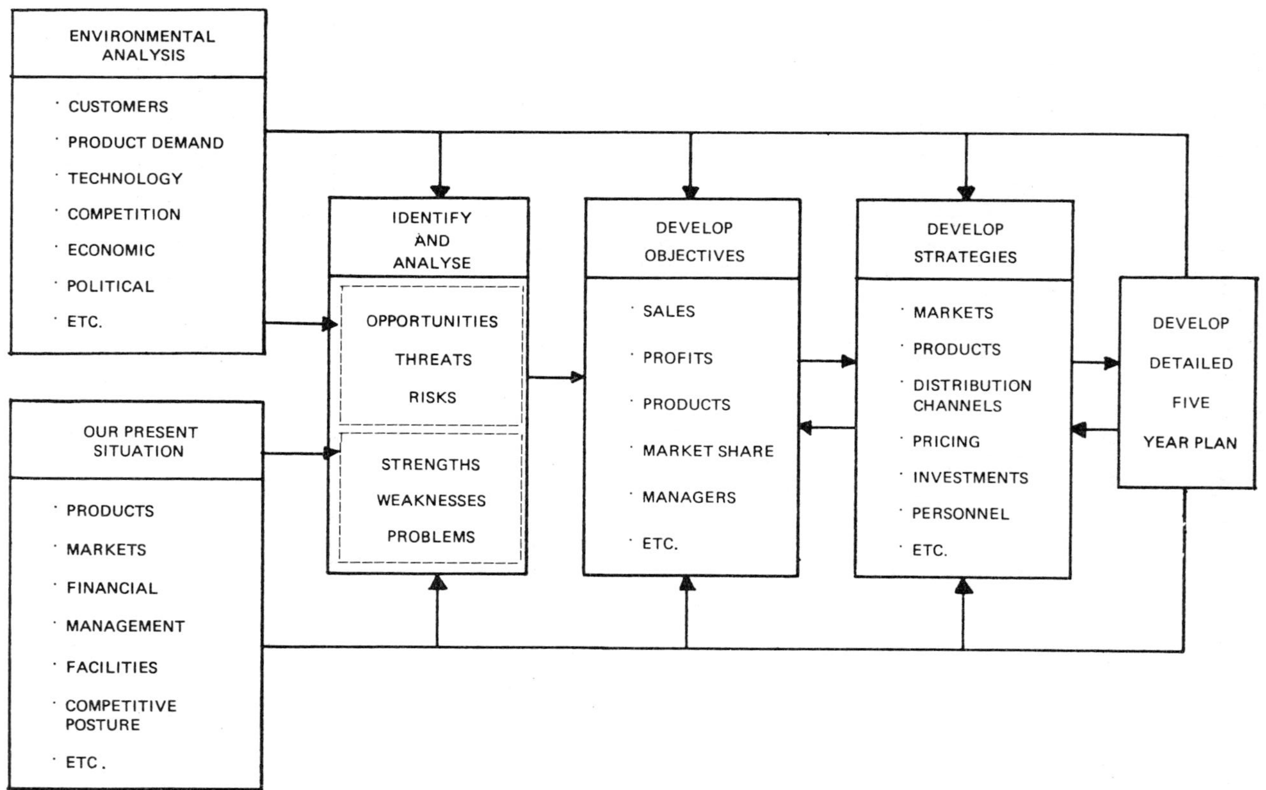

Chart II A model for business long-range planning.

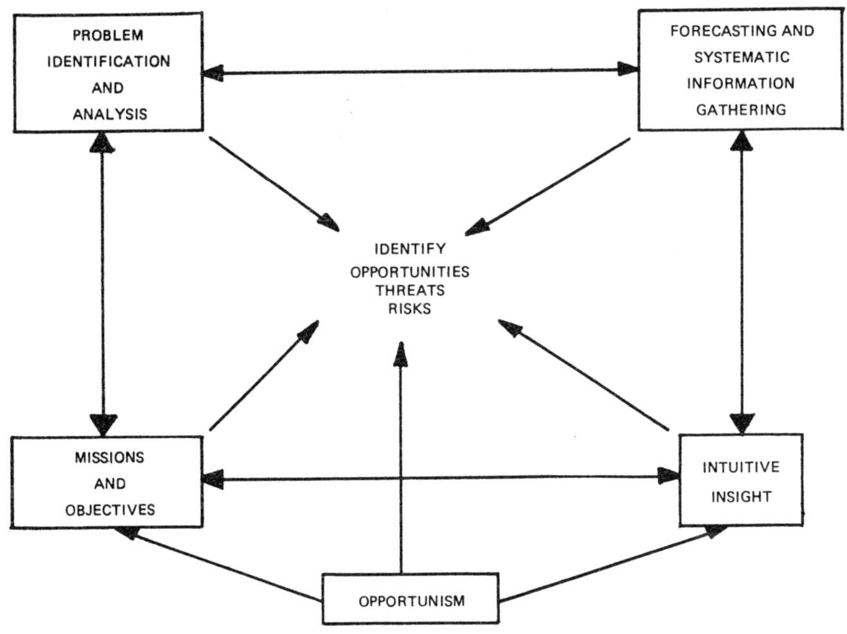

Chart III Opportunity—threat—risk analysis.

aerospace company. Threats to a beer producer are far different than those to a steel company.

Chart III illustrates different ways a company can approach identification of opportunities, threats, and risks. Problem identification in the upper left hand corner refers to results of simple observations or deep analysis. For instance, a company may note that its profit margin for product X is falling. This is a problem and the next step is to define precisely what is causing it. When that is understood what can and should be done in the future to correct it becomes clearer. Some companies begin the planning process by identifying opportunities and threats in this way.

Another approach is to ask what are the basic missions and objectives of the company and then determine what are the opportunities ahead to achieve them or the threats which may thwart their fulfillment.

Opportunism is a third approach. For example, the analysis of diversification opportunities of some companies is dependent upon "what comes over the transim." In other words they wait to see what offers are made and then analyze each one. This is in contrast to a careful examination of opportunities in the environment to find the best possibilities for diversification. McDonald-Douglas's movement into computer software systems resulted from such a systematic study.

Instinctive feel or intuitive insight into the future is always, of course, a potentially powerful approach.

All of these approaches can result in a determination to make sophisticated forecasts and to gather masses of other information. They also can follow this activity or parallel it.

There are five major types of forecasts made in and for the planning process. First, are survey-research type forecasts which involve the integration of many different areas of knowledge. For example, a quality forecast of the automobile market will rest not alone on economic analysis but upon changes in social values, technology, politics, and pollution standards. Second, are economic type forecasts. Generally, the most often made forecasts are of sales. While there is no standard methodology for making survey-research forecasts the tool kit of sales forecasters is very rich.[6]

Technological forecasts are a third type of futures information which are being made by more and more companies. Work has advanced importantly in recent years about how to make acceptable forecasts of technology. The methodology ranges from mathematical formulas to informed judgment.[7]

Forecasting what competitors are likely to do is something that all companies should do systematically but few do. For a large company a questionnaire to informed personnel is a simple and effective method to get such information.

Two other types of forecasts are now being made by very large companies but will be made increasingly, especially by large companies, in the future. They are forecasts of social values and social indicators. By social values are meant attitudes and views which people hold about such matters as social justice, comfort, human dignity, materialism, national pride, and so on. Everyone knows that values are changing importantly. A large company that can forecast changes in society's values which will affect it will obviously have an advantage.[8] Social indicators are measures of phenomenon associated with quality of life, such as personal safety, medical care, and different pollutions.[9]

Forecasts in these latter two areas will increase among the larger business and, for some, they will in the future stand beside the traditional economic forecasts as major considerations in corporate decision making. Important strides have been made in the past few years in making such forecasts.[10]

Return now to "Our Present Situation," on Chart II. There is no single way to identify and analyze a company's strengths and weaknesses.

They can, of course, cover a wide range from management talent to salesmen in the field. It is hardly necessary to comment that a company should move from its strength and avoid its weaknesses, and it should understand that a strength today may become a weakness in tomorrow's environment. Yet it is observable that companies fail because they ignored their weaknesses. Many have failed because they had a success syndrome which blindly assumed that present success was based upon a strength which would continue. Not enough companies systematically examine their strengths; fewer systematically study their weaknesses.

This is a much too brief and inadequate examination of how a manager can identify the right problem opportunity, and threat. The literature on how to solve a problem once it is discovered is mountainous. The literature on how to be sure to identify the right problem and how to see the best opportunity is extremely small. This is too bad because a businessman runs a far greater risk in not finding the right problem or opportunity than in determining how to solve the problem or how to exploit the opportunity once it is identified.

Developing Basic Business Missions

On the basis of premises developed in the above steps the strategic planning process then hammers out basic missions long-range objectives, and policies and strategies to achieve them. Each of these will be treated in turn. But first it is useful to point out that, contrary to so many elementary economic textbooks, there is no such thing as a single goal or objective of a company. Each firm has a network of aims which includes the basic socio-economic purpose of the company, value objectives of top managers, business missions, long-range objectives, and short-range targets and goals.[11] Each of these is different, has a different purpose in the planning process, and is developed in a different fashion. A surprising number of companies have developed creeds or philosophies for general distribution which encompass the basic ends which the top managements of these companies seek to achieve and, sometimes, how they wish them to be achieved.[12]

Basic missions should be stated in both product and market terms. A company may say that it is in the business of producing air conditioners. However, it will be in entirely different businesses if it chooses to make air conditioners for office buildings, or for home cooling, or for automobiles. Deciding upon a basic mission is a fundamental step in planning. If the Baldwin Locomotive Works had said its mission was to make tractive power for railroads, instead of sticking with the making of steam locomotives, it probably would still be in business. A company that says it is not in the business of making bricks for construction but is in the clay products business for construction widens its opportunities as well as its threats. Too broad a mission, however, may be dangerous. For instance, it is doubtful whether a company making lead pencils should say its mission is changed to making communications equipment. There is a sort of iron law of product-market development that says the further a company gets from its present products and markets the less likely it will make a profit. But if the product and market are very narrow, growth and prosperity can be enhanced by a judicious widening of the mission.

Long-Range Objectives

Objectives are desired results to be achieved, usually in a specific time. They are very important in the planning process because they are guides to the development of actions to assure their fulfillment. Behavioral scientists also conclude they are important motivators of people in organizations, because generally people in organizations like to try to achieve the objectives set for the organization. The more people in organizations participate in the objective-setting process the greater is their motivation to achieve them. Objectives can be used effectively, of course, as standards for measuring performance.

Objectives may be expressed for every element of a business which is considered to be important enough to be the subject of plans. There is no standard classification of objectives nor of the number of objectives which a company should have.

All companies that have a planning process set objectives for profits and sales. In addition to objectives in these areas one generally finds in planning systems of larger companies objectives for the following: marketing (e.g., share of market); finance (e.g., debt retirement, dividend objectives, new financing); stability (e.g., sales, profits, employment); personnel (e.g., developing managers, working conditions, employment levels); research and development; and survival. This does not exhaust the list and many subobjectives are possible in each category.

Peter Drucker says that objectives are needed in every area of a business where performance and results directly and importantly affect the survival and prosperity of the enterprise. Following are the areas where he says objectives ought to be set: market standing, innovation, productivity, physical and financial resources, profitability, manager performance and development, worker performance and attitude, and public responsibility.[13]

Objectives can be based on different considerations. They may be dictated by top management without any research analysis, or they may be based upon thorough analysis. They may be extrapolations from the past or set to exploit a foreseen opportunity or avoid a perceived threat. They may be derived from a settled strategy or designed to support other objectives.

However derived they should exhibit a few major characteristics. First, they should be able to lead and motivate and the more concrete and specific they are the more likely are they to have directive power. To say that "our company seeks to make a good profit," is far less powerful than to say, "our objective is to make $4 million in profits three years from today." Second, objectives should be actionable. Goals which are far too high or far too low do not lead to action. Objectives should be a little aggressive and require imagination and hard work to achieve. Third, objectives should be understood by those who are to develop means to achieve them. Fourth, objectives should conform to ethical and social codes accepted by society and by the business. Finally, objectives should correlate and be mutually supporting, to the extent possible. For instance, if the objective is to achieve a return on investment of 15 percent, after taxes, by the end of five years, the target is much more likely to be achieved if sub- and sub-subobjectives are linked to it. For instance, sub-objectives might be: increase sales to $10 million in 5 years, raise gross profits to $2.5 million in 5 years, build modern facilities and operate them at capacity over the next five years, and upgrade and maintain a skilled work force in specified ways. These objectives might also be linked to sub-subobjectives. For example, an increase in sales might be sought by setting specific objectives for market share, advertising expenditures, market penetration, product redesign, and research and development in specific directions. Similarly,, sub-subojectives might be set for achievement of the sub-objectives of gross profits, facilities, and work force. If the sub- and sub-subjectives are achieved, the achievement of the dominant objective is inevitable.

Devloping Policies and Strategies

Once objectives are established the logical sequence is to develop policies and strategies to achieve them. Policies are broad guides to action, such as a decision to allow divisions to acquire other companies, after approval of headquarters; or a decision not to require one division of a company to buy the products of another division unless it wishes to do so. Strategies are specific important actions, usually but not always the deployment of resources, to achieve an objective. In mind are major actions to distinguish them from minor tactics.[14]

Strategies, of course, can be associated with all kinds of activities in a business—markets, products, financing, diversification, pricing, and so on. There is no classification that has any common acceptance. Most writers would agree, however, that two broad classifications of strategies are personal and business. Personal strategies can influence business strategies, and vice versa. Karl von Clausewitz, when speaking about military success commented that "The best strategy is always to be very strong, first generally, then at the decisive point." This, of course, can apply to both personal affairs as well as to military and business strategy.

The most successful strategies turn out to be clusters of strategies. A strategic decision by a company, for example, to expand its foreign operations will result in substrategies for geographic area, financing, marketing, management, and so on.

A systematic stategic planning process in a formal planning system is a preferred approach to the development of effective stategies. The following specific approaches can be incorporated in a formal planning process or can be conducted in the absence of a formal system. Intuition, as pointed out earlier is an excellent approach if it is brilliant. For some activities, such as acquisitions, some companies use the *ad hoc,* trial and error approach. A successful invention is an unexcelled strategy. Another approach is to determine the really significant factors that are important in the success of a particular business and concentrate major decisions on it. For instance, a new imaginative toy is a critically strategic factor in the success of a toy company, but superior technical and fail-safe qualities are of dominant importance to the success of an airplane manufacturer. Finding a particular spot, a propitious niche, where a company can give a customer an irresistible value that is not being satisfied and at a relatively low cost, is a strategy that has made many companies rich. Finally, some companies are satisfied to follow the lead of other companies.

Two concluding points of importance should be added about strategies. What is a successful strategy for one company may turn out to be another's poison. Chances are that if Avon changed strategies with Revlon neither would do as well as it now does. Also, timing is very important. The Edsel automobile filled a niche for the Ford Motor Company but the timing was bad and the product failed.

MEDIUM-RANGE PROGRAMMING

Medium-range programming is the process where specific functional plans are related for specific numbers of years to display the details of how strategies are to be carried out to achieve long-range objectives and company missions. Many companies prepare manuals of procedures telling the divisions how to prepare their medium-range programs and plans. Typically, the planning period is for five years but there is a tendency for more technically advanced companies to plan ahead in some detail for seven or more years. In most companies the medium-range plans cover only the major functions and are quantified on comparatively simple forms, as shown in Chart IV. In most companies the functional plans are translated into financial terms in the form of a pro forma profit and loss statement, as shown in Chart V. Sometimes a pro forma balance sheet is also prepared. Sometimes, depending upon its importance, detailed forms are prepared for selected elements. This is especially true for facility programs.

SHORT-RANGE PLANNING AND PLANS

The next step, of course, is to develop short-range plans on the basis of the medium-range plans. In about half the companies that do formal planning the numbers for the first year of the medium-range plans are the same as in the short-range yearly operational budget summaries. Some companies feel that tightly linking budgets and medium-range plans will help to make long-range plans realistic. Others feel that a tight relationship will divert attention from the long-range to current matters, such as return on investment. This is especially so if a manager's compensation is based principally on yearly return-on-investment performance. If the linkage is very loose the long-range plan still can be reflected in and be of high importance to current budget making.

The current operating budgets will, of course, be in very great detail as compared with the numbers in the medium-range plans. There will also be covered many more subjects. The numbers of subjects will depend upon what management wishes to control in the short run. Some elaboration of this point is shown in Chart VI.

One should not leave this subject without at least commenting on the scope of short-range planning. While strategic and medium-range plans may provide the framework within which short-range planning is done, the different types of short range plans that can be affected covers a wide range. In mind are production plans such as plant location, layout of facilities, work methods, inventory plans and control, employee training, job enrichment, management education, and negotiations with unions. Space limitations prevent any further examination of these types of short-range plans, their nature, or how they are prepared.

ITEM	LAST YEAR	THIS YEAR FORECAST	NEXT FIVE YEARS				
			FIRST YEAR	SECOND YEAR	THIRD YEAR	FOURTH YEAR	FIFTH YEAR
SALES							
MARKETING EXPENDITURES							
ADVERTISING							
DISTRIBUTION							
UNIT PRODUCTION							
EMPLOYEES							
TOTAL							
DIRECT							
INDIRECT							
R & D OUTLAYS							
NEW PRODUCTS							
PRODUCT IMPROVEMENT							
COST REDUCTION							
NEW FACILITIES (TOTAL)							
EXPANSION PRESENT PROD.							
NEW PRODUCTS							
COST REDUCTION							
MAINTENANCE							

Chart IV Division five-year plans.

DIVISION: ____________

	THIS YEAR	19__	19__	19__	19__	19__
SALES - UNITS						
GROSS SALES - DOLLARS						
ALLOWANCES						
NET SALES						
COST OF GOODS SOLD						
GROSS PROFIT ON SALES						
G & A EXPENSE						
SELLING EXPENSE						
ADVERTISING EXPENSE						
R & D EXPENSE						
TOTAL OPERATING EXPENSE						
OTHER CHARGES, NET						
INTEREST ON LONG TERM OBLIGATIONS						
OTHER						
INCOME BEFORE DEPRECIATION						
DEPRECIATION						
INCOME BEFORE OVERHEAD ALLOCATION						
ALLOCATION OF GENERAL OVERHEAD						
NET INCOME BEFORE TAXES						
RATE OF RETURN ON ASSETS						

Chart V Financial summary.

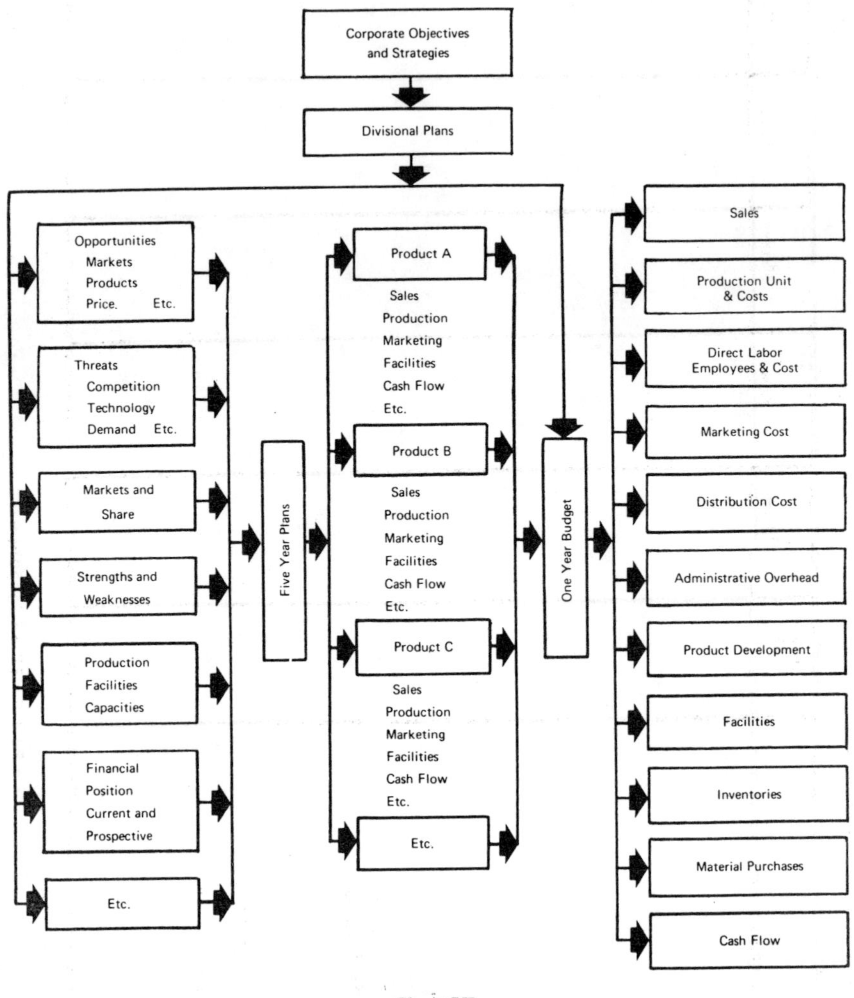

Chart VI

TRANSLATING STRATEGIC PLANS INTO CURRENT DECISIONS

Chart VI shows that corporate strategies can be reflected immediately in current plans or used as a basis for the development of medium-range plans which in turn are the basis for annual or shorter plans. There are several additional features of Chart VI worthy of note. In a divisionalized company where there is decentralized authority the general manager will be obliged to make studies of the environment for his product. This information will be used, with whatever directions he gets from headquarters about objectives and strategies, to make his medium-range plans. There should be, therefore, a close linkage between top management objectives and strategies, and subobjectives and substrategies forged by the division manager.

Also, the details of the one-year budget are considerably different from the main categories of the five-year plans. The two can be the same, but the budget is more concerned with coordination and control of critical internal flows of resources. The subject matter of the short-range plans, therefore, will be focused on these concerns rather than on the more aggregative functions in the medium-range plans. The aggregates of the short-range plans, however, can relate to medium-range plans, as noted above.

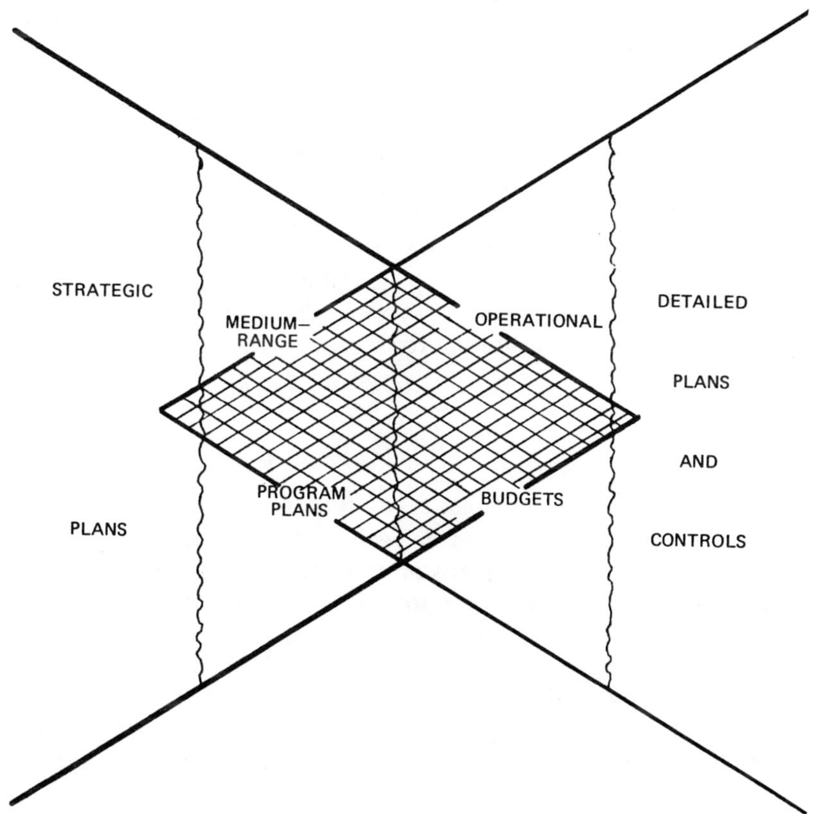

Chart VII Intermeshing of long-range planning and operational control.

In the formal planning process there is not a sharp distinction between strategic planning at one extreme and tactical planning at the other, or of planning at one end and control at the other. Each has a graduated impact throughout the planning process, as shown in Chart VII. This chart shows that traces of strategic planning are found in detailed short-range planning. Also, strategic planning and particularly medium-range programming is done in some reflection of control over operations.[15]

PLANNING STUDIES AND FEASIBILITY TESTING

Planning studies can, of course, be made throughout the planning process. I have noted how important are such studies in examining the environment. They also, however, can be important in analyzing such matters as current inventory replacement policy, or suitability of the present organization for planning.

Feasibility testing takes place throughout the planning spectrum. For instance, when lower-level managers are examining different alternative choices one may comment: "method A has great profit potential but I do not think the top management would like to use this method." He is obviously applying a feasibility test by appraising an alternative against the values of top management, as he understands them. At lower levels the testing can become completely quantitative and sometimes very sophisticated, as for instance in the applicability of a linear programming model to testing distribution routes for products to their markets.

REVIEW AND EVALUATION

Plans that are developed should be reviewed and evaluated. There is nothing that produces better plans on the part of subordinates than for the top managers to show a keen interest in the plans and the results that they bring. When comprehensive formal planning was first developed some fifteen years ago there was a tendency for companies to make written plans and not redo them until they became obviously obsolete. Now, the great majority of companies go through an annual cycle of comprehensive planning in which the plans are reviewed and revised.

PLANNING TOOLS

The range of tools available for making "rational" decisions in the planning process is very broad. It covers a spectrum ranging from non-quantitative tools, such as intuition, judgment, and hunches, to very complex and highly sophisticated methods such as systems analysis and computer simulation. In between are older quantitative tools such as conventional accounting techniques and newer quantitative methods like probability theory and linear programming.

I cannot do justice to this subject here, but there are several points that should be added to the present analysis. First, the applicability of different tools varies very much depending upon where and when they are applied in the planning process. For example, a sophisticated quantitative forecasting technique such as exponential smoothing is not very effective in making a forecast with great unknowns, such as the market for aspirin in China. Second, it is very important for technicians to find major business problems which their methods can solve for managers rather than to try to find problems which their tools can solve easily. Third, there is currently a virtual groundswell of use of more sophisticated quantitative tools at higher levels of corporate planning. For instance, computer simulation and risk analysis are being used widely in strategic planning.[16] Most of the computer simulation models are deterministic. They answer "what if" types of questions. But, increasingly, probability theory is being used in top-level decision making, as for instance David Hertz's risk analysis.[17] At the end of this chapter we include a few more comments concerning tools of analysis.

ORGANIZING THE FORMAL PLANNING PROCESS

There is no single method, or formula, or standard way to start and conduct a formal corporate planning system. What is done is a function of such factors as managerial style, size of organization, whether the firm is centralized or decentralized, managerial authority extended to decentralized managers, types of problems the company faces, managerial knowledge, types of products, and other comparable factors. So, each system is fitted to each company.

There are two fundamentally different approaches to doing formal planning. The first is the top-down approach. Comprehensive planning in a centralized company is done at the top of the corporation, and departments and outlaying activities are pretty much told what to do. In

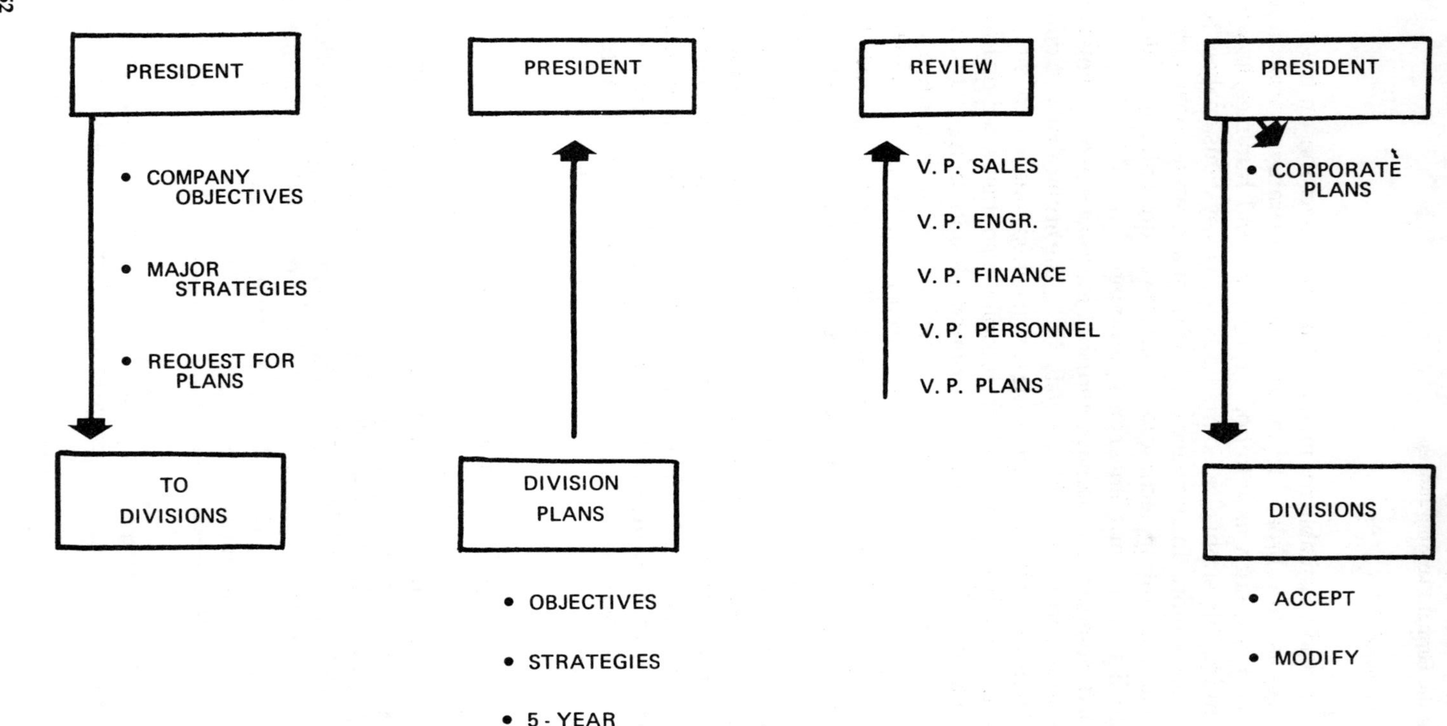

Chart VIII Top-down approach.

a decentralized company the flow of activity is shown in Chart VIII. The President gives the divisions guidelines and asks for plans. The plans are reviewed at headquarters and sent back to the divisions for modification or with a note of acceptance. If the division plans do not add up to what top management wishes there then are prepared additional corporate plans which may provide for acquisitions, divestment, or refinancing.

In the bottom-up approach the top management gives the divisions no guidelines and asks them to submit plans. Information such as the following may be requested: major opportunities and threats, major objectives, strategies to achieve the objectives, and specific data on sales, profits, market share sought, capital requirements, and number of employees for a specified number of years. This then is reviewed at top management levels and the same process as noted above is then followed.

A third approach, of course, is to develop a mixture of the top down and bottom up. This is the method used in most large decentralized companies. In this approach, top management gives guidelines to the divisions. Generally, they are broad enough to permit the divisions a good bit of flexibility in developing their own plans. Sometimes a top management may hammer out a basic objective by dialogue with division managers. Such objectives as return on investment may be derived in this way, especially if the performance of the division manager is measured upon the basis of this standard.

In smaller centralized companies the chief executive will often use his main line managers as staff in helping him to develop formal plans. In some very large companies the president will use his line managers in the same fashion. In many companies the president has a group of executives with whom he meets on a regular basis to deal with all the problems facing the company. In some companies, part of the time of this group is spent on long-range planning. Over time the group will develop written long-range plans.

Another organizational dimension is the scope of information accumulated. Some companies start the process simply by asking divisions and department heads to develop five year objectives for selected functions (e.g., sales, profits, markets, etc.,) and major strategies to achieve the objectives. Better results seem to flow, however, when enough information is requested so that decisions can be made and the plans can serve as a basis for preparing current operating plans. Also, it is better to initiate planning on a regular cycle, such as preparing written plans once a year.

Larger companies may appoint a director of planning, and give him a

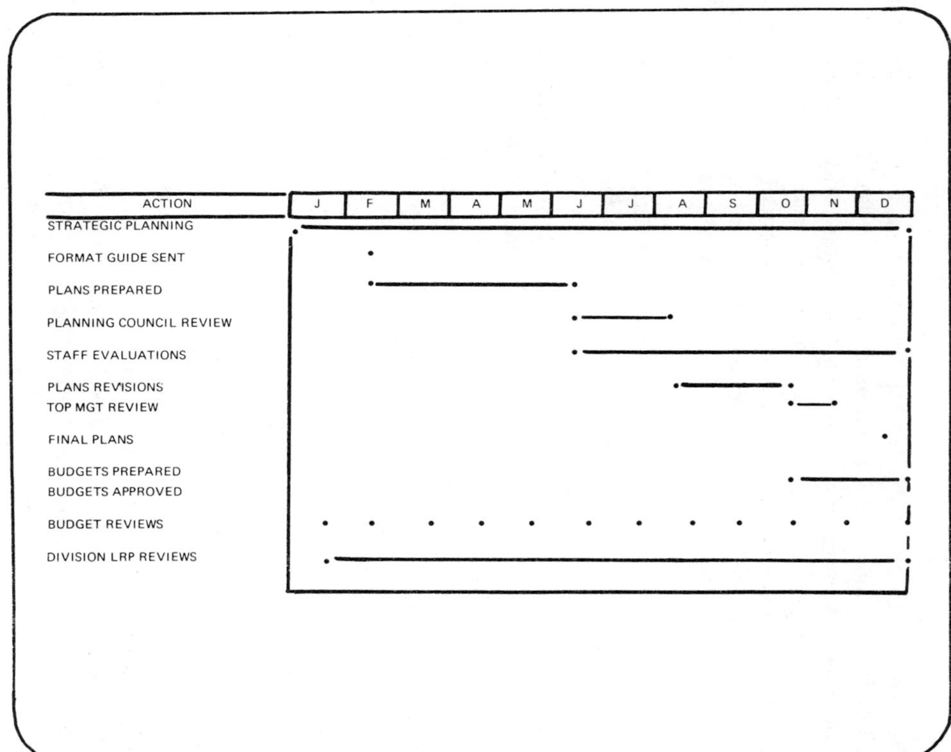

Chart IX   A planning time schedule.

small staff, to start and maintain the planning system. He should report to the top management. His basic functions are to help others, particularly line managers, to do an effective planning job and to coordinate the plans developed by different parts of the organization when that is desirable. He may help top management formulate goals, policies, and strategies to guide the planning process. When plans are received from others he may help top management evaluate them. He may make forecasts for others to use, help weak divisions make plans, show others how to develop effective plans, assist top management in making current decisions on the basis of long-range planning, and make recommendations concerning product development. He does not assume responsibility for doing the planning for either the top management or other line managers. Long-range planning is a line function and cannot be delegated to staff.[18]

One final observation on organization is that in all companies it is desirable to do a little "planning to plan" before actually starting the process. In larger companies this may result, and should, in a set of procedures which will tell everyone what is going to be done, how it is to be done, and when. Generally speaking it is better to prescribe as little as possible in order to permit those who are doing the planning a maximum of flexibility. But a minimum of procedure is required. In manuals it is desirable to define important words used in the planning process. This will very much improve communications. Chart IX shows a typical time schedule for comprehensive planning in a large decentralized company.

THE VALUE OF FORMAL CORPORATE PLANNING

Comprehensive formal long-range planning has been growing in use throughout the world simply because managers find that it is valuable. There are many reasons why this is so, a few of which are briefly noted below.

To begin with, the times demand it. Business environment is changing ever faster and becoming much more turbulent. In the product area, for instance, the typical life cycle is shrinking rapidly; but the average research and development time is lengthening and the costs to prototype are increasing. Technological threats to products are growing in numbers and coming from areas other than the industry to which they are related. Everyone is aware of shifting population movements, more and highly complex government regulations, changing consumer demands, and many other forces which make the evolving environment at one and the same time a world of opportunity and threat to every company.

Long-range planning is essential to discharging top management's responsibilities. Marvin Bower, a management consultant, wrote a book to describe the functions of chief executives and much of the book dealt with formal planning, particularly strategic planning.[19] Some companies that have job descriptions for their chief executive officer say explicitly the chief executive is the chief planner of the company.

As mentioned earlier, planning enables a company to simulate the future, on paper. If it does not like what it sees it erases and starts over. This is much less expensive than letting the future evolve on an *ad hoc* basis. It applies the systems approach. It looks at a company as a system composed of many subsystems. Looking at the company in this way prevents suboptimization of parts. It forces a company to set objectives and clarifies future opportunities and threats. It links decision-making between top and lower-level managers. Lower-level management decisions are much more likely to be made in conformance with the wishes of top management because plans are written and available to them. It sets standards of performance.

Formal planning answers some very significant questions for a manager, such as: what is our basic line of business? What are the company's long-range objectives? What products are or are not going to be obsolete? How shall we replace these products and when? What will be our cash flow over the next few years? What and where are our markets? What share of the market do we wish to get? How will we get it?

Long-range planning is a new and significant communications system. It permits people to participate in the decision-making process. People are more adaptable to change because they participate in making the change. It is a learning and mind-stretching exercise that increasingly is being recognized as a major tool for training managers.

Finally, a few recent studies are providing concrete evidence that long-range planning really pays off in cash. One study compared the five-year performance of firms that introduced formal planning with those that did not. It also compared the performance of the firms for the five years before introducing long-range planning with five years of long-range planning. Results were measured for sales, earnings per share, stock price, earnings on common equity, and earnings on total capital. In each instance those companies that did long-range planning had better performance in significant degree than companies in the same industry that did not formally plan. Also, in each case the record of the firms that did long-range planning was better after than before introducing the system.[20] Another study concluded that on virtually all relevant financial criteria companies that made acquisitions by a systematic planning approach did much better than those that went about it on an unplanned opportunistic basis.[21]

In sum, there are two types of values of comprehensive long-range planning—substantive and behavioral. Either set should be sufficient to convince management of the value of this new tool. When both are considered it is easy to see why formal long-range planning has been introduced into most medium-sized and larger companies.[22] More and more managers are agreeing with an old military assertion that says: "*Plans* sometimes may be useless but the planning *process* is always indispensable."

LIMITS OF FORMAL PLANNING

Comprehensive corporate planning is not, of course, without its shortcomings. It is an intimate part of the managerial process and if other parts of management are weak the planning process itself may be less than satisfactory. Long-range plans may not turn out well sometimes because of unexpected changes in the environment. Of fundamental importance, also, is the fact that long-range planning is virtually worthless in getting a company out of a major current crisis. Aside from such shortcomings, there are all sorts of problems which can arise in the development of a planning system. Many of these are suggested in the following array of pitfalls in planning.

PITFALLS IN COMPREHENSIVE LONG-RANGE PLANNING

Following are fifty major common pitfalls in starting, doing, and using long-range planning. They are the most important ones that I have detected. They vary in significance, but each can adversely affect the planning system and its value. Some of them were mentioned in the preceding discussion, but many were not. Space does not permit any comment about them.[23]

A. Pitfalls in Getting Started

1. Top management's assumption that it can delegate the planning function to a planner.
2. Rejecting planning because there has been success without it.
3. Rejecting formal planning because the system failed in the past to

foresee a critical problem and/or did not result in substantive decisions that satisfied top management.

4. Assuming that the present body of knowledge about planning is insufficient to guide fruitful comprehensive planning.
5. Assuming that a company cannot develop effective long-range planning in a way appropriate to its resources and needs.
6. Assuming that comprehensive corporate planning can be introduced into a company and overnight miraculous results will appear.
7. Thinking that a successful corporate plan can be moved from one company to another without change and with equal success.
8. Assuming that a formal system can be introduced into a company without an "agonizing reappraisal" of current managerial practices and decision-making processes.
9. Ignoring the power structure of a company in organizing the planning process.
10. Failure to develop a clear understanding of the long-range planning procedure before the process is actually undertaken.
11. Failure to create a climate in the company which is congenial and not resistant to planning.
12. Failing to locate the corporate planner at a high enough level in the managerial hierarchy.
13. Failure to make sure that the planning staff has the necessary qualities of leadership, technical expertise, and personality to discharge properly its responsibilities in making the planning system effective.

B. Pitfalls Related to a Misunderstanding of the Nature of Long-Range Planning

14. Forgetting that planning is a political, a social, and an organizational, as well as a rational, process.
15. Assuming that corporate comprehensive planning is something separate from the entire management process.
16. Failure to make sure that top management and major line officers really understand the nature of long-range planning and what it will accomplish for them and the company.
17. Failing to understand that systematic formal planning and intuitive (opportunistic, or entrepreneurial) planning are complementary.
18. Assuming that plans can be made by staff planners for line managers to implement.
19. Ignoring the fact that planning is and should be a learning process.
20. Assuming that planning is easy.
21. Assuming that planning is hard.

22. Assuming that long-range planning can get a company out of a current crisis.
23. Assuming that long-range planning is only strategic planning, or just planning for a major product, or simply looking ahead at likely development of present product. (In other words, failing to see that comprehensive planning is an integrated managerial system.)

C. Pitfalls in Doing Long-Range Planning

I. *Managerial Involvement*

24. Top management becomes so engrossed in current problems that it spends insufficient time on long-range planning, and the process becomes discredited among other managers and staff.
25. Long-range planning becomes unpopular because top management spends so much time on long-range problems that it ignores short-range problems.
26. Failure to assure the necessary involvement in the planning process of major line personnnel.
27. Too much centralization of long-range planning in the central headquarters so that divisions feel little responsibility for developing effective plans.

II. *The Process of Planning*

28. Failure to develop company goals suitable as a basis for formulating long-range plans.
29. Assuming that equal weight should be given to all elements of planning (i.e., that the same emphasis should be placed on strategic as on tactical planning, or that the same emphasis should be accorded to major functional plans).
30. Injecting so much formality into the system that it lacks flexibility, looseness, and simplicity, and restrains creativity.
31. Inability to avoid over-optimism and/or over-cautiousness in committing resources.
32. Extrapolating rather than rethinking the entire process in each cycle (i.e., if plans are made for 1972 through 1976, adding 1977 in the 1973 cycle rather than redoing all plans from 1973 to 1977.)
33. Developing such a reverence for numbers that irreverence for intuition and value judgments predominates the thinking going into planning.
34. Seeking precision of numbers throughout the planning horizon.

35. Assuming that older methods to choose from among alternatives should be discarded in favor of newer techniques.
36. Assuming that new quantitative techniques are not as useful as advertised.
37. Doing long-range planning periodically and forgetting it in-between cycles.

III. *Creditability of Results*

38. Failure to develop planning capabilities in major operating units.
39. Failure of top management, and/or the planning staff, to give departments and divisions sufficient information and guidance (e.g., top management interests, environmental projections, etc.).
40. Attempting to do too much in too short a time.
41. Failure to secure that minimum of system and information to make the process and its results creditable and useful.

D. Pitfalls in Using Long-Range Plans

42. Failure of top management to review with departmental and divisional heads the long-range plans which they have developed.
43. Forgetting that the fundamental purpose of the exercise is to make better current decisions.
44. Assuming that plans once made are in the nature of blueprints and should be followed rigorously until changed in the next planning cycle.
45. Top management's consistently rejecting the formal planning mechanism by making intuitive decisions which conflict with the formal plans.
46. Assuming that, because plans must result in current decisions, it is the short-run that counts and planning efforts as well as evaluations of results should concentrate on the short-run.
47. Failing to use plans as standards for measuring managerial performance.
48. Forgetting to apply a cost-benefit analysis to the system to make sure advantages are greater than costs.
49. Failing to encourage managers to do good long-range planning by basing reward solely on short-range performance measures.
50. Failing to exploit the fact that formal planning is a managerial process which can be used to improve managerial capabilities throughout a company.

NOTES

1. I have leaned heavily on my book *Top Management Planning* (New York, The Crowell-Collier Macmillan Company) 1969. This book contains a bibliography of about 700 items which, I think, included the best literature at the time of writing. For an earlier annotated bibliography of about 500 references see Melville C. Branch, *Selected References for Corporate Planning,* New York, American Management Association, 1966. A more recent brief resume of the best literature in the field, is Robert J. Mockler, "Theory and Practice of Planning," *Harvard Business Review,* Vol. 48, March-April 1970, pp. 148–150, 152–158. Another recent bibliography with good annotations is John P. Frazier, Ellsworth P. Ingraham, and William L. Kath, "Recent Publications on Planning," in Richard F. Vancil, Francil J. Aguilar, Robert A. Howell, and F. Warren McFarlan (eds.), *Formal Planning Systems* - 1969, Harvard Graduate School of Business Administration, Soldiers Field, 1969 (mimeographed), pp. 183–200. To this should be added a reference to the only journal in the world devoted exclusively to long-range planning. It is *Long Range Planning,* published by Pergamon Press Ltd., on behalf of the Society for Long Range Planning, Terminal House, Grosvenor Gardens, London, England. It first appeared in 1968.

Special reference should be made to surveys about what really is being done in business with respect to the formal planning process. Two of the earliest substantial studies were, first, David I. Cleland, *The Origin and Development of a Philosophy of Long-Range Planning in American Business,* doctoral dissertation, The Ohio State University, 1962. The second was William T. Newell, Jr., *Long-Range Planning Policies and Practices: Selected Companies Operating in Texas,* Research Monograph No. 25, Austin, Texas, Bureau of Business Research, The University of Texas, 1963. A more recent publication is Kjell-Arne Ringbakk, *Organized Corporate Planning Systems,* doctoral dissertation, The University of Wisconsin, Graduate School of Business, 1968.

Long-range planning in foreign countries has not been examined as extensively as in the United States. There are, however, exceptions. One is Toyohiro Kono, "Long-Range Business Planning in Japan," mimeographed, Tokyo, Japan, Japan Management Center, 1967. Another is Bernard Taylor and Peter Irving, "Organized Planning in Major U.K. Companies," *Long Range Planning,* Vol. 3, June 1971, pp. 10–26. Another is Raoul M. Elias, "State of the Art of Canadian Corporate Planning," mimeograph resume of MBA dissertation, McGill Faculty of Management, Montreal, Quebec. Special mention should be made of a large data bank of information concerning formal planning systems which is developing at Harvard University under the direction of Professor Richard F. Vancil. See Richard F. Vancil and Lewis B. Ward, "Formal Planning Systems: The 'Data Bank' Project," in Francis J. Aguilar, Robert A. Howell, and Richard F. Vancil (eds.), *Formal Planning Systems: 1970,* mimeographed, Boston, Massachusetts, Harvard University Graduate School of Business Administration, 1970.

2. I am using synonymously several words associated with creativity. Actually, there are differences among such things as intuition, judgment, hunch, instinct, invention, innovation, and entrepreneurship. See *Top Management Planning, op. cit.,* pp. 353–355. This footnote provides the occasion to make the comment that there is no general agreement on the many words and phrases used in planning. There is evolving, however, some consensus on some definitions.

3. See, for example, Robert N. Anothony, *Planning and Control Systems: A Framework for Analysis,* Boston, Graduate School of Business Administration, Harvard University, 1952; Frank Gilmore, and R. G. Brandenberg, "Anatomy of Corporate Planning," *Harvard Business Review,* Vol. 40, November-December 1962, pp. 61–69; and Robert F. Stewart, "A

Framework for Business Planning," Report No. 162, Long Range Planning Service, Menlo Park, California, Stanford Research Institute, February 1963.

4. One of the first good books in the field was Igor H. Ansoff's *Corporate Strategy*, New York, McGraw-Hill Book Co., Inc., 1965. This was followed by an excellent treatment in J. Thomas Cannon's *Business Strategy and Policy*, New York, Harcourt Brace & World, Inc., 1968. An earlier unique contribution to the field was A. D. Chandler, Jr., *Strategy and Structure: Chapters in the History of the Industrial Enterprise*, Cambridge, Massachusetts, The M.I.T. Press, 1962. This was an historical analysis and not operational like Ansoff's and Cannon's analyses. A recent short overview is Kenneth R. Andrews, *The Concept of Corporate Strategy*, Homewood, Ill., Dow Jones-Irwin, Inc., 1971. Important work has been done recently in the application of new quantitative tools to strategic planning. Reference will be made later to this literature.

5. Edward N. Cole, "Management Priorities for the 1970's," *Michigan Business Review*, Vol. XXII, July 1970, p. 1. See also Committee for Economic Development, *Social Responsibilities of Business Corporations*, New York, June 1971; and George A. Steiner, *Business and Society*, New York, Random House, 1971, Chapter 9.

6. See, for instance, William F. Butler, and Robert A. Kavesh, *How Business Economists Forecast*, Englewood Cliffs, N. J., Prentice-Hall, Inc., 1966; Robert S. Reichard, *Practical Techniques of Sales Forecasting*, New York, McGraw-Hill Book Company, 1966; and Norbert Lloyd Enrick, *Market and Sales Forecasting: A Quantitative Approach*, San Francisco, Chandler Publishing Company, 1969. See also John C. Chambers, Satinder K. Mullick, and Donald D. Smith, "How To Choose the Right Forecasting Technique," *Harvard Business Review*, Vol. 49, July-August 1971, pp. 45–74.

7. Note should be made of *Technological Forecasting*, a journal which began in 1969 and which is devoted to the methodology of the subject. Three good books on the subject are Erich Jantsch, *Technological Forecasting Perspective*, Paris, Organization for Economic Cooperation and Development, 1967; James R. Bright, *Technological Forecasting For Industry and Government*, Englewood Cliffs, N. J., Prentice-Hall, Inc., 1968; and Robert U. Ayres, *Technological Forecasting and Long-Range Planning*, New York, McGraw-Hill Book Company, 1969.

8. See Kurt Baier and Nicholas Rescher (eds.), *Values and the Future*, New York, The Free Press, 1969.

9. See *Toward A. Social Report*, Washington, D. C., U. S. Department of Health, Education and Welfare, 1969; and Nestor E. Terleckyj, "Measuring Progress Toward Social Goals: Some Possibilities at National on Local Levels," *Management Science*, Vol. 16, August 1970, pp. B-765–778.

10. For different forecasting methods see John McHale, "Typological Survey of Futures Research in the U. S.," (mimeographed), Center for Integrative Studies, School of Advanced Technology, State University of New York at Binghamton, N. Y., 1970. For futures forecasts see *The Futurist*, a journal which was created in 1967 to cover forecasts, trends, and ideas about the future.

11. Charles H. Granger, "The Hierarchy of Objectives," *Harvard Business Review*, Vol. 42, May-June 1964, pp. 63–74.

12. Stewart Thompson, *Management Creeds and Philosophies*, Research Study No. 32, New York, American Management Association, Inc., 1958.

13. Peter F. Drucker, *The Practice of Management*, New York, Harper & Brothers Publishers, 1954, p. 63.

14. Much confusion often exists in the use of these words. One reason is that different authors have different definitions for them. Another more important reason is that the

words are used in different connections in the planning process. For a good examination of this source of confusion see Bertram M. Gross, *The Managing of Organizations*, New York, The Free Press, 1964, Vol. II, Chapter 19, "The Matrix of Purposes."

15. For distinctions between strategic and tactical plans see Steiner, *Top Management Planning, op. cit.*, pp. 37–41.

16. James B. Boulden and Elwood S. Buffa, "Corporate Models: On-Line, Real-Time Systems," *Harvard Business Review*, Vol. 48, July-August 1970, pp. 65–83. See also Ernest C. Miller, *Advanced Techniques For Strategic Planning*, New York, American Management Association, 1971, pp. 32–33, for a tabulation of the use of newer quantitative techniques operational as compared with stategic planning.

17. David B. Hertz, *New Power for Management*, New York, McGraw-Hill Book Company, 1969.

18. George A. Steiner, "Rise of the Corporate Planner," *Harvard Business Review*, Vol. 48, September-October 1970, pp. 133–139; and Richard F. Vancil, "———So You're Going to Have a Planning Department!" *Harvard Business Review*, Vol. 45, May-June 1967, pp. 88–96.

19. Marvin Bower, *The Will to Manage*, New York, McGraw-Hill Book Company, 1966.

20. Stanley S. Thune, and Robert J. House, "Where Long-Range Planning Pays Off," *Business Horizons*, August 1970, pp. 81–90.

21. H. Igor Ansoff, Jay Avner, Richard G. Brandenburg, Fred E. Portner, and Raymond Radosevich, "Does Planning Pay? The Effect of Planning on Success of Acquisitions in American Firms," *Long Range Planning*, Vol. 3, December 1970, pp. 2–7.

22. From 1956, when the first survey was made of how many companies did formal planning, until the latest surveys, the number of companies purportedly doing formal long-range planning has increased rapidly. (See Steiner, *Top Management Planning, op. cit.*, pp. 14–15 for a resume of this data.) The most recent survey I have seen was made in 1970 by Marvin J. Cetron and concluded that 95 percent of the 1,114 companies surveyed had some sort of formal long-range planning activity. The range of comprehensiveness and coverage undoubtedly varies immensely among these companies. See Marvin J. Cetron, *Industrial Applications of Technological Forecasting*, New York, John Wiley, 1971.

23. Partly derived from Steiner, *Top Management Planning, op. cit.*, pp. 720–722. For other planning problems see E. Kirby Warren, *Long-Range Planning: The Executive Viewpoint*, Englewood Cliffs, N. J., Prentice-Hall, Inc., 1966.

3

A Survey of Information Services Planning Practices

This chapter summarizes the results of the McKinsey–UCLA long-range MIS planning conference survey and discussion, presenting some practical guidelines that should be considered by MIS executives in undertaking and carrying out their own planning activities.

THE SAMPLE POPULATION

To obtain a good cross section of various approaches to long-range MIS planning, the McKinsey–UCLA conference participants were chosen from a broad range of industries, including aerospace, airline, business equipment, chemicals, consumer goods, insurance, medical services, petroleum, and utilities, as well as governmental and educational enterprises at the local, state, and federal levels. As Figure 1 indicates, the "average" participant represented an organization whose annual revenues or total budget expenses were greater than $1 billion—in other words, larger than the average *Fortune 500* company in the United States. In addition, the "average" participant had been maintaining a formal MIS long-range planning effort for more than three years, and each plan encompassed an annual budget of approximately $15 million.

Most participants had their computer operations so well under control that their users were generally satisfied with the level and quality of service being provided. Half the participants also set quantitative production performance objectives and regularly communicated to users their experience versus these objectives. Surprisingly, although most of the users were satisfied with day-to-day activities, in approximately half the participating companies, the user community still had little confidence in the MIS group's ability to deliver major new information systems on time, within budget, and meeting required specifications. Yet essentially all the participants had well-defined feasibility assessment procedures, and some 65 percent required postimplementation audits of newly installed systems. In all cases these feasibility standards called for documentation of a range of tangible dollar benefits to be achieved by a proposed project. Moreover, all the participants established highly targeted, documented objectives for their individual employees, although fewer than half had established a strong follow-up or feedback system to monitor individual progress toward these objectives.

Thus the participants represented large MIS organizations that were relatively mature and experienced in long-term planning. However a certain subset of the participants from somewhat more sophisticated host organizations were clearly quite advanced in their degree of control over computer operations and systems development, and also had more years of planning practice to their credit. Another subset of companies represented what might be called a "novice" group, whose members were still struggling to bring individual system development projects under tight control, had been planning longer term for only a year or two, and were from what might be regarded as somewhat "unsophisticated" organizations.

Participants saw two quite different roles for themselves—the "reactive" service role and the "proactive" change-agent role. Although certain aspects of both roles were practiced by all participants in their day-to-day responsibilities, there was a clear division between them regarding major goals and plans. The reactive participants took a largely defensive posture, justifying their lack of regard for the strategy of the overall enterprise by stressing the importance of being responsive to users' immediate requirements. Their major problem ironically was a lack of credibility and confidence on the part of their respective user communities. On the other hand, the proactive group sought ways of actively interacting with the strategic planning effort of the host organization. This interaction gave them an overall strategic framework within which to link new computer systems to the most important needs of the host organization. Almost without exception, the more advanced planners were proactive and the novice planners were reactive.

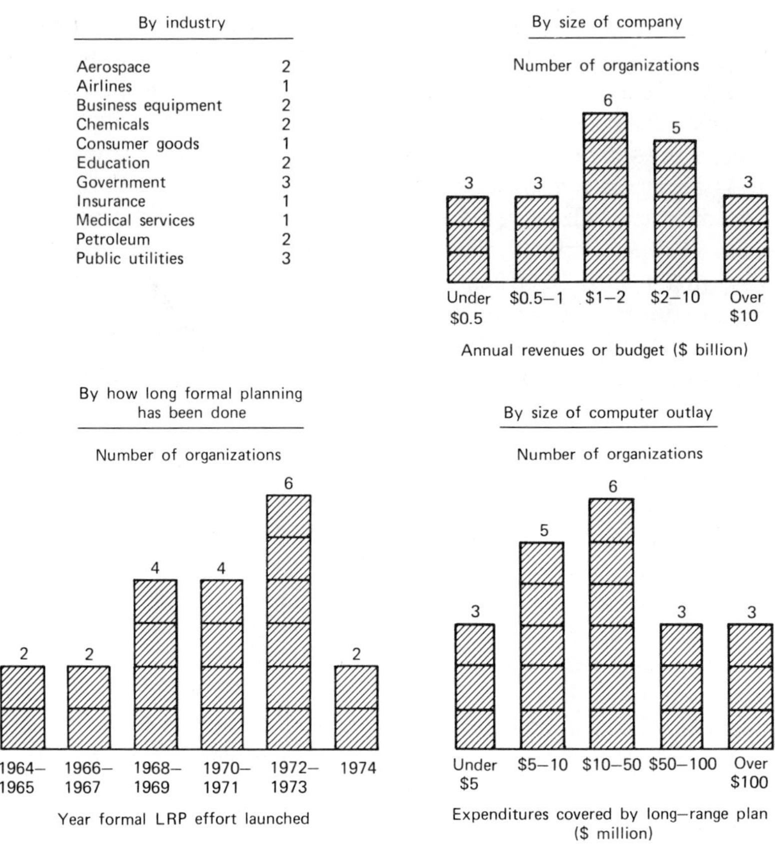

Figure 1 Profile of the survey participants.

PLANNING OBJECTIVES

The primary objectives participants had in mind in undertaking their long-range MIS planning efforts, as well as their estimate of how well they attained these objectives, are displayed in Figure 2. The upper bars reveal that the participants' primary objectives in planning are as follows:

1. To improve communications with users, to gain their cooperation.
2. To improve communication with top management, to obtain their support.
3. To improve resource requirements forecasting and allocation of resources (particularly for companies in the novice group).
4. To identify improvement opportunities internal to the information services organization.

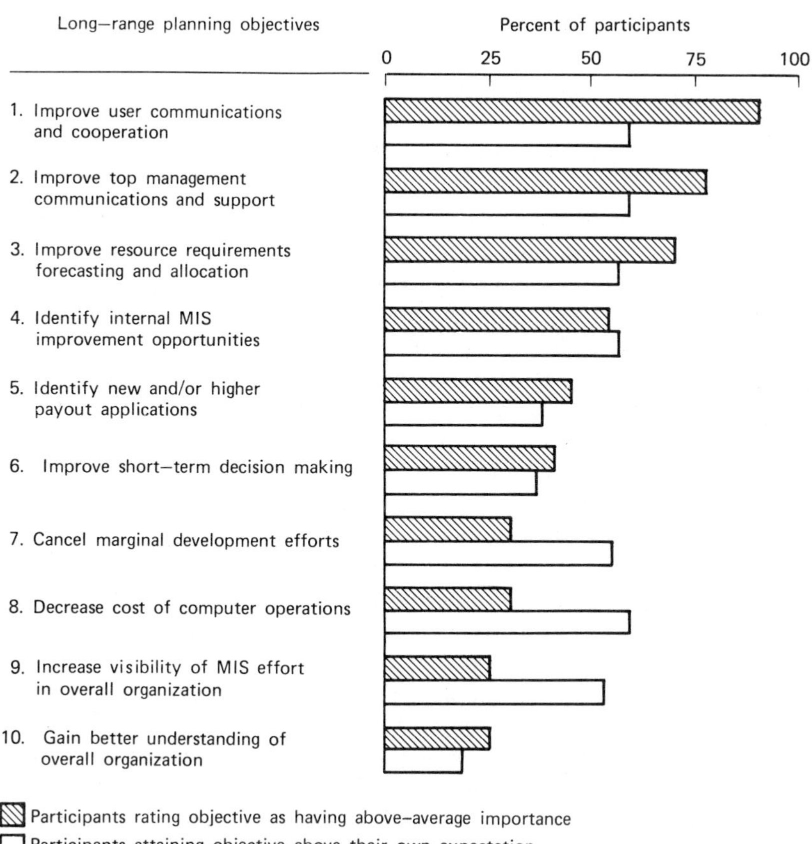

Figure 2 Long-range planning objectives and their degree of attainment.

5. To identify new and/or higher payout computer applications for the organization.

Item 5 may have been ranked lower by the MIS executives than might be expected either because they already had large backlogs of application ideas or because their planning efforts were primarily focused on making internal operational improvements. Unfortunately, the survey information was not sufficiently detailed to yield further insights on this issue.

A secondary group of objectives for these participants included the following:

6. To improve short-term decision making.

7. To cancel marginal development efforts.
8. To decrease costs of computer operations.
9. To increase the visibility of the MIS effort in the overall organization.
10. To gain a better understanding of the overall organization.

The tenth objective was rated as much more important by the advanced group of proactive participants, but was heavily discounted by the novice group. We believe that this objective will become increasingly important to MIS executives in the long term, as they strive to relate to their companies as businessmen rather than as functional specialists.

Roughly half the participants did better in achieving their stated objectives than they had expected initially. This was particularly true in the area of improving user and top management communications, where nearly two-thirds of the participants surpassed their own expectations. In general, the degree of attainment of these objectives was highly correlated with the importance they were given by the MIS executive, except for the relatively high attainment which occurred as fallout benefits of items 7, 8, and 9 (canceling marginal development efforts, decreasing cost of computer operations, and increasing the visibility of MIS effort). There was relatively meager achievement in the last item since gaining a better understanding of the overall organization is not necessarily a natural by-product of planning; also it was ranked by participants as the lowest priority objective. Underachievement here could well be a reflection of the general difficulty experienced by many in the MIS profession in integrating themselves into the mainstream of corporate life.

As part of the survey, the participants were also asked to judge the degree of satisfaction that their management, their users, and they themselves had with their MIS long-range planning. More than 40 percent of the participants indicated that their top management had a high degree of satisfaction. The remaining respondents evaluated top management's attitude as that of moderate satisfaction. In other words, none of the participants felt that top management had a low degree of satisfaction with their planning efforts. The participants' own degree of satisfaction with their planning efforts was quite similar to that of their respective top managers. However the degree of satisfaction with MIS long-range planning attributed to users in the participant companies was significantly lower. Only 20 percent of the participants rated their users as highly satisfied with the planning effort, and an equal number of participants indicated that their users had a low opinion of the effort. This somewhat disenchanted user viewpoint was supported by further analysis and discussions. The participants indicated that their communications with users had been significantly enhanced through planning, but the anticipated cooperation from, and understanding by, users still left much to be desired. Again, this was particularly true for the novice group, which apparently had not yet established a foundation strong enough to lend ongoing MIS efforts credibility among user management.

PLANNING END PRODUCTS

Figure 3 summarizes the contents, both ideal and actual, of the long-range planning document. The vast majority of the survey participants

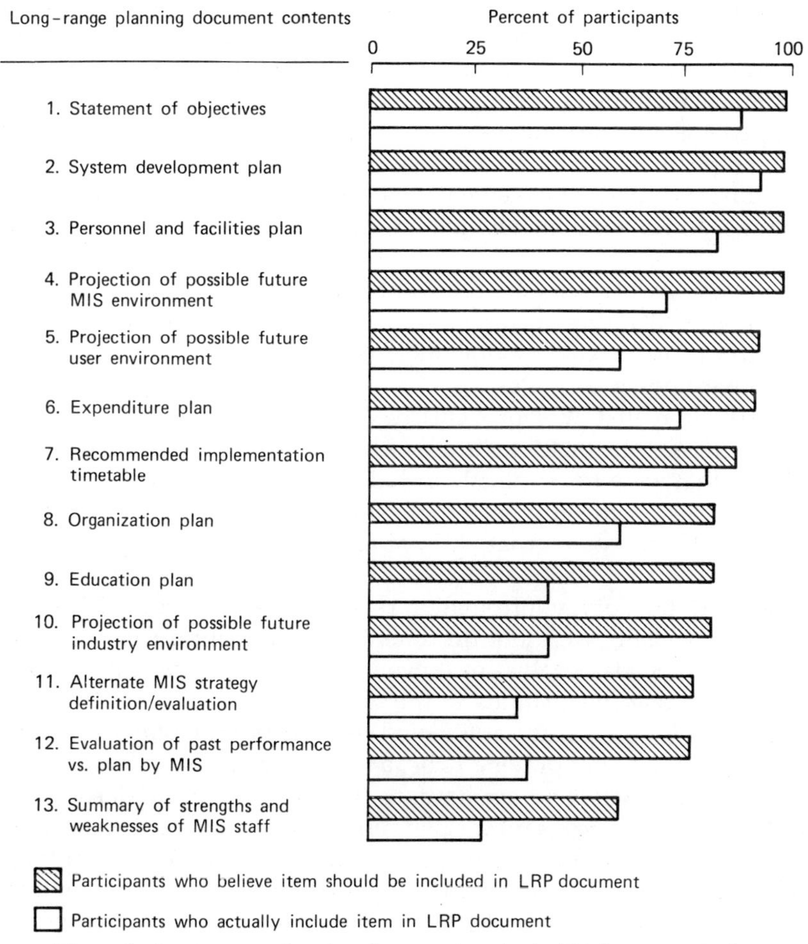

Figure 3 Long-range planning document content—ideal versus actual.

agreed that the basic contents of this document should include the following:

1. Statement of objectives for the MIS function.
2. Projection of the future MIS technology and user environments.
3. System development plan, including potential project descriptions with associated priority rankings, costs, benefits, returns on investment, and risk estimates.
4. Associated budget, equipment, personnel, facilities, education, and organization schedules.
5. Implementation schedules.

Unfortunately the survey did not pinpoint whether the participants believed that a section specificially listing their planning assumptions should be included in the document; later discussions, however, indicated that a majority of participants would have supported its inclusion.

In general, the participants performed relatively well in including in their respective documents the sections they themselves had said should be included. The elements that tended not to be included in the planning document generally fell into three categories:

1. Items the participants did not want to advertise explicitly in a widely circulated planning document—for example, evaluation of their past performance versus plan or documentation on their own strengths and weaknesses.
2. Information that was particularly difficult to obtain—for example, projection of the possible future industry and/or user environments.
3. Items that were not explicitly included in the document because of a lack of rigor in the approach to planning—for example, the definition and evaluation of alternate MIS strategies.

In addition, the survey information revealed that more than 70 percent of the participants were not documenting potential project returns on investment and risk evaluations, even though they agreed that this information should be included in the plan.

Importantly, the participants noted that the information system plan is not, and should not pretend to be, a three- to five-year schedule of the sequence in which new applications will actually be undertaken. In other words, the purpose of the planning effort should be to make better near-term decisions but not to become committed to long-term future actions that may not occur because of changes in the environment in the intervening period. Naturally there is some value in constructing a scenario that might occur, given a certain resource commitment. For this reason, most information system plans are reasonably specific with regard to near-term system development activities and provide some valuable insights by generally describing the likely activities of later time periods.

Finally, the long-range planning document for these participants varied in length from 12 to more than 300 pages; the average size was in the range of 30 to 50 pages of text plus supporting data attached as appendices.

PLANNING APPROACHES

The approaches taken by the conference participants in developing their longer range MIS plans varied widely. Figure 4 portrays differences in the level of participation by various groups in the planning effort, in the relation of long-range MIS planning to overall business planning, in the length of the planning horizon itself, and in the effort expended in the initial MIS long-range planning effort.

As one would expect, the MIS group generally participated quite heavily in the planning effort, with somewhat less involvement by users and even less on the part of top management. Interestingly, only a very few of the participants reported any involvement whatsoever in their longer range MIS planning effort by members of the business planning staff of the corporation. One might conclude from this that the MIS planning activities were not closely tied to the strategy of the overall corporation—a hypothesis that is further supported by the observation that only one-third of the participants linked their MIS planning process to the overall business planning effort of the enterprise. Unfortunately another one-third represented organizations that had no overall formal plan to which the MIS effort could be related.

Most of the participants tended to use a five-year horizon in their long-term planning. All of those using horizons longer than five years represented companies in which the overall business planning horizon was either six or seven years; thus their MIS plan was made consistent with the period already established. In general, the number of man-years of effort expended in developing the initial MIS long-range plan varied widely, the median effort being somewhat less than two man-years. Understandably, this first effort took longer than the subsequent revisions of the plan.

Somewhat surprisingly, the novice group spent about as much time in developing a list of potential computer application project ideas as did

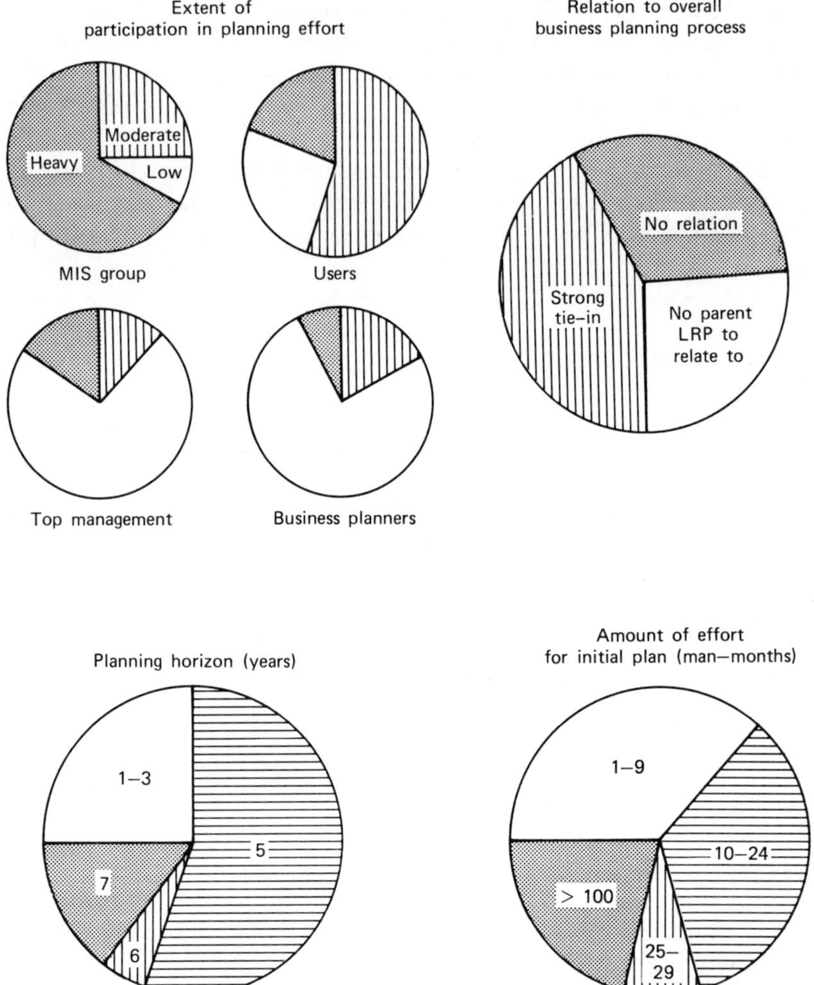

Figure 4 Attributes of planning approaches.

the more advanced group. Apparently this was because the novice group had not perfected the procedures to perform such a ranking and therefore required considerable time to do so. The advanced group on the other hand had to spend relatively more time searching out new project ideas and analyzing overall business functions because they had already skimmed the cream from their existing backlog.

It was particularly difficult to categorize the different planning approaches employed by the conference participants, since they represented such diverse environments with substantial differences in the following factors.

1. *Nature of the host organization,* including the stability of the overall organization's strategic thrust, the sophistication and openness to change of management, the competitive importance of computers to the strategy of the overall company, and the maturity of its overall business planning processes.
2. *Nature of the MIS function,* including its capabilities, operating responsibilities, and objectives.
3. *Status of the existing information systems.*

More than 90 percent percent of the participants adopted a combination "bottom-up, top-down" approach in carrying out their planning efforts. However lack of precision in terminology made it unclear as to which of the following aspects of top-down planning the effort was related.

1. Development of a statement of overall information services division objectives before undertaking the planning effort.
2. Performance of business analysis to identify key company profit leverage areas in which to focus efforts to generate new application ideas.
3. Interviewing of top management early in the planning process to develop an understanding of the overall company and its strategic direction.
4. Direct linking of the information services plan to support the formal business plan of the overall enterprise.
5. Support of, and pressure from, top management to expedite user involvement in the MIS planning effort.

Although all these have some element of top-down direction, a combination of items 3 and 4 probably provides the best definition of the approach used by these particular participants.

The participants also confirmed that the pressures to carry out formal MIS long-range planning were growing and included the following:

1. A mandate to develop a plan to comply with overall organization planning or regulatory body requirements.
2. A directive to lay out a plan to strengthen the MIS effort as a result of general discontent with the progress, performance, and economic contribution of the ongoing MIS effort—and to provide a basis for beginning to measure and control these aspects of the effort.

3. The need for top management to make multiyear commitments to provide resources to ensure, for example, that the MIS organization can be built up, computer equipment can be expanded, and orderly growth guaranteed.
4. An interest in improving short-term decisions that entail longer lead-time commitments; such decisions would include, for example:
   A. The acquisition of computer equipment.
   B. The launching of a particular application development effort, while delaying other efforts.
   C. The provisioning of specialized personnel in technical support areas for the MIS effort.
5. The requirement to communicate prospective actions and priorities to those outside the MIS division, so that multidepartment considerations can be taken into account, users can plan to utilize the possible new systems, and alternate shorter term means can be found by those who need to satisfy their immediate information requirements more rapidly.
6. A concern for increasing communications, cooperation, and coordination within and between the MIS group, its users, and top management.
7. The need for the MIS organization to gain a better understanding of the overall organization, and the need for executives within the overall organization to increase their understanding of how the MIS function might be better able to assist them.
8. A recognition of the value obtained from having the MIS organization setting a good example for the overall enterprise that does not yet plan formally.
9. Desire for self-protection of the MIS division from undue criticism.

Thus the participants were unanimous in their support for formal long-range planning.

PLANNING PITFALLS

Figure 5 portrays the pitfalls encountered by the participants in carrying out their long-range planning efforts, both as beginning planners during their initial effort and as planning practitioners following three or more years of planning experience. As the figure indicates, the following major pitfalls were encountered in *launching* the planning effort:

- Lack of free communication and commitment to change throughout the host organization.

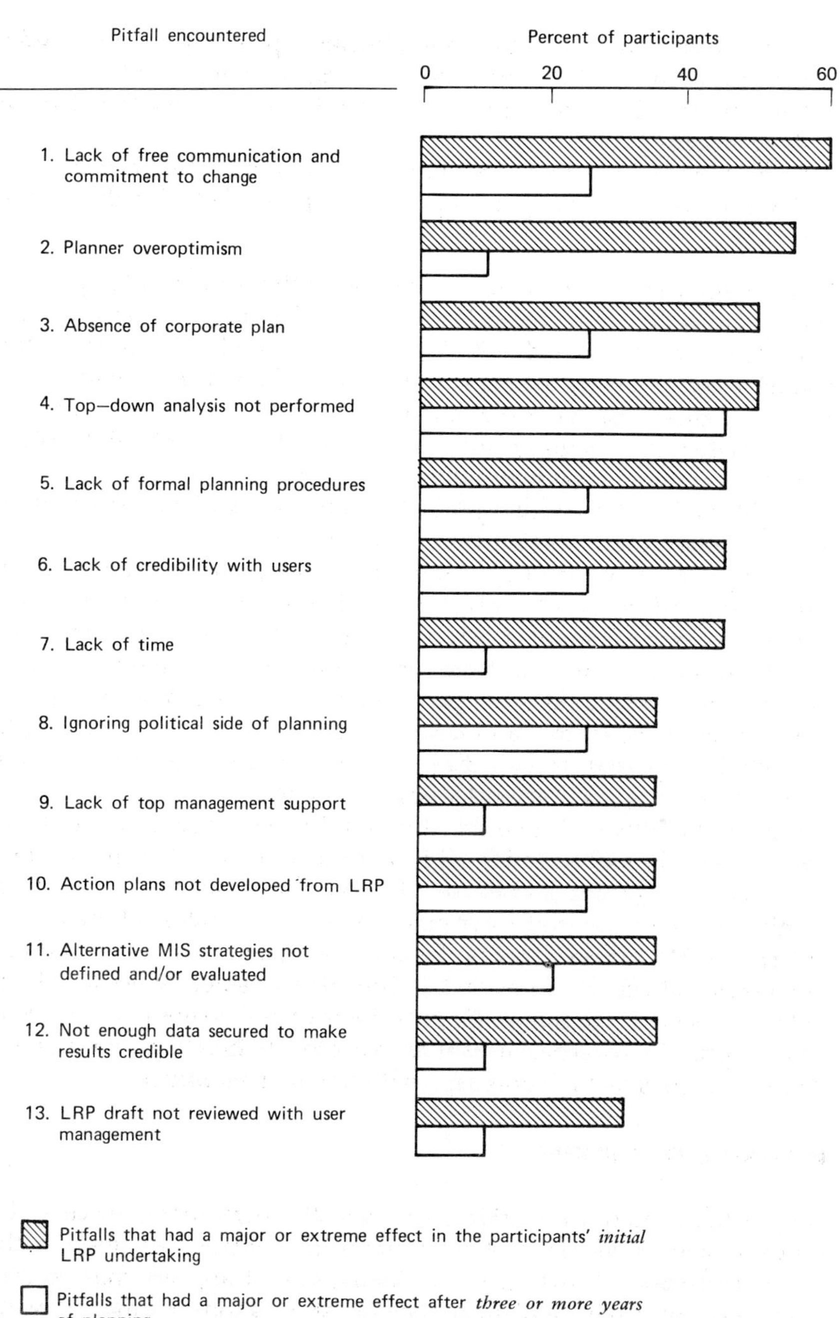

Figure 5 Long-range planning pitfalls—initial versus experience after three years.

- Absence of an overall organization business plan to provide a model for, and input to, the information systems planning effort.
- Lack of formal planning procedures to define precisely the steps in the planning process.
- Lack of credibility with users, due to past lack of control over systems development and computer operations (particularly for the novice group).

The major pitfalls experienced in *developing* the plan included planner overoptimism, ignoring the political side of planning, not performing a "top-down" analysis to identify high-potential application areas in the organization, and not defining and evaluating alternate information systems strategies. The major pitfall noted in *using* the plan was not translating it into tactical action plans, which would have permitted the planned strategy to be implemented in small steps.

It is likely that these major pitfalls stem from lack of maturity both of the MIS effort and of the host organization, as well as from the procedures used. Lack of maturity of the MIS effort results in low credibility with users, and inmaturity or lack of sophistication of the host organization results in the absence of a clear-cut corporate plan, overall corporate objectives, open communications, and commitment to change. Lack of information services planning procedures, or the use of an inappropriate planning approach, can likewise create these problems. As would logically be expected, these pitfalls were significantly reduced after the MIS group had gained several years of experience.

Clearly the MIS executive can, through his own direction over time, overcome the lack of maturity of his division and the lack of an information services planning procedure. However the same executive cannot by himself overcome the lack of maturity or sophistication of the overall enterprise. Yet he need not be fatalistic, resigning himself to such an organizational climate because it is difficult to change or because he is not responsible for this area. He must instead seek to improve the overall enterprise by whatever means are available to him (e.g., through his day-to-day personal relationships with line management).

PLANNING GUIDELINES

During the conference working sessions, the participants discussed a number of possible ways of overcoming the pitfalls described in the previous section. Based on those discussions, it appears that an MIS executive undertaking a planning activity should consider the following guidelines.

1. Recognize the growing need for formal MIS planning as computer systems grow more complex and costly, require longer to develop, involve multiple functions or departments, and become increasingly more important to the success of the overall company.
2. Admit that a set of extrapolated budget, personnel, and equipment schedules routinely submitted to the overall organization planning department does not constitute an MIS plan of any substance.
3. Acquire familiarity with the literature on overall business planning, the specific business planning approaches taken by the parent company, and what others have written about their MIS planning experiences.
4. Develop documented proposals on, and seek to gain top management's agreement with, the objectives for the overall organization's use of information services resources, as well as a simple set of MIS policies regarding the organization of, setting expenditure levels for, and allocation of, scarce resources in the MIS function, and the strategies by which the objectives can be achieved. All these should be accomplished before the detailed planning effort is undertaken.
5. Recognize the importance of communication with and support from top management for the detailed planning effort.
6. Tie the plan into the overall organization's business plan if at all possible, to enhance the contribution of MIS to the enterprise.
7. Do not let the absence of a formal business plan for the overall organization stop the MIS organization from planning its own efforts, but do recognize that its absence will make these efforts significantly more difficult.
8. Define the specific objectives of the planning effort at the outset and "plan the plan" around achieving these; do not attempt a great leap forward.
9. The purpose of the plan is to make better near-term decisions; therefore think through what these decisions must be, and how best to reach them.
10. Carefully structure a means by which the parent organization management, not just the MIS division, sorts out and sets priorities for the undertaking of new application or service projects.
11. Make sure the plan will be driven by the business needs of the organization and its management, not by technology.
12. Remember that a model long-term information system architecture is a dynamic working tool for the system development effort not an end result to which top management should commit itself.
13. Always plan to review the attractiveness of modifying existing sys-

tems to meet new needs; do not assume that new needs automatically require completely new systems.

14. Select a planning approach suited to the practicalities of the situation and, if possible, develop a conceptual model of the planning process to be used, along with a well-defined set of end products.
15. If the MIS organization is relatively underdeveloped in terms of standards, computer operations effectiveness, individual project management capability, and the like, concentrate on the short term, and severely limit concern for the long term, until the near-term situation has been substantially improved.
16. Make the plan focus on the overall organization's use of the computer, not on internal MIS department considerations, and involve users in its development, orienting the language of the plan to the user as much as possible.

Most important, one should remember that as helpful as formal long-range planning can be, it cannot replace the political sensitivity, entrepreneurship, conceptual contribution, and basic business leadership required of the successful MIS executive.

4

Top Management and Strategic Planning for Information Services

In 1968 McKinsey & Company, Inc., published *Unlocking the Computer's Profit Potential,* a research report that pointed out the larger payoffs being achieved by successful computer users through improved overall planning. This report, coupled with the continuing advice of other observers and the growing maturity and importance of the MIS function, spawned numerous MIS planning efforts. Certainly many of these planning efforts have aided top management in making key decisions that could not have been reached otherwise. Our impression, however, is that many of these efforts have been ill conceived and weakly implemented, producing a new wave of executive frustration in attempting to direct the MIS function.

This chapter provides a more comprehensive view of the role top management can and must play in directing the development of MIS strategies and plans that support the business objectives of the enterprise. We will give examples of underachieving MIS planning efforts, summarize the planning challenge from the MIS executive's point of view, portray the vital role the chief executive officer must play in establishing an MIS strategy, discuss the contents of the MIS strategic statement in more detail than in Chapter 1, review the various types of planning to implement MIS strategies and the techniques involved, and suggest steps the chief executive can take to enhance the enterprise's MIS planning effort.

PLANS TO AVOID

There are many varieties of weak MIS plans. For convenience, we have labeled a few of these as the squeaky wheel, straightedge, ivory tower, silver platter, conceptual smorgasbord, and tinker toy approaches.

The *squeaky wheel* MIS plan probably occurs the most frequently in business today. Actually it is no plan at all, rather, it is the frantic top MIS executive scurrying to meet day-to-day crises in dealing with disgruntled users and alienated line executives. This activity results in a series of start-stop projects that fritter away corporate resources with little resulting benefit and much frustration. In spite of the damage to present efforts, however, this very mess often provides the impetus for the initial long-term formal MIS planning effort, if only because of the inevitable realization that the chaos cannot be allowed to continue. But as the following examples point out, the resulting initial long-term formal planning is more difficult to carry out successfully than one might first suspect.

The most frequently occurring formal long-range MIS plan can be called a *straightedge* plan. Not a "plan" in the true sense of the word, it is simply a linear extrapolation of past MIS expense trends. It can be visualized as placing a straightedge on a graph of past MIS expenditures and simply drawing a line into the future. This budget extrapolation is often supported by numerous pages of descriptive material which, when boiled down, fail to provide any insights into the capability of the MIS group, the needs of the user community, the business objectives of the MIS organization, or general policy regarding the allocation of scarce resources or reasons for top management to continue to fund new computer systems development activities. The straightedge information services plan can be indicative of a superficial overall corporate business planning effort, lack of interest by top management in the MIS effort itself, and/or an underachieving MIS executive.

A large number of information services organizations have graduated from straightedge planning into what might be called the *ivory tower* approach, in which the information services organization performs a rather extensive analysis of its own forecasted computer equipment needs, personnel needs, transaction volumes, and the like—all focused on internal MIS division concerns. There is little communication with the user community or with top management on policies, objectives, or matters of resource allocation. The ivory tower plan certainly is a more thoughtful approach than the straightedge plan, but it contributes little to the total enterprise, since the identification and evaluation of potential new information systems or services is not addressed, and even the evaluation of existing systems is narrow and self-serving.

The *silver platter* plan often follows on the heels of the ivory tower planning effort, when top management begins to question the value of this approach for the overall business enterprise. It is also chosen when the need for a long-range information service plan is mandated by government regulation or by corporate policy, without a corresponding set of practical guidelines for preparing the plan and/or the format for it. In the silver platter approach, MIS personnel present their thoughts about the types of computer-based systems that might benefit the organization in the future. This set of application ideas is documented, then put forward as a long-range plan—but without the involvement, contribution, and understanding of the user community, or commitment from it. Generally taken under the pressure of a short lead time, this approach often reflects the attitude of the MIS organization—namely, that the user community does not have the interest or competence to contribute to the effort.

A number of executives have recognized the shortfalls of the straight-edge, ivory tower, and silver platter approaches, and have committed substantial resources in an attempt to enlist the meaningful involvement of the user community in the planning process. In a number of well-intentioned but poorly directed planning efforts, the result can be called a *conceptual smorgasbord.* The conceptual smorgasbord involves a massive series of interviews with company executives and operating personnel to help interpret business requirements and forecast the use of advanced computer techniques and technology. These efforts often result in a number of conceptual ideas for new computer applications without corresponding documentation of their likely costs, benefits, risks, or fit with corporate objectives. Thus top management is left with no way to evaluate the inevitable requests for accelerated funding of MIS, other than a philosophical commitment to managing "better" through the use of "newer" techniques. The conceptual smorgasbord approach also tends to result in suggestions that the corporation completely revamp its operating MIS to yield better management information, even though such a comprehensive "cure" is seldom necessary. The conceptual smorgasbord is expensive in terms of the cost of developing the so-called plan and in the lackluster investment decisions that executive management risks making at the conclusion of the effort.

The *tinker toy* plan is a request for management to fund an unspecified multiyear effort that purports to transform the company's information systems into a magnificant architectural design, represented on a chart by numerous data base circles, interconnected with information flow arrows, and interpersed with transaction boxes and report wingdings. This approach may appear similar to the conceptual smorgasbord, but there is a major difference. Whereas the former often lacks an integrating or unifying principle, the tinker toy plan, as its name suggests, is so integrated and interrelated that it becomes virtually impossible to implement—even if there exists a documented, tangible business rationale for doing so. This architectural diagram is held up as the five- to ten-year target for the company's information systems, and management is asked to agree to it conceptually and to become committed to moving toward it, based on a philosophical commitment that the new technologies and techniques for storing and representing data are worthy objectives in and of themselves.

These are only a few examples of the many MIS planning pitfalls that we have observed. However each of these examples exhibits certain elements of good planning approaches, albeit masked ones, that must be salvaged if the computer's profit potential is to be realized by top management.

VITAL ROLE OF TOP MANAGEMENT IN SETTING MIS STRATEGY

In most organizations the chief executive officer is responsible for establishing the strategic direction of the enterprise. In *The Will to Manage: Corporate Success Through Programmed Management* (McGraw-Hill, 1966), Marvin Bower emphasizes the vital importance of a strategic point of view to the successful business executive. Bower's convictions, gained from several decades of behind-the-scenes comparisons of leading companies with those comprising the rest of the pack, are that the top management executives of the leading companies:

- Have a deeper understanding of their strategic facts.
- Look at strategic facts more objectively.
- Are determined to lead rather than follow.
- Believe in their strategies and follow them.
- Have more resolute will to manage.
- Think and act in strategic terms.

The importance of a strategic point of view to the chief executive officer carries over into the MIS function because, presumptuous as it may sound, the use of computers is vital to the competitive success of many enterprises. MIS is naturally of more strategic importance in certain industries than in others, but computer-based, operationally oriented systems are becoming more evident everywhere in the competitive jostling for leadership in American business today. For example, consider the number of banks, thrift institutions, and credit card issuers now wrestling with the legislative, technical, economic, and competitive issues surrounding electronic funds transfer and the impact of this phenomenon on traditional service delivery. Again, the availability of point-of-sale devices, coupled with the use of the Universal Product Code, now offers the retail industry the capability to obtain vital, accurate information on store profit and loss, inventory control, and the like. This information can significantly alter the management style and strategic viewpoint of, say, the food processing and retail grocery industries.

But how does one go about developing a strategic plan for MIS? Refer again to Figure 4 of Chapter 1, where we introduced our conceptual framework. Recall that we defined strategic planning as involving the following sequence of steps:

1. A setting of the mission or charter of the MIS organization.
2. A formal environmental assessment to identify the MIS opportunities, threats, and risks of concern to the enterprise.
3. The establishment of MIS objectives that define the desired results to be achieved by the function, related as much as possible to the strategic objectives of the overall enterprise.
4. The development of MIS strategies, which are broad courses of action describing how the previously set objectives are to be achieved.
5. The definition of MIS policies as guidelines to be used in carrying out the strategy, giving particular importance to policies relating to the organization of the MIS effort, the allocation of scarce resources, and the setting of expenditure levels for the function.
6. The translation of these objectives, strategies, and policies into long-, medium-, and/or short-range plans.
7. The implementation of the plans, the measurement of progress against them, and the recycling of the appropriate planning effort over time.

Naturally, the ways in which these tasks can be or are being accomplished are subject to untold variations. Unfortunately, all too often the critical strategic issues that top management and the MIS executive must consider together are sloughed off and the company charges into the development of what is called a long-term MIS plan without a guiding strategic point of view. The chief executive must prevent this from occurring, since correct, precise objectives, strategies, and policies create the top-down pressure and decision framework within which the planning effort can best be carried out. Moreover, these objectives, strategies, and fundamental policies, which should be accomplished in any case, is a challenge in its own right, particularly for organizations that have not yet begun to plan formally for their MIS activities. In addition, the most appropriate approach to longer term planning itself is closely related to the choice of strategic objectives, as we discuss in a later section of this chapter. Finally, the longer term MIS planning effort often requires an investment of company resources much more substantial than is involved in setting these initial objectives, strategies, and policies. Thus by focusing on strategy first, we reduce the risk that the MIS organization will become involved in a massive amount of information gathering and will miss the forest for the trees.

Naturally management will need to assess the past performance and capability of the MIS group, as well as the company's management systems and related information needs. Part of this task can be initially accomplished by requesting that the MIS executive develop a brief environmental assessment, along with his recommended objectives, strategies, and policies. Once this strategic statement has been reviewed and refined by top management, the longer term planning effort for information services can be carried out to align the MIS activities with its "new" objectives and policy guidelines.

The MIS strategy can be established in either a "reactive" or "interactive" mode with the overall enterprise's planning efforts. In the reactive mode, the enterprise's objectives and strategies are determined, and the MIS strategic plan is derived from them, to make the MIS activity responsive to the needs and activities of the enterprise. In the interactive mode, the MIS function and all other areas of the enterprise develop their strategies simultaneously, and exchange tentative strategic statements with one another. These tentative statements are revised to reflect more precisely the impact that each of the activities the enterprise has on all the others. This helps ensure that the final strategies are in concert and that the effect of each on the others is noted, agreed on, and included in the resultant plans. For the novice MIS or business planner, however, the reactive mode is likely to be an easier initial approach.

MORE ON THE STRATEGIC STATEMENT

As we have said, *top management bears the sole responsibility for defining an MIS strategy statement.* It must answer, at a minimum, five critical interrelated questions.

1. What are the objectives for the MIS effort in the enterprise?

2. By what strategy will we seek to achieve these objectives?
3. How are we going to organize the MIS effort to carry out these objectives?
4. How are we going to decide how much to spend on MIS?
5. How are we going to decide how to allocate scarce MIS resources to various projects and services?

The precise resolution of these issues regarding objectives, strategies, and the three major policy concerns—organization, budgeting, and allocation of resources—is basic to the success of the MIS effort in every organization. From time to time other strategic questions arise to complement these five key issues. Such additional concerns are often technological and difficult for the top executive to resolve. Thus we believe that he should postpone decisions on these until the five principal issues just enumerated are well in hand.

Objectives

The choice of appropriate strategic objectives for the MIS effort is critical, since all subsequent planning efforts are oriented to successfully implementing or achieving these desired end results. The objectives should be tied as specifically as possible to the strategic objectives and plans of the enterprise. Importantly, although the MIS objectives should be strategic, they need not be long term. In other words, it is often advisable to have the objectives spell out what the MIS organization should accomplish in the short term, particularly if its day-to-day performance is not yet up to par. Although objectives should be as precise and quantitative as possible, consideration of the very general objectives in Table 1 should help management begin to refine its thoughts regarding the appropriate, unique strategic role for its own MIS organization.

Strategies

A strategy or set of strategies should be developed for each MIS strategic objective, to describe *how* the objectives will be achieved, but not necessarily *when*. Criteria for evaluating alternate strategies should also be defined and agreed on. Top management must be careful to ensure that strategies are forward looking but practical in light of the existing MIS environment in the enterprise. In other words, a key criterion should be the degree of risk that would be assumed to execute a particular strategy.

Table 1 Possible MIS objectives

1. Contribute to the development of, and seek to maximize achievement of, overall organization objectives, strategies, policies, and plans
2. Develop information systems and services for management that
   - Are necessary to the business as a result of external requirements imposed on the organization, have high strategic value, support business planning and decision-making efforts, and/or provide benefits in automating routine activities
   - Help meet the projected customer service levels to be attained by a major competitor
   - Pay for themselves through tangible benefits achieved as a result of their implementation
   - Utilize proven and up-to-date technology
   - Are adaptable to organizational and nationality changes without major modifications
   - Can be transformed into projects lasting less than 18 months and requiring less than 30 man-years development
   - Will support a doubling or halving of organization size and volume of business without major modification
   - Ensure integrity of data and, where justified by need, ease of their accessibility
   - Eliminate the generation of routine reports unless they serve a specific, valuable purpose not easily satisfied in other ways
   - Evolve toward an interlinked network of management support systems and services on a pay-as-you-go basis
3. Provide effective data processing services, defined as, say, a 3 percent annual reduction in costs per transaction
4. Keep appraised of trends in, and competitive uses of, information processing technology, but stress contribution to management needs rather than technical excellence in applying this knowledge
5. Educate overall organization personnel in worthwhile uses they could make of information systems technology
6. Achieve excellence in the development of personnel under MIS division control
7. Preserve and secure organizational assets that are under MIS division control
8. Represent the overall organization in MIS-related market, community, professional, and industry associations
9. Maintain, with the chief executive officer, formalized strategies, objectives, policies, and plans for the MIS division to achieve

Policies

Policies relating to the *organization* of MIS resources are a familiar topic to most executives. Basically, establishing these policies involves considering where the MIS function will reside, how it will interrelate with other staff, line, and computer activities in the corporation, how the carrying out of major computer projects will be organized, what coordinating entities (e.g., steering committees) are to be instituted to aid in the effort, and so on. In addition, the potential impact of the recent advances in distributed processing are becoming an area of major concern. Here again, specific policies depend largely on the management philosophy of the company, the capability of key executives, and the past experience of the existing management team. In many large companies the crucial point is ensuring that the role of the corporate staff of critiquing and controlling is carried out without conflicting with the operating role traditionally assumed by the MIS organization.

Setting the policy for how the company is going *to decide how much to spend* for MIS is seldom directly addressed, and it is an area of particular frustration for top management. Sometimes a mixture of techniques is decided on as a means to fix the MIS budget, ignoring, for the moment, the arbitrary budget cutting that occurs from time to time in corporate life. These include, for example, taking a fixed percentage of sales or assets; comparable expenditures of similar companies, adjusted for size and profitability; whatever the major company profit centers will agree to pay for; base amounts plus discretionary increases for high-potential projects; and/or the amount spent last year plus adjustments for inflation. Too often lack of policy in this area leads the chief executive to concentrate his attention on evaluating requests for major computer equipment changes. On the surface this may appear to be pragmatic, but it generally reveals that the existing equipment is "filled up" and commitments already made for new computer system projects preclude intelligent planning for increased equipment needs in the near term. The MIS executive should play an active role in coming to grips with this issue, helping top management to understand the bottom-line benefits to be gained at different levels of spending.

Policies for the *allocation of scarce MIS resources* are particularly critical because they provide guidelines for effectively deploying existing resources and for making commitments that will lead to additional future resource acquisitions. These policies generate guidelines for the means by which the portfolio of current and potential projects will be funded and managed. Hence they are similar to certain aspects of managing applied research and development efforts for new products, selecting bond and stock portfolios, and acquiring or divesting operating companies under a corporate holding company umbrella. These policies should be stated in terms of attributes of proposed projects, such as their business necessity, their estimated tangible return on investment, the economic and technical risks associated with undertaking them, the relation of the projects to overall corporate, geographical, or functional area strategy, and/or the relation of the projects to MIS organization technical objectives regarding, say, data storage and retrieval.

Unfortunately, in many companies where these resource allocation policies have not been established, MIS and its user management have little incentive to perform disciplined economic evaluations of new project proposals, and corporate strategies often are not precise enough to relate to proposed projects. Thus in these organizations the implicit resource allocation policy frequently becomes one of allowing the MIS division the professional self-indulgence of selecting projects on the primary basis of the division's interest in utilizing information processing technology, since most projects can be loosely "justified" using crude economic forecasts and drummed-up political support. This shortcoming is readily apparent if the MIS organization is found to be using an information systems' architectural structure as the overriding stragetic objective rather than as a working document for technical system design.

Top management may, on occasion, become involved with other highly important, but generally somewhat lower level, technically oriented policies at the strategy level. These include, for example, guidelines related to the organization and accessibility of data; the worldwide standardization of applications, equipment, and/or systems software; the acquisition of computer equipment from various vendors; the selling of computer services to customers outside the corporation; the security of company data; and the charging of company profit or cost centers for the use of common MIS resources. Selecting which policies to focus on, as well as determining the policies themselves, involve judgmental decisions that depend on the specifics of the individual company, plus the experience, interest level, and technological orientation of its executive management. If the company has not formally fixed its objectives, strategies, and policies in the MIS area, however, it would do well to limit its concerns to the five issues laid out initially in this section as a first step in planning its efforts. As in the development of strategies, care must be given to planning the implementation. This is the subject of the next section.

PLANNING TO IMPLEMENT STRATEGIES

Turning our attention to Figure 1, we note that the plans developed to implement strategies can be of several types.

1. *Long-range conceptual planning* is concerned with portraying the general courses of action and broad types of resources to carry out strategies. The time horizon here is generally five to ten years.
2. *Medium-range managerial planning* is focused more on specific projects that might be carried out to achieve medium-range MIS objectives. Objectives are translated into goals, and strategies into project portfolio priorities for, say, three to five years.
3. *Short-range operational planning* spells out the performance targets, specific tasks, related schedules, and necessary resource requirements (budgets) to achieve short-range objectives. The time horizon is generally one to two years.

In addition, there are detailed individual project plans that can be short and/or medium range. Ideally, the MIS strategy statement should be translated into current-day decisions by sequentially developing the long-range conceptual, then the medium-range managerial, and finally, the short-range operational plans. However top management should exercise considerable judgment in selecting an appropriate type of MIS plan and a time horizon for it. Our experience indicates that companies with short-term MIS strategic objectives (e.g., to build credibility, to "get away from the crocodiles") should concentrate on simple annual plans that include very specific quantitative performance measures for effectiveness and efficiency. Once the MIS organization has mastered its short-term challenges, it can extend its planning horizon because it has built a resource that can convert opportunities into contributions, rather than into continuing economic and performance liabilities. However, practically speaking, the MIS organization is sometimes caught in the web of having to comply with requirements from the headquarters planning staff of carrying out longer term planning, even if it not well prepared to do so. It is our judgment that relatively few enterprises would find a major investment in long-range conceptual planning for MIS to be particularly beneficial. Thus it seems appropriate to focus the remainder of our attention on medium-range planning.

When the medium-term managerial and technical goals for the organization's use of MIS have been set, the development of information services medium-range plans to carry out the agreed-upon MIS

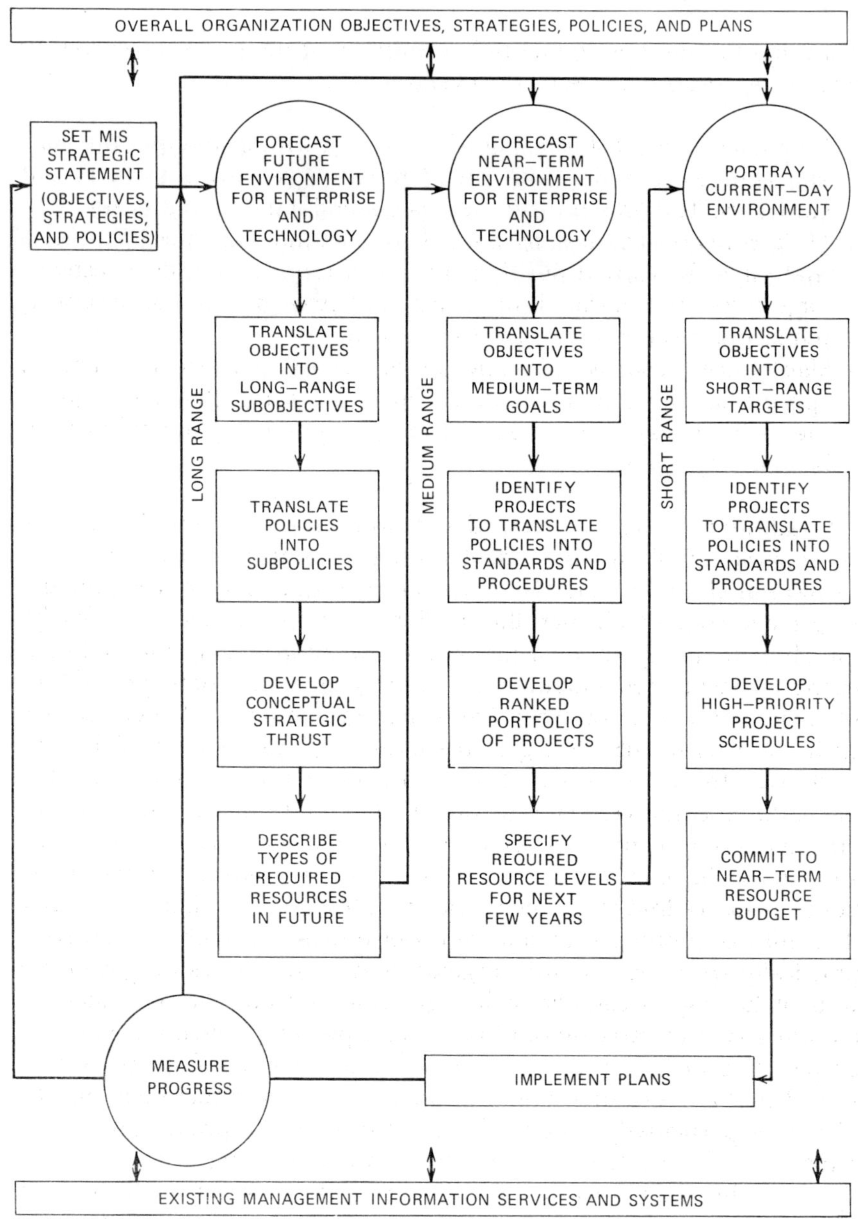

Figure 1 Implementation of MIS strategic planning.

strategy generally involves a series of activities that can be categorized as follows.

1. *Identify potential projects.* Fill a "hopper of opportunity" with ideas for projects to help achieve the medium-term goals. These projects will relate to, say, new computer system development efforts, enhancements to existing computer services, pilot tests of new systems services, standardization of data terminologies, construction of networks, upgrading of ongoing MIS management procedures, and/or strengthening of the MIS organization and personnel.
2. *Evaluate and rank projects by priority.* Filter the contents of this hopper of opportunity by using the resource allocation policies and overall MIS objectives previously set by top management in its strategy statement; this allows selection of the projects to be undertaken next and identification of the types of projects that might be undertaken in future years.
3. *Translate projects into time-phased profiles of tasks, resource requirements, and action steps.* Define the means and requirements for implementing the selected projects to achieve the company's strategic MIS objectives.

One of the key roles for the MIS organization is the development of new computer-based applications and/or services that contribute to the overall benefit of the enterprise. Thus the planning for information system development activities is a major aspect of the overall MIS planning job itself, both in terms of its importance and in terms of the commitment of planning resources to perform an adequate job in this area.

Identifying Potential Projects

A first step in the development of an information systems plan is an identification of potential information system projects of merit. As Table 2 reveals, a wide variety of approaches can be used to scan for new opportunities to invest system resources. They can be briefly summarized as follows:

1. *Isolated* approaches in which the MIS organization reacts to environmental necessities by modifying existing systems to meet new legal requirements, proposes retrofits to existing computer systems to enhance their cost and/or operating characteristics, operates on the basis of its own "intuition" regarding new opportunities, and/or consolidates requests for changes to existing systems already submitted by user managers.

Table 2. Examples of New Project Opportunity Scanning Approaches

Opportunity Scanning Approach	Activity	Summary Description	Major Benefits	Possible Shortcomings
Isolated	React to environmental necessities	Certain forces outside the corporation (e.g., governmental agencies) dictate new requirements that must be acted on	Aligns MIS activity with requirements	No real opportunities uncovered
	Review existing computer systems	Staff reviews costs and operating characteristics of existing computer systems to identify improvement opportunities	Can be accomplished quickly; should lead to ideas for lower ongoing operating costs or enhanced performance for existing systems	MIS communications with top management and users not enhanced; many new opportunities not identified
	Summarize organization's intuition	MIS personnel summarize their own judgment regarding possible high-potential projects	Can be accomplished quickly; should lead to many ideas in areas of company familiar to personnel	MIS communications with top management and users not enhanced; many new opportunities not identified
	Synthesize existing user system	An existing file of user ideas is reviewed and updated	Can be accomplished quickly; is apparently responsive to user desires	Many new opportunities not identified

Emulative	Emulate similar companies	Projects previously completed by similar companies are identified through surveys, site visits, and/or vendor presentations	Can be accomplished quickly; should lead to many, somewhat proven ideas if company is not already an industry leader	MIS communications with users not enhanced; may not generate ideas aligned with specific company plans
Bottom-up	Interview selected users	Selected company personnel are interviewed regarding their management systems and related information needs and desires	Offers opportunity to enhance communications between users and MIS; provides MIS personnel with greater exposure to apparent company needs	Not all new ideas generated—particularly if users or interviewers not highly skilled
	Document all user requirements	Exhaustive interviews and analyses are carried out for essentially all company personnel, functions, and data flows—perhaps translated into a conceptual MIS architecture diagram	Exposes a full range of project ideas; offers MIS personnel good grounding in company activities while opening communication channels	Requires very heavy time commitment of MIS and user personnel
Reactive	Receive executive mandate	Top management dictates new idea(s), perhaps as a result of meeting a competitive need	Aligns MIS activity with overall corporate strategy if CEO mandate is properly focused	Restricted scope of scan by CEO may result in numerous missed opportunities

Table 2. Examples of New Project Opportunity Scanning Approaches *(continued)*

Opportunity Scanning Approach	Activity	Summary Description	Major Benefits	Possible Shortcomings
Derived top down	Seek to impact existing company profit levers	Financial analysis of company operating characteristics is carried out to identify key decisions having highest profit impact and projects are hypothesized to support these decisions	Focuses planning effort on high potential areas; broadens business understanding of MIS personnel somewhat	Not all new ideas are generated, since the selected search is focused only on high-potential area
	Support hypothesized company plans	Industry performance trends, structure, profit economics, and environmental conditions are analyzed to document overall company needs; projects are hypothesized to help meet challenges	Focuses planning effort on range of high-potential areas with stategic importance; broadens business understanding of MIS personnel	Requires large time commitment of high-caliber analysis team; can often lead to incorrect strategy assumption without heavy top management involvement

Top down	Support existing company plans	Documented, well-verbalized, or clearly understood company plans are reviewed and MIS projects are identified as necessary and desirable to support management actions	Aligns ideas for MIS support with overall company plans and related user needs	Existing company plans must be substantive or ideas generated will be poor; does not force consideration of possible impact of MIS on company plans
Interactive	Interact during company planning effort	The identification of MIS and project needs, desires, and impacts is integrated into the required planning activities of overall company management	Makes idea generation everyone's conscious responsibility	Requires particularly sophisticated MIS and company management and planning techniques

2. *Emulative* approaches in which the MIS organization picks up ideas for new projects from the successful computer systems of other, somewhat similar companies.
3. *Bottom-up* approaches in which MIS systems analysts interview either selected user executives or, in certain company situations, all major user executives and operating personnel, to identify the major decision areas, management and/or operational systems needs, possible information gaps, and operating inefficiencies that could be improved with computer-based systems efforts.
4. *Reactive* efforts in which the MIS organization simply responds to decisions made by the chief executive officer or higher level corporate officers specifying new computer system projects to be undertaken.
5. *Derived top-down* approaches in which the overall company business strategy, being missing, must be synthesized by financial analysis of the company's operating characteristics, a full-blown industry and/or company analysis, or the specification of a new approach to managing the business. From this synthesis, new high-priority computer system ideas can then be selected.
6. *Top-down* efforts in which the MIS organization identifies services to be provided by examining the existing company business plans for potential support requirements.
7. *Interactive* efforts in which the MIS organization interacts with other business functions during the normal company planning cycle, ensuring that the identification of MIS project ideas and assessment of the likely business impact of each are integrated into the required planning activities of management throughout the company.

All these approaches can and should result in what are called "need-driven" plans, since the creativity of the individuals involved in the planning effort is employed in idea generation regarding the possible use of new technology without use of technology itself becoming the overriding objective.

The creative task for top management is to ensure that the MIS executive selects the scanning approaches that best fit the company's unique needs at a particular time. In doing this, several points should be kept in mind. First, if the MIS strategic objectives are primarily focused on the short-term building of credibility and capability of the MIS function itself, a more introspective and/or emulative approach to planning is probably advisable. Second, the absence of a substantive business plan for the corporation or for major functional areas is likely to hamper significantly medium-term systems development planning, even though efforts to develop a derived company strategy partially help to

Application/ service identity	Brief description	Operating expenses estimate	Operating benefits estimate	Resource allocation criteria							
				User sponsor	Develop– ment cost estimate	Develop– ment time span estimate	ROI estimate	Risk assessment	Corporate strategy fit	MIS archi– tecture fit	Other consider– ations
1. 2. . . .				(Funded, already undertaken)							
1. 2. 3. . .				(Funded, not yet undertaken)							
1. . . .				(Not funded, under consideration)							

Figure 2 Sample project portfolio overview.

offset this weakness. Yet few EDP organizations possess the skills to scan aggressively for new opportunities in this derived top-down manner, even though it may seem desirable for them to do so. Finally, the interactive approach to information systems planning requires that the company be dedicated to interactive planning for the entire enterprise; it is an approach that the MIS function cannot pursue independently, despite its desirability.

Evaluating and Ranking Projects

Invariably at some point in the planning effort, the collected ideas for new projects must be sorted out so that the highest priority applications or services can be undertaken in the near term. Many planning efforts, however, fail to perceive in advance the need to establish a means for the company's management to conduct such a screening both within and across functional areas. Since the MIS effort is a service function to the entire enterprise, this sorting out of priorities is difficult, even when well-chosen resource allocation policies have been established as guidelines within which management's best judgment can be exercised. A simple framework for carrying out this ranking is shown in Figure 2, where the project ideas are listed and the previously selected resource allocation criteria are applied to each project. The major challenge is to obtain a summary evaluation of these project characteristics without entering into a detailed project feasibility study, since the primary objective is to decide which projects should initially be allocated feasibility study resources. Yet this desire to defer an exceptionally detailed analysis of new system ideas should not preclude the well-managed enterprise from making precise evaluations of the priorities for investing resources in new systems.

Many corporations have established computer applications steering committees in which selected members of management make judgments regarding alternate new system investments on an ongoing basis. These committees should be supported by well-defined, phased, project-development funding commitment policies. In this way, a "rolling" consensus regarding the need for new system development activities is obtained; furthermore, more fact-based quantitative rankings of projects can be made, using the resource allocation criteria, as documented project feasibility studies are completed. Unfortunately, many of these committees have not been successful in carrying out their prescribed role; some of the reasons for this are summarized in Table 3. More often than not, however, the overriding problem with underachieving applications steering committees is the absence of a precise

Table 3 Selected MIS Steering Committee Pitfalls

Pitfall	Description
Premature establishment	The committee is set up either before the company has a long-term view of where it is heading or before the MIS organization has developed proven procedures (e.g., individual project planning and control methodology) for effectively implementing committee decisions
Wrong charter	The committee attempts to administer and monitor the design of individual computer systems instead of either managing a portfolio of potential computer system investments to the maximum benefit for the overall enterprise or acting as a counterpart awareness vehicle
Wrong members	The committee is composed of too high or too low a level of operating management, or is overstocked with MIS personnel who attempt to direct the committee rather than work behind the scenes to provide required support to the committee
Unnecessary meetings	Meetings are held regardless of need, which wastes time and loses the interest of involved executives
Wrong spokesmen	MIS personnel attempt to sell newly proposed projects to the committee rather than having company personnel who will benefit from the new system act as spokesmen for the proposed investment
Poor preparation	Muddled premeeting documentation and preparation is carried out, and needed information for conducting a crisp committee meeting is not forwarded to participants in advance so that they can carry out their necessary premeeting discussions and jockeying
Poor across-the-broad communication	Lower level MIS and user personnel do not maintain active day-to-day communication about proposed projects so as to be in a better position to aid in premeeting briefings of individual committee members

Table 3 Selected MIS Steering Committee Pitfalls *(continued)*

Pitfall	Description
Technical smokescreens	Committee members use technical jargon rather than more straightforward business terms in discussing potential projects
Fuzzy feedback	Tracking data and reports are not prepared to show the committee explicitly how it is performing relative to its primary objectives
Priority dithering	The committee indiscriminately changes the priorities for ongoing system development work while it is in midstream
Weak investment tracking	Commitments to major development projects are not routinely reviewed at predefined project milestones so that the committee can reevaluate the incremental return on investment from continuing with the project (assuming this is the objective of the committee)
Lack of training	Committee members are not exposed to general, but highly selected, background briefings, seminars, and the like, so that they can gain a modicum of computer systems awareness

charter and a simple means of translating MIS resource allocation policies into the business characteristics of new computer application proposal ideas. In other words, the MIS function does not provide good staff support to the establishment and operation of the committee.

Developing Action Plans

If an appropriate approach to scanning and ranking information system development projects is taken, the third step in planning—the development of associated resources and activity schedules—is somewhat more mechanical, although vital in considering such important issues as the amount of computer equipment that is likely to be needed. Generally, these project schedules are quite precise for the near term and somewhat more general in nature for future years. This is as it should be, since the primary purpose of the planning effort is to make near-term decisions that are consistent with a longer term direction, not to agree on the specific computer system projects that are to be undertaken three to four years hence.

NEXT STEPS FOR THE EXECUTIVE

Given the brief description in the foregoing sections of the various aspects of MIS planning, the chief executive officer should be in a better position to reassess the MIS planning efforts of his own organization. Certainly there is no one right way to carry out this planning effort. Even if there were a single best approach, there is insufficient experience at this time to define this approach with precision. As a first step, the chief executive officer can recognize that *he* is responsible for setting objectives, agreeing on strategies, and laying plans for the entire enterprise, including the MIS area. Then, in considering how—or whether—to launch a new and/or revised planning effort, the chief executive, with his MIS executive, should seek answers to the following questions:

1. Are we reasonably adept at estimating the costs, benefits, and risks of proposed new computer projects?
2. In general, do our MIS project postimplementation audit reports indicate that we were able to carry out projects within cost and timetable estimates, and that we were able to capture the dollar benefits committed to at the outset of the project?
3. Is the MIS function now operating above average from an effectiveness and efficiency standpoint? How is this being measured?
4. Have we agreed on documented objectives, broad strategies, and policies for the MIS function?
5. What decisions need to be made that require long-term planning and what information will we need in order to make these decisions?
6. How can we integrate the MIS strategy and plans with our overall corporate strategy and plans?
7. Are we taking the appropriate approach to scanning for new computer investment opportunities in the corporation?
8. What role should the chief executive officer play in the launching and conduct of the planning effort?
9. What will be the end product of our planning effort?
10. How can we make sure that the plan will focus on the company's—rather than the MIS division's—use of computer resources?
11. Will top management be given interim progress reports during the planning effort?
12. Can we monitor the planning itself, putting us in a position to improve our effort the next time around?

Admittedly, the answers to some of these questions may involve

technical evaluations that top management often is not in a position to give. We believe, however, that in using these issues as guidelines for channeling discussions with, and directions to, the MIS executive, the chief executive officer could go far in targeting the planning effort to better unlock the computer's profit potential. The following chapters provide examples of how a number of enterprises have approached this goal.

II
Information Services Planning in the Private Sector

The first group of participant contributions come from firms doing business in the private sector. The seven chapters represent companies engaged in a wide range of activities. CIBA–GEIGY is in petrochemicals and pharmaceuticals, TRW Systems and Hughes Aircraft are in aerospace and electronics, Mobil and Standard of Indiana are prominent petroleum companies, and IBM and Xerox are major producers of information processing equipment.

As there is diversity in the products of each of these companies, so is there in their planning efforts. Some have begun formal long-range planning for information services only fairly recently, while others have had much longer experience. Similarly, some companies have planning efforts that are relatively limited in scope and time horizon, whereas others are quite comprehensive and long ranging. The following section describes briefly each of these companies' efforts.

In going through the chapters, the reader is advised to avoid searching for *the* right answer or *the* best approach. Each company represented has different circumstances and aims and, consequently, has evolved a type of planning that is appropriate—and feasible—within its particular environment. Read in this light, each chapter should offer something of value, even though the planning approaches described are quite different.

PRIVATE SECTOR MIS PLANNING

CIBA–GEIGY was faced with a number of unique problems when two separate companies, Geigy and CIBA, merged together in 1970. Geigy, which had been growing at a rapid rate, combined with CIBA, a more stable organization, into a major international company with sales of $2.5 billion.

The first order of business after the merger was to integrate these dissimilar organizations; as a result, corporate long-range planning was quite unstable for a time. Without a clear set of overall corporate objectives, planning for management services—which included information systems—was largely reactive. However the merger solidified remarkably well, and in 1971 the company began "a formal worldwide planning system . . . [with] each division and company department . . . [to] develop annually a five-year plan (now a three-year plan) and a one-year plan." By 1973 the Management Services Department was able to produce its first five-year plan, which stressed the importance of stabilizing the information system environment within the company and of regaining the confidence of users.

The planning process within CIBA–GEIGY is a combination of top down and bottom up; opportunities, problems, and objectives are developed for a three-year horizon, then strategies are devised to meet the objectives. The one-year plan, or annual budget, is the first year of this three-year plan, made more specific with additional financial details. In this way the long-range plan is kept more realistic than it might have been if this plan and the annual plan were prepared independently.

For individual projects within this three-year planning horizon, a project life cycle system is used, bringing together both Management Services personnel and user management. Finally, for company-wide projects, an advisory committee is convened to review and make recommendations on major systems expenditures.

TRW Systems Group is the electronic and scientific software subsidiary of TRW Inc., a multinational corporation with annual sales in excess of $2 billion. TRW Systems' contribution to this figure is about $400 million.

The first long-range plan for the Management Systems Department was developed in 1969; this plan was revised and further refined in 1971. At each stage every attempt was made to make the plan "consistent with and responsive to the overall company business planning and objectives." From these top management objectives, an "MIS concept" was devised to guide the Management Systems Department "in viewing any one requirement and any one system as a part of a total company information flow."

The planning process is designed to produce three outputs: a long-range plan (up to five years in duration), an annual operating plan, and a portfolio of individual project plans. In all these aspects heavy user involvement is stressed. In fact, for many individual projects, a manager from the user group serves as the project manager, and since 1971 every project has had a "lead executive" who accepts overall responsibility for the success of the venture.

The responsibility for developing the long-range plan within Management Systems is assigned to the manager of planning and analysis. He coordinates with both user groups and with the Computer Technology Department, the latter to ensure that hardware and software trends are adequately taken into account.

Hughes Aircraft's business is closely tied to the various governmental agencies it serves. As a result, corporate long-range planning is intimately interwoven with the procurement plans of the federal government. Internally, Hughes consists of some 40 divisions, each operating in a highly decentralized fashion, and with revenues ranging from $20 million to $200 million each (total corporate sales are $1 billion). The combination of these factors, of course, makes the task of information systems planning extremely difficult.

Planning is basically bottom up in nature. Individual project requirements, some projected out over several years, are summarized every six months, and one of the semiannual summaries serves as input to the annual operating plan. From the user's standpoint, the horizon for most computer and data processing planning is one year. "From top management's point of view, the most important objective is to keep the cost effectiveness of data processing high and its absolute cost as low as possible." Internally, however, the computer department has had to undertake longer range planning, first for the scheduled consolidation of its computer equipment, and second, for desired improvements in performance standards. As more experience is gained with this effort, it is expected that the planning horizon for all computer-related activities will be expanded to five years.

Mobil Oil, with annual sales exceeding $20 billion, was the largest company in terms of revenues to participate in the conference. The company has a well-established Corporate Planning Department, which prepares both five-year and one-year plans to guide Mobil's business. These corporate plans are inputs to the Computer Systems and Management Sciences Department's own planning efforts, which parallel the corporate planning cycles. The resultant planning is thus a combination of top down (key assumptions and guidelines coming from top management) and bottom up (detailed planning coming from the individual information systems groups within the various corporate divisions).

Long-range planning for information systems was first begun in 1969, with the creation of the first five-year and one-year plans; each of these plans has been revised or redone every succeeding year. As an indication of the amount of attention devoted to information systems planning at Mobil, in 1973 an estimate was made that the creation of that year's five-year plan absorbed more than 200 man-months.

The chief aim of the initial planning was to achieve control and guidance over computer activities. Mobil feels that they have been quite successful in this, although "most of the credit must go to the short-term items, even within the long-range planning document."

Because of some early "failures with certain large operations research-type development projects, large and long-duration management science projects [including information systems] fell into disfavor." As a result, most projects are now planned on a modular basis, with the planning horizon for these applications rarely extending beyond two years. The long-range information systems planning is, therefore, "for computer equipment alone, not for applications."

The one-year plan is a direct part of Mobil's regular budgeting cycle, and the approved plan becomes an integral part of the parent organization's budget. Since 1972 these separate one-year plans, like the five-year plan, have been consolidated at a corporate level to provide an opportunity for greater coordination and control.

Standard Oil of Indiana, another international oil company, has sales of approximately $6 billion annually. The company has engaged in formal long-range planning for more than 20 years. The first long-range plan for information services, prepared in 1964–1965, covered a five- to seven-year period and has been updated annually since 1967. These annual updates devote particular attention to the budget implications of the long-range plan, especially for the first two years of the planning horizon.

The plan is prepared by the general manager of the corporate Information Services and Management Sciences Department, with assistance from Information Services Coordinating Groups in each of the Standard Oil subsidiaries. It is carried on "throughout the year as a series of studies addressed to pertinent subjects as they arise. . . . The results of these individual studies are incorporated into a brief two- or three-page report as changes or additions to the previous year's plan." Thus it is "the most complete and up-to-date plan that is practical to prepare."

Although both corporate planning and information systems planning have been established for a relatively long time, "there is no formal relationship between [them]. . . . It is not felt to be worth the major effort needed to integrate them." The coordination is handled informally by the general manager of Information Services.

IBM, the largest manufacturer of computer equipment in the world, is also a major producer of a wide range of other information processing equipment. Its sales are slightly more than $11 billion annually, and about half of this comes from abroad.

IBM began its long-range business planning in 1959. The company's two-part effort consists of a two-year operating plan prepared in the fall of each year, and a seven-year strategic plan prepared in the spring. When the company began planning for information systems in 1966, the same pattern was adopted. The operating plan is directly tied to the budget, while the strategic plan addresses longer range issues. A key aspect of the decision to undertake information systems planning was the feeling by top management that data processing should develop "information systems to support key business decisions, with emphasis on supporting the planning, measurement, and control processes of the corporation." This was in sharp contract to the company's earlier approach, which merely focused on individual applications.

The first information systems plan, issued in 1967, was an integral part of the overall corporate business plan. It soon became apparent, however, that something more was required to "ensure that information systems were planned and implemented in such a way that they supported overall business goals." Out of this concern grew the establishment of an information systems architecture function and, later, a data management function.

The responsibility for information systems planning resides with the vice president of plans and controls, who is supported by the director of Corporate Information Systems. Each year assumptions, goals, and objectives are passed down to the various business units and subsidiaries to guide them in their planning efforts. Then each level "develops its own objectives, strategies, and actions through which it will meet its commitment to the overall corporate goals."

To make sure that the plans are kept on target, there are requirements for status reports on various aspects of the plan, as well as scheduled audits on the performance of individual information systems departments. "There are no steering committees *per se;* the planning process itself is the primary means for project selection and approval."

Xerox Corporation has experienced rapid growth for a number of years, with 1973 sales of $3 billion—an increase of 24 percent over the previous year. This growth has led to a recognition of the need for, and the importance of, long-range planning.

Because of its decentralized character, Xerox maintains some 35 independent information systems organizations throughout the company, with combined budgets in excess of $70 million. Because of the importance of having these activities coordinated, however, in 1972 the Information Services Division was established at the corporate level. This division provides data center operations services, programming, management sciences, and telecommunications to most of the domestic operations within Xerox. To monitor systems development and data center operations, a Performance Assurance Audit Group was established as a part of corporate internal auditing. This activity "has proved to be one of [Xerox's] most successful organizational moves."

The planning for information systems closely parallels the overall corporate planning and control process. This is a two-year operating plan and a seven-year long-range plan. The operating plan establishes specific projects to be funded, ongoing service objectives, and profit goals. It is a "one-year commitment with a second-year projection," developed within the basic strategy of the division. The long-range plan is "viewed basically as a *communication* vehicle. . . . While it does attempt to highlight issues, it is *not* intended necessarily to provide definitive solutions." It includes long-range organizational and application strategies, major projects to be undertaken in support of these strategies, resource requirements, and key planning issues for management awareness.

CONCLUDING REMARKS

In addition to the chapters in Part II, samples of some of the planning vehicles used by these companies are reproduced in the appendices of this book. IBM's Information Systems Planning Requirements are shown in Appendix A, copies of Mobil Oil's planning forms are in Appendix B, and a statement of Xerox's Information Systems Long-Range Plan is shown in Appendix D.

The chapters in Parts III and IV are drawn from organizations functioning in either the regulated or public sectors. Some of these chapters describe planning activities quite similar to those described in this part; others, of course, are different. Thus it is quite likely that several of them will contain information that will be of interest to even those readers whose primary concern is the private sector.

5 ANTHONY J. CRAINE

CIBA–GEIGY Corporation

Today CIBA–GEIGY is wrestling and overcoming the problem of long-range planning for information systems. The company, the United States affiliate of an organization whose headquarters are in Switzerland, is active in the research, production, and sale of pharmaceuticals, dyestuffs, plastics and additives, agricultural herbicides, and consumer products. The affiliate companies are organized by selling divisions supported by company staff departments, such as Personnel, Controller, and Planning. Information systems, along with scientific systems, operations research, and data processing are all parts of the Management Services Department (see Figure 1). Worldwide sales exceed $2.5 billion. The company is active in about 100 countries and employs more than 65,000 persons. The United States sales are approximately $600 million.

CIBA–GEIGY differs from many other large organizations in one critical area. It is the product of a merger of two previously successful, but quite different organizations, CIBA and Geigy, in 1970. Somewhat surprisingly, the merger has been extraordinarily successful. The resultant organization has settled down quickly, and sales and profits have remained strong. One of the last areas still reverberating slightly from merger tremors is information systems, and this was expected.

INFORMATION SYSTEMS BACKGROUND

When considering the information systems background, one cannot overlook the merger and the different personalities of the individual

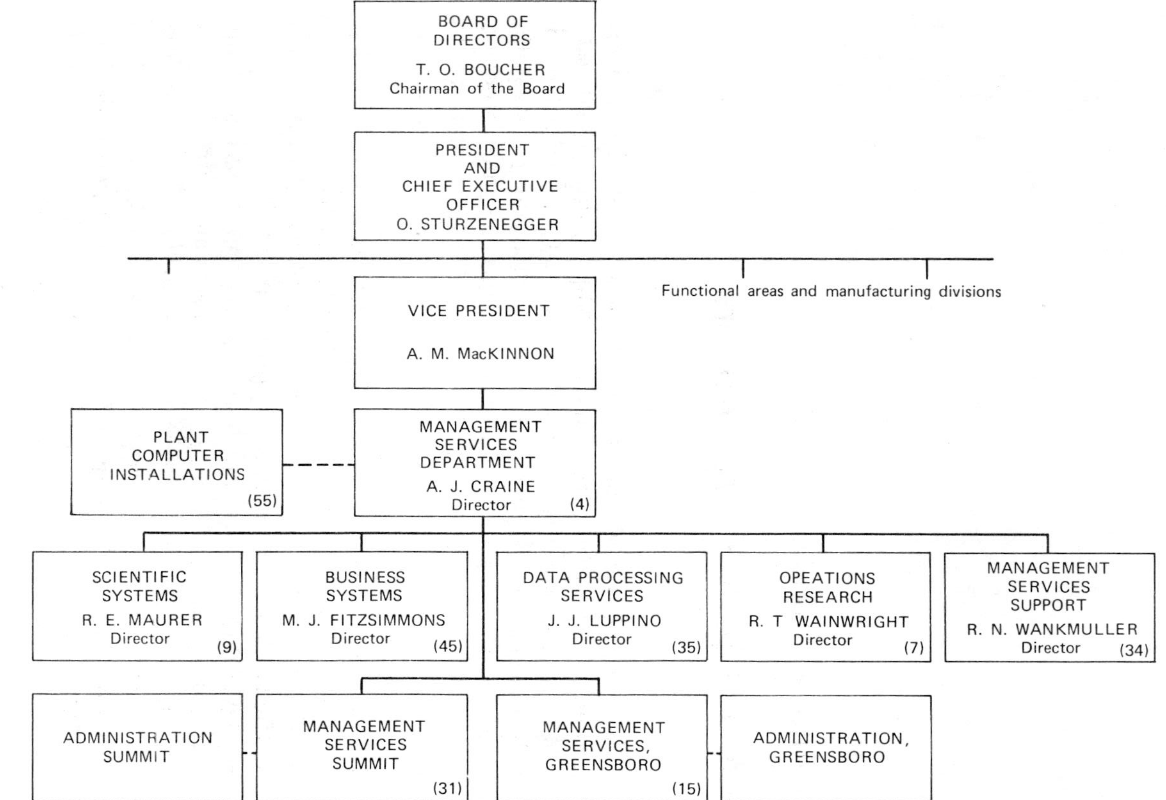

Figure 1 Organization chart, CIBA-GEIGY Management Services Department. Number of personnel indicated in parentheses. Total personnel, 235.

companies. Geigy became active in information systems in the early 1960s while caught up in a very strong growth cycle. Sales doubled from 1960 to 1965, and doubled again from 1965 to 1970. The organization was young and aggressive, and systems development lagged behind sales. The growth caused a dynamism and a positive kind of instability. Rather than concentrate on challenging budgets, the problem was to get out information and to support groups making decisions. Systems and programming personnel were in a continuous, explosive, overtime, catch-up phase. CIBA, on the other hand, was a smoother running, more mature company. Sales were high, profits good, and the organization was stable. The information systems were outgrowths of the 1950s; and although they were not exciting, they were stable. The challenge of the systems effort was to satisfy requests while minimizing data processing costs. The divergent needs, personalities, styles, and systems of CIBA and Geigy were fused into one company. By the end of 1970, the data processing effort had an annual budget of approximately $5 million, a staff of about 175, two major computer locations, and strained relations with users caused by the unstable environment and incompatible information systems.

INFORMATION SYSTEMS HISTORY

The group at Geigy was under constant pressure to catch up to the needs of the organization. For instance, report systems were developed using maximum field sizes provided by the user, but before the system could be installed, these maximum lengths had already been exceeded. One user stated that the customer master file would never exceed 10,000. One year later the file contained the names of more than 20,000 customers, doubling the time needed to pass the file through all the systems using the data. Planning became pragmatic, and developed on a one-on-one data processing–user relationship. All users' requests were ascertained, then all requirements were summarized. The estimated personnel and expense budgets based on this summary were always too high, and data processing then had to renegotiate with each user. Documentation and control requirements were also caught up in this push for output and were rushed through as well. Attempts were made to develop long-range plans, both for applications and hardware; but the effort was very general and covered immediate needs more than future requirements.

At CIBA, the developments were more calcified than explosive. The approach emphasized the service bureau type of support for user needs rather than overall systems development. Segmented, single-purpose jobs were developed based on individual requirements. The user was responsible for the controls. There was enough capacity to ensure that the bulk of the jobs ran like superswift, unit record equipment applications. This approach did not call for too much planning. Once agreement to undertake a given project had been secured from the user, all that was necessary was a programming staff and sufficient computer capacity.

Both Geigy and CIBA had a form of pro rata chargeback technique that passed on annual expenses to the user departments, but it was impossible to break the charges down in any meaningful way. It is interesting to note that although both systems had shortcomings, each company developed a style that accommodated each approach. However the merged company, with the added ingredients of a volatile organization and an urgent need for quick information systems at the time of the merger, caused an explosive atmosphere.

MANAGEMENT SERVICES OBJECTIVES

Although the merger was most successful, the years immediately following 1970 were bumpy for Management Services. One of the first systems installed in the new company was a planning system, and Management Services attempted to establish its own long-term plan. This program broke down quickly because the users were not yet stabilized. The basic objective of each operating area at that time as to establish its individual identity. This confused period clearly reenforced one basic axiom; that is, it is impossible to design information systems in an unstable environment with poorly defined or missing objectives.

Management Services was quickly forced into a reactive position. The mission for the department became simple and pragmatic—keep things going and stabilize the operation. After two years of turbulence, the Management Services problems and opportunity began to solidify. Following is a list of the formal objectives excerpted from the department's five-year plan, approved by the corporate management in 1973 and updated in 1974.

1. *Long-term work plan.* By June 1974, begin fact finding and by December 1974, recommend an extension of the present work plan for achieving a savings of at least 10 percent of Management Services costs, or causing an increase in the productivity of the operating units by this amount, or defining a comparable approved nonquantifiable justification. The work plan will also include personnel and hardware utilization, based on a coordinated approach for all remote sites.

2. *Data base management in a multicomputer environment.* By January 1975, establish the philosophy of data base management to assure a coordinated development of corporate data bases and to protect them from accidental misuse, destruction, or duplication. This should also reduce programming costs by giving the department the opportunity to forward copies of data bases to Switzerland rather than developing output systems, and to reduce systems and programming efforts through expanded use of interrogation packages. The objective is, with the collaboration of Swiss headquarters, to install a pilot application using a common formal data base management system during the first quarter of 1975. This would encompass four different areas, one scientific and one commercial, in Switzerland and in the United States. Then, by January 1976, we would determine the effectiveness of this approach and develop a future plan of action.
3. *Management services reorganization.* As the first phase of this plan, reorganize Data Processing and support; also define the overall size and responsibilities of each of the component areas. By January 1976, complete all phases of installing the new organization concept.
4. *User involvement and coordination.* By January 1974, establish a coordination program for all remote locations for the plants. This would involve close collaboration on the development of their work plans, expenses, and hardware requirements; and for all remote locations this would involve a CIBA-GEIGY computer sciences work group, perhaps with subgroups in the scientific and commercial areas.

   By June 1974, a users' work plan review team should be formed, made up of members of all the major operating units to discuss the work plans. By the end of 1975, have an active program of shifting personnel; of enhancing accessibility of software and hardware; and of using outside resources at all key locations, based on the company's priorities through collaboration with the newly formed Advisory Group. Also, there should be increased involvement of users as project managers and a strong overall coordination program.

These objectives were taken from the long-term plan almost verbatim to illustrate the formality and, hopefully, the commitment of Management Services regarding these objectives. Perhaps the most critical objectives for Management Services, however, are those that were unstated: redeveloping a professional posture in the department, getting control over the increasing personnel and other expenses caused by firefighting, and rebuilding confidence and credibility with users.

THE PLANNING PROCESS

In 1971, shortly after the merger, CIBA–GEIGY installed a formal worldwide planning system. It was decided that each division and company department in every major country would develop annually a five-year plan (now a three-year plan) and a one-year plan. An annual financial and personnel budget would also be prepared. As a company department, Management Services came under these guidelines. The process was based on experience in both premerged companies and thus was well thought out. In fact, the planning process was one of the major stabilizing influences after the merger. However this progress was also very volatile in the beginning. Principles had to be defined, misunderstandings clarified, timings changed, marginal sections discontinued, and certain segments added. The very base for planning within the company was shaky, causing special difficulties for support groups like Management Services. Managers were unfamiliar with products, markets, processes, and behaviors of the newly merged company. One potential major problem that was tracked carefully from the beginning was the danger of forgetting the objective of the entire effort, and making the planning process a bureaucratic staff exercise and an end in itself, time-consuming and only marginally productive.

The company planning process was a substantial tool for Management Services. However it was only one of many techniques needed to manage the department. Additional techniques had to be developed within this framework, including the following:

- Long-term work plans.
- Project management.
- Systems development and installation guidelines (project life cycle).
- An advisory committee for project acceptance.
- Chargeback and performance system.

A few of these have recently been developed and are being installed. This cluster of techniques has had a strong influence on the stabilization gains made by Management Services since the merger. Departmental expenses and personnel growth are now under control, and the attitudes in the group have improved markedly. Firefighting has been drastically reduced and planned for, and the department has regained the confidence and credibility of the users.

The planning process for Management Services is clearly a series of interrelated processes having many aspects, time horizons, and levels of detail. It is too simplistic to say that planning is top down, bottom up, or some combination thereof, or that each phase is discrete. Depending on the segment under discussion, any one of the three could apply.

Planning is a continuous process, but it is not an effort performed solely by planners. In fact, the company has few formal "planners." In the United States perhaps fewer than five persons are assigned full-time to the planning process throughout the organization. Even they do not plan, but coordinate the efforts of others and assure that the process is performed consistently and within established time constraints. A key point in CIBA–GEIGY is that planning is an integral part of operating management's responsibilities.

The Three-Year and One-Year Plans

Since planning is a continuous process, with specific dates when "snapshots" are taken, perhaps we should begin by considering it as a top-down process and discuss the development of the three- and one-year plans, outlined in Table 1. The formulations of the three-year and one-year departmental or division plans, although done at different times, are instituted by "planning letters" written by management. These letters establish the major assumptions to be used, including the cost-of-living index; the average percent salary and benefit increases over the planning period; the energy, raw materials, and supplies and positions; the possibilities for acquisitions; and the company's sales contributions and total expense targets.

Table 1 CIBA–GEIGY Planning Outline

Three-year plan
- Chapter 1, Introduction
- Chapter 2, Assumptions (specific to department)
- Chapter 3, Opportunities and/or problems, objectives, and strategies
- Chapter 4, The three-year plan data
- Chapter 5, Problems for higher management attention
- Appendix

One-year plan
- Chapter 1, Assumptions
- Chapter 2, Action programs
- Chapter 3, Major deviations from the first planning year of the three-year plan
- Chapter 4, The one-year plan data

The three-year plan concerns itself with opportunities, problems, and objectives, and the strategies to reach them, as well as the indicated financial impacts if the objectives are reached. The plans are usually submitted for approval at the end of the first quarter.

The one-year plan deals with deviations from the first year of the three-year plan and contains a detailed financial forecast. These plans are usually submitted toward the end of the last quarter of the preceding year.

The Three-Year Plan. The receipt of the planning letter triggers discussions within Management Services on the formulation of the plan. The letter is reviewed to determine the "stretch targets" management has established. In developing the three-year plan, the background materials used are the previous three-year and one-year plans, the active long-term work plan, the present expense-versus-budget outlook, and the knowledge of future areas of impact.

At the first meeting, held with the managers of Management Services and a staff assistant, a plan of action is established for the development of the planning document within the given time constraints. This is followed by a series of meetings at which the managers discuss assumptions to be used. Even such a simple process as establishing assumptions becomes involved, for they are key factors. And, by definition, assumptions are factors over which Management Services has no control. They can be external to be organization, such as cost of living and energy, or they can be internal matters such as acquisitions. While these first group meetings are taking place, each manager is meeting with his key personnel, covering the same ground.

After the assumptions are more or less established, work begins on the opportunities and problems. Again conferences are held concurrently by each manager with his key personnel. Sometimes groups are pulled together from all areas within Management Services, disregarding organizational lines. Discussion leadership is not related to a person's position in the organizational hierarchy. The goal is to use everyone's full intelligence to arrive at the eight to ten major opportunities or issues. These opportunities or issues are not stereotyped. One may be an opportunity for a reorganization; another, a summary of the impact of an entire long-term operating work plan. One opportunity may be a very significant single application that affects the entire organization, like an MIS or a data bank; another may be concerned with internal personnel development. These conferences within Management Services are intended to get the significant subjects to the surface. They also serve to involve all the key members of the department with the planning process.

When a group of major opportunities or problems have been determined, there is discussion of plans that will enable the department either to take advantage of the opportunity or to overcome the problem. The plans are quantified as much as possible, including monetary goals and completion dates. There are different opinions regarding such quantifications. Some argue that stress on quantification is unrealistic, since many types of benefits and expenses, and their impacts on organizations, cannot be quantified. They say that frequently systems can set the general working postures in an organization for as much as a decade; thus they have far more impact than the quantification of a budget or the expense to a user would indicate. I agree with this, and on some occasions qualitative statements must become part of the plan. However, as much as possible there must be measurable targets to strive for, even if they are not as neat or exact as one would desire. Without such targets, it is difficult to arrive at a final plan.

From these targets, strategies are developed. The strategies are the major efforts needed to reach the objectives, including specific areas of responsibility and agreed-to target dates. Regarding objectives and strategies, a cascading principle is used; that is, a strategy developed in the overall departmental plan becomes the objecive for a subunit. Then the subunit establishes its strategies to arrive at this objective. Finally, after all the opportunities, problems, objectives, and strategies are decided on, and their effects on personnel, hardware, software, and expense are estimated, the plan is submitted to top management for approval.

All this may appear to involve a great deal of extra, time-consuming activity. However active members in any organization cannot help but be continually aware of possible opportunities and problems. In most organizations conditions are discussed informally by responsible dedicated professionals through the year. This allows ideas to surface constantly for review. Furthermore, since the three-year plan is developed annually, new ideas evolve from presently active projects as well as from changes in the environment. Therefore the process does not start from ground zero each year. It would be a serious weakness for a department to attempt to develop a new, unrelated long-term plan each year.

The One-Year Plan and Budgets. A planning letter also initiates the development of the one-year plan. The first meeting defines the time constraints within which the plan must be developed and the objectives that management has established. The major concern of the one-year plan is to establish a clear outlook for the coming year and to delineate any major differences from the approved first year of the long-range plan. Also, the long-range plan, although quantified, is concerned mainly with major areas and trends. The one-year plan, however, becomes quite detailed and is a specific financial commitment for the next year.

A review process then takes place, as with the three-year plan, although the period and effort is reduced. Finally, the plan is submitted to management, and once approved, it becomes a commitment. As a follow-up, formal quarterly management reports are developed by all divisions and departments on the status of their actual performance against plan.

As was noted earlier, each division and department must also develop financial and personnel budgets for the year. These budgets are a vital end product of the planning process. The financial budget is prepared by department, by specific segment, by month, and by quarter. It is one of the principal tools used by management to control the company operations.

Remaining Key Planning and Control Instruments

In addition to planning, other control techniques are used by Management Services. Long-term work plans are developed as a result of the user–Management Services dialogue that continues throughout the year.

The department uses the "requested services" concept to charge out costs to other units within the organization. This requires that the user be in agreement with the estimated services charges for the coming year. However this is budget information and does not mean that the user has an absolute commitment. These forecasts simply become part of each user's expense forecast in the one-year plan and may be challenged by management.

Therefore ceilings may develop from this exercise. The firm commitment for the user comes when a project is undertaken, the first phase of the "project life cycle system" (see Table 2). After a request is made or a project proposed, agreements are reached on the objectives and scope, a feasibility study is made, and developmental expenses are calculated. Then manpower requirements, both from Management Services and the user, are established and a project manager named. It is strongly urged that the user manage all the projects. The project life cycle demands that the project be divided into phases having objectives, expenses, benefits, and manpower forecasts clearly stated; reports must be sent to all involved, including the internal auditor, permitting all projects to be tracked and deviations to be spotted before they become major problems.

Each major operating unit has an information liaison representative who coordinates all projects in his areas, reports the financial and personnel impact on his division or department, and reviews the status and operating charges with Management Services. Thus division management committees are made aware of the commitments of their divisions based on divisional requests. The chargeback and performance system, through the information liaison representative, reports to all users the

Table 2 Project Life Cycle Phases

1.0. Prefeasibility
  1.1. Purpose
    1.1.1. To demonstrate mutual understanding of the project request
    1.1.2. To indicate disposition of request
    1.1.3. To develop preliminary plan and attendant time and cost estimates
    1.1.4. To obtain user authorization
  1.2 Product
    1.2.1. Work statement
    1.2.2. Work plan
    1.2.3. Activity checklist

2.0. Feasibility
  2.1. Purpose
    2.1.1. To analyze and define project requirements
    2.1.2. To identify alternate solutions
    2.1.3. To present alternatives
    2.1.4. To obtain user authorization
  2.2. Product
    2.2.1. Project team responsibility chart
    2.2.2. User's organization chart
    2.2.3. Current information flow
    2.2.4. Design alternatives
    2.2.5. Proposal
    2.2.6. Phase-end report

3.0. Design
  3.1. Purpose
    3.1.1. To analyze processing requirements of project
    3.1.2. To design systems to meet requirements
    3.1.3. To develop appropriate specifications for programming and procedures
  3.2. Products
    3.2.1. Systems functional specification
    3.2.2. Program/module specifications
    3.2.3. Procedure specifications
    3.2.4. Initial installation plan
    3.2.5. Initial conversion plan
    3.2.6. Phase-end report

4.0. Development
  4.1. Purpose
    4.1.1. To develop programs and procedures specified in design phase
    4.1.2. To conduct test of developed programs
    4.1.3. To prepare draft systems documentation
    4.1.4. To obtain user authorization

Table 2 Project Life Cycle Phases *(continued)*

- 4.2. Products
    - 4.2.1. Test plan for program, job, and system
    - 4.2.2. Tested programs
    - 4.2.3. Draft systems documentation
    - 4.2.4. Final installation plan
    - 4.2.5. Final conversion plan
    - 4.2.6. Training plans
    - 4.2.7. Specifications modifications
    - 4.2.8. Phase-end report

5.0. Installation
- 5.1. Purpose
    - 5.1.1. To educate all users of the system
    - 5.1.2. To test all aspects of the system to ensure the quality and accuracy of output and the ability to meet proposed schedules
    - 5.1.3. To have all system documentation reviewed by appropriate operational units
    - 5.1.4. To convert all files
    - 5.1.5. To install the system in production mode
    - 5.1.6. To obtain the user's authorization
- 5.2. Product
    - 5.2.1. Final user's procedures
    - 5.2.2. Final systems documentation
    - 5.2.3. Final project documentation
    - 5.2.4. Successfully installed system

specific charges to each department for scientific, operations research, business systems, and data processing work. This includes developmental, operational, or retrieval projects. Also, on developmental projects, total costs to date are given.

As major developmental programs come to light that need a company-wide review, an advisory committee is convened to help determine a project development schedule. This group, of approximately eight members, is made up of divisional vice presidents of administration and key corporate department heads. All active and requested projects are presented, along with the recommendations of Management Services. This material is reviewed, and recommendations of the advisory group are established. If these recommendations necessitate increases in staff, expenses, or hardware, Management Services presents this information to management as a company recommendaion. This cuts down the one-to-one negotiations that so often are not reflective of overall company needs.

Based on the foregoing procedures, it is a simple step to summarize the status of all the projects into a single input for the one- or three-year plan, with consideration given to future projects not yet begun.

IMPROVEMENT OPPORTUNITIES

Manufacturers, computer professionals, and consultants must share the guilt for the many mediocre installations today. We have all become so involved in techniques, programming languages, software, core, speed, teleprocessing, buzz words, tricks, hardware, and plain being busy that we have forgotten the objectives. The information science discipline supposedly came about to improve the profit-making capabilities of an organization. It started with professionals called "efficiency experts," who began using unit record equipment, then computers. They joined forces with economists and statisticians who had an affinity for the computer and banded together under the titles of management scientists or operations research specialists. This tremendous talent, however, all too often lost sight of the objectives and became wrapped up in the techniques. This is a major concern at CIBA–GEIGY and a problem throughout the industry. The professionals confuse staff work with making things happen. Being busy is not the mission; it is productivity and profit. Writing a plan or a budget is just the beginning. Implementing it, motivating personnel, developing credibility to try new ideas—this is management. This is also in too short supply. If there is one objective for our discipline, it must be to get back to the basic objectives. We must remember that information systems encompass the entire organization and do not start and stop at the computer room door. All the techniques are available. We now must become responsible members of the management group of an organization by helping it reach its objectives through increased sales, cost reduction, and profit improvement.

6 JACK B. GEARHART

TRW Systems Group

TRW Systems Group has evolved during the last 20 years from a systems engineering–technical organization in the ballistic missile business to a leading spacecraft, electronics, and scientific software contractor. The corresponding annual sales growth has now reached the $300 to $400 million level.

TRW Systems is a member of a multinational corporation that includes such diversified product lines as automotive and aircraft parts, oil drilling equipment, transportation systems, and computing equipment. TRW Inc., the parent corporate entity, has annual sales in excess of $2 billion.

TRW Systems is comprised of four operating divisions and six central staff elements. The divisions deal with products and services that are all based on advanced scientific and engineering technology and therefore employ a high percentage of professional personnel. In addition, each division and most staffs have developed quite independently of the others, resulting in a wide array of information systems, often "in triplicate." As the TRW Systems Group matured and a systematic approach was implemented for information system development, a sound stable of systems has evolved and the long-range plan objectives are being realized.

The information system planning is consistent with and responsive to the overall company business planning and objectives. In addition, several models are now in regular use by business planning as decision-making aids.

The functions of information systems planning, development, and implementation have reached a fair level of maturity in approach and practice, although a good deal remains to be done in achieving a complete complement of such systems.

INFORMATION SYSTEMS BACKGROUND

As the company grew from a modest labor-oriented environment to the current hardware and software producing environment, including sophisticated development and production techniques, hundreds of subcontractors and suppliers, dozens of associated contractors, and many small research and analysis tasks, the information systems grew from simple labor reporting to complex parts control systems, cost control systems, resource allocation systems, and others.

Business information processing is now considered by top and line managers to be an important company resource. As the company has grown, the sophistication and usage of the various business systems has become more sophisticated, effective, and responsive to increasingly complex user requirements.

The computing equipment within the company has evolved from early accounting machines to RCA 301's, IBM 7090's, RCA 3301's, IBM 360/50, 360/65, 370/155, and recently to the 370/158. Concurrently, the associated information systems technology not only included IBM's IMS, but also time-sharing, data collection terminals, minicomputers, and remote terminals. Approximately 200 people are engaged in the management, development, and operation of management systems within the company.

The Management Systems Department and its related organizational structure are designed to respond to the established long-range plan. As requirement trends change, the organization is expected to be appropriately adjusted. Figure 1 portrays the 1974 organizational arrangement.

As we have entered our planned on-line environment, the major new applications are concentrated in the area of interactive inquiry and update. Typical of these applications are a cost data base, a product data base, manpower information, manpower planning, and a project forecast system.

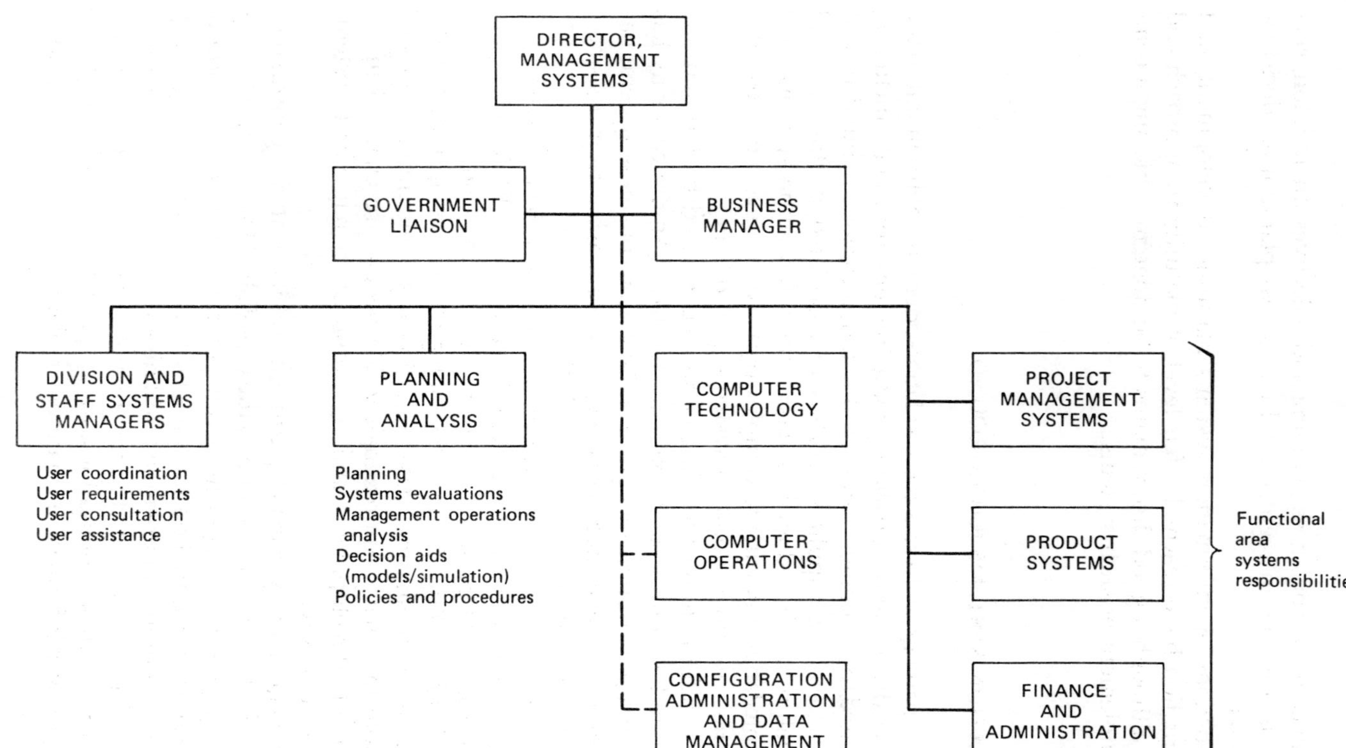

Figure 1 Organization chart, TRW Management Systems.

INFORMATION SYSTEMS OBJECTIVES

To pursue immediate and long-term plans in the most effective manner, specific information systems objectives are developed and maintained. These objectives are periodically reviewed and approved by TRW management to assure that the requested budget allocations are consistent with overall company objectives and with competing requirements for budget allocations.

The top level objectives are depicted in Table 1. From these objectives, an "MIS concept" was derived (Figure 2). Within TRW, "management information system" is defined as the aggregate system of all policies, procedures, forms, reports, files, computer systems, and decision aids that facilitate the processing and utilizing of business data for all levels of management. Our MIS concept guides us in viewing any one requirement and any one system as a part of a total company information flow. Thus each solution to a requirement is tailored to serve all anticipated actual needs. We also view the MIS concept as a technical and management discipline that minimizes firefighting reactions and maximizes a rational approach in planning our projects. Each of our existing

Table 1 Approach to Information System Development

Objectives

- Satisfy external requirements
  - Legal
  - Customer
- Improve support to business operations
  - Timely, relevant, and economic management information systems
- Improve cost effectiveness of MIS
  - Usage
  - Processing
- Provide special management support

Planning

- Management Information System concept
- Strategic planning
- Thrusts
- Lead executive concept

Understanding unique user problems

- Analysis
- Design
- Development
- Implementation
- Training

System evaluation and audit

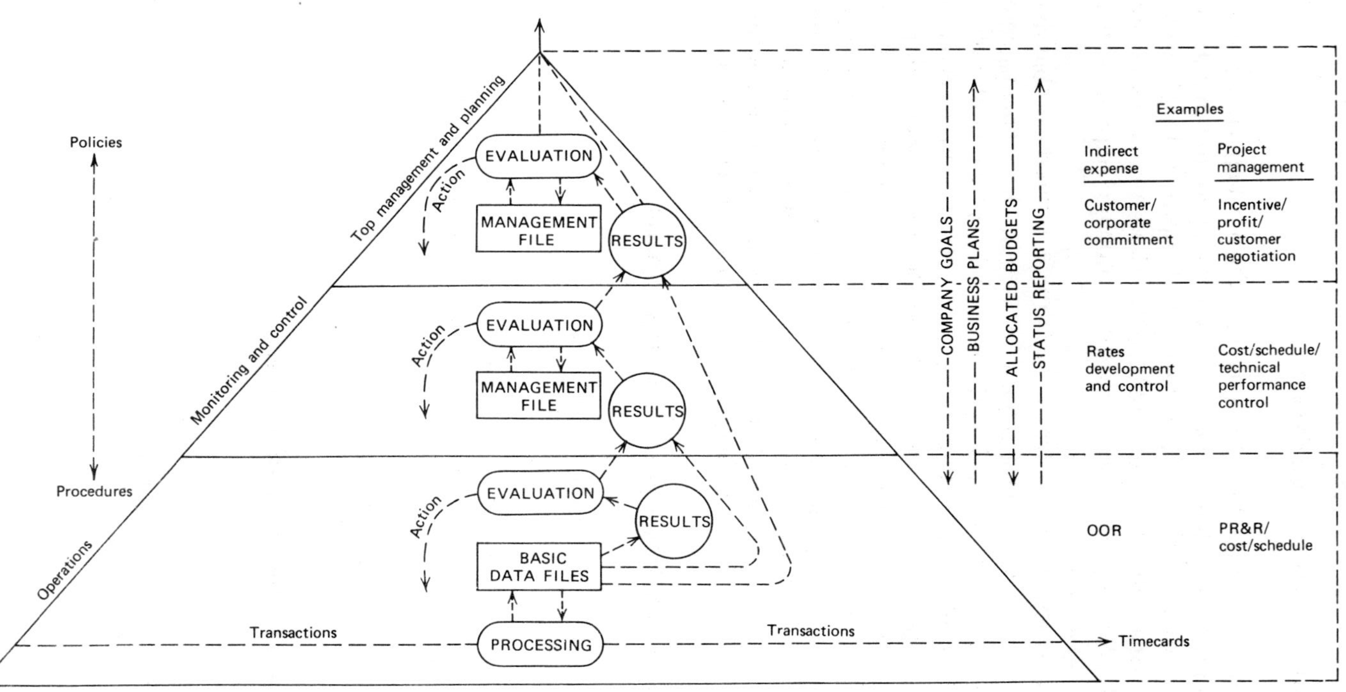

Figure 2 MIS concept.

and proposed systems is continually evaluated against this concept. As specific achievements are made, the relative emphasis of technical efforts change. Six specific MIS thrusts have been identified, and these underlie our long-range plan.

1. Modular data bases.
2. Departure from batch reporting.
3. Direct access teleprocessing.
4. Management by exception.
5. Improved policies and procedures.
6. Timely, relevant, and cost-effective information to decision makers.

INFORMATION SYSTEMS PLANNING HISTORY

The first formal TRW Systems management systems long-range plan was developed in 1969, reflecting a detailed system requirements analysis (SRA) of the company's information needs. The SRA examined the requirements from a functional and organizational viewpoint. To evaluate individual requirements and new project proposals, an overall company functional framework was developed. No one technique can guarantee that *all* requirements have been categorized, but a reasonable framework serves as a valuable tool. At TRW Systems we developed our requirements framework from three viewpoints: first, we examined the basic functional requirements and responsibilities of the company. One method of portraying this viewpoint was a requirements tree (Figure 3). The second viewpoint was that of continuous evaluation by the user of the requirements and the current operating information systems, coupled with a data processing efficiency assessment. The third was testing the results of the first two against "typical" functions that might be found in any company.

The 1969 plan effectively assessed the existing situation and laid the groundwork for subsequent improvement in the longer range approach. In 1971 a revised long-range plan was issued (Table 2 gives its table of contents). The planning process to achieve the previously discussed objectives and concepts is a mechanism for the integration of all major factors. This process produces a tangible, meaningful, and acceptable long-range plan, an annual operating plan, and individual project plans. These plans serve as flexible but consistent road maps for our work and contain a five-year projection of specifically planned projects to achieve established objectives and meet identified requirements. As requirements change, this road map needs to be adjusted. Our planning staff

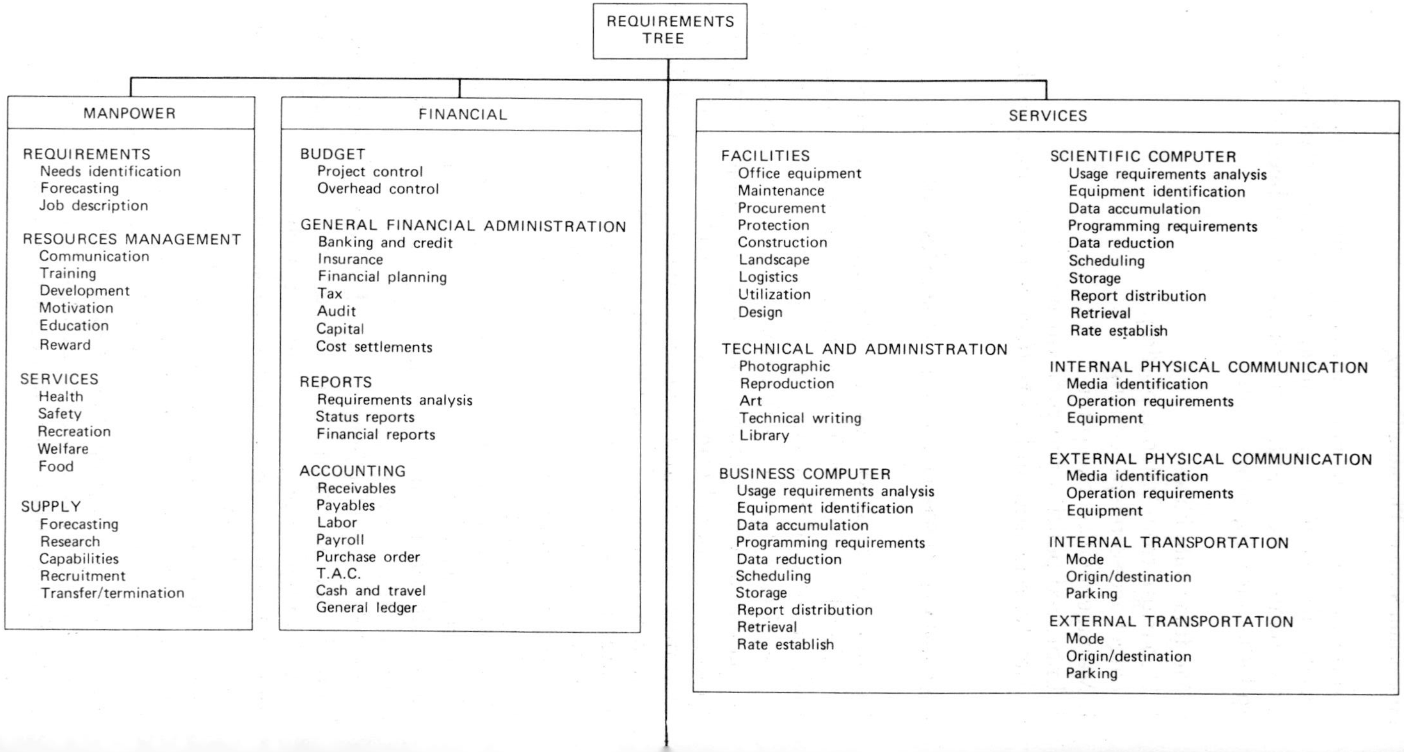

REQUIREMENTS TREE

MANPOWER

REQUIREMENTS
- Needs identification
- Forecasting
- Job description

RESOURCES MANAGEMENT
- Communication
- Training
- Development
- Motivation
- Education
- Reward

SERVICES
- Health
- Safety
- Recreation
- Welfare
- Food

SUPPLY
- Forecasting
- Research
- Capabilities
- Recruitment
- Transfer/termination

FINANCIAL

BUDGET
- Project control
- Overhead control

GENERAL FINANCIAL ADMINISTRATION
- Banking and credit
- Insurance
- Financial planning
- Tax
- Audit
- Capital
- Cost settlements

REPORTS
- Requirements analysis
- Status reports
- Financial reports

ACCOUNTING
- Receivables
- Payables
- Labor
- Payroll
- Purchase order
- T.A.C.
- Cash and travel
- General ledger

SERVICES

FACILITIES
- Office equipment
- Maintenance
- Procurement
- Protection
- Construction
- Landscape
- Logistics
- Utilization
- Design

TECHNICAL AND ADMINISTRATION
- Photographic
- Reproduction
- Art
- Technical writing
- Library

BUSINESS COMPUTER
- Usage requirements analysis
- Equipment identification
- Data accumulation
- Programming requirements
- Data reduction
- Scheduling
- Storage
- Report distribution
- Retrieval
- Rate establish

SCIENTIFIC COMPUTER
- Usage requirements analysis
- Equipment identification
- Data accumulation
- Programming requirements
- Data reduction
- Scheduling
- Storage
- Report distribution
- Retrieval
- Rate establish

INTERNAL PHYSICAL COMMUNICATION
- Media identification
- Operation requirements
- Equipment

EXTERNAL PHYSICAL COMMUNICATION
- Media identification
- Operation requirements
- Equipment

INTERNAL TRANSPORTATION
- Mode
- Origin/destination
- Parking

EXTERNAL TRANSPORTATION
- Mode
- Origin/destination
- Parking

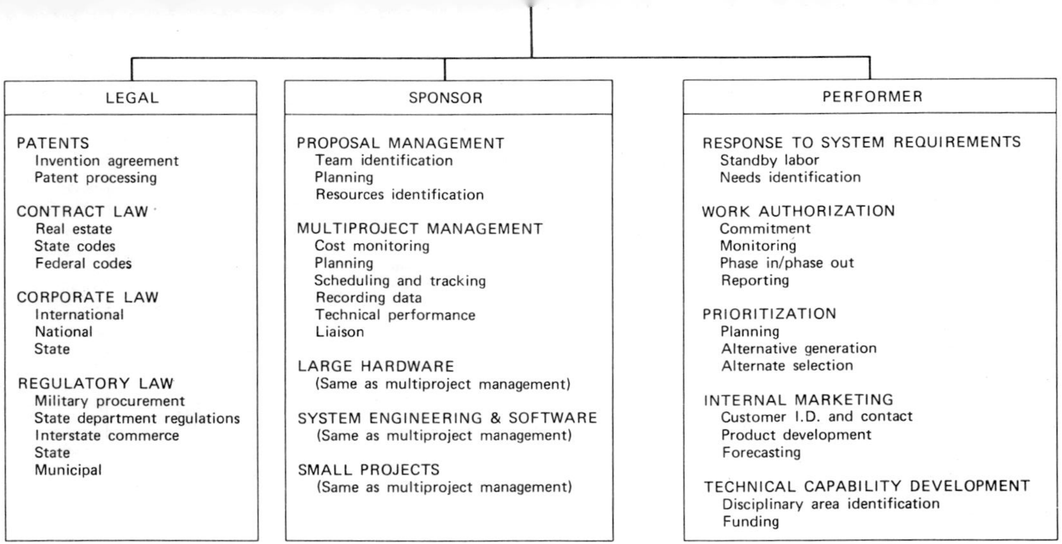

LEGAL

PATENTS
- Invention agreement
- Patent processing

CONTRACT LAW
- Real estate
- State codes
- Federal codes

CORPORATE LAW
- International
- National
- State

REGULATORY LAW
- Military procurement
- State department regulations
- Interstate commerce
- State
- Municipal

SPONSOR

PROPOSAL MANAGEMENT
- Team identification
- Planning
- Resources identification

MULTIPROJECT MANAGEMENT
- Cost monitoring
- Planning
- Scheduling and tracking
- Recording data
- Technical performance
- Liaison

LARGE HARDWARE
- (Same as multiproject management)

SYSTEM ENGINEERING & SOFTWARE
- (Same as multiproject management)

SMALL PROJECTS
- (Same as multiproject management)

PERFORMER

RESPONSE TO SYSTEM REQUIREMENTS
- Standby labor
- Needs identification

WORK AUTHORIZATION
- Commitment
- Monitoring
- Phase in/phase out
- Reporting

PRIORITIZATION
- Planning
- Alternative generation
- Alternate selection

INTERNAL MARKETING
- Customer I.D. and contact
- Product development
- Forecasting

TECHNICAL CAPABILITY DEVELOPMENT
- Disciplinary area identification
- Funding

Figure 3 Requirements tree.

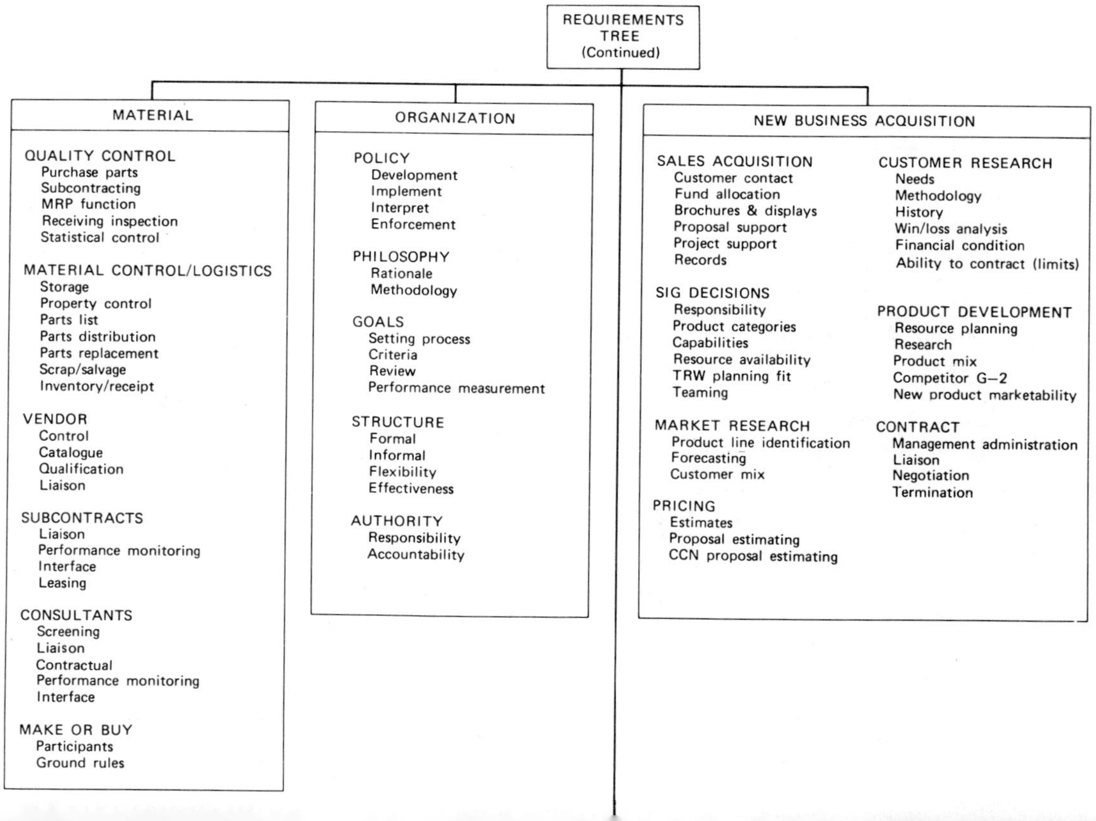

REQUIREMENTS TREE (Continued)

MATERIAL

QUALITY CONTROL
- Purchase parts
- Subcontracting
- MRP function
- Receiving inspection
- Statistical control

MATERIAL CONTROL/LOGISTICS
- Storage
- Property control
- Parts list
- Parts distribution
- Parts replacement
- Scrap/salvage
- Inventory/receipt

VENDOR
- Control
- Catalogue
- Qualification
- Liaison

SUBCONTRACTS
- Liaison
- Performance monitoring
- Interface
- Leasing

CONSULTANTS
- Screening
- Liaison
- Contractual
- Performance monitoring
- Interface

MAKE OR BUY
- Participants
- Ground rules

ORGANIZATION

POLICY
- Development
- Implement
- Interpret
- Enforcement

PHILOSOPHY
- Rationale
- Methodology

GOALS
- Setting process
- Criteria
- Review
- Performance measurement

STRUCTURE
- Formal
- Informal
- Flexibility
- Effectiveness

AUTHORITY
- Responsibility
- Accountability

NEW BUSINESS ACQUISITION

SALES ACQUISITION
- Customer contact
- Fund allocation
- Brochures & displays
- Proposal support
- Project support
- Records

SIG DECISIONS
- Responsibility
- Product categories
- Capabilities
- Resource availability
- TRW planning fit
- Teaming

MARKET RESEARCH
- Product line identification
- Forecasting
- Customer mix

PRICING
- Estimates
- Proposal estimating
- CCN proposal estimating

CUSTOMER RESEARCH
- Needs
- Methodology
- History
- Win/loss analysis
- Financial condition
- Ability to contract (limits)

PRODUCT DEVELOPMENT
- Resource planning
- Research
- Product mix
- Competitor G–2
- New product marketability

CONTRACT
- Management administration
- Liaison
- Negotiation
- Termination

ENGINEERING

DESIGN ENGINEERING
Standardization
Test
Maintainability
Producibility
Production engineering
Simulation modeling

ENGINEERING SUPPORT
Configuration management
Value engineering
Data management
Engineering release
Hardware definition documentation
Design review
Reliability

MANUFACTURING

TEST/INTEGRATION
Subsystem
Components
Environmental
Systems

OPERATIONS
Cost/budget
Production control
Methods & process
Plans & estimates
Scheduling
Standards
Parts control

EQUIPMENT
Requirements
Priorities
Methodology
Maintenance
Accountability
Procurement
Disposal

QUALITY
Standards
Procedures
Reports
Methods
Processes

ADMINISTRATION

ENVIRONMENTAL INTERFACE REQUIREMENTS
Internal to external
External to internal

OFFSITE OPERATIONS
International
Intranational
Military
Nonmilitary

SECURITY
Area control
Personnel clearance
Document control
Personnel orientation

OVERALL PLANNING
Near term
Long range planning

Figure 3 *(Continued)*

Table 2 Table of Contents for Management Systems Long-Range Plan

Executive summary

I. Introduction
   A. Requirements and the role of management systems
   B. Management systems objectives
   C. Management systems approach
   D. Management systems long-range planning process

II. Planning assumptions
   A. Business assumptions
   B. MIS requirements
   C. State-of-the-art projections
   D. Budgetary guidelines

III. MIS concept
   A. Purpose of the MIS
   B. Evolution of the MIS—past and future
   C. Five key thrusts
   D. Computer hardware and software trends
   E. Contingency planning

IV. Planned projects

V. Resources plan
   A. Management systems manpower plan
   B. Management systems facilities plan
   C. Management systems training plan
   D. Management systems financial plan

IV. Glossary

maintains a current and accurate picture of the developing requirements and how they fit into our long-range picture.

Throughout our analysis, design, development, implementation, and training efforts, a heavy user involvement is achieved by assigning user personnel to responsibilities ranging from project manager to analyst to implementation manager. In addition, users participate as members of the project review board and are required to sign off acceptance of a new system before it is declared operational.

A major improvement in our 1971 plan was the introduction of the "lead executive" concept. Our strong emphasis on meaningful and committed involvement of top management has been achieved by obtaining the concurrence of management in our basic concept and approach, and by requiring that each individual project must be sponsored by one of our executives. The key features of this arrangement are outlined in Table 3.

Table 3 The Concept of the Lead Executive

Purpose

- To achieve real management involvement and thereby realize meaningful guidance and direction in the information system development program
- To maintain a sense of user ownership in the new and productional systems
- To obtain the proper support for information systems development and operation consistent with other company needs

Each information system project must be sponsored by one or more company executives at the division general manager or staff director level.

Assignment as lead executive is based upon the executive who is most affected, has primary area of related responsibility, and/or has the major source of experience.

Support executives are those who may be substantially involved and/or interested in the results of the project.

Over the years this concept has been extremely important and valuable. Our top management has, in effect, teamed with us to ensure that the management systems expenditures are at an appropriate level with other key discretionary commitments. We thus have assurance that every project we undertake continues to be an important and supported building block not only of the management systems objectives but of the company's objectives as well.

INFORMATION SYSTEMS PLANNING RESPONSIBILITIES

As indicated in Figure 1, the responsibility for developing our long-range plan is assigned to the manager of planning and analysis. It is his continuing responsibility to update, coordinate, and publish our long-range plan and to maintain an up-to-date portrayal of the current picture of requirements and projects with reference to our long-range objectives. He ensures that the plan is compatible with current company planning trends, such as sales levels, product mixes, customer trends, emerging legal requirements, and internal requirements.

Appropriate user participation in our planning process is one responsibility of our division and staff systems managers (Figure 1), who serve as management systems representatives to the division and staff organizations we serve. They are our key points of communication with user requirements. Such planning must reflect the cognizance and support of our top management team.

The manager of planning and analysis is also supported in these efforts by our Computer Technology Department to ensure that hardware and software state-of-the-art trends are considered. He also closely coordinates with the various functional managers who are responsible for the actual implementation of the planned projects. Similarly, joint planning is conducted with our computer operations, thus keeping equipment planning fully integrated with evolving requirements.

INFORMATION SYSTEMS PLANNING PROCESS

Although our planning process is continuous, discrete individual steps are taken to reflect the previously discussed objectives, requirements, and operations. As Figure 4 indicates, the three major paths continually iterated are the long-range plan, the annual operating plan, and the individual project plans. As an individual requirement is identified, it is documented by means of a management systems action request (MSAR). This request reflects a user's statement of the requirements; our validation of the requirement; a proposed project description,

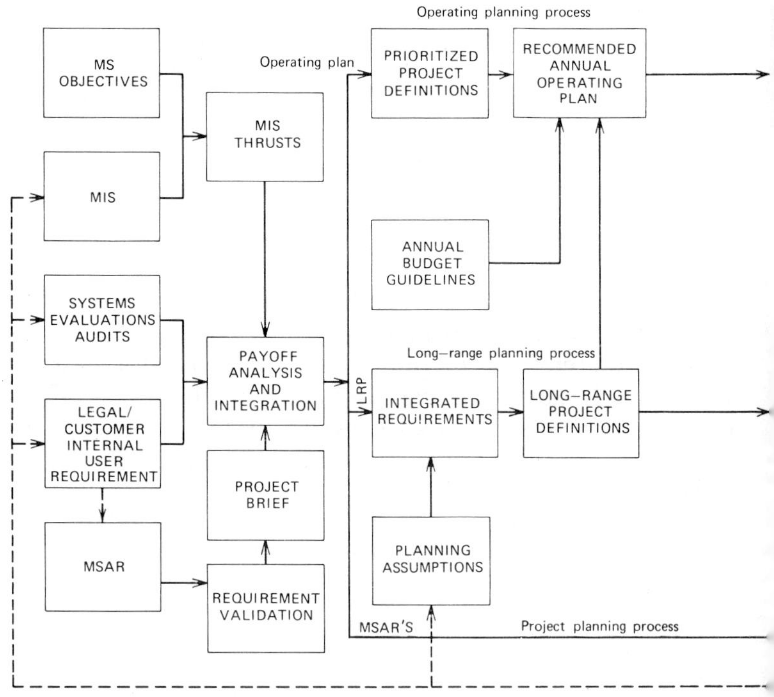

Figure 4 Management systems planning process.

analysis, and integration of this requirement/project into overall planning; a budget analysis; and the lead executive approval to proceed when appropriate priorities have been set (Figure 5).

As this individual project activity continues, it is reflected in the current annual operating plan, the budget, and the long-range plan. The annual operating planning process is summarized late in the year to become the budget proposal for the following year. One way to portray this relationship is illustrated in Figure 6. Since we keep our planning current, we are able at any time to take a slice out of our long-range plan and propose a budgetary planning package. This is formally accomplished in the September-to-December time frame, to obtain funding from the next year's budget.

During this period our head executives are contacted, and their guidance and concurrence is requested. At this point we have achieved tentative top management approval of our proposal and the final budget is worked out based on management systems budget requirements and those of other discretionary resource requirements.

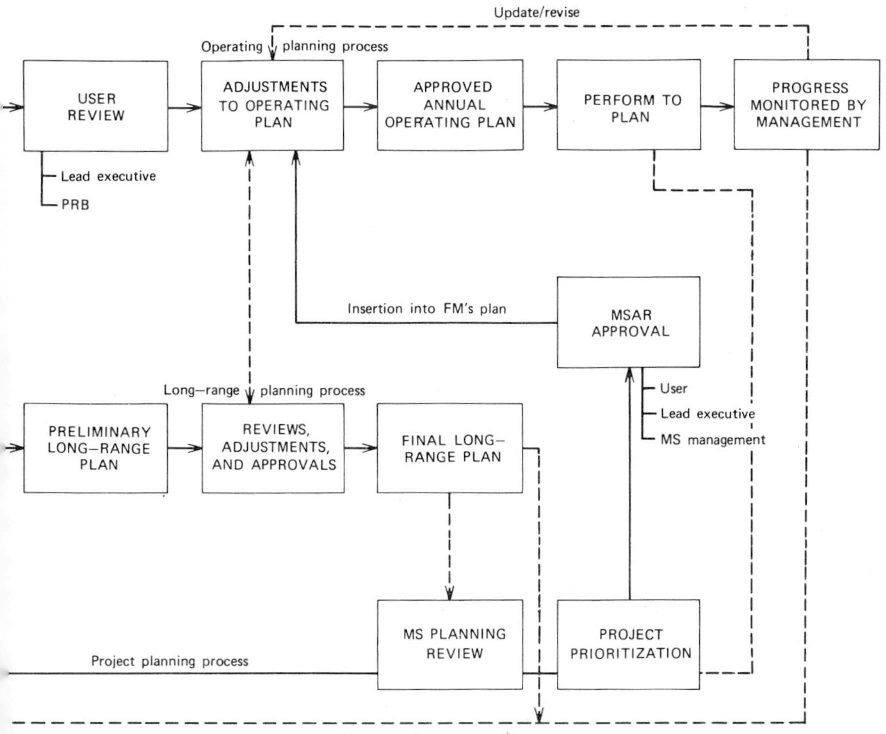

Figure 4 *(Continued)*

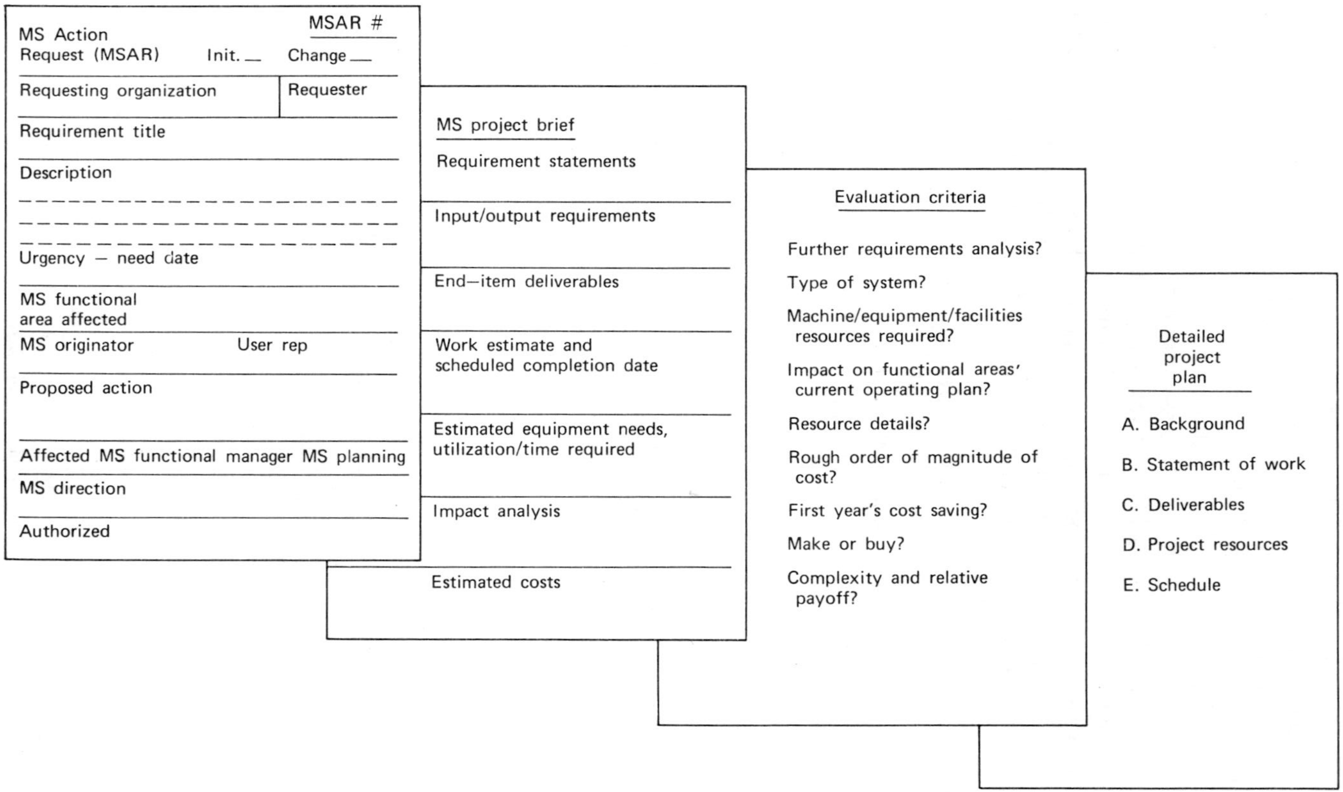

MS Action
Request (MSAR) Init. ___ Change ___
MSAR # ___

Requesting organization | Requester

Requirement title

Description

Urgency – need date

MS functional area affected

MS originator User rep

Proposed action

Affected MS functional manager MS planning

MS direction

Authorized

MS project brief

Requirement statements

Input/output requirements

End–item deliverables

Work estimate and scheduled completion date

Estimated equipment needs, utilization/time required

Impact analysis

Estimated costs

Evaluation criteria

Further requirements analysis?

Type of system?

Machine/equipment/facilities resources required?

Impact on functional areas' current operating plan?

Resource details?

Rough order of magnitude of cost?

First year's cost saving?

Make or buy?

Complexity and relative payoff?

Detailed project plan

A. Background

B. Statement of work

C. Deliverables

D. Project resources

E. Schedule

Figure 5 Management systems action request (MSAR), including backup documentation.

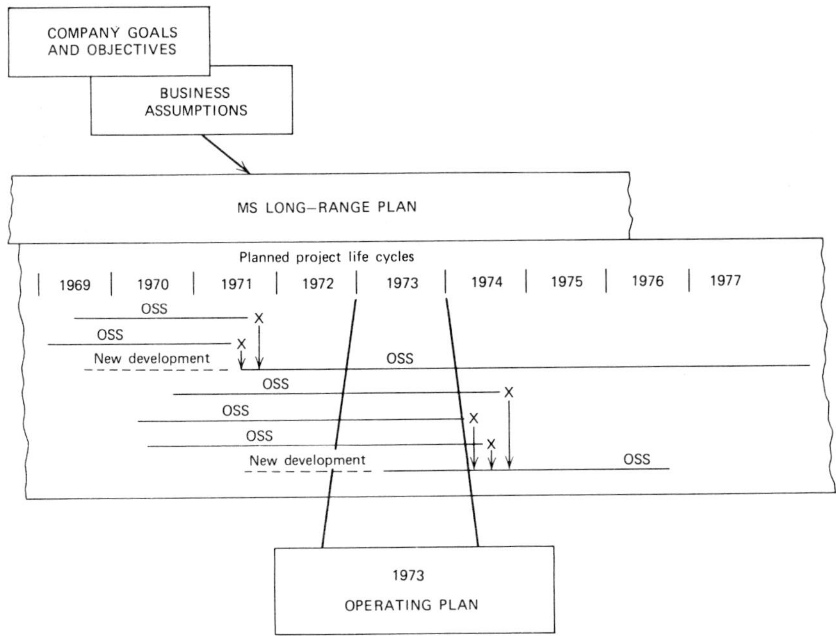

Figure 6 Results of planning process.

IMPROVEMENT OPPORTUNITIES

The temptation to conclude that planning is done when the plan is completed must be resisted. Every one of the last five years brought a new challenge in requirements and planning. Some of the challenges came in the form of new legal or customer requirements. Other challenges included decisions to bring in new technology, such as virtual storage, computer output microfilm (COM), and Entrex input technology.

Since 1969 we also have been fortunate enough to be able to demonstrate cost savings levels well above expenditures. Top management is satisfied with our approach to information systems planning, but we continue to search for improvements and better communications with all levels of users, better response to user requirements, better resource utilization in meeting user requirements, and better personnel career development opportunities. We feel that the very essence of good planning is the search toward greater improvements.

In summary, TRW Systems has carefully defined its objectives and goals regarding its MIS, considering current and expected characteristics of the business and the business environment. Second, an explicit concept guiding the evolution of the MIS was established. Third, an integrated process of planning, budgeting, evaluating, and controlling has been put into practice. Fourth, top managers of TRW Systems and the users are involved directly and specifically in managing the evolution of the MIS. We believe this strategy assures that TRW Systems' MIS flexibility supports the operating and managerial needs of the business in a most cost-effective manner.

7 CARL H. REYNOLDS

Hughes Aircraft Company

Hughes Aircraft Company, established in the early 1930s, took on its current business complexion about 1950, when it made a major move into aerospace electronics. Since that time it has had its ups and downs like most aerospace companies; but over the last six or seven years it has maintained a reasonably steady growth. We now have about 35,000 employees and sales of about $1 billion. We are organized into four separate groups quite different in size, and almost all are engaged in some facet of the electronics business. Our products range from cable connectors, which cost in the neighborhood of $2 to $3 a piece, to full-scale weapons systems and satellites costing several million dollars each. The operational unit in the company is the division, of which we have approximately 40. The management organizational philosophy is decentralization to the greatest extent possible.

The Hughes corporate data processing organization must therefore serve a large number of relatively independent entities of varied size, each having normal business information system needs as well as highly technical computational requirements. In addition, much of our work is development and project oriented in a highly competitive, low-margin market. These last factors place great demands on our project, technical, and financial control systems, many of which are computer based.

Because so much of our work is in new technologies and is government connected, our business is closely tied to the long-range development plans of various government agencies. There is routine long-range planning implicit in the contracts we win and in the ones we work for. Semiannually, the long-range financial and manpower implications of every division's projects and expectations are summarized into a corporate five-year plan. One of these semiannual projections coincides with the development of the annual operating plan. The key to long-range success, however, is not this plan—it is necessary, but not sufficient. The key management decisions are the selection of technology for our research efforts and the selection of the projects for sales effort that will survive the government's selection process. The current role of information systems in these critical decisions is minimum and indirect.

COMPUTING BACKGROUND

Computing started at Hughes in the middle 1950s on IBM 650's, each in separate scientific and business computing organizations. Through the late 1950s and early 1960s, this dichotomy continued; and as the company grew, it started to differentiate and decentralize its organization. During this period the growth of several decentralized computing centers, though entirely in keeping with the fundamental organizational philosophy of the company, was probably not very cost effective. In the late 1960s, centralization within one of the major groups was started. This was the first step toward complete organizational centralization and two machines were maintained, one for open shop and one for closed shop. In 1970 a decision was made to centralize all computing (except that which was not directly tied to physical processes like testing and flight tables) into one organization and to bring onto one set of equipment both open shop (engineering) and closed shop work. A plan was developed to take the work that existed on two separate IBM 360/65's, a GE 635, a 360/30, and two 360/20's onto one dual 370/165 complex.

Our current organization, called Computing and Data Processing (C & DP) is a corporate function reporting to the executive vice president. We do essentially all the routine business data processing in the company, about two-thirds of all the open shop scientific computing, and about 90 percent of the business systems design and implementation. Our network is also quite extensive. We have more than 200 low-speed terminals scattered from Malibu to Tucson for applications such as ATS, IMS, and TSO (Administrative Terminal System, Information Management System, and Time Sharing Option); and we have approximately 12 remote job entry terminals ranging in capability from 300 lines a minute to 1100 lines a minute.

There are also other data processing and computing capabilities around the company. We have an IBM 370/145 installed in Tucson. There is a 370/158, for a special contract in one of the groups that is not under our direction, and a Xerox Sigma 8 that is used to drive a flight table. A Sigma 5 serves in conjunction with analog computers to do hybrid computing that is also not part of our organization. All these systems are capable of, and on occasion do, some of the work for which we are responsible. It is interesting to note the contrast between the basic organizational philosophy of decentralization and the implementation of a strong central data processing organization. One of the most difficult parts of our operation is that we are one organization trying to offer complete data processing service to 40 different entities ranging in size from $200 million revenue a year down to $20 million or less per year.

The original objectives of the central organization were as follows:

1. Increased technical competence.
2. Increased cost performance.
3. Flexibility in responding to a fast-changing business environment.
4. Security of corporate records.
5. Compliance with government ASPR regulations with respect to the lease and/or buy of equipment.

INFORMATION SYSTEMS PLANNING

Our first long-range plan was the one developed to centralize our computing capabilities into one organization in place of the previous four, and to concentrate on one set of hardware and software instead of three. In the process of implementation, this single goal was the overriding objective. Since then we have had to develop more specific, user-oriented objectives. Besides budget objectives, there has been a need to quantify performance objectives and to set levels of performance acceptable to our users. We have been successful in both these endeavors, though the latter keeps getting more difficult. For 1974 our key objectives were measured in terms of report on-time delivery, teleprocessing system up-time, and open shop turnaround time as a function of program resource requirements.

From top management's point of view, the most important objective is to keep the cost effectiveness of data processing high and its absolute cost as low as possible. Generally, users want to optimize a system of which computing is only a part. This can lead to "inefficient" use of the computer. On the other hand, data processing people have their own ideas about how their hardware and software "ought" to be used. In light of this, the management of C & DP has taken on the task of trying to make the impact of its activities on all these goals as visible as possible. One major element in this effort is the system requirement specification, which requires C & DP, users, and their management to agree on the objectives and benefits of every significant project undertaken by C & DP.

Planning in small data processing installations tends to be *ad hoc* and informal. But when the decision was made to form a large central organization, a relatively detailed plan of attack had to be developed. It was, however, more related to how to build the organization than how to service the company. The organization is now built; and for several reasons stemming from our being centralized, the need for a long-range plan has become evident.

First, the growth of computing has been higher than anticipated. We must make a decision within the next 12 months about the way in which we are going to handle time-sharing and open shop computing. This is necessary because our present situation is barely satisfactory and will be clearly unsatisfactory and inadequate over the long pull. Second, it has become clear that as the company grows and as investments in application programs become larger in scope, such investments must take place over more than a single year. If we are to avoid wasting money by turning projects on and off, and if we are properly to plan the hardware to support applications as they are developed, we must lengthen the time over which we forecast our requirements. Finally, government auditors are increasingly requiring longer range plans to justify our lease-versus-buy decisions. To date we have only a system for developing annual plans. However the long-range planning procedure we intend to follow is almost the same as our annual one. Therefore the explanation of our annual planning process will be given first, followed by how we hope to extend it to the longer term.

THE PLANNING PROCESS

Essentially, we develop two plans in parallel. The first is a sales forecast, and the second, an operating plan. The sales forecast is made by categorizing the services we provide into four manageable groups: business systems production, business systems development, teleprocessing, and open shop. Business systems production is further divided into approximately 12 categories, each consisting of several systems, which in turn comprise the 100 or so systems we run. In accounting for our programming activity, we identify the amount of effort required for maintenance and include that in production costs. In addition, anything costing $5000 or more is a "development," whereas anything less than $5000 is a "small improvement." For each group of services we prepare the expected dollar expenditure by division for that service for the current year. This is done during the late summer. We also try to identify, for as many of the systems as possible, the parameter or parameters that seem to affect resource utilization or the cost of that system. For example, the key element in payroll is the number of people.

We then assemble a forecast for each division of its requirements for all these services for the next year, based on the information we furnish plus whatever the division knows about its own expectations. Development projects are somewhat harder to account for, since often several divisions share the development cost; and this may require coordination, not only between divisions but also between groups. But for every development project we have an identifying name and line-item number in our plan and an estimation of manpower and computing costs for the following year. Of course, for the major developments, much more detailed plans are prepared.

After each division forecast has been put together, they are added up in terms of total dollars. In the meantime our operations personnel and our systems programming department have been analyzing trend data on the number of jobs per day, the size of jobs, the number of lines printed, storage used, and so forth. We also look at performance data such as mean time to failure. We then make some rough judgments about what our objectives for the next year should be. From this review we develop a preliminary resource plan that includes hardware, software, and programming, plus a cost breakdown for each. Large deviations from previous history are reviewed by the staff that prepared the sales forecast and by the operating people. In 1973 we came within 0.5 percent of being correct; but that was after several large compensating changes. The 1974 figures are a better test of the effectiveness of this scheme.

We expect to follow the same general procedure in developing a five-year plan. Additionally, we will try to forecast the logical implications of current development activities into the future before we ask for the users' own requirements. For example, several large data-base-oriented systems under development are expected to call for increasing numbers of terminals, numbers of transactions, and so forth. Thus the first element of our five-year plan will be a logical extrapolation of what is already happening. We think this will also help the user in figuring out what he may want to do. Once we have completed this forecast of our own, we will go to the major users and ask each one to develop his own forecast. In this way we hope to ensure that no emerging need is overlooked.

IMPROVEMENT OPPORTUNITIES

There are several major problems that are easy to foresee but hard to resolve. First of all, for the first time we are using a bottom-up approach to the development of the plan. I will be very surprised if this does not generate budget requests for the future years that are quite high in comparison to management's current expectations. Second, it is very difficult to forecast the impact of the minicomputer revolution. I foresee the day, not very far away, when it will be cheaper for the user to do many jobs on dedicated minicomputers rather than on large, central computers. Third, for the large jobs we do have, it is difficult to forecast when we should move to the next generation of new hardware or what we should do to prepare for this transition. Finally, if we are to create a C & DP plan that is meaningful to line management and anticipates and reflects their goals and objectives, more of their attention and commitment may be required than C & DP has been able to obtain in the past.

8 ALAN H. GEPFERT

Mobil Oil Corporation

In Mobil Oil Corporation the term "management sciences" (MS) connotes the full spectrum of information systems and computer-related activities. Specifically included are the activities of operations research, systems analysis and programming, computer operations, and the ancillary responsibilities in hardware and software technology assessment, resource and applications planning, controls and standards, training, and education. "MS" is used in this sense throughout this chapter.

COMPANY BACKGROUND

As a fully integrated, international oil company, Mobil has interests in crude oil exploration, production, and transportation; in refining; and in marketing gasoline, fuel oil, lubricants, and other petroleum products. It also has sizable research, development, and engineering interests that address product and process innovation and facility design and construction. In addition, Mobil has interest in energy resources such as uranium and coal. It has a large chemical division, whose products range from paints to plastic consumer products. Finally, it has real estate interests to develop properties worldwide.

In 1974 Mobil's revenues were $20.5 billion, with personnel totaling 73,100; assets are in excess of $14 billion.

The whole Mobil organization is decentralized physically. Domestic interests (i.e., exploration and production, refining, and marketing) are organized functionally, whereas international interests in affiliates are organized by country and, as appropriate, functionally within country (e.g., in some countries affiliates may engage only in marketing operations). Two key interests tend to overlay the foregoing structure, centering on crude oil: (1) exploration and production, and (2) supply and distribution.

The business is guided by five-year and one-year plans, generated annually. Guidelines and assumptions are provided starting with specifications by Mobil's Corporate Planning Department. The plans are then formulated and consolidated; the ultimate tests of consistency and feasibility are executed by the Corporate Planning Department and tests of directional correctness and desirability by the corporation's Executive Committee (ExCom), consisting of the chairman, the president, division heads, and certain other top-level executives.

The Mobil group of companies is very capital intensive. It is faced with extremely large individual investments, including those for governmental leases of possible sources of crude oil, for refineries, and for oceangoing tankers.

The operating environment has always been characterized by risk and uncertainty, resulting mainly from crude oil exploration activities. New challenging dimensions recently added include shortages of crude supplies and escalating costs, constraints by national governments to protect the product supplies for their own citizens, the emergence of direct government-to-government negotiations to secure crude oil supplies, moves by crude-rich producing countries to enter the refining and marketing segments of the business, environmental restrictions on product specifications and on facility design and location, and governmental mandates on product prices and allocation.

MS BACKGROUND

Computers have been used for many years in the Mobil organization, with early applications in both process control and financially oriented EDP.

Operations and systems development are physically and functionally decentralized along the lines of Mobil's business structure. Also, the same annual cycles are followed for one- and five-year planning, with the same approach of top-down specification of guidelines and assumptions, and bottom-up formulation of the detailed plans. In this context the principal MS unit is the Mobil's Corporate Computer Systems and Management Sciences Department (CSMSD).

The senior executive for MS is the general manager of CSMSD; he reports to the senior vice president, finance, who reports directly to chairman of the corporation. Each of Mobil's divisions also has its own MS coordinator to give direction to all the division's MS activities and to be the focal point for interfacing with CSMSD. In the two larger divisions, the reporting relationships are coordinator to controller, to division president (for the domestic division) and coordinator to vice president, planning and finance, to division president (for the international division).

At Mobil's corporate-division level there are six MS functions, with the staffing and budgets for 1974 shown in Table 1. The budget is stated in net costs after cross-charging for services between divisions. The seventh function, "Other Corporate Departments," is strictly a user of such services. Relative to the Mobil group of companies overall, these totals are roughly 3.0 percent of the organization's personnel and 0.4 percent of its revenue, respectively. Over the next five years the total costs are expected to grow at a rate of approximately 5 percent a year.

Table 1 Staff and Budgets for Major Management Science Activities within the Mobil Oil Organization (1974 Data)

Unit	Staff Size	Budget ($ Million)
1. Domestic Division	923	$36.9
2. International Division	813	24.1
3. CSMSD	222	4.7
4. Chemical Division	125	3.8
5. Mobil Research & Development Corporation	40	3.6
6. S & D Division	4	0.8
7. Other corporate departments	—	1.9
Total	2127	$75.8

Based on the 1974 year-end annual inventory, the Mobil organization's stock of computers is as follows:

16 large	IBM 360/50, 370/145, and up
4 medium	IBM 360/40, 370/135
27 small	IBM 1401, 360/20
204 mini	
251	

Most of the minis are used in process control and for order entry. About 20 of the grand total are in special purpose use, as for processing credit cards, or geophysical data. Roughly 30 are in general purpose use.

Each of the dual operating centers of CSMSD has an IBM 370/158; the CSMSD development staff of 84 is located at Mobil's headquarters. These centers serve all headquarters departments and Mobil's corporate units and the central management and staffs of the divisions. They also serve, to differing degrees, MS units and users within the divisions.

The Mobil organization has 46 computer centers, including CSMSD's two centers. Of this total, 13 have at least one large computer (as defined previously). In another dimension 23 centers are primarily general purpose types, and 23 are special purpose, including one for credit card processing. Some have no operations staffs as such, especially where minicomputers or remote job entry (RJE) are involved. Some have no development staff; on the other hand, some small development staffs within the Mobil group are not associated with a computer facility.

The organization's MS plans cover the total budget and all the personnel, centers, and associated resources indicated earlier. The budget breaks down to about 49 percent for personnel, 26 percent for equipment, 12 percent for outside services, and 13 percent for supplies and all other items.

Through commercial and private facilities, the Mobil group has worldwide communications services. The strictly data part is covered in the organization's MS plans, being handled by three specialists for planning and providing for such services as RJE. The bulk of the telecommunications, including cable, microwave, and satellite, is devoted to voice and message transmissions. The responsibility for all types of communications is vested in a department within CSMSD consisting of 40 people.

All these resources have produced a very large set of applications. Some examples are as follows:

1. (Remote Job Entry)
    - Geophysical processing
    - Linear programs for refinery planning
2. Real time, interactive
    - Facility planning
    - Order entry, billing, and inventory control for marketing operations

- Engineering design and cost calculations
- A library of financial, statistical, and other service programs

3. Batch

- Accounting and commercial systems
- Crude oil allocation planning
- Cash management, investment planning, and other financial systems
- Credit card processing
- Crude oil lease sale bidding
- Product distribution planning

MS OBJECTIVES

In 1970 Mobil's senior vice president, finance, as a member of ExCom, endorsed the objectives for MS listed in Table 2. These have governed MS planning throughout the Mobil organization in each succeeding year. They are supplemented each year by more extensive statements developed in view of the particular conditions in the environment and of the overall performance of Mobil and of its individual divisions and their affiliates.

The annual objectives address items such as particular issues of cost control; standards and standard approaches for equipment requests and approvals; project authorization, documentation, or charge-out for MS services provided; rationalizing diverse approaches to order entry for marketing operations; and searching out opportunities for new applications to serve business areas facing new challenges.

The Mobil organization's business plans are subject to approval from both formal line management and, ultimately, ExCom. Therefore the MS objectives statements contained in them are similarly approved formally. The responsibilities as well as the planning objectives of the CSMSD are documented and formally approved.

MS PLANNING HISTORY

The long-range MS plan was instituted in 1969. It has a five-year horizon and covers MS throughout the Mobil organization. The impetus for this plan was a concern for the extremely high rates of growth then being experienced with MS costs (in excess of 20 percent annually), and more generally, the suspected inadequacy of knowledge about, and control of, MS throughout the organization.

Table 2 Mobil Oil Corporate Level Objectives for MS Planning

Primary

- To assure that the Mobil organization's management sciences programs and operations produce the best cost/benefit performance.
- To identify, develop, and implement, new management sciences applications consistent with the overall strategy of the Mobil organization when justified by their cost/benefits.

Secondary

- Continuity of business

  To operate the Mobil organization's management science function in such a way as to assure continuity of the Mobil organization's business, and to assure that services that have a direct impact on employees, customers, and stockholders will be of fully acceptable quality.

- Effectiveness of service

  To provide management science services to meet approved requirements of users at the lowest cost.

  To standardize languages, equipment, applications, and operating practices to the extent commensurate with the efficient carrying out of management sciences functions.

  To assess the status of the function by reference to equivalent functions in competitors, to the extent to which such data are a matter of public record.

  To determine the optimal degree of consolidation of management sciences facilities consistent with the required standards of service and security.

- Career development

  To recruit, design, and implement career development of key employees through a planned program of training, broadened job experience within the management sciences functions of the Mobil organizations, and rotational assignments to and from other functions.

- Security

  To implement security measures and practices consistent with the best interests of the Mobil organization.

Thus the first and principal aim was to achieve control and guidance. This was accomplished with several actions:

- Singling out MS for separate attention within one- and five-year business plans.

- Developing explicit definitions governing MS, including personnel outside formal MS units if they were mainly doing MS work (90 percent or more of their time).
- Requiring that plans be submitted to Mobil's CSMSD and be approved, in consolidated form, by ExCom.
- Focusing, within the five-year framework, on the current year's program and the past year's accomplishments, with special attention to control and guidance issues in both cases.

Other operational control and guidance steps were taken as well, aimed at ensuring user awareness of, and commitment to, MS projects. Initially, for example, Mobil's International Division MS Department designed a project review procedure, backed by specified dollar review levels for various user executives. CSMSD instituted a similar procedure, as well as a charge-out scheme for all computer usage and for about half the total budget of the development staff.

The combination of all these efforts—the long-range plan, the annual plan, the controls and guidelines, and so forth—achieved the aim of control over cost growth. Realistically, however, most of the credit must go to the short-term items, even within the long-range planning document. For example, Mobil's headquarters MS resources were cut back as service requirements were correspondingly reduced.

The long-range aspects of the plan indicated a direction, but this was based mostly on extrapolation. There was little in the way of precise programs keyed to specific applications or to computer center strategies for better capitalizing on economies of scale through, for example, equipment consolidation. Therefore comprehensive long-range planning for individual applications has not generally been done.

Long-range planning is called for where the following criteria are present:

- Acquired resources have an extended life.
- Resource commitments are not readily reversed in the short term.
- Projects run for long, rather than short, terms.
- Potential future technological, economic, or other environmental developments dictate which of present actions are to be preferred, even when these actions span only a short term, as long as they are individually costly or risky relative to measures such as the organization's profit or capital budget.
- Some desired future action is contingent on identification and accomplishment of a sequence of intermediate actions.

Partly because of some failures with certain large operations research-type development projects, large and long-duration MS projects fell into disfavor within the Mobil organization. At the very least, major ends were to be accomplished through modular efforts, with each phase permitting a meaningful go/no go decision and, generally, yielding an incremental benefit of its own.

Based on the foregoing criteria, long-range MS planning has been done for computer equipment alone, not for applications. Only secondarily are associated facilities involved, along with operating staffs and programming and analysis personnel. (Realistically, staff levels can be revised in the short term, unlike major items of computer equipment. However major costs, both tangible and intangible, might be incurred.)

The challenge, of course, is that all these equipment and personnel resources are called for only because of applications—supporting existing ones, developing new ones, and supporting the latter once they, too, become operational. Therefore the fundamental issue for long-range MS planning is determining how to project the computer work load without being trapped in the false precision of detailed application plans extending several years into the future. The planning of applications is, of course, important in its own right, to ensure that MS is effectively serving the information and analysis needs of the users. It seems, however, that this can be accomplished only with a horizon of, perhaps, two years at the most. Although it is not a solution, this issue is addressed in the Mobil organization by identifying it and insisting that each center try to deal with it whenever equipment plans are made.

This issue will be of importance as long as new computer equipment continues to provide increasing benefits of economies of scale, and as long as capacity must be added in large increments. However a counter-development could be the increased competitiveness of very low cost minicomputers for dedicated use.

MS PLANNING RESPONSIBILITIES

All MS units within the Mobil group participate in MS planning, following the cycles described earlier. The larger computer centers and divisional staffs at Mobil's headquarters have one or more persons formally designated as MS planners; otherwise the responsibility is discharged generally as part of regular management responsibilities. The MS planning unit includes some six people in CSMSD.

In 1973, as part of an ongoing effort to monitor the time taken by planning and to keep it reasonable, a check was made on the time spent in producing the last five-year plan. Results indicated that all MS organizations combined spent nearly 200 man-months on the project. This shows that many people besides those formally designated as MS planners participate in the planning effort. Some of this effort, of course, goes into formalized exchanges between applications organizations and their clients, to characterize the anticipated use of the MS services, at least in dollar terms and by generic categories.

MS PLANNING PROCESS

The timetable for preparing the latest five-year MS plan appears in Table 3. The cycle starts with two preliminary steps. One is a stock taking, arranged by the CSMSD planning unit to get feedback, particularly on procedural problems or requests for changes in scope or definitions. Guides for this stock taking are drawn from experiences in recently completed planning efforts.

The second preliminary step is the preparation of a comprehensive set of planning guidelines and assumptions. These are compiled from a number of sources by various units of the CSMSD function. In the quantitative area, they cover the outlook on computer hardware and software technology and economics and on inflation rates for projecting personnel and other resource costs. They include position statements covering issues such as dealing with the many vendors supplying minicomputers or the vendors of large computers, and the outlook about adopting given languages as programming standards. They also address the business environment and take into account counterpart guidelines and asumptions of the Corporate Planning Department, especially as they pertain to MS applications planning.

These MS guidelines and assumptions are distributed in August and September within the Mobil organization to CSMSD and to the MS coordinators in the divisions in a package, together with the timetable, guidelines, and forms for the forthcoming planning cycle. This material is used as reference by the divisional MS coordinators in developing detailed planning packages for use within their respective divisions.

It is at this point that the planning effort picks up within the individual MS units. These units specify any unique guidelines and assumptions they may have locally; they formulate their particular objectives with reference to the respective division or corporate guidelines, as appropriate; they develop the programs to achieve these objectives; and they project costs, resources, and the other data required by the planning packages. This step of developing the individual plans and con-

Table 3 Corporate Management Sciences Projected Planning Timetable

Event	Lead Time Before Next Event (weeks)	Projected Date
ExCom presentation	0	5-13-75
Report sent to ExCom	2	4-29-75
Management control of computer usage meeting	1	4-21-75
Consolidated MS objectives report completed and approved	1	4-14-75
ID objectives report submitted to P & A	2	3-31-75
Divisions (excluding ID) and CSMSD objectives reports completed, approved, and submitted to P & A	3	3-24-75
CSMSD Department objectives reports completed, approved, and submitted to P & A	2	3-10-75
Preliminary drafts—CSMSD Departments to P & A	2	2-24-75
Interdivision and CSMSD client charges—*final* reconciliation	2	2-10-75
Inflation and wage escalation factors—*final* issued	—	Feb. 1975
MS profit plan report completed, approved, and issued	—	2-3-75
Divisions and CSMSD profit plan reports completed, approved, and submitted to P & A	—	12-16-74
Interdivision and CSMSD/client charges—*preliminary* reconciliation	—	11-18-74
Inflation and wage escalation factors—*preliminary* issued	—	11-11-74
CSMSD charge rates issued	—	Sept. 1974
Profit plan and objectives instructions issued	—	Aug. 1974

solidating for the respective divisions takes an elapsed time of four to six months. As part of this process, the individual plans at each step are subject to approval by the managers responsible for the corresponding business functions.

The consolidation for the Mobil group starts in April. This, and the balance of the process, is carried out by the CSMSD planning unit; there is coordination with the divisional MS coordinators, to clarify certain material as necessary. The result is a document some 30 pages long, formally presented for review and endorsement at an ExCom meeting in May.

A week or two beforehand, a meeting is held at which the consolidated plans of the divisions (including CSMSD) and the total corporation are highlighted. At this meeting are the president, the senior financial officer, the controller, and MS coordinators of each division; other selected MS personnel may also attend. The divisional MS coordinators deliver their own reports, answer questions from the executives, give a picture of MS throughout the organization, and provide a preview of the forthcoming presentation to ExCom.

In general, the planning guidelines and the resulting plans focus on four items. One relates to assessments of the level and trend of MS costs and resources. A second relates to issues for attention in the next cycle, such as a further appraisal of MS efforts relative to those of other very large companies. A third relates to endorsement of recommended potential new strategic directions, such as the selective consolidation of computer centers. The fourth item relates to endorsement of procedural and other proposals on the planning effort itself.

One recent example of the latter item was a modification to the definition of "MS personnel." The aim was to avoid reporting outside staff members who extensively perform MS activities, but for their own purposes as, say geophysicists, and not as a service to others. Another example is the intended proposal to formalize the annual plan as the main vehicle for (1) comparing accomplishment against plan, and (2) mapping out the slate of applications. The five-year plan would then be the focal point for attention to resources and resource strategy, and for any special issues on applications.

One-year plans, prepared in the fall and winter as part of Mobil's regular budgeting cycle, are approved as integral parts of the MS unit's parent line organization. The consolidations made for MS starting in 1972 were largely informational and to set the stage for the coordinated actions on the one-year and five-year plans already mentioned. (The time seems particularly ripe for this, since at a recent presentation ExCom acknowledged the accomplishments in the areas of cost control and user involvement. The members then raised questions about the adequacy of the applications thrust in selected areas of the business.) Both the annual and five-year plans are supported by computer programs to aid with consolidation. These consolidations are not just mechanical. For example, throughout the cycle for the five-year plan the CSMSD planning unit interacts with divisional coordinators on selected items to preview while awaiting final submission of the division plans.

MS PLAN FORMAT

Each Mobil division has its own format for its five-year plan. They are all compatible with the format of the ExCom report, but frequently they are much longer than the latter's 30-pages report. At a minimum, they all have the following sections:

1. Assumptions.
2. Objectives.
3. Past and projected costs (at a minimum in the categories of personnel, equipment, outside services, and all other).
4. Resources (staff numbers and computer counts, by type).
5. Recent accomplishments as to costs, applications, and managerial practices.
6. Plans for resources and applications.

The plans frequently have extensive information on applications, but there is no complete listing of applications that comprehensively covers anywhere near the full five years of the long-range planning horizon.

The main categories of the ExCom report are as follows:

1. Accomplishments in planning, control, and review activities.
2. Security.
3. Applications.
4. Administration.
5. Resource plans.

Under resource plans are included costs, head counts, and so on, for the past year (e.g., 1974 actual), the current year (e.g., 1975 budget), and the upcoming five years (e.g., 1976–1980 plan, but showing figures only for the 1976–1977 and 1980). The forms used for the resource data part of the ExCom report are shown in Appendix B.

MS PLANNING IMPROVEMENT OPPORTUNITIES

Within the context of the Mobil organization, the following items are areas for change that might help to improve MS planning's contribution to overall business effectiveness. Note that some are as much inherent challenges as they are acknowledged opportunities for improvement.

Planning Aims

1. The identification of potential applications should build on joint user-MS surveys that document each business function's responsibilities; decision processes; information needs and flows; uses of formal analytical methods; and impacts on revenue generation, cost incurrence, and asset acquisition and utilization.
2. Plans for MS resources should allow for hardware and software technology and economic trends, and they should reflect explicit projections of work loads. These projections, as stated earlier, should address the current production base and new production to result from new applications. Detailed application slates for the full long-range horizon are not realistic requirements. Methods for planning under uncertainty should be used, making sensitivity calculations for costs associated with different work loads, technologies, and economics.

Planning Practices

1. MS technology units find it difficult to make preliminary judgments on new and potential developments and to generate concrete, unambiguous guidelines for timely inputs to resource planning.
2. Some resource, software, and applications proposals are made with inadequate identification and cost-benefit weighing of alternatives. And the alternatives that are considered may address the issue in isolation (e.g., a new computer versus an old one within a given center) rather than in view of the interactions (e.g., redistributing loads between certain centers, thereby changing the need for computer power in the involved centers).
3. Resource strategies requiring extended terms for implementation may imperfectly allow for updating and redirection of the plans as events unfold. On the other hand, individual steps such as selecting the operating system for a new computer might be swayed by short-term assessment of an opportunity to provide a new service (e.g., an in-house time-sharing service).
4. Users may still play an inadequate role in developing the slate of applications for their area. Understandably, this can be caused by preoccupation with business operating problems, frequent staff turnover that hampers continuity of working relationships with MS, and disenchantment with MS due to past failure in developing or using some application, as well as educational or intellectual orientation that does not foster MS use.

Planning Attitudes

1. Computer center staffs or applications units may still wish to see adoption of new developments because they are viewed as the "way of the future" or as a means for making their own jobs easier, while possibly conflicting with the goals of cost control or user service.
2. The plans may be viewed more for their use in formal communication to ExCom than for their role in guiding the further development of MS locally.
3. The cost-control orientation of the long-range plan can cause insufficient attention to issues of strategy and to the proper thrust of applications. An aspect of the latter may be an unwillingness to put forth application proposals that admittedly entail sizable risk and uncertainty of success.
4. Some units may delay communicating about new projects or present them as thoroughly researched and virtually approved. This can result from the desire to position themselves as *the* focal point for MS in the business entity they serve.

In general, the achievement of progress on the problems cited in these three major areas is considered to be a feasible goal. Action programs, albeit evolutionary, have already been established to deal with them.

9 F. A. GITZENDANNER

Standard Oil Company (Indiana)

Standard Oil Company (Indiana) is one of the major integrated international petroleum companies. Established in 1889 as a regional oil company, it has expanded to become a nationwide (although currently withdrawing from West Coast marketing activities) and international oil company, with a rapidly expanding international petrochemical business including the world's largest producer of synthetic carpet backing and other minor but growing interests in international mining and in domestic real estate development and insurance. Annual sales and total investment are slightly over $6 billion apiece. There are currently about 45,000 employees. For the past decade, annual revenues have grown at about 5 to 6 percent per year, and 90 percent of this is currently in the conventional petroleum industry.

From a highly decentralized and autonomous group of subsidiaries, the company has changed over the past 10 years to an organization in which the subsidiary line functions are still decentralized and largely autonomous, while the staff services, such as law, public affairs, accounting, personnel relations, and information services, are organizationally centralized in parent company staff departments with increasing functional control over the physically decentralized units carrying on these functions in the subsidiaries.

The company has made formal long-range plans for the past 20 years, updated annually. Interestingly, for about 15 of these years, there have been significant developments, such as the discovery of North Dakota crude, a major commitment to expand in petrochemicals, large-scale programs abroad, and the like, with the result that planning has had to face important questions; and top management has had to participate actively in the process, since mere lip service to the idea of having annual updates is impossible.

Over the last five years the questions to be faced have been of such magnitude that the trend has been toward a two- to three-year update of the strategic plan, with less emphasis on the detailed revision of a long-range plan *per se.* Generally, however, the top and line operating managers of the company consider that realistic and effective long-range and strategic plans do exist and are met to a consistently high degree.

In this climate there has been tacit acceptance by top management of the merit of planning for information services; but it has been a relatively small aspect of the overall picture and, until the early 1960s, little was actually done.

INFORMATION SERVICES BACKGROUND

Under the previous arrangement of highly decentralized subsidiaries, information services were undertaken by each subsidiary, and departments within subsidiaries, whenever they were felt to be necessary and by whatever means were felt to be appropriate. The parent company controller exercised a degree of functional control over the financial information system by specifying what the subsidiaries had to furnish to the parent; but in practice this was a very loose control in that the official merely specified the information that was to be supplied to him, leaving the internal practices of the subsidiaries alone. With respect to all other operational information needs, the determination of these needs and the furnishing of them was left entirely up to the subsidiaries and their departments.

During this period practices varied all over the spectrum. Punched card equipment was introduced at some points as early as 1926; and stored program computers were first used when they became available. In 1963 the consolidated company (then considerably smaller and less complex than today) had 43 computers at 40 locations. They ranged from IBM 7044's for scientific work, IBM 705's for large office accounting work, IBM 1710's for process control work in refineries, IBM 650's in regional sales offices, and equipment manufactured by a host of vendors for use in the oil fields, pipeline and ocean terminals, credit card offices, and the like.

Information Services Background

In 1966 information services costs were $13 million per year. The data processing equipment and organizations at each location represented the local management's view of what was needed, with little similarity between locations. Since then, this has changed considerably to a more centralized structure (Figure 1). Also in 1966 a communications network was established within each subsidiary (often with duplication between different subsidiaries), but there was almost no company-wide teleprocessing. Communication of data, except for a few cases, was by mailed hard copy.

At this time (1966), relationships between EDP and users were very close because the users ran their own data processing. The accounting area was the largest single user; and each accounting activity (general office accounting, refinery accounting, sales division accounting, and division production accounting) designed, established, and operated its own data processing. Stored program computers made scientific and technical computing practical, and use of such applications by operating management was large and expanding. The analysis, programming, and computer operation of these applications were done by the Research & Development Department; but through longstanding tradition in the company, the department, in effect, "sold" these services to the operating departments. Here, too, there was a close and effective relationship with the user. If the user did not endorse an application, its undertaking was terminated. Applications covered the entire range of operating data, technical design, modeling, and operations research.

INFORMATION SYSTEMS OBJECTIVES

There was one difficulty with the situation just described. Although it was characterized by effective relations with users, high satisfaction by users with their applications and service, and many profitable applications, it was nevertheless needlessly expensive. There was little generalized use of applications that had proved effective at one location, little abandonment of marginal applications, almost no integration of information needs, general proliferation of costs, and perpetuation of poor practices. An information systems planning function was accordingly established by top management to prepare a long-range plan and to recommend a course of action.

Inasmuch as the orientation of the top management of the company was predominantly operational and technical—rather than financial—there was general acceptance of the proposition that the goal of effective information systems should be to improve operating decisions by

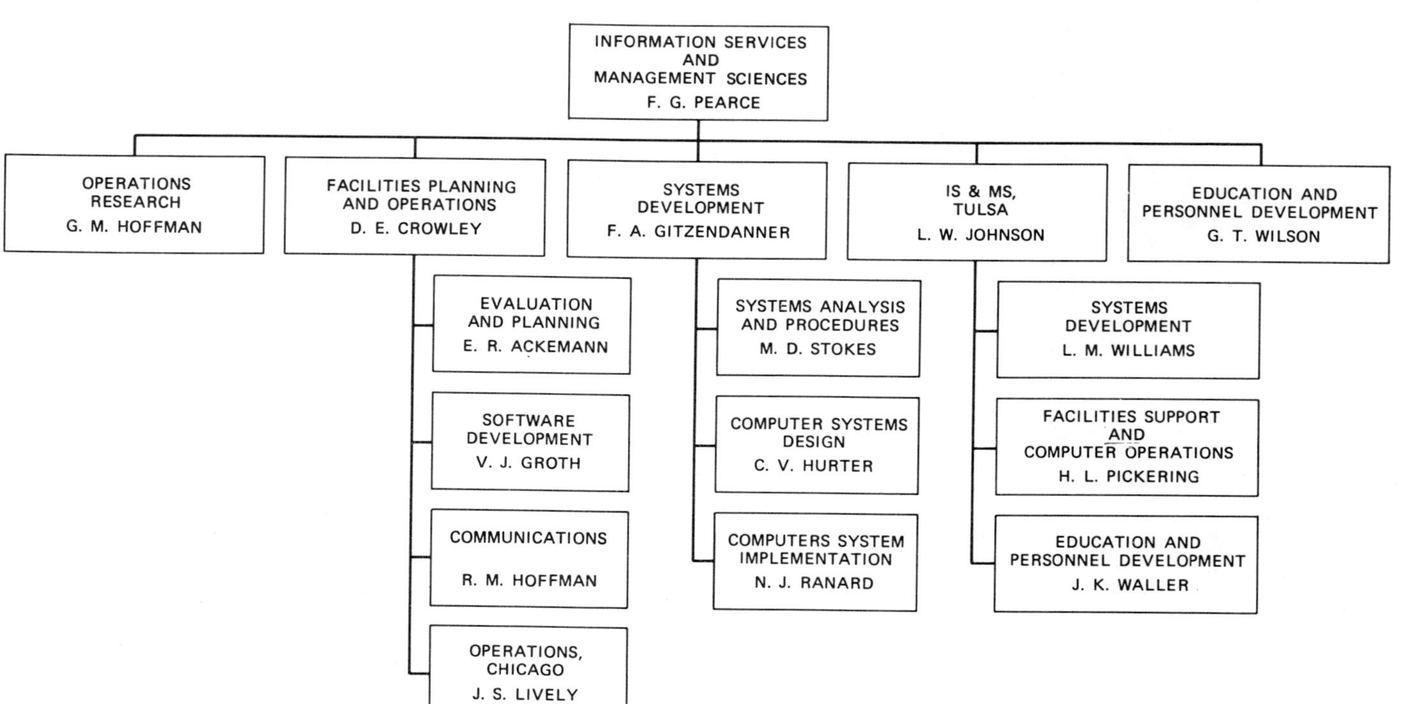

Figure 1 Organization chart, Information Services & Management Sciences, Standard Oil Company (Indiana), October 1, 1972. Not all positions are shown.

better information, and any direct information processing cost reductions would be desirable, but secondary. This was the first attempt to prepare a consolidated long-range plan addressing information processing specifically. The result of that initial study, largely in the form of a charter for continuing work, is reproduced as Table 1 at the end of the chapter.

INFORMATION SYSTEMS PLANNING HISTORY

The initial information services long-range plan prepared during 1964 and 1965 broadly charted a course for the next five to seven years.

The first shortcoming that became evident during this period was excessive optimism regarding what could be accomplished at a given cost. The implementation of this planning began during the early days of IBM System/360 hardware and software; and the problems of that era are familiar to many. Suffice it to say that the estimates that were made of the time required to develop applications and to operate them were naïvely optimistic. Although this was partly due to hardware and software problems, largely responsible, as well, were personnel who were inexperienced with the analysis and design problems associated with integrated systems using elemental data bases (although nothing approaching present-day data base design problems). Interestingly, the difficulty was not due to system specification problems; that is, the systems, as originally conceived to accomplish a given purpose, ultimately proved to be suitable for that purpose. The problem was in seriously underestimating the effort required to get there.

The problem was further aggravated by the extreme mobility of programmer-analysts in the Chicago area in the 1966–1969 period. Fortunately the problem has markedly abated since then, and the mobility of these people is now little different from that of others employed in the petroleum industry.

These apparently negative design efforts were fortunate in certain respects, however. First, the initial projects were small rather than very extensive; thus many were able to get "on stream" and start producing rather than being interminably mired in nonperformance. Second, since some of the early projects were financially more productive than originally had been estimated by the users, the cost-benefit ratio remained attractive despite expenses that exceeded estimates. Third, in each of the years after 1967, the long-range plan was updated, at least for budgeting purposes. Thus without completely redoing the entire long-range plan, there was a realistic, working plan each year; and with these revised plans, performance was far closer to plan than might otherwise have been the case, thereby building credibility with top management.

It must be recognized that although top management was closely interested and involved in information services planning because of its organizational and financial impact, the effect of such planning on overall company affairs was relatively small. During the same years formal long-range plans were formulated for the company as a whole; but top management did not direct that information services features be included. Instead they preferred to look at the plans separately and subjectively integrate their combined effect into the company's overall plans.

INFORMATION SYSTEMS PLANNING RESPONSIBILITIES

The general manager of Information Services & Management Sciences (IS & MS) is responsible for preparing the information services' long-range plan. He reports to the vice president, finance. To assist him from the users' standpoints are Information Services Coordinating Groups in each of the subsidiaries. These groups have the responsibility of coordinating activities, communications, and plans between information services and the operating and top management of the various subsidiaries.

The bulk of the planning work is carried out within the information services organization and is summarized each year, in terms of the budget requirements, for the next two years. Periodically the general manager, IS & MS, may choose to submit additional information to the top management of the parent company and respond to specific questions from them. Top management has not yet directed that a formal long-range plan for information services be incorporated in the company's overall formal plan.

INFORMATION SERVICES PLANNING PROCESS

The planning process is carried on throughout the year as a series of studies addressed to pertinent subjects as they arise or as they need to be addressed. It is not a major x-month effort carried out during the y-quarter of every year. Rather, the results of these individual studies are incorporated into a brief two- or three-page report as changes or additions to the previous year's plan, which was prepared at budget time. By this mechanism, the IS & MS Department considers that it has in hand, at any time, the most complete and up-to-date plan that it is practical to prepare—and top management shares this view.

Subsidiary companies are involved in this process in that they buy information services from the parent company staff group and, therefore, there is close coordination required between the two. This coordination and agreement is reflected in the final budget. The planning horizon varies with the project being considered; some items are very long undertakings, whereas others are relatively routine and represent only a two- to three-year horizon.

As mentioned earlier, there is no formal relationship between information systems planning and the parent long-range planning effort. This is because of the differences in size, proportional relationship, and character between the two. It is not felt to be worth the major effort needed to integrate them formally. The general manager, IS & MS, is kept appraised by various means of the company's general long-range plans, and this advice is relied on to keep the plans consistent.

IMPROVEMENT OPPORTUNITIES

The two-year planning effort that was completed in 1966 resulted in a plan that was considered at that time to be reasonably firm for five to seven years. However it has been modified, updated, and revised in varying degrees as new requirements, capability, and technology have developed. This process has produced a working long-range plan that is reasonably accurate, given the difficulties in forecasting the future.

Naturally there are shortcomings in both format and content. A uniform format would make it easier to assimilate mentally the changes that occur over time. The problem of content hinges on the impossibility of being omniscient. Omniscience is obviously too strong a word—but the basic problem in a field that changes as rapidly as computing is the inability to foresee very clearly what will happen next.

On balance, the problem of a nonuniform format is not considered to be serious enough to warrant much effort until the ability to foresee technological changes is significantly better than it is now. And even if we had the ability to foresee these changes, there is still a very large problem associated with predicting how the changes can be incorporated into better ways of running the business, that is, what information systems will lead to better decisions and profits. In summary, the concern is not with the planning process itself but with the ability to develop increasingly better data to go into the plan. It is not an easy task, but certainly a necessary one.

Table 1 Statement of Information Systems Planning

The following statement and recommendations have been adopted by the Policy Committee and the Office of the Chairman and shall be considered in effect until further notice.

During the last half of 1965, personnel in Standard, American Oil, Pan American, and Service engaged in intensive planning activities for the modernization and consolidation of our data processing and telecommunication facilities and for the provision of more timely, complete, and better organized information to aid in management decisions. The results of these studies have been presented to and approved by the affected managements.

Management of Amoco Chemicals, American International, Tuloma, and Imperial Casualty decided that the urgency of other areas of activity precluded such a detailed planning study during that period. However, some degree of planning was accomplished in all subsidiaries so that a nucleus of personnel exists that is aware of the incentives for the program, the results of the studies of those companies which did engage in intensive planning, and the steps which are required before final planning and implementation of improved information systems can be initiated.

All agree that the modernization and consolidation of our presently compartmentalized and dispersed automatic data processing facilities is a technically feasible and economically attractive course of action which will require five to seven years to consummate. At that time, most of our data processing activities will be conducted at two centers (Chicago and Tulsa) which will be connected by telecommunications to remote installations, providing them with direct access to the computing centers. Although the data processing activities of the Central Credit Card operations and Imperial Casualty may not be consolidated by that time, the revised systems for these installations will be designed with the possibility of eventual consolidation in mind.

If we were to structure a separate telecommunications system for transmission of data to and from the centers, the annual charges by the Bell companies would exceed $2 million. However, the incremental cost for data communications by expansion of a Consolidated Company voice and message telecommunications system would be only $500,000 per year. Consequently, negotiations are continuing with Bell system personnel to determine the performance and cost of a Consolidated Company voice and message telecommunications system to replace our present privately owned facilities and individual subsidiary arrangements with the Bell companies. At the present stage of development, it appears that such a system would (1) be no more expensive than the current systems, (2) provide better service, (3) allow for expansion in service at a lower rate of increase in cost, and (4) result in the lower data transmission costs referred to above.

Although significant cost reduction is possible through the modernization and

Table 1 *(continued)*

consolidation of our telecommunications and automated data processing facilities, these cost reductions are minor as compared to the value of the resulting more complete and timely information made available to all levels of management. This comparison in evident from the following estimates of savings and profit improvements at the time when presently planned systems are expected to be operational.

	Annual Improvement 1965 vs. 1973
Personnel savings	$ 3,000,000
Improved operations	23,000,000

At that time, total data processing plus telecommunications cost will be higher than current by about $1.3 million (10 percent). One-time implementation costs (mostly salaries and wages) are estimated to total about $20 million over this same period. The overall project reaches a positive cash position during 1968, after a minimum negative cash position of about $3.5 million during 1966 and 1967. The overall economics are extremely favorable with a profitability index so high as to have little meaning.

Further detailed planning of the systems is required before actual implementation can start. This will require continued involvement of responsible operations personnel and periodic review of specific systems by management for final approval before implementation. However, an excellent base has been established during this phase so that the system can be viewed in total rather than in parts.

It is recommended that:

1. Negotiations be continued with the Bell system to further define and evaluate a Consolidated Company system for voice, message, and data to replace our present privately owned telecommunications facilities and individual subsidiary arrangements with the Bell companies. The resulting Bell system proposal will be presented to the Policy Committee for review and approval—probably during the third quarter of 1966.
2. American Oil, Pan American, and Service managements be advised to continue into the detailed planning for and implementation of improved management information systems as defined in their Phase I reports.
3. Standard Oil personnel be organized to do the same for the parent company management information systems.
4. Amoco Chemicals, American International, and Tuloma managements be advised to reevaluate their ability to spare the manpower necessary to determine information needs and to report their plans in this area at the May quarterly budget review meetings.

10

P. DUANE WALKER

International Business Machines Corporation

International Business Machines Corporation (IBM) is a leader in the information handling industry. Its products range from electric typewriters and copying equipment to computer main frames and a comprehensive line of data entry and data storage devices.

In 1973 IBM had 274,108 employees organized into 12 divisions and 2 wholly owned subsidiaries. The consolidated gross income amounted to approximately $11 billion, of which overseas sales accounted for $5.1 billion. To underscore the dynamic growth the company has experienced, let me point out that in 1964 IBM's income was $3.2 billion. Thus we have an increase of $7.8 billion in a decade.

A number of characteristics make IBM singularly difficult to manage. Chief among these are (1) its growth rate, (2) the changing technology, (3) the extraordinary communications required to ensure compatibility among various engineering designs, (4) the worldwide disbursement of engineering and manufacturing, and (5) the leasing of a large percentage of the equipment, which makes the inventory and accounting processes unusually complicated.

Because of its dynamic growth and the complexities just cited, IBM had to develop definitive, formal management practices. Indeed, in anticipation of the growth potential and unique problems related to the products, IBM began developing its long-range business planning processes as early as 1959.

INFORMATION SYSTEMS PLANNING

This chapter discusses IBM's information systems planning process and its tie to the long-range business planning processes.

Let us begin with business planning. IBM's business plan has two time horizons: an operating plan covering two years and a strategic plan that covers seven years. The planning process has varied between (1) doing a single strategic-operating plan as one continuous process throughout the year, and (2) doing the strategic plan as a separate process in the spring and doing the operating plan as a separate process in the fall. Although IBM is currently planning with the strategic emphasis in the spring and the operating horizon in the fall, at the inception of information systems planning in 1966, the first (continuous process) approach was in effect. This business planning cycle is illustrated in Figure 1.

Each January the process begins with the corporate office establishing assumptions and goals. These statements are passed on to the business units (profit and loss centers) and subsidiaries. Each business unit, and the major divisions within the business unit, defines its strategic programs and transfers the basic statements down through the organization to operating management to confirm operating plan programs and resources. Each level develops its own objectives, strategies, and actions through which it will meet its commitment to the overall corporate goals.

It takes five to six months to complete the downward communication. The commitment or requirements takes an additional five or six months to resolve as the plans are aggregated from the bottom up. During this period, the various functions, both line and staff (engineering, manufacturing, marketing, finance, information systems, etc.) have the opportunity to review one another's plans and either concur or take "issue" with other functional plans that have impact on their performance. Final negotiations are completed, and nonconcurrence or "issues" are resolved during November and December. The result is a comprehensive operating plan covering two years and a strategic plan with a seven-year outlook.

The two-year plan is tied directly to the budget, whereas the seven-year plan presents statements of how marketing, engineering, manufacturing, personnel, services, and 14 separate functional programs will

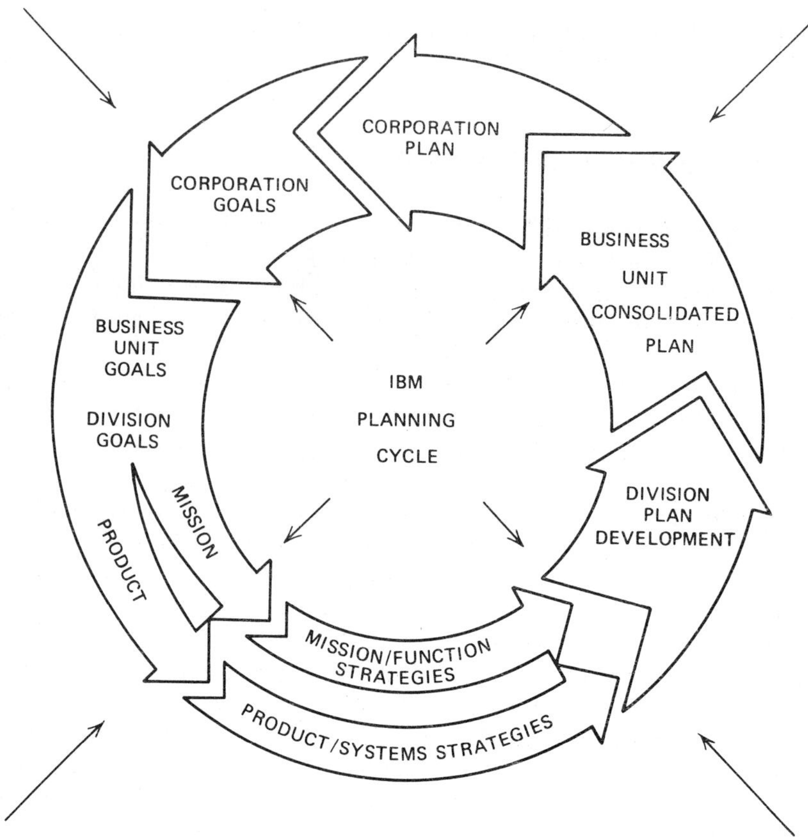

Figure 1 IBM planning cycle.

interrelate and support one another over the longer program period. The business plan has proved to be an effective tool for controlling planned versus actual performance, for delegating specific responsibilities to specific functions, and for communicating among functions when a given function is not attaining its plan and there is impact on other functions that will require adjustment.

Tieing Information Systems into the Business Planning Cycle

In 1966 considerable effort was mounted to formalize IBM's management system. The management system is concerned with formally defining the key decision processes: product introduction, capital spending, the organization plan, and the planning and control process. At that time two other dimensions were emphasized: (1) responsibilities for data management and (2) the need to design information systems in such a way that they would support the management system. This represented a major change in the use of data processing in the company. In essence, it said that over and above traditional programs and operational services, data processing would develop information systems to support key business decisions, with emphasis on supporting the planning, measurement, and control processes of the corporation.

Background of the Decision

Why did IBM make this significant information system decision?

Data processing in IBM started much as it did in most other large corporations. Each individual plant, laboratory, and regional marketing location had its own data processing facility. The emphasis was on individual applications, with a strong thrust in the financial areas. There was no overall control or direction in assigning priorities to applications under development, although from the beginning there were mechanisms to control equipment allocation. Since the priorities for the applications were not spelled out, however, the rationale for committing equipment to those applications was relatively weak. The company had a good record of where equipment was but lacked application justification for why it was there.

The introduction of the System/360 in 1964 made it apparent that the company, particularly within the Data Processing Group (including the engineering, marketing, manufacturing, and service divisions that supported the computer product in the United States), had to initiate some top-down planning and control procedures. The recognition came almost simultaneously from the top and the bottom of the organization. In the period from 1965 through 1967, user organizations in manufacturing, marketing, engineering, and services began to define what information they required to do a better job of managing their functional areas. These groups worked diligently through 1965 and 1967 to define what they needed to respond to the company's business needs.

In 1967 executive management issued a policy letter stating explicitly the need for "developing a unified control and information system encompassing all segments of the company and for developing and maintaining a corporate master plan to coordinate the information systems needed to support the business measurement, planning, and control processes." The same policy letter said, "We can combine the advantages of decentralized management with the economy of a unified corporate-wide information system. A total corporate approach is required." This letter provided the impetus for IBM to formulate planning, controlling, and measurement conventions to guide the information systems activity. The letter articulated the general information systems goals, which had to be translated into more specific information systems objectives. The following is an outline of these more detailed objectives.

Information Systems Design Objectives

1. Functional information systems
   A. *Objective:* To support functional management with that information required to manage large integrated functional divisions in a manner that is consistent with a large unified business.
   B. *Strategy:* Create and maintain a divisional information systems architecture that encourages the development and installation of division-wide systems that share hardware, software, communications, and data. The architecture will be flexible enough to allow local developments and centralized or decentralized processing (1964–1974).
2. Unified group-wide information systems
   A. *Objective:* To understand the critical information requirements at all levels of management and the information processes that support them. To design information flow networks that will improve management support and reduce the cost of handling information.
   B. *Strategy:* On a longer time frame (1967 and continuing), work toward broadening the previous strategy from its basic functional scope to a total business scope.
3. Data management
   A. *Objective:* To develop a system that will improve the control, availability, and integrity of the data required to support all levels of management and operations.
   B. *Strategy:* Develop a single dictionary/directory of data commonly required by the Data Processing Group divisions. Develop uniform data management practices and standards for the interdivisional data of the Data Processing Group. It is expected that the long-term goal of data-managed information systems will evolve from this work on information systems centers.
4. Standards development
   A. *Objective:* To develop standards in those areas where
      - Business planning demands it.
      - Economies of operation make it right.
      - Business effectiveness benefits significantly.

Such standards will also

- Aid communications between the divisions and the information systems centers.
- Reduce programming conversion time and expense.
- Make better use of programming resources.
- Ensure more efficient utilization of communication resources.
- Ensure economic and efficient data processing facilities construction and utilization.

B. *Strategy:* In business standards, analyze, define, develop, and implement

- Data classification structure and codes that consistently identify the key divisional activities and resources.
- Reporting techniques that directly relate operational performance to management goals and objectives.
- In technical practices, manage the growth and development of general purpose, terminal-oriented systems. Provide a central operational facility to support the requirements of operating facilities within the Data Processing Group where such services are not provided. Program products will be utilized wherever they are compatible with the Data Processing Group information requirements. Data Processing Group-wide programs will be selected and/or developed as required.
- Analyze, define, and develop group-wide technical practices to support common programming and operating requirements.
- In support standards, define, develop, implement, and maintain standards required to supply the necessary support services.

Information Systems Management Objectives

1. Planning

   A. *Objective:* To ensure information systems plans that are interfaced with business plans.

   B. *Strategy:* Establish and maintain an information system master plan in accordance with the provisions in the Data Processing Group and information systems planning instructions. Improve the existing information system management system by developing necessary practices and procedures.

2. Organization

   A. *Objective:* To evolve an organization with the responsibility for planning, controlling, and measuring the development, operations, and maintenance of the group-wide information systems management system.

B. *Strategy:* Create and sustain the interdivisional communications and liaison required to keep all participants aware of the requirements, changes, and direction of the group-wide information systems.

3. Measurement and control development

A. *Objective:* To present consistent information in a time frame that will allow management to act on situations to minimize and/or prevent problems.

B. *Strategy:* Design and implement a set of development criteria that will ensure timely installation of information systems.

4. Operations

A. *Objective:* To measure the effectiveness of existing information systems.

B. *Strategy:* Develop a set of operational criteria to make certain that the system
- Utilizes resources efficiently.
- Verifies the necessity of the work being performed.

5. Physical resources

A. *Objective:* To ensure effective management planning, control, and utilization of resources associated with data processing equipment, facilities, and telecommunications resources. This control emphasis extends beyond the Data Processing Group information systems to all internal use of data processing equipment throughout the corporation.

B. *Strategy:* Plan total IBM internal data processing equipment to
- Ensure adequate internal system and critical box supply from manufacturing.
- Establish and control systems allocations for each group division.
- Extend allocation control to nongroup divisions.
- Measure internal equipment utilization.
- Ensure effective planning, ordering, control, and utilization of telecommunications resources.
- Promote optimal facilities for data processing equipment, services, and support operations.
- Review, evaluate, and approve equipment justifications, system design, and machine application.

INFORMATION SYSTEMS PLANNING EVOLUTION

The corporate information systems planning function was officially instituted in 1966. A formal organizational structure evolved, beginning with corporate and group information systems planning activities in 1966; division and major location information systems planning activities followed in 1967, as the processes became better defined. The first accomplishment of these functions was to generate an information systems plan covering the entire corporation. First issued in 1967 as part of the overall corporate business plan, the information systems plan summarized all major information systems projects under way and the resources being expended for systems operations, development, and maintenance. It was primarily a project and resource document that delineated expenditures across the organization. It identified major projects but did not make a judgment of whether the projects were valid investments for the corporation, nor was there any attempt to set priorities for resource commitments.

It is not surprising that the best development of information systems planning, control, and measurement activities occurred within the Data Processing Group. In 1966 that group represented close to 65 percent of the total IBM corporate business and nearly 120,000 people. Activities were distributed among engineering, manufacturing, marketing, services, and the components development and manufacturing activities. In 1966 an information systems planning and control function was established within the Data Processing Group. During the first 15 months the activity's staff increased from three to eight professionals—three concerned with the planning process and five with the control process. The following planning and control activities emerged during the period 1966–1971.

- Plans and audits
    - Master plan
    - Assessments
    - Phase reviews
    - System audits
- Control
    - Data processing equipment
    - Data processing facilities
    - Telecommunications
    - Equipment/application justification

Information Systems Architecture

In late 1967 it became apparent that IBM lacked an overall activity to ensure that information systems were planned and implemented in such a way that they supported overall business goals. The information systems architecture function, which grew out of this realization, included information flow design, value analysis, information systems center planning, information systems management system, and business standards. Table 1 shows the relationship of the information systems architecture function to other architectural activities within IBM. The primary architectural thrust was to improve information flow among and between business functions in support of major corporate decisions. To do that, the architecture group concentrated on developing a strategic design goal that would serve as the basis for allocating resources in the information systems plan. The emphasis was on the development of major management control systems to support general management's planning, control, and measurement processes. With this thrust, data processing emerged from a pure service function which supported the needs of individual operational managers and became a force in changing the entire business operation. When you begin to be integrally involved in the business management system, you become a central part of the decision systems of the business. The information system function contributed to the overall organization, product, and resource planning decisions across the business.

Figure 2 highlights the major tasks performed by the architecture staff during the period 1967–1971.

In 1969 the architecture staff expanded to 14 members. The information systems control and planning organization, which also included an architecture function, grew to 16 in 1967, 33 in 1968, and peaked at 36 in 1969. In 1974 20 people were concerned with information systems control and planning, exercising worldwide responsibility for maintaining the information system in a manner consistent with the architectural design.

Data Management

In late 1967 it became clear that data constituted an important resource in the business and that this resource was not being well managed. It was apparent that data management systems activities were required. Accordingly, a data management function was formed to define the disciplines necessary to manage the data elements within the corporation. This included responsibility for the data dictionary/directory, MIS/360 and PSG (Planning System General), advanced MIS planning and development, and technical standards. Emphasis was placed on developing a "chart of accounts" that would tell the user where data were located in the many systems throughout the corporation; attention was also directed at clarifying the definition of the data and its use among the various functions. From the "chart of accounts" activity came the requirements for what is known today as a Data Dictionary/Directory System, which is an integral part of the data management processes within IBM.

Table 1 Architect Hierarchy

Level	Architect	Resulting Program	Instruction set	Processor
1	Computer system	Computer system	Design logic	Computer
2	Programming system	Operating system, language processor	Machine instructions, basic symbolic coding system	Computer
3	Application system	Single business function (billing, inventory management)	Program languages (PL/1, COBOL)	Computer
4	Information system	Information flow design and basic data definition	Business functions, computer applications, data elements	Information systems resources
5	Organization	Organization definition	Business functions, management practices, departments	Management system
6	General manager	Return on investment, profit	Product programs, business objectives, budget	Business unit resources

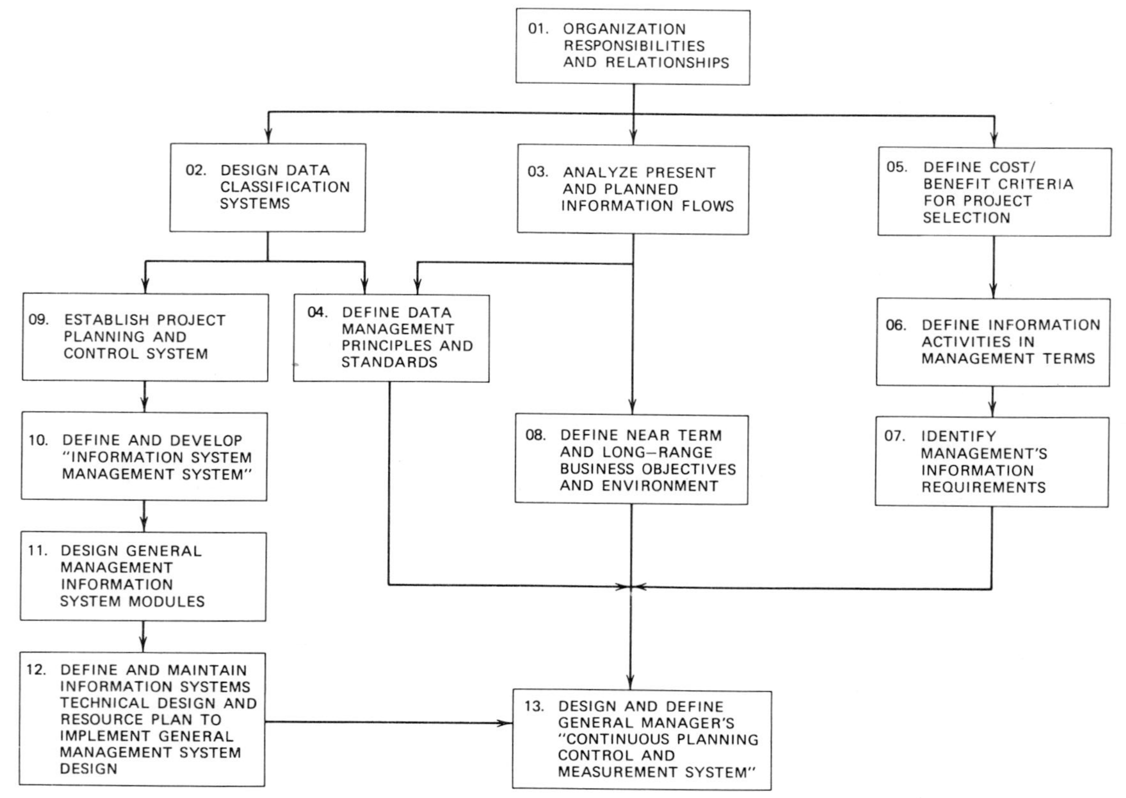

Figure 2 **Information Systems architecture tasks.**

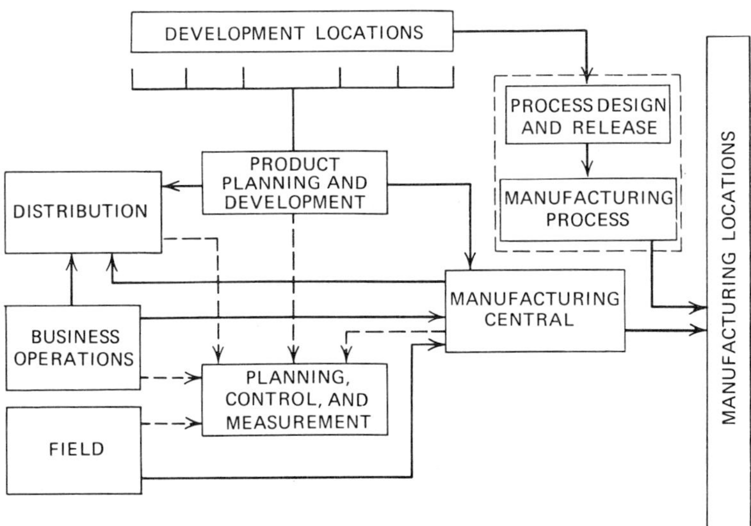

Figure 3 Information Systems Center relationships.

In 1968 the architectural function began to bear real fruit when the definition of a logical network of information systems evolved. The network defined the major data bases and the business processes that would share data from those data bases. These logical groupings were termed "information systems centers." By 1969 an information systems center plan had been developed to define that network and to assign priorities in the development sequence. As the plan became more firm, the management of respective competency centers was delegated to divisional management with corresponding plans for physical facilities. Figure 3 illustrates the first logical definition of information systems centers in IBM.

INFORMATION SYSTEMS PLANNING RESPONSIBILITIES

As mentioned previously, there are information systems planning activities at each major level of the corporation. Responsibility for the overall information systems plan resides with the vice president of plans and controls, who is supported by the director of corporate information systems. The information systems plan is coordinated with the business plan. A set of goals and instructions, spelling out content, input-output procedures, and change procedures, is issued yearly by information systems management. The instructions are given to the group organizations, and each group organization disseminates the material to its product divisions, plants and laboratories, and marketing and service locations. Each major location or division has assigned responsibility for maintaining and supporting key data bases within its organizational responsibility. Plans emerge from the base operation to each higher level. These plans indicate resource requirements, project plans, schedules, and other resource information.

How does IBM track the plan to make sure it is on target? One device is the scheduled audit, conducted to assess performance of individual information systems departments. In addition, status reports are prepared periodically and presented to top management, indicating progress toward scheduled phases of project implementation, and including a financial analysis of whether the program is meeting its financial objectives. There are no steering committees *per se;* the planning process itself is the primary means for project selection and approval. The plan is complemented by these other auditing review functions, which are part of the plans and audits staff.

INFORMATION SYSTEMS PLANNING PROCESS AND PLAN FORMAT

The information systems planning process, as defined in the instructions sent out to "inputters," has been under development and refinement since 1966. Today, activity is not "extraordinary"; it is a matter of fact and good business sense. (A copy of the instructions for the information systems plan and a representative plan schedule appear in Appendix A.) The process has not undergone a major change in the last three years, testifying to how well the foundation was laid. Four other characteristics of the process should be understood.

1. The information systems resource allocation is built into the corporate chart of accounts as a line item that can be reported by the accounting system.
2. All major information systems efforts are subjected to financial analysis to determine return on investments, payback, and business objectives fulfilled through the project.
3. The information systems are designed to support major business processes (activities and decisions). Conversely, they are organizationally independent, thus giving IBM a great deal of organizational flexibility.
4. In conjunction with point 3, organization planning and design is integral with information systems architecture. The rationale for major information system activity often comes from the displacement

of organizational levels and/or the integration of business organizations and/or functions.

In summary, the information systems planning process is a way of life within IBM. It offers control of the information systems resource, development of information systems that support major business activities and decisions, a way of organizing development according to priorities, and real user participation. It is our belief that business success depends on the effectiveness of management's decisions, and management decisions are as good as the information on which they are based.

Does it pay off? We believe the impact is evident in reviewing the operating expense and profit margins between 1964 and 1973. As previously indicated, IBM's revenues grew by a factor of 3.4 during this period. During the same period, manpower grew by a factor of only 1.8, and most important, the operating expense grew at a controlled rate comparable to the revenue. This challenging accomplishment during a period of uncertainty explains why IBM is so heavily committed to the information planning process. It supports the business planning, measurement, and control systems in a way that allows us to maintain better management controls in a dynamically changing external and internal environment.

11 LAURENCE S. WEINSTEIN

Xerox Corporation

The Xerox Corporation is dedicated to continued progress in the growth of our revenues and profits, our product lines, and opportunities for our people. Accomplishing this requires significant attention to planning for the future.

Information systems play an important role throughout the corporation by providing Xerox operating people with the tools they need to manage their responsibilities effectively. In information systems, as in the corporation as a whole, careful attention to planning is essential.

THE CORPORATION

Revenues, Profits, and Products

The 1973 operating revenues of Xerox were $3 billion, an increase of 24 percent over 1972. Worldwide net income was $300 million, an increase of 20 percent over the preceding year.

Marketing of Xerox copiers, duplicators, facsimile equipment, and related supplies and services in the United States accounted for $1.56 billion in revenues. This was 52 percent of our worldwide revenues. Some 100 branch offices throughout the United States provide marketing, technical service, and administrative and billing support to Xerox customers.

International operations are conducted through Rank-Xerox Ltd., Fuji-Xerox Ltd., Xerox of Canada Ltd., and our Latin-American group operations. Revenues for international operations in 1973 were $1.2 billion. This was 40 percent of our total worldwide revenues. At the end of 1973 close to half our machines were installed outside the United States and about the same proportion of our 94,000 Xerox employees were citizens of other countries.

Worldwide revenues for other operations, including the following, were just over $250 million:

- In the education field, marketing textbooks, microfilm services, magazines, and bibliographic reference materials to schools and libraries.
- Production of Xerioradiographic equipment for medical institutions to detect breast cancer.
- In the computer field, marketing Sigma equipment, primarily to time-sharing services, education institutions, and real-time users. Recently we delivered a custom-built communications system to the Los Angeles Police Department.
- Marketing computer printers and Diablo disk drives, primarily for the original equipment manufacturers (OEM) market.
- Providing through Xerox Computer Services in Los Angeles, a fully interactive accounting service for small and medium-sized businesses and a utility billing service for municipalities. This service is rapidly being extended nationwide.

Geographic Decentralization

Geographic decentralization has a particular impact on the information systems community, heightening the need to provide data processing services without excessive increase in expense, and making essential a modern, efficient voice and digital data network.

Geographic decentralization is proceeding rapidly within Xerox. At the end of 1973 we were doing business in more than 100 countries. By 1975, we will be manufacturing in 10 countries around the world. We have active research centers in the United States, England, and Japan and soon will have one in Canada. During 1973 construction of our new training center in Leesburg, Virginia (near Dulles Airport) continued, ground was broken for a new research center in Palo Alto, and we acquired a site in Dallas for an advanced product development and manufacturing facility.

Construction was begun on a consumables plant in Spain and a machine manufacturing plant near Lille, France. A machine manufacturing plant was opened in Canada, and a research laboratory will begin operations there in 1974. These will supplement existing manufacturing and assembly facilities in the United Kingdom, Holland, Brazil, Mexico, and Japan.

INFORMATION SYSTEMS WITHIN XEROX

Mission

The mission of information systems within Xerox is to provide data processing and telecommunications services to maximize the operational effectiveness and decision-making capability of operating management throughout the corporation.

Specific information systems objectives are as follows:

- To improve administrative productivity.
- To provide effective tools for tactical and strategic decision making.
- To support our rapidly expanding manufacturing and development facilities.
- To strive for the highest level of technical competence within the development staff.
- To ensure that information systems personnel receive qualified and thoughtful leadership and are provided with suitable challenges.

Another extremely important aspect of our mission is to provide a test site in which potential new products and information handling technology developed by Xerox may receive controlled evaluation and tryout.

Personnel and Budget

Worldwide, there are 35 independent information systems organizations responsible for data processing services, systems development and programming, telecommunications, and management sciences within Xerox. The 1973 budget, exclusive of telephone expense, was $70 million worldwide. There are 4300 personnel employed in information systems activities: 2000 or 47 percent, are in systems development and programming; 1600 or 36 percent, are in data center operations; and the remaining 16 percent are in management, personnel, training, financial control, telecommunications, and management science. Only 20 people are specifically identified as planners. Every line manager is, in fact, involved in the planning process.

Facilities and Equipment

Xerox data processing installations range from the Xerox Computer Center in Webster, New York, to small installations in countries such as Venezuela and Brazil. We had more than 30 separate equipment installations at the end of 1973.

Xerox Sigma equipment is installed extensively throughout the corporation for a wide variety of applications, including message switching, equipment control, inventory accounting and sales control, manufacturing applications, on-line program debugging, educational research, and time-sharing services for the technical and financial communities.

The Xerox Computer Center in Webster services all our marketing headquarters and manufacturing operations in nearby Rochester. It houses $37 million worth of IBM, Univac, and Sigma equipment and employs more than 300 people. Each month the center handles 5000 batch production jobs, 12,000 time-sharing jobs, 400,000 on-line time-sharing transactions, and 17,000 remote-site service jobs.

A second Xerox Computer Center is under construction to consolidate our West Coast operations. Internationally, we are consolidating our operations in 11 individual countries into three regional data centers to be located in the United Kingdom, France, and Germany.

Telecommunications

With our total telephone voice and data communications expense approaching $25 million in 1974, we are taking aggressive steps to make the most economical use of communications facilities through consolidation of our present diverse networks and systems into two major Xerox corporate communications networks with international coverage. These are as follows:

1. A line-switched ("dial-up") analog network, mainly for voice and analog facsimile.
2. A time-division switched and multiplexed digital network for data, telegraph, and digital facsimile.

An interim tie-line voice network serving our major headquarters locations is scheduled for May 1974. Requests for bid have been let for the corporate voice network, and installation is expected in late 1975 or early 1976.

Systems Development

Systems development efforts are taking place in many application areas throughout Xerox. During 1973 more than 1000 software development projects were undertaken.

Several major projects having implications for the entire corporation are under way. The following are a few that have special significance.

- *Project COIN (Communications-Oriented Information Network).* This project will place intelligent terminals with visual displays and printers in all our branch sales offices. Communicating through a hierarchy of Sigma computers to duplexed host processors at the Xerox Computer Center, COIN will provide for the rapid editing and inputing of order entry and equipment control data, billing adjustments, and accounts receivable transactions and the outputing to the branches of commissions, revenue analysis, and equipment status information. For the first time it will provide a single data base maintained in a completely consistent fashion. COIN objectives are to furnish improved customer service and to increase administrative productivity. The first phase, Branch Data Entry, is to be implemented in 1974 with full interactive capability to follow in 1976-77. Internationalization is projected for the late 1970s and early 1980s. This is our single largest systems development effort.
- *Common multinational manufacturing systems architecture.* The intent of this project is to standardize and integrate all the facets of our worldwide manufacturing operations. Currently in the conceptual phase, this multinational, cross-divisional venture is one of the most complex undertakings in Xerox. If successful, it will save many millions of dollars in redundant manufacturing efforts and duplicated toolings.
- *Integrated in-house time-sharing service.* Xerox has pioneered in the large-scale use of APL for strategic planning, budget preparation, revenue and expense forecasting, and capital investment analyses. As a result, utilization of time-sharing services by the financial community has grown within three years to several million dollars. It is our intent to provide a reliable, economical in-house service for all Xerox users.

INFORMATION SYSTEMS PLANNING

Philosophy and Objectives

Information systems planning reflects both the character of Xerox and its products and a planning philosophy developed and refined over a number of years.

Information systems organizational and management philosophy can be summarized as follows:

- Responsibility for system specification and operation lies with operating management.
- Programming and data processing services are to be provided by an information utility, operated as a profit center.
- Information utility business area managers are to be measured on the attainment of service objectives and profit-loss objectives, on overall customer satisfaction, and on personnel development and technological leadership.
- Strong emphasis is to be placed on professional and managerial development.

In Xerox it is clearly recognized that responsibility for meeting business objectives, whether they be sales quotas, unit manufacturing cost targets, or product introduction dates, rests with operating management. Information systems exists as a service organization to give operating management the tools required to do the job. At the same time it is recognized that a competent systems and data processing community is not a passive function. It must generate ideas, work closely with the user, and often lead the way in introducing new approaches to solving business problems.

Organizational Implementation

To implement the philosophy just outlined, the Xerox Information Services Division was formed in March 1972. The division general manager reports directly to the president of United States Operations. All operating organizations, such as manufacturing, marketing, and planning, have their own systems analysis staffs. Working with personnel directly responsible for an application area, they identify systems needs, translate them into specifications for programming, negotiate schedules and budget, and accept and implement delivered systems. The operating department is responsible for input of data, maintaining of controls, timeliness and accuracy of output, and error resolution. Services are purchased from the Information Services Division based on competitive rates.

The Information Services Division provides data center operations services, programming, management sciences, and telecommunications services to most of the domestic operations within Xerox. It operates with its own financial and personnel organizations and a small division staff. Profit objectives are established for the division during the operating plan cycle just as for each of the other operating divisions of the company.

To ensure that the Information Services Division managers place appropriate emphasis on meeting technological and professional objectives, the following actions have been taken.

- Each business area manager is given one or more technological leadership missions and goals. For example, Computer Operations is responsible for capacity planning, specialized hardware interfacing, and maintaining knowledge of advanced hardware technology.
- A separate personnel organization totally devoted to information systems personnel, employing its own education and training staff, has been established.
- A dual-ladder concept, allowing personnel either to advance through a managerial or professional career path or to move into a user functional area, is in place.

Checks and balances to both systems development and data center operations are provided through a Performance Assurance Audit Group established as an integral part of Xerox Internal Audit. This group, which is independent organizationally and managerially from operating unit systems groups as well as the Information Services Division, performs data center audits and audits of systems critical to the business. The establishment of this group has proved to be one of our most successful organizational moves.

Our international operations and certain domestic operations are not yet organized under the Information Services Division concept. We have just taken a major step in this direction on the West Coast with the formation of our second Xerox Computing Center. With two years of experience behind us, we are convinced that the approach is sound, although certainly not without its problems. It permits the establishment of and measurement against precise, quantifiable targets. It forces a businesslike approach to the solution of problems. It prevents user management from running over information systems management, and it prevents data processing management from avoiding objective measurement of their results.

THE PLANNING PROCESS

Overview

Planning and control of Xerox information systems closely parallels the overall Xerox corporate planning and control process, in scope and in timing. The elements of the planning process include an operating plan (two-year commitment) and a long-range plan (seven-year projection).

Operating Plan

The operating plan which focuses on specific resource requirements and commitments during the coming years, establishes the following:

- Specific development projects to be funded.
- Specific ongoing service objectives and expense, capital, and manpower levels necessary to meet these objectives.
- Commitment by the Information Service Division to revenue and expense, and hence profit, objectives.

The operating plan is a one-year commitment with a second-year projection. It tends to focus on approval of specific plans for the coming year rather than on broader issues. Operating plan discussions generally are limited to manning requirements, funding levels, and timing. It usually is assumed that the basic strategic decision to initiate a project has already been made. Operating plan submissions tend to quantify alternatives and to array various competing projects and equipment proposals for setting of priorities against realistic funding levels and other competing business requirements both inside and outside the information system community.

The operating plan cycle extends from the June issuance of initial instructions until final submission, normally in October.

Long-range Plan

Long-range planning seeks to establish four principal goals:

- Long-range applications, technological, equipment, facilities, and organization strategies.

- Major projects that should be undertaken in support of these strategies.
- Expense, manpower, and capital resources to support these strategies and projects, plus ongoing operations.
- Key planning issues for division, group, and corporate management awareness.

The long-range plan is viewed basically as a *communications* vehicle. Through the long-range plan it is possible to focus on issues, establish goals, and provide for an awareness by user and systems management of potential resource needs that often would be bypassed under the day-to-day pressures of running the business. The guidelines and formats for the preparation of the long-range plan are included in Appendix D.

Though the long-range plan does attempt to highlight issues, it is *not* intended necessarily to provide definitive solutions. Rather, it may identify a need for an intensive study or an executive review before preparation and approval of the forthcoming operating plan. For example, the Multinational Manufacturing Study was undertaken as a result of an issue identified initially in the long-range plan. By focusing on such an item and bringing it to the attention of corporate and group management during the long-range planning process, sufficient pressure can be brought to bear at the appropriate levels to initiate action.

Long-Range Planning Process

Within Xerox, long-range planning instructions are issued in February, and the formal submission is due in June or July.

The methodology used varies somewhat depending on the group or division, its size, and the sophistication of operating and systems management. But a typical schedule is as follows:

JANUARY: Issue preliminary guidelines via corporate planning office.

FEBRUARY: Issue final guidelines.

MARCH: Review guidelines with division systems manager. This is normally a personal visit.

APRIL: Division systems manager meet with key operating management to identify strategies, projects, issues, and resource requirements. Prepare draft plan and submit.

MAY: Corporate information systems feedback. Presentation by division systems manager to division operating management. Submission of final plan to corporate information systems.

JUNE: Consolidation of all group and division plans. Identification of key corporate issues.

JULY: Presentation to corporate management.

AN ASSESSMENT AND SOME OBSERVATIONS

Does the approach we are using at Xerox work? We believe the answer to be a definite *yes,* although clearly there are areas where we can and will improve.

Before we initiated the operating plan process for information systems in 1969, and the long-range plan in 1970, every organization had its own systems and programming staff, its own hardware plans, and its own set of systems objectives. As a result, two, three, or more groups were often embarked on parallel programs, but in different ways. True data processing expense was at best uncontrolled and at worst unknown. There was little or no visibility regarding how our information systems dollar was being spent.

Today the operating plan process forces each systems and operating manager to take a close look at expenditure plans for the coming year, to justify projects, to evaluate expenditures being devoted to non-project-related activities, and to consider expenditure tradeoffs.

The "business area" concept within the Information Services Division forces each manager to establish service objectives and to be responsible for profit objectives. The manager negotiates with users and his performance in meeting the commitments he makes is measured. His people are motivated to perform. In short, by introducing and carrying through the information utility approach, we have made information processing a professionally managed business.

The long-range planning process forces operating and systems management, including our own technology staff, to take a hard look at the question of where do we want to be two, five, and even seven years from now. The long-range plan has contributed significantly to the success of our information systems activities, especially when viewed as a vehicle to force constructive thought; to make issues visible; to identify key issues for corporate management; to establish and obtain approval at the appropriate management level of planned resources and the strategic direction in which the information systems community is headed; and to obtain visibility at division, group, and corporate levels of the most essential decisions that must be made relative to systems activities.

Improvements and Recommendations

But, where can improvements be made, and what recommendations can be offered to others? There are several.

1. *Do not allow the formalized structure—the paper work, if you will—to be the focus of the planning process.* It is essential to have a formalized structure. Without it, operating and systems managers alike can too easily duck their responsibilities. But the true value is in the thought process, the review procedures that sharpen the thinking of division and group managers, and in the visibility that is afforded by the process.
2. *Make certain that user and systems managers do not confuse the objectives of the various planning processes.* This is a difficulty we still have with some of our divisions and with many of our newer managers.
   The long-range plan formulates strategies, estimates gross resource requirements, and raises key issues. It does *not* solve the problems, and in some cases it does not even come up with the right answers; but it does place issues squarely in front of a level of management that can and thereby forces them to be addressed.
   The operating plan commits to projects, service objectives, and resource levels. It does not ensure accomplishment of the projects, meeting of service objectives, or adherence to budgets. These are the functions of Project Control, Internal Audit, and normal budgetary controls and operating reviews within the corporation. But even here, the mechanical aspects of the system should not be overemphasized. Only through the placement and training of competent line management, given proper technological tools and properly motivated personnel, will tasks be accomplished on schedule, within specifications, and within budget.
3. *Quantify goals and objectives.* We are placing greater emphasis on this area during the 1974 planning cycle. Thus it is not, "improve administrative productivity in branch offices," but "improve administrative productivity by 10 percent within the next three years as measured by number of transactions handled per administrative person."
   Nor is it, "improve cost-efficient use of hardware," but "obtain an increase of 20 percent annually in the number of transactions processed with an increase in payroll operations budget no greater than 15 percent annually."
4. *Effective communication and visibility are essential.* Within Xerox, informa-

> tion systems instructions are not issued by the director of Information Services. Operating plan instructions are issued by the corporate controller. Long-range plan guidelines are issued by the corporate planning office. Everything possible is done to encourage division systems managers to involve key operating management, and before submission, to obtain concurrence from division financial management and division presidents. When the plans are consolidated, we present them to the entire corporate staff for review and to the corporate office for approval. Without this, the plans are little more than incestuous exercises, subject to change at the whim of the next operating manager with a "today" problem.

This background and information should give some insight into how Xerox information systems planning works. Motivating managers to plan is difficult. Putting the proper mechanism in place to make it happen and establishing the proper controls to ensure that the plans are translated into results is also difficult. But it is essential to accomplish these tasks if effective information systems are to be established and maintained.

III

Information Services Planning in the Regulated or Quasi-Private Sector

Part III contains chapters on four organizations: Consumers Power, Pacific Gas and Electric, Trans World Airlines, and Kaiser-Permanente Medical Group. Although each of these organizations is "private" in the sense of its ownership, they are all deeply affected with the public interest and are, therefore, regulated in one or more ways by some branch of government. Both Michigan's Consumers Power and California's Pacific Gas and Electric, being public energy utilities, are regulated by their respective state regulatory or public utility commissions. Trans World Airlines is subject to the rulings of the CAB, FAA, and other federal agencies. Kaiser-Permanente, a nonprofit medical foundation, depends heavily on grants from the Department of Health, Education, and Welfare to underwrite its various computer-based systems. Thus their ability to undertake comprehensive long-range planning is affected by outside forces not under their control. Of course, even private companies, such as those described in Part II, are not free from such outside influences; but the overall impact is usually much less.

MIS PLANNING IN THE REGULATED SECTOR

Consumers Power serves the gas and electricity needs of the "outstate" area of Michigan. In 1973 its revenues were $835 million. As with almost all utilities, its chief concerns are energy resource availability, the construction of new facilities, the acquisition of capital needed to finance such construction, and the rate-setting process, as determined by the state regulatory commission. Taken together, these uncertainties make the job of long-range planning extremely difficult.

For some time planning within the Computer Services Department "consisted mainly of the work associated with the preparation of an annual budget. The department took a somewhat autocratic position in determining what projects would be initiated and on what schedule, and there was little long-range planning and a minimum amount of user involvement." The shortcomings of this attitude were soon realized, however, and an advisory (steering) committee was formed, consisting of seven line managers and the computer manager. This committee was given broad responsibility to review projects, set priorities, and recommend policies and courses of action. Unfortunately the committee met with little success, primarily because "the level of authority of its members was too low, and no long-range development plans existed."

The latter deficiency led to the formation, in 1972, of a planning group given the "specific responsibility of developing a company information system plan." This group not only began to work with users within the company, it also joined the Utilities Information System Association, a five-company effort to develop "a corporate information system for a natural gas and electric utility." The flow model that resulted from this effort now serves as a road map for Consumers Power's information systems development activity.

Within this framework, short-range or operational plans are made. These are typically one to two years in scope and are prepared by the user organizations; the Computer Department functions mainly in a coordinating role. The short-range plans focus on the individual projects of interest to the user groups. Longer range planning within the department is concerned primarily with hardware acquisitions and systems software planning.

Pacific Gas and Electric, operating in the northern California area, shares many of the problems that face Consumers Power. New construction is a particularly important area for the company, and much of its corporate planning is directed toward this activity.

As far as information systems are concerned, a major impetus occurred in 1966, when the chairman of the board called for the "development and implementation of a comprehensive coordinated management information, planning, and control system . . . utilizing such data processing and communications systems as prove feasible." This led to the creation of the corporate Information Systems Department in 1968, the year in which the first long-range plan was produced. Since this plan was for a three-year period, a new plan was issued in 1971 and another in 1974. The horizon for this last plan has been shortened to one or two years, with the intention of creating a new long-term plan for a five- to ten-year period. This latter activity is now getting started.

The first planning efforts were aimed at creating a slate of applications, and the 1968 plan included "a list of some 140 projects needed to develop a comprehensive company-wide information system." The planning horizon was shortened partly to make the planning for these projects more concrete and realistic.

The responsibility for both short- and long-range planning is in the hands of a planning analyst in the development section of the Information Systems Department. The short-range plan is prepared annually and consists of "preliminary studies for projects reflecting the current needs of the company. . . . The resulting studies form a basis on which senior management decides priorities for development." The guide for this effort is the control plan for information systems projects, which spells out the ground rules for preparing the plan. Although a comprehensive long-range plan (i.e., five to ten years) is not presently in hand, work is actively under way on its development.

Trans World Airlines, like most of the major United States airlines, has had a long association with computers. With revenues of $1.4 billion per year, TWA is not only one of the leading American air carriers but is also a major hotel operator (Hilton International) and food service vendor (Canteen Corporation).

The first comprehensive long-range plan for information systems was prepared in 1968. It was the result of a substantial effort by the planning group within the corporate Systems and Data Services Department. It had a horizon of seven years and consisted of two massive volumes, covering projects that had a total price tag of $300 million! However it did not contain any savings data or return on investment calculations. Not surprisingly, "the plan appeared to be extremely overwhelming" and it "probably was not read by anyone who did not have a direct interest in a particular part of it."

In an effort to salvage some of the plan, the first volume, containing the general objectives, was revised in 1969 and forwarded to the corporate Planning Committee for consideration. Although it still did not include any information on cost savings, it brought to light a number of important points. In early 1970, however, a major reorganization of the Systems and Data Services Department took place, a new vice president in charge was appointed, and the planning group was eliminated! This has meant that until the planning and control staff was reestablished in 1974, planning has been conducted by the individual data centers.

During this four-year period the main mechanism for overall planning has been through project review, conducted by the Data Services Request Review Committee. The committee, composed of the president, senior vice president for finance, and vice president for systems and data services, screens all major projects (those costing more than $25,000) and approves those meeting the appropriate criteria.

Within the individual centers, the Commercial Data Processing Department prepared its first five-year plan in 1972. The plan was eight pages long and focused on hardware, software, and manpower considerations, as well as on application development and scheduling. The Reservations Data Processing Group created its first plan in 1970 and updated it in 1973. Because both these departmental planning efforts were fairly specific, they tended to be well received by top management and by their respective user groups.

One final planning activity consisted of inputs from all major departments and user groups within TWA. This general planning document discussing "potential future data processing applications" was first produced in 1972 and again in 1974.

Kaiser-Permanente is composed of a number of entities. It is a health plan which, in the San Francisco Bay Area, has more than a million members; it is a medical group of more than a thousand physicians who provide care to the health plan members; it is a hospital organization that furnishes a site for the physicians to practice; and finally, it is a research institute that conducts and supports medical research. Nationally, Kaiser is the largest prepaid medical practice in existance, and it has served as a model for a number of similar ventures.

As far as computing activities are concerned, Kaiser has long been a pioneer in the development of medical information systems. However most of the funding for this work has come from the Department of Health, Education, and Welfare; thus Kaiser is at the mercy of HEW's decisions as to whether or not grants will be approved. For the period 1964–1973, substantial grants were obtained; but this funding has ended, and the systems that were developed during this period are "in transition."

The author sums up the planning situation at Kaiser as follows: "Kaiser-Permanente in northern California does not have a medical information system master plan, nor a formal long-range plan for computer systems. Year-to-year planning and budgeting activities have been based on management's decisions relative to its objectives, priorities, and available funding, year to year. . . . Medical Methods Research departmental planning and operating activities have been considerably influenced by the Department of Health, Education, and Welfare through several grants and contracts directed toward implementing a prototype medical information system."

In discussing medical information systems, the author describes a number of their component parts and how they function. Finally, because of the lack of a long-term planning horizon, he stresses the importance of designing systems in a modular fashion, to permit their implementation within a reasonably short time frame.

CONCLUDING REMARKS

Although the differences among power utilities, airlines, and medical care organizations are great, it is instructive to see how each of them has come to grips—or is still struggling—with the problems of planning for information systems. In Part IV, which deals with the public sector, these problems are shown to be even more serious and the planning results more variable.

12 JOHN R. FREY

Consumers Power Company

Consumers Power Company is a combined electric and gas utility serving about 900,000 gas customers and 1.2 million electric customers in the "outstate" Michigan area. The company has about 11,750 employees, and 1973 annual revenues of approximately $835 million. Historically, revenue growth has been about 10 percent per year.

As an energy distribution company, Consumers Power exists in an exceedingly dynamic and not always predictable environment. The limited supply of fuels, either for resale as in the case of natural gas, or for the generation of electricity as in the case of other petroleum products and coal, pose problems in obtaining supplies and in the rapidly escalating costs of these supplies.

Huge construction programs are necessary to meet the forecasted energy requirements in the next decade. Since utilities require large capital expenditures relative to revenues, the company must obtain large amounts of capital at a time when money costs are high and the economy is inflationary. Today, the social implications of large construction projects also require formal approval by many state and federal agencies, resulting in longer lead times and higher initial costs.

The result of these factors is an increase in the price of the energy sold. The detailed and complex process of justifying rate increases before the state regulatory commission is almost continuous, and the adverse effect of these increases on customer relations is not unexpected.

This rapidly changing environment makes operating planning, and at times even corporate strategic planning, difficult and sometimes prohibitive. It also directly affects the planning and operating environment of the Computer Services Department.

Paralleling the experience of many utilities, computing was introduced within Consumers Power during the late 1950s as a direct machine replacement of clerical effort to accomplish the customer billing function. Other cost reduction accounting functions and minor engineering work soon followed. The 1960s were characterized by a proliferation of applications in all areas of the company. Most of the efforts were devoted to promoting machine use, with minimum emphasis on controls of any type. Centralization of development and production functions was established during the latter part of the decade, and there was growing concern about rapidly increasing costs. By the early 1970s tight control of both machine and manpower resources was established, and the need for more detailed and broader scope planning was recognized.

COMPUTER SERVICES DEPARTMENT

The Computer Services Department is organized with three basic areas of responsibility: the application development function, the production function, and the staff function, including planning (Figure 1).

Computer Systems Development is staffed with about 130 analysts and programmers who work on engineering systems development, administrative systems development, and systems extension and maintenance. It is responsible for the design and programming of all administrative data processing projects, engineering applications, and maintenance of production programs; and it assists on request in the programming of process control and time-sharing applications. Personnel from sponsoring departments are deeply involved in all development work. All major projects (more than $50,000 total cost) are accomplished by a team in which user personnel participate full-time. The project manager is normally from the sponsoring department(s).

Computer Systems Processing is staffed with about 125 analysts, operators, and key punchers, all in a centralized environment. It is responsible for the operation of the computer center, for the technical support of that operation, and for the terminals connected to it. The data entry group operates both a key-to-disk system and conventional keypunch equipment.. The use of optical scanning, introduced in 1962, is steadily increasing. The principal computing equipment consists of

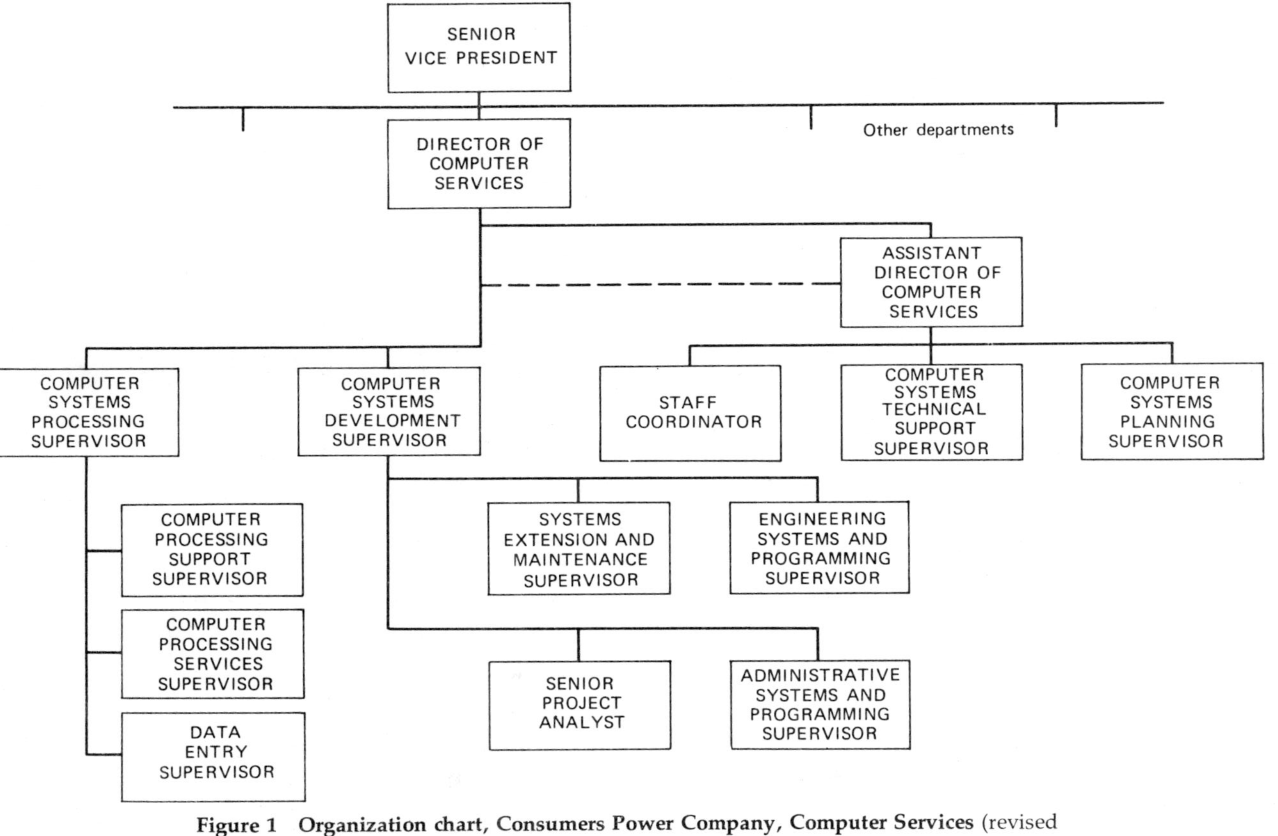

Figure 1 Organization chart, Consumers Power Company, Computer Services (revised March 1974). Not all positions are shown.

two IBM 370/158's with switchable peripherals. About 180 terminals on the communication network are scattered throughout the service territory. Another 100 terminals will be added in the fall of 1974. Computer output microfilm (COM) equipment is helping to reduce the quantity of paper output. Substantial use of an outside time-sharing service is also being made.

A relatively small staff group of about 10 people, reporting directly to the assistant director of the department, is responsible for personnel and facilities administration, technical support, and strategic (long-range) planning for computer services.

The foregoing description of the department's organizational structure and the concomitant responsibilities paraphrases and elaborates on the formal statements contained in the company's general orders. In addition, the department is regarded as a true service organization. As such it is expected to provide developmental and/or processing services as needed and justified by any department. The policies and procedures that define "need" and "justification" are now an integral part of the planning process. This process has been evolutionary and is still developing.

INFORMATION SYSTEMS PLANNING HISTORY

Planning in the department originally consisted mainly of the work associated with the preparation of an annual budget. The department took a somewhat autocratic position in determining what projects would be initiated and on what schedule, and there was little long-range planning and a minimum amount of user involvement. In a period when the objective was the promotion of computer use, and very little cost control was being exercised, this policy was adequate. However it soon became evident that the more successful systems had extensive user involvement in the system definition phase. People also began to ask how this proliferation of programs would fit together in the processing environment, whether new programs would be cluttering the files with identical data, how large a staff would be required to maintain and modify these programs, and so forth. In beginning to determine answers to these questions, a planning effort was started but was not formally recognized as such.

At this time, the need was also noted for more user department involvement in the decision-making process, principally in determining priorities for development. An advisory or steering committee was formed, consisting of seven line department managers and the manager of the computer area, and given the following responsibilities:

1. Review all proposals for major data processing projects (more than six man-months of effort) and recommend a priority relative to the total needs of the company. Factors to be considered in the review are economics and other qualitative and quantitative benefits, urgency of need, manpower available within the company, manpower available from outside service organizations, impact on projects currently under way, and impact on computer hardware systems.
2. Review policies and practices for providing computer services to all company departments and, when appropriate to ensure good service, recommend changes in such practices and policies to the Computer Services Department. This duty includes but is not limited to applications development and routine and priority production scheduling.
3. Review the evaluation and selection of outside data processing support services and recommend, where appropriate, changes in evaluation procedures to the Computer Services Department. This function includes but is not limited to consulting services, time-sharing services, and computer processing.
4. Review the computer systems hardware acquisition plans and schedules as developed by the Computer Services Department and, when appropriate to ensure good-quality service, recommend changes in such plans and schedules to the department.
5. Review interdepartmental computer-related problems and recommend courses of action.

Although intriguing in concept, the committee had very limited success. It was a communication vehicle of sorts, promoting some general understanding of problems. It was not as successful in its other responsibilities for two reasons—the level of authority of its members was too low, and no long-range development plan existed. Requests for development work that had vice-presidential support were "rubber stamped" on a first-come basis. Brush fire reaction techniques were employed in attempting to supply the needed resources for the approved projects.

In 1972 a two-person planning group was organized with the specific responsibility of developing a company information system plan. The primary objectives were to identify the information system needs of the various departments of Consumers Power, to identify the time frames within which the systems were desired, to estimate the resources required to develop and implement the desired systems, and to identify the interrelationships of departmental needs and the potential for common systems development.

The individual assigned to lead this effort was an experienced super-

Table 1 Current Applications by Department

Consumers Power Company Information Systems Planning Matrix, March 30, 1973

Department	Corporate System (CRP)	Construction and Maintenance System (C & M)	Customer System (CUS)	Employee System (EMP)
Accounting	1. Integrated plant in service 2. Property tax 3. Work order ledger and budgeting 4. Payroll system 5. Responsibility accounting system		Customer accounting system	Payroll system
Buildings services			1. Customer count configuration 2. Customer density center	
Bulk power supply				
Customer service			1. Meter services magnetic tape billing (WR-4) 2. Misc. meter services processing	
Economic and financial planning	1. Financial Model 2. Misc. economic and financial planning applications			
Electric construction		1. Contractors' file 2. Construction scheduling 3. Project management system 4. Material tracing and cost tracking reports		

Table 1 *(continued)*

Equipment System (EQP)	Facilities System (FAC)	Procurement and Stores System (P&S)	Gas production Operation System (P&O)	Electric Production and Operation System (P&O)
1. Integrated plant in service 2. Responsibility accounting	1. Integrated plant in service 2. Property tax	Materials and supplies	Customer accounting system	Customer accounting system
	1. Customer count configuration 2. Customer density center			
	Misc. bulk power supply applications			Misc. bulk power supply applications
			Miscellaneous economic and financial planning applications	Miscellaneous economic and financial planning applications
		Material tracing and cost tracking reports		

Table 2 Future Applications by Department

Consumers Power Company, Information Systems Planning Matrix, March 30, 1973

Department	Corporate System (CRP)	Construction and Maintenance System (C & M)	Customer System (CUS)	Employee System (EMP)
Accounting	1. Responsibility accounting study 2. Depreciation tax study		Customer service system project	
Area development	Building and site system			
Building services	Budgeting system	1. Room, building, and property system 2. Project cost monitoring system 3. Preventive maintenance system	Customer forecasting	
Bulk power supply	Budgeting system	1. Facilities maintenance backlog 2. Preventive maintenance system 3. Deferred maintenance versus forced outage analysis 4. Maintenance manpower requirements and availability program		
Customer service			Customer service system project	
Economic and financial planning	1. Corporate model 2. Stock and bond analysis			

Table 2 *(continued)*

Equipment System (EQP)	Facilities System (FAC)	Procurement and Stores System (P & S)	Gas Production Operation System (P&O)	Electric Production and Operation System (P&O)
	1. Room, building, and property system 2. Customer forecasting 3. Travel time study		Travel time study	Travel time study
	Forecast future load requirements			

visor in the Computer Services Department who was respected by his peers and who had good rapport with the users. The team was given nine months to give birth to a plan.

Major department heads were asked for assistance in specifying their departments' information needs. Personnel from Computer Services subsequently contacted the designated departmental representatives to obtain their views regarding the present situation, proposed plans, and problem areas. These interviews were the initial steps in the formulation of the development plan.

In April 1972 the company joined the work meetings of the Utilities Information System Association (UISA), hoping to define a corporate information system for a natural gas and electric utility. The UISA, which consisted of representatives of five utilities,[1] confined its efforts to the development of an information flow model that describes the activities involved in the gross transactions of the business. This model defines the nine basic activities that must be performed by a utility regardless of the extent of computerized assistance. The model was then tailored to Consumers Power and adapted as the basic frame of reference for the company's information systems planning.

The resulting development plan defined all proposed systems in terms of this basic frame of reference. It also analyzed and defined all existing programs and systems in terms of this same reference. Other useful outputs were charts of current applications by department and future applications by department (Tables 1 and 2). All this information is updated annually.

The net result of the information systems plan is a rather complete road map for development. It defines interrelationships between present and known future developments. It tells where the company wishes to go but does not attempt to prescribe the exact route nor the speed of travel. It is a strategic or long-range plan without established priorities.

INFORMATION SYSTEMS PLANNING PROCESS

Once direction is established by the long-range plan, complementary short-range or operational planning is necessary. Typically these plans have one- to two-year objectives and are initiated by the department or group bearing line responsibility for that function. Thus the priority of applications development is determined solely by those who have the

[1]Consumers Power Company, General Public Utilities Service Corporation, Niagara Mohawk Power Corporation, Public Service Company of Oklahoma, and Public Service Electric & Gas Company.

functional responsibility. This places Computer Services in a coordination and service position. It also necessitates clearly defined policies and procedures for developmental activities. These policies have been designed to utilize existing company control and approval methods wherever possible without creating practices unique to computer applications.

A project may be initiated at any time by a line department, but it must follow a formal procedure. It is submitted to Computer Services on a project request form (Figure 2) describing the project, quantifying the benefits, and establishing a project class (priority). It is then costed by Computer Services and authorized for implementation by the appropriate level of user management. A rather rigid system of authorization and scheduling (Table 3) is followed once the priority has been established. No projects having a cost-benefit ratio exceeding 2.0 are undertaken, and all projects are subject to postimplementation audit by the Internal Audit Department.

The development cycle is divided into three parts for control purposes, with management approval required before initiation of the succeeding phases:

1. *The feasibility study* results in enough conceptual definition to permit estimation of reasonable ranges of costs and benefits. At this time the project is checked for adherence to the long-range plan.
2. *The general design requirements study* defines all input, all output, and enough detail of system design to cost the project within approximately 10 percent and to estimate the benefits accurately.
3. *The implementation phase* covers all other aspects of implementation and conversion.

All major projects (more than $50,000 total cost) are reviewed for approval by the same company officer-director committee that controls all other large company expenditures.

Although this philosophy for application development is characterized by a lack of formal short-range planning, it provides extreme flexibility for the functional manager to exist in a dynamic environment where his destiny is often controlled by outside influences such as regulatory commissions and availability of fuels. From the standpoint of Computer Services, the limiting factors are the available resources. Even though the work load is subject to stringent review and justification criteria, it has at times exceeded manpower available. When this happens, outside contract services are employed to handle the ballooning effect as long as the cost-benefit ratio does not exceed 2.0.

CONSUMERS POWER COMPANY

COMPUTER SERVICES DEPARTMENT PROJECT REQUEST

SYSTEM NUMBER ______ PROJECT REQUEST NUMBER ______

1. REQUESTING DEPARTMENT ______ CHARGE NUMBER ______

☐ NEW SYSTEM ☐ EXISTING SYSTEM ☐ CHANGE ☐ ADDITION ☐ STUDY

PREPARED BY ______ DATE DESIRED ______ DATE PREPARED ______

2. SYSTEM NAME ______

PROJECT DESCRIPTION ______

3. EXPECTED BENEFITS OR REASON FOR CHANGE

ESTIMATED ANNUAL BENEFITS	
MATERIAL	$ ______
EQUIPMENT	$ ______
LABOR	$ ______
COMPUTER USAGE	$ ______
TOTAL BENEFITS	$ ______

4. AUTHORIZED - DEPARTMENT MANAGER ______ DATE ______

FOR COMPUTER SERVICES DEPARTMENT USE ONLY

5. ESTIMATES	ESTIMATED
REQUEST RECEIVED BY ______ DATE ______	COMPLETION DATE ______
SYSTEM IDENT ______ *PROJECT CLASS ______	MAN HOURS $ ______
EST PREPARED BY ______ DATE ______	COMPUTER DEVELOPMENT $ ______
REVIEWED WITH USER ______ DATE ______	TOTAL DEVELOPMENT $ ______
	ANNUAL OPERATING $ ______
DISPOSITION ______	PAY BACK RATIO ______
6. COMPUTER SERVICES REVIEW	**SCHEDULED**
DATE ______	START DATE ______
DISPOSITION ______	FINISH DATE ______
7. IMPLEMENTATION	**ACTUAL**
ASSIGNED TO ______ DATE ______	COMPLETION DATE ______
AUTHORIZED BY ______ FOR DATE ______	MAN HOURS $ ______
FINAL REVIEW BY ______ DATE ______	COMPUTER DEVELOPMENT $ ______
ACCEPTED BY USER ______ DATE ______	TOTAL DEVELOPMENT $ ______

* 1. MANDATORY - SYSTEM ERROR; REGULATORY, LEGAL OR CONTRACTUAL REQUIREMENT
2. SAVINGS
3. UNCLASSIFIED (INCLUDING PROJECTS OVER 2 MAN-MONTHS)

Figure 2 Consumers Power Company Computer Services Department Project request form.

Table 3 Classification and Scheduling of Computer Projects Computer Services Department, Consumers Power Company

Project Class 1: Mandatory

Definition. A Class 1 project is any project for which urgency is established because of a given pressing date by which the project must be completed. Such a project is established because of the following requirements:

- To satisfy regulatory bodies.
- To meet legal or contractual provisions, or industry standards or commitments.
- To correct program malfunctions—defined as the difference in actual system performance relative to the specified performance as stated in the approved systems documentation.
- To make modifications or extensions to systems in order to conform to new company policies or practices—defined as policy changes documented in the company's general orders or division accounting bulletins.

Authorization. Class 1 projects may be authorized by the supervisor responsible for the function.

Project 2: Savings

Definition. A Class 2 project is any project for which savings can be quantified. Only projects with computed payback periods equal to or less than two years will be considered.

Authorization. The requesting department manager's or director's approval is required for projects whose estimated total cost is less than $15,000; a company officer's approval is required for projects whose estimated total cost exceeds $15,000; and approval of the Budget Review Committee is required for projects whose estimated total cost exceeds $50,000.

Project Class 3: Unclassified

Definition. A Class 3 project is any project that is not classified as Class 1 or 2.

Authorization. A company officer's approval is required for Class 3 projects exceeding $15,000 and Budget Committee approval is required for projects costing more than $50,000.

Scheduling of Projects

As personnel become available to work on projects, projects shall be selected in a general priority order as follows:

1. Class 1 projects shall be started first.
2. Class 2 projects shall be started in order of payback period after all Class 1 projects have been started.
3. Class 3 projects shall be started after all Class 1 and Class 2 projects have been started.

Planning for hardware follows a similar pattern. The previously described strategic plan dictated that Computer Services expansion would utilize IBM central processing units (CPUs) with continual consideration of other vendors for peripherals. It determined that hardware would not be purchased but would be leased wherever possible. It defined a method of providing computing power closer to the user (i.e., minicomputers versus various telecommunication methods). Although long-range application priorities are not firmly established, the goal is always clearly defined; and hardware planning provides for various combinations of operating software and hardware for improving the information systems capability.

Line responsibility and functional management of the computer equipment rests with the Computer Services Department. Even though short-range application development planning is not formalized, normal lead times in development cycles allow detailed and formal operational hardware planning. These plans last between 12 and 18 months and encompass changes to provide increased processing capability for newly developed systems and changes to reduce operating costs.

Planning for increased capability follows the long-range plan for CPU additions, but it must determine the best method of obtaining intermediate increases from such options as operating software improvements and selected peripheral changes. It also accomplishes the detail installation planning.

Planning for reduction in operating cost considers such factors as scheduling changes, price advantages in competitive peripheral equipment, and different operating procedures. It also must accomplish installation planning for all changes adopted.

Planning for personnel, their education, and facilities is also a part of the annual operational plan.

OPPORTUNITIES FOR IMPROVEMENT

A formal and more rigid short-range application development plan certainly would promote a more placid atmosphere within the Computer Services Department. And to the extent that adherence to such planning does not prohibit the using departments from effective action in their hectic and changing environment, it is highly desirable. Direct chargeback of development costs is being studied as one means of improving this situation. Presently all computer processing costs are charged to the user. However, only part of the development costs is directly charged; the balance is memo billed.

The utility industry has some unique opportunities in the area of information exchange, planning, and even application system design, which are not always exploited. Utilities are not in direct competition with one another and have a great deal of commonality in the functions they perform. Therefore it should be possible to exchange detailed information or jointly perform a number of activities within the data processing area. Although this has been accomplished to some extent (e.g., the joint development of a frame of reference for information systems planning described earlier), many other opportunities surely exist.

13 ROGER W. BARBEY

Pacific Gas and Electric Company

The Pacific Gas and Electric Company is a an energy utility supplying northern California with electric power and natural gas. The company employs 26,000 people and has revenues of $1.8 billion, of which roughly two-thirds is from electric power sales and one-third from natural gas. Its physical plant is worth around $6 billion.

The headquarters in San Francisco houses all staff functions, and policy and major procedural matters are developed there. Thirteen geographical divisions handle all contacts and direct service work for the company's 5 million customers.

A major function in utility operations is construction; both at the local level, to provide gas and electric service to customers, and at the corporate level, to direct the development of major facilities such as power-generating stations, gas compressor stations, and gas and electric transmission lines. The company's construction program is now on the order of $600 million annually.

Planning at the corporate level is primarily directed toward scheduling the addition of major facilities, with the associated fallout in terms of financing requirements, equipment purchases, land acquisitions, and manpower planning. Four major company headquarter functions independently determine, then reconcile, their respective positions on the expected growth in power needs over the next 15 years. This growth is the input to planning for the establishment of plant additions.

The same process goes on at a lower level in the geographical divisions, where the planning results are used to schedule local plant additions over the next two to four years.

INFORMATION SYSTEMS BACKGROUND

Computer-supported information systems began at Pacific Gas and Electric in the mid-1950s with the centralization of the customer billing process. Along with this came the establishment, in the comptroller's organization, of an Accounting Methods and Procedures Group to handle the system development work and an Operations Group to handle the production processing.

During the late 1950s and early 1960s, new systems were developed to support payroll, inventory, and other volume data handling operations. Organizations running these EAM operations were for the most part centralized. Also during this period, the engineering function at the corporate level developed a growing reliance on computer support for design matters. At first requiring outside time-sharing companies, the engineering people are now served by inside time-sharing services.

In 1966 Robert H. Gerdes, the chairman of the board, initiated a comprehensive review of the company's information needs. He called for the creation of "a senior management committee to give overall direction to a program with following objectives:

> Development and implementation of a comprehensive coordinated management information, planning, and control system together with the application of advanced decision making and operating systems and techniques—utilizing such data processing and communication systems as prove feasible.

"This committee will consist of myself, as chairman, and [members from a number of functional areas]. The functions of this committee will be review and approve actions to be undertaken by the staff in executing the program; passing on policy questions involved in systems changes; and approval of commitments for electronic data processing equipment and related communication systems. A staff is being assembled to participate on a full-time basis in the conduct of the studies required in the execution of the program."[1]

[1]R.H. Gerdes, *Interoffice Memorandum to Officers, Heads of Departments, and Division Managers*, Pacific Gas and Electric Company, February 9, 1966.

This group set about developing a comprehensive information system based on requirements stated in numerous interviews conducted through the company. In 1968 this effort culminated in a list of projects to be undertaken over time and the establishment of an Information Systems Department to accomplish the work. The development staff within the comptroller's organization was merged into the new Information Systems Department, which reports to the vice chairman of the board.

There are currently three computer-related groups:

1. Information Systems reports to the vice chairman of the board and has a staff of 125 people and a budget of $2 million.
2. Computer Operations, reporting to the comptroller, has a staff of 360, of which 110 support the computer production process and 250 are in data reduction. The annual equipment rental is about $3.8 million, and the total staff budget is $4.2 million.
3. Engineering Computer Applications, reporting to the vice president, planning and research, has a staff of 37 persons and a budget of $0.6 million.

The computers within the department consist of two IBM 370/168's supported by smaller IBM computers for such peripheral functions as printing and scanning. Video and printer terminals number about 130, with a majority concentrated at or near corporate headquarters; 95 terminals support a customer services function.

Major systems work has been done in a number of functional areas; but new systems or major enhancements to existing systems have been designed for all areas experiencing considerable data flows. Supporting this main functional development work has been a major software development effort that provides functional users with rapid responses to their requests for reports. The introduction of data base management systems and special reporting capabilities has greatly enhanced the usefulness of the new systems to the functional departments.

INFORMATION SYSTEMS OBJECTIVES

The original objective, stated in the board chairman's 1966 letter, remains the basic goal of the Information Systems Department. A more detailed list of objectives, expanding on the foregoing, appears in Table 1. A further expansion of the objectives can be found in the tasks and

Table 1 Information Systems Objectives

1. Provide user organizations with information systems they can justify, accept, and handle, as well as providing data to all who need it.
2. Complete projects within budget and schedule.
3. Develop integrated information systems.
4. Design the computer processing to make most efficient use of the available hardware resources.
5. Design the programs to permit modifications with relative ease.
6. Provide opportunity for personal growth by project managers, analysts, and programmers.

responsibilities listed in the functional organization chart for the department (Figure 1).

Close ties are maintained with the Computer Operations and Engineering Computer Applications departments by means of monthly coordination meetings. In this manner the meshing of objectives of all three groups is assured. It is this coordinating group that serves as the medium for discussion of future plans and how new or enhanced systems and new equipment will blend effectively.

INFORMATION SYSTEMS PLANNING HISTORY

From the mid-1950s to the mid-1960s, planning for new systems and equipment was confined principally to accounting-oriented applications. The development staff did, however, prepare long-range plans. These plans typically had a two- to three-year horizon and detailed the projects likely to be considered in that period. The comptroller reviewed outstanding requests for development work and decided on the projects to be undertaken and the sequence of the development.

When a comprehensive study was undertaken in 1966, senior management became more involved in the project selection process. Two years later they were presented with a list of some 140 projects needed to develop a comprehensive company-wide information system. About six medium-to-large projects were selected from the list and were authorized for development at that time.

In 1971, and again in 1974, projects were submitted to senior management for authorization to proceed. The 1968 and 1971 submissions were of significant size and involved a planning horizon of about three to four years.

The present approach is to reduce the current short-term planning

INFORMATION SYSTEMS

Develop, design, and program management authorized, computer–based information systems, new and modified.

INFORMATION SYSTEMS DEVELOPMENT

1. Plan the design and development of information systems to assure best possible sequence, effectiveness, and integration.
2. Review proposed major modifications to operational systems to assure continued system integration.
3. Plan development of company data base and allied glossaries.
4. In collaboration with departments affected, design, develop, and install new information systems.
5. Assure that new projects are integrated with overall system development.
6. Assure overall precedural efficiency in new projects.
7. Review data privacy and physical security requirements to assure that these are met before project segments are installed.
8. Work closely with Computerized Systems Technology and Computer Program Maintenance Sections to assure the best possible computerized system design and operational effectiveness in new projects.
9. Work with departments affected in preparing their personnel to operate new information systems.
10. Develop, maintain, and publish appropriate standards for project development and performance.
11. Maintain contact with other utilities and companies on their latest thinking and practice in corporate systems development.
12. Evaluate commercially available application software packages pertaining to projects under development.

Figure 1 Information Systems responsibilities.

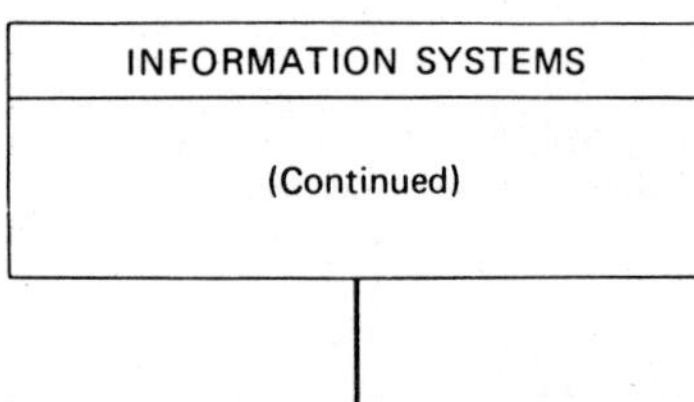

COMPUTER PROGRAM MAINTENANCE

1. Ensure operational readiness of business data processing programs; correct program malfunctioning, modify programs to accommodate changed requirements, and rewrite programs to optimize data input or computer processing, where economic and feasible.

2. Maintain appropriate records of all business application computer programs in the company.

3. Maintain record of company data bases content and publish glossaries.

4. Administer data base control procedures and assist users in accessing data stored in machine-readable form.

5. Control changes made in data base file content and dynamic tables.

6. Audit systems development and adequacy of job stream, programs, and documentation to assure operational readiness results.

7. Audit high-level tests and ensure that external clarances are received prior to implementation.

8. Maintain physical security of programs and program documentation.

9. Administer computer file space allocated for programs and related tables and test data.

10. Ensure recovery of systems in case of disaster.

11. Publish and maintain programing standards.

12. Work with Computer Operations Department in establishing effective schedules and procedures.

Figure 1 *(Continued)*

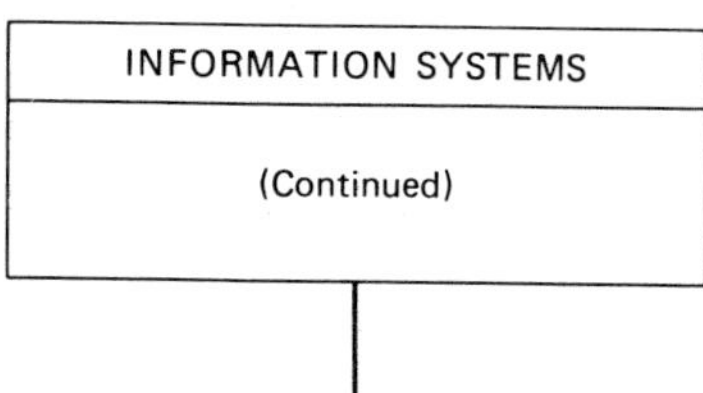

COMPUTERIZED SYSTEMS TECHNOLOGY

1. Adapt or develop, document, and maintain appropriate systems programs (software) for computer file management, teleprocessing, resources management, and utility routines.
2. Identify and evaluate available systems software and programing languages.
3. Provide technical assistance in using the company's software and in program design, in developing computer processing strategy, and in systems control; work closely with information System Development to assure best possible computerized system design.
4. Assure that systems programs and allied teleprocessing requirements are synchronized with application requirements.
5. Assist in simulating proposed computer applications.
6. Evaluate capabilities, costs, and configuration of computer equipment.
7. Work with Computer Operations in the evaluation and generation of computer operating systems and allied control and utility programs.
8. Work with Computer Operations, Communications, Information Systems Development, using departments, and vendors, in selecting and installing equipment to assure adequate and reliable teleprocessing.
9. Forecast computer file storage requirements; allocate file space for company data bases.
10. Compile forecasts of computer test time requirements; arrange for computer test time and direct test job queues.
11. Issue standards for guidance in designing computerized systems and enhancements to systems.
12. Maintain Job Control Language (JCL) procedure library for company informations systems.

Figure 1 *(Continued)*

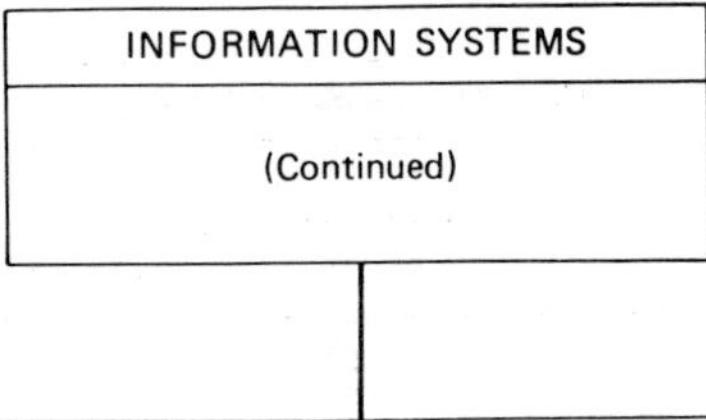

COMPUTER SUPPORT SERVICES

1. Investigate availability and capability of equipment peripheral to the computer that will support and provide the most economic and reliable service to the company's computer–based information systems.
2. Provide to appropriate company organizations pertinent, detailed, and timely information on peripheral equipment that will complement the company's computer–based information systems.
3. Investigate and provide pertinent and timely information on computer software services to appropriate units of information systems.
4. Respond to external requests for information concerning the company's information systems development.
5. Arrange to issue periodic reports on progress made in implementing the company's information systems projects.
6. Complete special studies and assignments as assigned to support the company's information systems.
7. Coordinate and arrange departmental training programs.

Figure 1 *(Continued)*

horizon to one to two years, while at the same time developing a long-term plan covering five to ten years for the general guidance of the development staff effort. The principal reason for reducing the horizon of the short-term plan is that numerous new project requirements developed during the three-year cycle, and fitting these new requirements into the ongoing development process caused delays in the original projects, as well as dismay on the part of the users affected.

Work on the long-range plan is now being pursued aggressively, although several initial efforts had been set aside earlier because of the lack of agreement on the objectives for such a long-range plan.

INFORMATION SYSTEMS PLANNING RESPONSIBILITIES

Both long-range and short-range planning are the responsibility of a planning analyst in the development section of the Information Systems Department.

The preparation of the short-range plan, formerly a periodic effort (every three years), is now to be an annual activity. It encompasses the preparation of preliminary studies for projects reflecting the current needs of the company. In preparing these studies, the planning analyst coordinates the work of several other analysts, assigned to the task temporarily for periods of up to three weeks and working with representatives from user organizations. In this team approach, the analysts are responsible for general design proposals and for estimates of the costs of development. The users supply the general requirements and the estimated benefits. The resulting studies form a basis on which senior management decides priorities for development.

INFORMATION SYSTEMS PLANNING PROCESS

Perhaps the most convenient way to discuss the present approach to the long-range planning process is to start by discussing the present high-level "Control Plan for Information Systems Projects" (see Table 2). This plan spells out the ground rules for preparing the short-range plan. Although the plan is self-explanatory for the most part, each of the steps in Table 2 is supplemented by comments to tie that step to other long-range planning considerations within the company. (Several other steps to the control plan, not appearing in Table 2, do not relate directly to short-range planning, but instead to the review steps that must be undertaken during project development.)

Table 2 Control Plan for Information Systems Projects

Control Plan Step	Comments
1. Each year the Information Systems Department will publish a list of projects that have been authorized or that have been requested but not yet authorized. Scheduled dates for beginning or completing the authorized projects will be shown.	It is the planning analyst's responsibility to maintain an updated list of projects basing the projected start and end dates, where appropriate, on current manpower availability forecasts.
2. All officers, department heads, and division managers will be asked, in connection with the published list, what new projects should be added, whether any projects already authorized should be discontinued, and for suggestions on priorities for undertaking or completing old or proposed new projects.	At this point, the Information Systems manager or planning analyst will start receiving calls from various staff people asking questions and generally asking for help in preparing responses.
3. The Information Systems Department will review these proposals for new projects and priorities to ascertain how they interrelate with other information requirements. The department will identify additional projects it believes are in the best interests of building integrated systems. Recommended changes, based on Information Systems Department studies, will be reviewed with the officers functionally concerned.	The planning analyst reviews all new requests submitted to determine if requests submitted appear to have any economic benefits. Recognizing the wide range of requests submitted by corporate officers, the Information Systems Department also prepares its own recommendations for projects to ensure that a logical sequencing of projects will emerge, leading to an integrated system. The sequencing within project development is in most cases flexible, but depending on the sequence selected, it can result in a greater or lesser degree of redo or redesign work. Proposals for new projects are not limited to system development but may also include new software requirements necessary to support new system needs. Typical of the latter type of proposal is one to study the current state of the art in distributed processing. A review of user requests at this point also serves to sort out those that have only marginal benefits.

Table 2 *(continued)*

Control Plan Step	Comments
4. New projects identified in steps 2 and 3, together with suggested changes in priorities, will be described in general terms and circulated to all officers for their recommendations and comments.	The planning analyst pulls all the descriptive material together and prepares another report to company officers.
5. The Information Systems Department will review with the officers functionally concerned these additional recommendations and comments to assess the practicability and desirability of including the proposed changes.	Here, and also at step 3, discussions are held on the most logical developments within a functional area (i.e., personnel, materials, equipment, customer information, etc). User representatives review the most desirable approach from their point of view; the Information Systems Department does the same. The goal is always to try to work out satisfactory development steps, to minimize redesign at a later stage of development.
6. Feasibility studies will then be made to explore generally the scope, sequence of implementation, content, costs, and benefits to provide management with better estimates on which to base decisions on priorities of project initiation.	At this point studies are made that provide a more solid base for determining, among other things, whether the proposed sequencing of development will result in the most logical and economical development of the functional area involved.
7. On completion of the feasibility studies, results will be furnished each officer for further review to determine his interest and to elicit his comments.	None.
8. If substantial changes in the results of the feasibility studies are required as a result of step 7, the feasibility study will be expanded to cover the additional requests stated.	To date, there have not been significant modifications to proposed projects. Generally the preceding discussions with functional representatives have ensured understanding and agreement on the path to be followed.
9. The results of the feasibility studies and the Information Systems Department recommendations for undertaking the proposed projects	Based on economic and other factors, projects supported by the officers are recommended to senior management for undertaking in a sequence that will

Table 2 Control Plan for Information Systems Projects *(continued)*

Control Plan Step	Comments
will be submitted for senior management decision on what projects are to be authorized and priority of work on the authorized projects.	give the greatest benefit first.

As brought out in the Comments portion of Table 2, considerable discussion throughout the process is aimed at ensuring that the projects, as defined, will fit together to form an integrated whole. This is done by reviewing existing documentation, created in 1968, which identifies all system interfaces. Well-informed persons are consulted to ensure that no loopholes or gaps exist. But in spite of this review process, some system interfaces are missed and some redesign work is necessary.

This experience with short-range planning has led to the development of improved objectives for long-range planning. These may be summarized as follows:

1. Provide analysis tools to facilitate the development of projects to ensure that there are smooth and complete data flows and that there is effective systems integration.
2. Provide suitable means of communicating long-range information systems goals to functional management and to the analysts in the Information Systems Department.

At the present time, there is no comprehensive plan showing what is planned for the next five to ten years; there are, however, plans or studies describing proposed developments in specific areas. Work on the long-range plan is being pursued as a continuing effort until all the necessary displays, analysis tools, and aids are current. When this has been accomplished, it is expected that the long-range plan will become a central part of the overall planning activity and will be updated annually.

AREAS FOR IMPROVEMENT

As mentioned earlier, the long-range planning process has evolved from a significant planning effort every three years to one that occurs annually. Also, in the development of new projects, because of the size of Pacific Gas and Electric and the trauma caused by the installation of relatively large systems, there is a tendency to undertake the installation of major projects in relatively small steps. These two factors have made it necessary to develop better tools for evaluating whether the projects, as proposed and developed, will correctly and effectively fit together. It is vitally important that all interfaces be provided for and that the data flows be smooth. These improved tools are taking many forms and may in themselves be termed long-range plans, for each must look into the future to predict what it might look like.

It is premature to state in detail what these tools will comprise, but the current work points to the following characteristics:

1. An information processing and flow diagram showing
   A. Significant information processing modules and their frequency of occurrence.
   B. Data flows—types of data and their volume.
   C. The sequence of processing through time (i.e., daily processes feeding weekly or monthly processes, and weekly processes feeding monthly processes).
2. A data precedence chart showing
   A. The stages through which data are summarized from the state of elemental identification, through transformations or combinations, to the most highly summarized state.
   B. The different functional areas through which data move within the corporation.

If tools such as these are developed, they will have a significant impact on the way in which the company approaches long-range planning for information systems.

14 ELDON G. NICHOLSON

Trans World Airlines, Inc.

Through mergers of various companies long forgotten, such as Western Air Express, Standard Airlines, Maddux, and Transcontinental Air Transport, came the original TWA, "Transcontinental & Western Air, Inc." Further growth and expansion of routes overseas justified another corporate name change. The initials TWA were retained, but they now stand for Trans World Airlines, Inc., a name in fact but also a description of the company's position in the ever-expanding airline industry.

The following information about TWA and the services we provide appeared in the *1973 Annual Report*.

Reflecting our commitment to the consumer to provide the best in transportation service, we adopted in 1973 as our principal advertising theme: "TWA is what travel should be." In support of this commitment, we introduced or expanded a number of customer service programs discussed below.

Automated Ticketing/Seat Selection

In 1973, with the introduction of automatic ticket imprinters in St. Louis, Chicago, and San Francisco, we made further progress toward automated passenger processing at the airport. These imprinters provide customers with both faster ticketing service and the highest degree of accuracy in computing fares. This system is currently being installed in Los Angeles, and an additional ten domestic airports will be equipped during 1974 to offer this new convenience.

1974 also will mark the introduction of automated passenger flight check-in, whereby passengers may check in, select a seat, and receive a boarding pass any time before departure, at a number of locations in the air terminal. With this fast and convenient one-stop check-in system, passengers only have to proceed to the gate and, without further processing, board their flight. Twelve domestic airports will have this capability by mid-1974.

Security Program

During 1973, TWA continued to provide one of the highest levels of security in the industry. By introducing an X-ray baggage inspection system, we effectively minimized passenger inconvenience attributable to time-consuming hand searches of carry-on baggage. This facilitated examination of items not easily opened for inspection (e.g., gift-wrapped packages) and reduced departure delays due to security inspections. X-ray equipment is installed at 17 airports in the United States, with expansion to other airports planned for 1974. Our units meet all radiological standards of both federal and state authorities.

Demand Scheduled Flights

On October 1, 1973, we introduced Demand Scheduled Flights, a new concept in leisure travel. This program offered a service between selected East Coast and West Coast cities for travelers willing to commit themselves in advance to a specific date and destination, with substantial savings on regular coach/economy fares. As a result, we could tailor capacity to meet demand, thereby improving fleet utilization.

Ambassador Programs

Ambassador Express, a service concept in short-distance air travel introduced in 1972, was expanded in 1973 through refurbishment of the airline's DC-9 fleet and extension of the service to 13 new domestic routes. The combination of X-ray security equipment and carry-on luggage compartments were the key promotional features of this service in 1973, and enhanced existing Ambassador Express convenience of gate-area ticketing, twin-seating in coach, and same-day "out-and-back" scheduling. In addition, we expanded our Ambassador Service by utilizing newly acquired L-1011 aircraft.

Favorable consumer response to these Ambassador programs has improved traffic levels during the past few years, and we are confident these trends will continue.

Getaway Programs

During 1973, we produced five major tour programs—Getaway Adventures: Europe, Orient, Fly/Drive, U.S.A., and Ski—which comprised a wide selection of prepackaged vacations to meet the demands of today's traveler. To complement these tour packages, we developed a program for the individual traveler, Europe on Your Own.

For the first time, each of our Getaway Adventures tours in the United States and Europe was covered by our unique Tour Warranty. Pursuant to this warranty, TWA guarantees that an appropriate refund will be made for any element of service not delivered to the passenger as advertised due to causes within the reasonable control of the tour operator and provided the passenger presents a claim within 60 days after completion of the tour.

As a reflection of consumer confidence, tour bookings increased approximately 6 percent over 1972 in spite of adverse market conditions during the fall of 1973.

The Little Black Book—containing discounts on gifts, tours, car rentals, and related travel services—was introduced to fulfill the airline's commitment to providing the best dollar value for the pleasure traveler. In addition, we continue to publish the most widely read travel books in the industry, *Getaway Guides,* of which there are over 2 million copies currently in circulation.

TWA's Getaway cardholders during 1973 topped the one-million mark, making our personal airline credit card the most widely circulated in the airline industry. 1973 Getaway credit card sales for airline, hotel, car rental, and other services exceeded $60 million and brought travel within the reach of numerous new consumers.

Cargo Activities

1973 saw inauguration of cargo jet service in the Pacific. System cargo commercial charter activities more than doubled over 1972, with a resulting revenue increase from $1.0 million in 1972 to $2.7 million in 1973. With the expansion of combination wide-body cargo capacity, a new level of containerized air freight service was developed offering a greater choice of frequencies, containers, pricing, and interline transfer capabilities. Despite the 45-day flight attendant strike, total cargo revenues improved slightly over 1972.

Aircraft Programs

During 1973, TWA took delivery of eight L-1011's and also canceled its options to purchase six Concorde SSTs. Aircraft on firm order include 19 L-1011's for delivery in 1974 and 1975, and 17 B-727-200's for delivery in the 1974–1976 period. The decision to purchase the B-727-200's was based on fuel efficiency and environmental considerations as well as the planned phase-out of the CV-880 fleet of 25 aircraft.

TWA's all-Jet Fleet

	Actual as of December 31		Additions/(Retirements)			Total
	1972	1973	1974	1975	1976	
Lockheed 1011	6	14	11	8	0	33
Boeing 747	19	19	0	0	0	19
Boeing 707 (passenger)	90	90	(1)	0	0	89
Boeing 707 (cargo)	13	13	0	0	0	13
Boeing 727	72	72	3	6	8	89
Convair 880	25	25	(25)	0	0	0
Douglas DC-9	19	19	0	0	0	19
Total	244	252	(12)	14	8	262

Energy Conservation

TWA has been energetic in introducing and following policies and procedures designed to conserve energy. Among the programs to save jet fuel are lower cruising speeds, reducing flap settings during takeoff and landing, deferring engine startup while in the gate-hold area, taxiing aircraft with one engine shut down, conducting flight training in simulators to maximum extent possible, and absorbing most traffic departure delays at the gate. These measures are estimated to save approximately 32 million gallons of jet fuel a year.

Other corporate conservation measures include a limitation on running of ground equipment engines unless in immediate use, proper maintenance of ground equipment to maximize performance, reductions in interior and exterior lighting and, where practical and controllable, reduction of heating levels in offices and other facilities. We also are urging all employees to cooperate with local, state, and national efforts to control personal energy consumption by reducing home electrical power and by utilizing car pools as well as public transportation.

Hilton International Operations

1973 marked the twenty-fifth anniversary of Hilton International and the eleventh consecutive year in which its earnings reached record new highs. Starting with a single hotel, the Caribe Hilton in Puerto Rico, consisting of 300 rooms at its opening in 1949 and now enlarged to over 700 rooms, Hilton International at the end of 1973 had 59 hotels in operation, 12 under construction, and many more in the planning and development stage.

The company's growth has been worldwide, spanning six continents, including Australia, in which two large hotels will be completed during 1974 in Sydney and Melbourne. Of the hotels presently in operation, 17 are in the Western Hemisphere, 20 in Europe, 14 in Africa and the Middle East, and 8 in the Far East. As a consequence, the market served by the company has grown from one largely oriented to the United States to one in which a large majority of its clientele come from other countries. In fact, operations in a new country inevitably bring a substantial increase in the number of guests from that country to the company's other hotels.

We are highly diversified not only geographically but in the types of hotels operated, ranging from city convention hotels to airport hotels to resort hotels. The company is, of course, engaged in major food and beverage operations, catering both to guests of its hotels and to residents in the localities in which it operates. It operates a total of 351 lounges and restaurants in its various hotels. In addition, it has successfully operated for many years the 20 bars and restaurants in the Place Ville Marie complex in Montreal, Canada. During the past year, it was awarded by the Port of New York Authority a contract to operate all public food and beverage facilities at the New York World Trade Center which, it is estimated, will have a population of 50,000 workers and 80,000 visitors a day.

Canteen Corporation Operations

When Canteen Corporation joined the TWA family on August 10, 1973, we looked forward with great anticipation to our new association with TWA. We too are a service-oriented company, greatly aware of people and the importance of the public to the success of our operations.

Founded in Chicago in 1929, Canteen now conducts operations in 44 states, the District of Columbia, and Canada, through approximately 150 local distribution centers, 435 manual food locations, and some 66 independent franchised distributors. Distributors also operate in Milan, Italy, and Stockholm, Sweden.

Canteen continues its leadership of the food service industry through industrial, commercial, and institutional feeding as well as vending operations, and fine restaurants. The food service industry is today one of the highest growth service industries. In 1970, one out of every four meals in the United States was eaten away from home. Conservative estimates predict that this will double to one out of every two by 1980, and Canteen is well positioned to take advantage of this growth because we strive to feed people wherever they are.

We distribute food and beverage products, cigarettes, and other items through our own vending machines, and we operate dining rooms, cafeterias, and other manual food services for businesses, institutions, and the public. Canteen also leases vending machines and furnishes services to independent franchised distributors who provide vending and manual food services.

We are particularly proud to have been chosen to operate the restaurants at some of the nation's most distinguished showcases, including the Kennedy Center for the Performing Arts in Washington, D.C., and the Metropolitan Opera at Lincoln Center in New York. We also own and operate the distinguished Jacques Restaurant Group in Chicago.

. . .

Consumer Products Division

In 1973, TWA established a Consumer Products Division as part of its overall diversification program. The function of this division is to develop new profitable business ventures in consumer products. In addition to directing the expansion of the flight catalogue and on-board sales program, a new company, Chateau Wine and Cheese Shops, Inc., was formed to take advantage of the rapidly expanding public interest in wine and cheese. The first of a planned chain of similar stores was opened in Costa Mesa, California, in March 1974, and additional openings are scheduled throughout the remainder of the year.

Special Services

In 1973, TWA continued successfully to provide assistance to Ethiopian Airlines, Saudi Arabian Airlines (Saudia), and Trans Mediterranean Airways. In addition, TWA Services, Inc., completed the first season of its ten-year concession contract with the U.S. Department of the Interior for the operation of visitors' support services and facilities at Bryce, Grand Canyon (North Rim), and Zion

National Parks. TWA Services undertook interim operation on November 21, 1973, of Scotty's Castle, Death Valley National Monument, in California. Trans Arabian Technical Services Company, Ltd., in which TWA Services held a 51 percent interest during 1973, has been awarded a five-year contract by the Arabian American Oil Company to provide vocational training to Aramco's Saudi Arabian employees. TWA continued to operate visitors' services for NASA at Kennedy Space Center in 1973, welcoming over 1.3 million visitors. At the end of 1973, TWA established a new wholly owned subsidiary, TWA Associates, Inc., to engage in selected technical projects, including acquisition of TWA Services' interest in Trans Arabian Technical Services. Effective January 1, 1974, TWA Services became a wholly owned subsidiary of Canteen Corporation, and it will in the future concentrate its efforts on tourist-related service activities.[1]

THE INDUSTRY

TWA airline system operating revenues in 1973 were $1379.5 million, 2.7 percent below 1972, reflecting the impact of the November–December strike of flight attendants. Operating revenues have grown from $575 million in 1964 to $1098 million in 1969 to the present level of $1380 million.

Despite this attractive growth rate, substantial problems face TWA and the industry. For example, an article in *Fortune* in January 1974 contained the following comments.

> The carriers suffer the double disadvantage of heavy regulation combined with intense competition. They are told not only where they can fly but how much they can charge. Still, the government has lacked power to regulate how many flights go, or how often. So within each market the airlines generally compete for traffic as fiercely—and sometimes as recklessly—as barnstorming dare-devils once competed for trophies.
>
> In their zeal to woo customers with fancy new planes, the airlines have piled up mountainous debts, like public-utility companies. But their profits have proved to be erratic and often elusive. Annual variations of plus or minus 30 to 50 percent are common. Only once since 1955 have the trunk airlines as a group attained what the CAB considers a fair return on their total investment. That was in 1965, when the CAB guideline was 10.5 percent and the industry earned 11.2 percent. Three years ago, the CAB raised its profit guideline to 12 percent, but since 1967 the industry's return has never exceeded 6 percent.
>
> . . .
>
> Considering the range of difficulties that have long plagued the industry, it is remarkable that any airline makes money. Passenger and freight traffic fluc-

[1]*Trans World Airlines Annual Report, 1973.*

tuates widely, according to the hour of the day, day of the week, the season, and the cyclical swings in the nation's economy. Yet airlines must maintain enough facilities to serve their markets during peak periods. If a company must slash costs, it takes two or three months to realize the savings. The only available sources of big reductions are layoffs or major reshuffling of airplane maintenance arrangements. But layoffs require both advance notice and severance pay, which postpone the financial impact, and maintenance changes involve complex, time-consuming planning. Thus, some 70 to 85 percent of an airline's total costs are not subject to quick change, and the operation is characterized by a high degree of leverage. Small variations in traffic or in the nonfixed costs make a big difference to the bottom line. TWA calculates that if just one more paying passenger had boarded each of its 1973 flights, earnings per share would have risen by nearly $1.25.

. . .

The airlines' shaky financial situation raises serious questions about whether they can raise enough money to meet the demands of tomorrow's markets. Wide swings in earnings have made it difficult for many carriers to sell more common stock or convertible debentures. And now sources of long-term loans are drying up as well. Insurance companies, which have invested some $4 billion in the air carriers since the 1950s, have reduced their future commitments to the industry from $414 million in 1969 to a recent level of about $25 million. William A. McCurdy, vice president of Equitable Life, asks: "Why should I give away my policyholders' money when we can get the same return from another industry without so many problems?"

As their load of debt has risen, the airlines in the last decade have turned to leasing as a way of obtaining new planes. But lenders generally require airlines to confine leases to a third of their fleet, and all the five largest carriers —American, United, TWA, Eastern, and Pan Am—are approaching that limit. So they have had to turn to bank loans at towering 10 percent interest rates to finance the purchase of new planes.

To escape the borrowing trap, airlines would have to raise more equity capital. But first an upturn in profits is needed. Unfortunately, the prospect, reinforced by the energy crisis, is that rising costs will continue to squeeze earnings. Total expenses have been growing at a recent annual rate exceeding 8 percent. Even before the dramatic jump in fuel prices, the carriers had been hit with a rapid rise in the costs of such items as labor, food, landing fees, spare parts, insurance, and even plastic swizzle sticks for stirring cocktails.[2]

SYSTEMS AND DATA SERVICES BACKGROUND

The challenges of data processing coupled with those of the airline itself produce a tempo that occasionally ranges between a quiver and a quake,

[2]Michael B. Rothfeld, "New Downdrafts for the Airlines." Reprinted from *Fortune*, Vol. 89, No. 1, January 1974, by special permission. Copyright © Time Inc., 1973.

or perhaps mild excitement to exacerbation. Our industry is such that data processing departments have been forced into leading-edge technology, both in terms of systems software and applications development.

Systems and Data Services is a major corporate department within TWA. Our mission is to be responsible for the operation, allocation, and control of data processing resources for all other major corporate departments and to ensure that these resources are used in a manner that is consistent with total corporate objectives.

History of EDP at TWA

The data processing group originated within the Controller's Department, utilizing punched card technology to support the major accounting functions. Expansion into inventory control resulted in acquisition of our first computer, an IBM 650, in the late 1950s. Data processing technology has since been applied to reservations and various functions within flight operations, technical services, marketing research and planning, financial analysis, scheduling, and other areas of finance.

During the late 1950s and into the mid-1960s our data processing resources were departmentalized (decentralized). Data systems design groups established in each major division were given primary responsibility to perform feasibility studies and develop design specifications for new applications. In the case of the Technical Services, Flight Operations, and Reservations divisions, computer hardware was dedicated to specific applications; at various times the groups also exercised organizational control over the computer resources.

In the late 1960s the Systems and Data Services Department was established and assigned complete responsibility for all computer resources. The departmental data system design groups were gradually phased out, resulting in total consolidation of all data processing resources in a single major corporate department. Other major departments retain coordinators for data processing activities, and Technical Services has a small staff that provides policy directives and user specifications for new applications development.

Current Role of Systems and Data Services

The Systems and Data Services (S & DS) Department is a major corporate department responsible for the allocation, control, and expenditure of all data processing resources within TWA. Organizational reporting relationships are given in Figure 1. As the department name implies, we

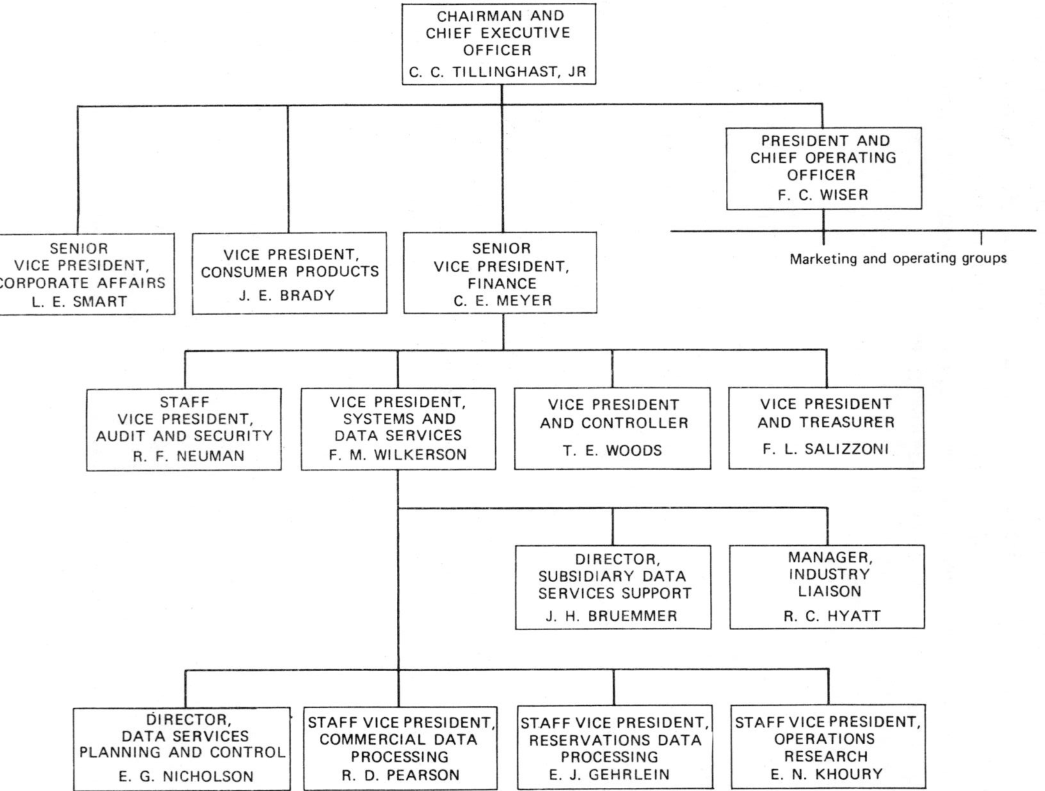

Figure 1 Organization chart, TWA Systems and Data Services.

develop system solutions to specific problems, either manual or automated, depending on the problem under study.

The user departments work with S & DS in a partnership to identify the areas within TWA that offer potential future benefits from the application of data processing and management science techniques. The jointly agreed-on potential projects are compiled in a management summary, including gross estimates of S & DS developmental manpower requirements and an order-of-magnitude estimate of the benefits. At this level of investigation, it is stressed that these are gross estimates that will undoubtedly change as the study develops; however they are useful in setting priorities for planning.

The three major subdepartments within S & DS, are Commercial Data Processing, Reservations Data Processing, and Operations Research.

Commercial Data Processing

The Commercial Data Processing Department services every major department within the airline, dealing with all levels of management with respect to service, problems, and creation of new systems. This responsibility requires, in the short term, the providing of consistent and adequate services, as well as quick responses to problems as they arise. Long-range planning, as it relates to new systems development and changes to the existing computer environment, necessitates a total awareness by Commercial Data Processing in the areas of industry trends, new computer technology, long-range department goals, and the overall goals and objectives of the corporation. This information must be determined and analyzed far in advance of the implementation of major systems, to develop the best overall man-computer environment at the least cost.

Additionally, since this department is so vitally involved with the day-to-day activities of all the major departments within the airline, it is imperative that we have the ability to react quickly to such problems as changes to union contracts, new and changed CAB reporting requirements, payroll rules that vary according to federal, state, county, and local government regulations, maintenance requirements as they relate to new aircraft systems, and new competitive billing and service enhancements for major credit billings. We must also be able to meet the mandatory closing requirements each month for presentation of these data to the CAB and other federal agencies.

The largest portion of Commercial Data Services' processor power is utilized in a series of financial systems, including passenger revenue accounting, cargo accounting, credit card systems, budgeting, and payroll. In addition, the Commercial computers support marketing reporting, airframe overhaul scheduling, maintenance base inventories, and a wide variety of operational and control systems.

The system also handles such on-line applications as on-board aircraft monitors, flight planning, data collection for flight crew payroll, and labor cost reporting from terminals throughout TWA's maintenance base.

The hardware system utilizes an IBM 370/168 as the support processor to an IBM 370/165-II using ASP (Attached Support Processor) Version 3. ASP supports the coupling of the two central processors and provides the scheduling and supervising of the operations for the entire complex.

Reservations Data Processing

The TWA reservation system was developed to control and manage the airline's seat inventory and to sell these seats as a product. Tremendous growth in air passenger traffic in recent years has made it necessary to install a system that not only sells seats but has the capability to perform all the other tasks needed to serve the public effectively. We now provide a comprehensive reservation service with our Passenger Name Record (PNR) system, which is constantly being enhanced to incorporate improvements.

In the PNR system, each customer's booking is contained in a passenger record filed on disk storage in the computer system. The record contains such data as the passenger's name, the flight segments sold, the class of service, the number of seats, a telephone contact, ticketing information, and the name of the person who booked the reservation. If the passenger subsequently wishes to change his itinerary, the PNR record can be recalled instantly for display on the agent's terminal, and adjustments can be made. In addition, the system can automatically generate messages to sell or request seats on other airlines, process waitlists as seats become available on a flight, display schedule and availability information, calculate fares, maintain current flight information, and handle other travel-related information about rental cars, hotels, and ground transportation, and so on.

TWA is required to handle an immense number of telephone calls each day. The traveling public has adopted the telephone as the simplest and quickest means to make reservations, and the telephone has become the major revenue pipeline for the airline. At busy periods we average 150,000 telephone calls daily. It is the responsibility of Reservations to serve the needs of these customers efficiently and effectively. Thus it is extremely important to have a computerized reservation system that can respond promptly, completing a reservation in a minimum amount of time. An agent using the programmed airline reservations system (PARS) can complete an average booking in less than four minutes; this involves an average of 10 separate entries, each requiring a response from the computer before the transaction can be continued. The current TWA PARS is based on an IBM 360/75, with a model 360/65 as a backup computer, and a third 360/65 for test purposes.

From the beginning, the reservation system has been undergoing improvement to supply better service and additional capabilities to aid TWA in its marketing position and operational activities. Some examples of its growth are extensive applications for fare quotation and ticketing, seat assignment and boarding control, weight and balance computation, and the flight operations-oriented COMMAND system. These and other functions will continue to increase the load on PARS, along with the growth expected in the basic reservation function. These new features will play a major part in our maintaining efficiency and keeping our competitive position in the marketplace.

To withstand the expected growth in messages entering the system, and to handle surges caused by perturbations in the economic and/or fuel situations or by industry strikes, it is important to upgrade the current hardware to a more powerful system, to be operational by the summer of 1975. The most viable alternative is the IBM 370/168 computer coupled to a twin backup computer, and this approach is being presented to TWA's management for approval.

A number of new applications have been approved for implementation.

1. *Fare quote/automated ticketing.* This system is being implemented on our real-time computer complex and will initially be capable of automatically pricing and producing 90 percent of all tickets at our 10 largest Automatic Ticket Offices (ATOs) and 80 percent of all Telemail tickets produced by the area reservations sales offices.
2. *Credit authorization.* This system has been operational for merely a year for TWA's Getaway Cards and will be expanded this fall to include blacklist capability for UATP, American Express, Diners Club, BankAmericard, and Carte Blanche. This system will give TWA agents the capability of checking all blacklists by computer (using the agent sets planned for automated stations) and by the reservations office for nonautomated cities.
3. *Seat assignment system.* An experimental seat assignment system will be installed and, in conjunction with automated ticketing and credit authorization, will provide "one-stop service to our customers." This means that a customer can proceed to a single point in the airport, purchase his ticket, have the flight coupon lifted, and receive a seat

assignment for any flight departing that station during the next four to six hours.

4. *COMMAND.* This system will automate the current dispatch and operational planning functions, providing automated flight watch displays and an automated information system that will give current status on flight departures and arrivals.
5. *Schedule planning system.* This system is being developed by Operations Research and consists of a number of modules that will accelerate the entire schedule planning process and will include aircraft routing, gate planning, line maintenance planning, profitability determination, ground equipment planning, and crew penalty planning.

Operations Research

The Operations Research Department function is dedicated to maximizing TWA's revenue and minimizing its costs, to increasing its efficiency, and to improving the productivity of labor and the quality of service. For example, Operations Research has been involved in almost every area of the corporation, with programs ranging from those involving the overall corporation to those for specific departments or operating units. Operations Research has developed and implemented programs in a number of areas. Almost every department within TWA is seeking Operations Research support in solving complex problems. In short, Operations Research, by its contributions, by the acceptance it has received throughout the organization, and by the increased demand for its services, has been recognized as an important function within TWA.

Cost Trends Within Systems and Data Services

An idea of what we have achieved since 1970 can be obtained from our total expenditures and number of personnel (Figures 2 and 3). Our expenditures in 1970 were in excess of $25 million, and staffing comprised approximately 586 people (programmers, analysts, operators, and administrative personnel). In 1971 a decision was made to consolidate all data processing activities, which previously had been geographically dispersed, into a single facility. That consolidation and reconfiguration of equipment produced a substantial reduction in expenditures during 1971, as well as a small reduction in employees. The $8 million or 30 percent drop is somewhat misleading though, since equipment acquisitions tended to distort our expenditures and make them unusually low. However 1972 was more representative of our true yearly expenditures, and they were still $7 million below 1970, or approximately 26 percent. As we have added new applications and ac-

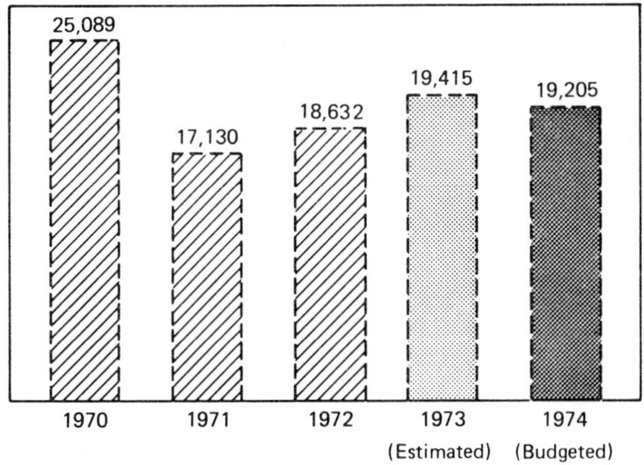

Figure 2 Systems and Data Services total expenses (millions of dollars).

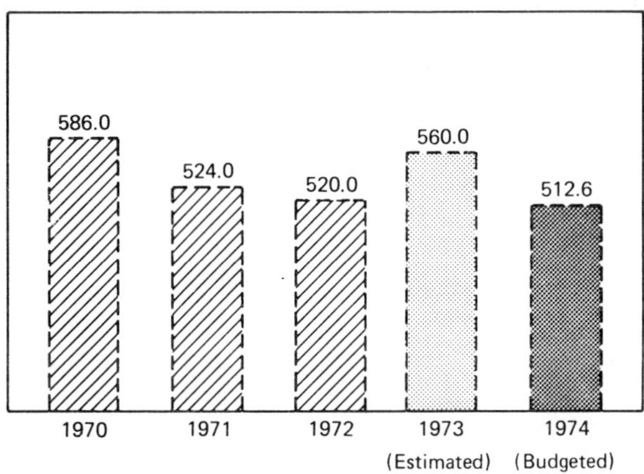

Figure 3 Systems and Data Services number of personnel (as a December 31).

quired additional equipment, our total costs have gradually increased, although unit costs have gone down. In 1974 we initially projected an expenditure of over $21 million, but that figure was subsequently reduced to $19.2 million.

SYSTEMS AND DATA SERVICES LONG-RANGE PLANNING HISTORY

The first comprehensive long-range plan for TWA data services was published in late 1968 by the planning department for Systems and Data Services, located in corporate headquarters in New York City. At this time the S & DS was decentralized; corporate headquarters was in New York City and data centers were in Rockleigh, New Jersey, and in Kansas City, Missouri. The plan, which covered the period 1968–1975, can be summarized as follows:

1. Identification of overall system requirements.
2. Identification of S & DS program goals in each of the major TWA operating areas.
3. Determination of the operating systems and equipment requirements necessary to accomplish these goals.
4. Identification of the dollar requirements needed to meet these goals.

The report was intended to be the first in a continuing planning effort to revise and improve the program as the Systems and Data Services Department developed closer communications with user groups.

The plan was the result of a substantial effort by a large staff of the Systems and Data Services planning group. It was developed through a rigorous study process involving a large part of TWA management. In addition, we had professional help from the Midwest Research Institute.

Presentation of the plan was in two massive volumes, bound separately. Part I summarized and highlighted the general objectives of the plan and the approach taken to achieve these objectives. A time frame for development and implementation was provided, with a summary of resources and decision points necessary to accomplish the plan within the specified time frame.

Part II included details, supporting techniques, and features of the plan, including equipment, facilities, software requirements, data communications and remote terminal descriptions and projections, and necessary administrative and technical controls.

The plan was presented to the corporate Planning Committee, which in turn solicited input from all major user departments.

In retrospect, the plan appeared to be extremely overwhelming. Since the two volumes contained such a great amount of data, the plan probably was not read by anyone who did not have a direct interest in a particular part of it. In addition, the cost projections to meet these program goals and develop the necessary internal systems during the period 1968–1975 were estimated to be about $300 million. From a corporate point of view, this was certainly unreasonable. Also, the user departments did not submit any savings data as related to any program goal; thus no return on investment was calculated, and no financial and economic savings were estimated for the company. An exhibit from that plan (Table 1) depicts program goals and their priority ranking.

Table 1 Program Goals Priority Ranking

Rank	Program Area	Man-Years to Complete	Estimated Completion Date	Data Processing Center
1	Passenger Reservation System	54	12/69	Rockleigh
1	Market Information	45	6/73	Kansas City
2	Hotel Reservations	5	6/69	Rockleigh
2	Fare Construction	5	6/70	Rockleigh
2	Passenger Services	95	6/71	Rockleigh
2	System Schedule Development	21	6/71	Rockleigh
2	Flight Operations Planning	18	6/71	Rockleigh
2	In-Flight Control	10	6/72	Rockleigh
2	Flight Schedule Performance Analysis	10	6/71	Rockleigh
3	Engineering Configuration and Process Planning	15	6/71	Kansas City
3	Maintenance and Overhaul Production Planning, Scheduling, and Control	75	12/75	Kansas City
3	Aircraft and Equipment Performance Analysis	55+	12/75	Kansas City
3	Maintenance and Overhaul Performance Analysis	10	6/74	Kansas City
3	Personnel Management	40	6/73	Kansas City

In addition to the pitfalls already listed, some of the comments that were fed back from corporate officers included the following:

1. A project that falls within the general area of maintaining TWA's competitive position is not automatically more valuable than another project. The project itself might not be justifiable, and this is an indication that all projects need to be evaluated in terms of corporate objectives.
2. The proposed criteria in the plan did not lend themselves to identification with the many functional objectives generated by the departments as they try to do their jobs better. Also, as the plan related to individual programs, there was no good justification or operational goals given to relate a particular program with identifiable corporate needs.
3. The validity of the status of current systems presented in the long-range plan was doubtful. Some of the programs listed were questioned as to whether they were really operational; and if not, they could not be considered to be available for use with the proposed data base system.
4. It was not certain whether a universal discipline for data management systems had been agreed on; this seemed to be an essential step before work could begin.
5. There were some comments that we should not be irrevocably committed to centralized data control, and some serious questions were raised that suggested a need to examine the practicality of moving toward decentralization before going ahead in the area of centralized data control.
6. The vice president, controller, had serious reservations about adopting a plan as expensive as the one proposed without some attempt to address ourselves to the economics involved and to seek out an independent opinion.

In late 1969 Part I of the Systems and Data Services long-range plan was revised and forwarded to the Planning Committee of TWA. This was the second edition of the plan, which was originally created with the help of all TWA user departments in an attempt to ensure that company needs were identified. Members of the corporate Planning Committee and major department heads were again asked to review the Data Services plan as an aid in making policy decisions concerning Systems and Data Services.

As a result of that review, several major points were discussed and some decisions were reached. Concern was expressed about the large data processing expenditures and the need to examine alternative ways to reduce costs. On the other hand, it was noted that the expense projections were gross estimates and did not reflect the cost savings that were to be gained by the use of EDP. Finally, the corporate Planning Committee suggested the possibility of joint development efforts with other air carriers.

Some of the conclusions and decisions reached were as follows:

1. A review was to be made of the needs for the various projects relating to the operating departments and priorities established for them.
2. Data Services was to explore the possibility of working with another airline in joint development of data processing programs.
3. A listing was to be developed of possible proposed programs that could be contracted outside.
4. Data Services was asked to develop a rough estimate of the savings attributable to new programs.
5. Data Services was requested to separate the costs associated with ongoing operations from those attributable to new programs.

In early 1970 a memo to the secretary of the corporate Planning Committee expressed the feeling that the Data Services program was so intertwined with the long-range plans of the operating divisions that one could not be addressed without looking at the other; as a consequence, efforts to develop them had to go hand in hand. In response to that general directive, the secretary of the corporate Planning Committee instructed Systems and Data Services to include in their long-range plan three additional items:

1. A projection of costs for the planning period, broken down by programs currently active, programs under active development, and proposed projects.
2. The status of individual projects regarding degree of completion and remaining costs.
3. The identification of the programs and projects that would be affected if projected expenses were to be reduced by 10, 25, 33, and 50 percent.

At about this time a major reorganization took place in the Systems and Data Services Department, and a new vice president was appointed. He expressed serious doubts regarding the method of projecting long-range user needs. During the same period, the development of the new PNR system was in serious jeopardy because of problems with the hardware manufacturer. Therefore any consideration of a review of the long-range plan was postponed. In the course of the succeeding months, the Systems and Data Services planning group was eliminated and the whole department was reorganized.

Two major decisions then were made: (1) all data processing centers and administrative personnel were to be centralized, and (2) the effort to implement a new reservation system with the current equipment vendor was to be abandoned and a new equipment vendor selected. When this was accomplished, a new reservations system was to be installed.

From this point on, the planning activities took place within the individual data centers of Systems and Data Services. At the same time, however, substantial efforts were also under way with a large task force composed of members from each data center to coordinate the centralization of all the data centers.

ALLOCATION OF SYSTEMS AND DATA SERVICES RESOURCES AND ASSIGNMENT OF PRIORITIES

The Systems and Data Services Department operates principally with a fixed budget. We present our case for additional resources during the annual budget preparation period; and, in extreme cases during the calendar year, we take advantage of the quarterly operating plan (QOP) adjustment vehicle. Since 1970 we have kept those increases to a minimum; therefore the allocation of our limited resources to the many requests for services becomes a matter of extreme importance to our users and to TWA's continued profitability and operating performance. In many cases our operating performance has direct bearing on the level of customer services we are able to provide.

The vast majority of our resources, 70 to 80 percent, are committed to the ongoing operation and maintenance of existing applications (e.g., the reservations system, payroll, accounts payable, numerous financial applications, and the flight planning system, MOC-I). Approximately 40 percent of our systems and programming staff is reserved for the development of new applications. This is consistent with other large data processing departments throughout the United States and has normally provided us with adequate resources to undertake the most profitable and urgent projects during the past two to three years.

All projects are divided into three major categories: maintenance, small projects, and large or major projects. Maintenance applies to the required changes in existing applications resulting from policy, procedure, or regulatory changes. Minor projects are defined as those costing less than $10,000 to accomplish in the case of new projects or less than $25,000 in the case of major revisions to existing applications. Major projects are those which cost more than $10,000, or $25,000 in the case of major revisions to existing applications.

The allocation of resources and the assignment of priorities to minor data services requests (DSRs) is normally accomplished by Systems and Data Services personnel in consultation with user representatives. Allocation and priorities for major projects are determined by the DSR Review Committee consisting of the president, the senior vice president for finance, and the vice president for systems and data services. This committee meets as required and reviews the recommendations of the requesting departments and Systems and Data Services in making final determinations. In 1973 and 1974 the only projects receiving approval were those that were cost justifiable (i.e., those providing a return on investment of 12 percent or more). Other forms of justification have not generally been adequate to secure approval since 1970 because of the extreme cost pressures existing in our industry and specifically within TWA.

One significant factor in assigning priorities and timing of projects is related to the availability of personnel who have experience and knowledge in a given application area. For example, maintenance and small DSR work on existing applications normally take from 2 to 16 man-weeks. Because of the short duration of these projects, it is seldom economical to spend 2 to 6 weeks familiarizing a new individual with the application so that he is qualified to make the necessary modifications. For projects of longer duration (major DSRs) we have the flexibility of assigning people who are skilled in data processing but lack specific experience in a given area. We include in the overall schedule adequate time for orientation and training; this has some impact on the total cost of the project, but normally it is not significant.

Aside from the allocation of manpower and existing computer resources, many projects require additional equipment or communications lines. When additional assets or resources are required, TWA's normal expenditure authority approvals are also required. In the case of capital expenditures, this includes preparation of appropriation request summaries (form A-559) and board approval if the amounts exceed $500,000. Normally the capital appropriation brief, with comments from the Finance Department, is prepared prior to the DSR Review Committee meeting. This requirement applies only to projects in the "implementation phase," since capital expenditures are not authorized during feasibility and design phases.

DSR Life Cycle

The evaluation and development of information systems within TWA assumes increasing importance as the size and number of the applications to be developed increases. This increase is further amplified by a corresponding increase in sophistication. Thus the cost of implementing both computer-based and manual information systems becomes formidable. Recognizing that these conditions exist, a systematic method for evaluating and developing systems proposals has been developed within Systems and Data Services, to provide greater assurance that the resources expended in implementing such systems will not be wasted. To accomplish this goal, a set of procedures has been established, giving a logical step-by-step progression, from initial awareness of a problem or of an area of potential profitability, to approval from top management for the allocation of resources to implement a specific plan of action.

Data Services Request Form. The vehicle for controlling requests and channeling formal communications between Data Services and the user, the DSR, furnishes the user departments a means for formally requesting Systems and Data Services to commit resources to a given effort. The DSR form is divided into three phases:

1. Feasibility phase.
2. Detail design phase.
3. Implementation phase.

By establishing these distinct phases within the evaluation and development of an information system study, Systems and Data Services and their respective users can control the progression of actual events at logical breaking points. Thus management decisions can be made to determine whether sufficient justification exists for initiating the current phase or for going forward with the subsequent phase of any project under investigation.

DSR Review Committee. User departments work with S & DS to identify areas within TWA that offer potential future benefits from the application of data processing and management science techniques. DSRs are evaluated on one or more of the following criteria:

- Direct cost reductions.
- Cost avoidance.
- Incremental revenue generation.

- Satisfying a critical operational need.
- Improved information for planning and control.

The final establishment of priorities is controlled by the DSR Review Committee, which deals with major expenditures only ($10,000 and above). Because top management serve on this committee, it is an effective and responsive means of assuring that new major application developments are consistent with corporate goals and objectives. Of course the committee also functions as a forum for users to contend for resources on an equal basis. The final decision rests primarily on the presentation of the request for implementation, and these estimates are used during postaudit of the project. The postaudit study is conducted by a team with representatives from the user group and S & DS and is chaired by the Audit Department.

Basis for System Justification

Mandatory Requirements. Many new systems, and major modifications to existing systems, result from legislative action or regulatory body decisions. The most costly examples in recent years were the CAB's ER 586 and ER 597, which presented major problems for the Commercial Data Processing Department. Major changes in corporate organization or philosophy can also result in mandatory modifications, particularly in our accounting and budgetary systems. In such instances we try to minimize the cost of data processing efforts, but economic justification is not required.

Economics. The most desirable basis for justifying new developmental work during the past three years has been economics. It assumes reduction of direct costs, and such reductions are reflected in budgetary commitments on the part of the affected departments once the system is implemented. Examples are as follows:

- A reduction of fixed or variable costs at any location in the domestic or international system.
- Elimination of older, and more costly, systems.
- Cash flow improvements resulting from earlier receipt and/or deposit of funds.
- Reduction in direct non-personnel-related expenses such as damage or delay claims, fuel costs, operating supplies, and maintenance expense.
- Reduced capital investment in facilities and equipment.

Critical Operational Needs. Normally our critical operational needs involve the daily operation of the airline and the achievement of reasonable control over aircraft, crews, and spare parts. The most recent example was approval of the Flight Times System, which introduces a single source for all out-off/on-in times as a basis for tracking usage on aircraft rotatable parts, flight crew pay and utilization, and eventually flight information for reservations and station personnel. This system was not economically justifiable in its own right, but it is an essential building block for many other systems that will be economically defensible.

Meeting Competition in the Market. We are constantly seeking out marketing innovations that will improve our market share. Occasionally, we find ourselves in the position of responding to improved services offered by our competitors. When it is determined that those services will effect our own revenues, we try to meet or slightly exceed those offerings. For instance, our current plan to install agent sets in travel agent and commercial account offices is designed to improve TWA's revenues and profits. However, if every major carrier offered such sets to travel agents, this marketing advantage might be lost and the project would no longer be justified on the basis of economics, though it would remain justified in terms of maintaining our market share.

Incremental Revenues. Incremental revenues are the most difficult of all to quantify, both before implementation and during postaudit evaluation. This factor is most often used in conjunction with meeting market competition. Unless the competitive pressures are extremely strong, projects covered under the first three categories receive the great majority of all Systems and Data Services resources. This tendency was especially noticeable during the period 1971–1972.

SYSTEMS AND DATA SERVICES PLANNING PROCESS

One of the key elements in aiding the planning activities of Systems and Data Services has been the development and refinement of the data services requests and the DSR Review Committee. Through these procedures, the projects included in the five-year plans are documented with costs and savings, from a Data Services point of view and from that of the user department. The projects either have been approved by the DSR Review Committee or are pending approval by the committee. Of course sufficient flexibility is maintained within the yearly operating budgets to permit us to respond to the changing data processing needs of the major departments, especially in the dynamic environment of the airline industry.

Five-year Plan—Commercial Data Processing

The first five-year plan for the Commercial Data Processing Department, which involves a $10 million budget covering some 500 EDP-related employees, was developed in 1972. Since a planning staff within Commercial Data Processing did not exist, the plan was developed through intensive planning sessions involving the directors of Computer Systems Development, Systems and Programming, and Computer Operations. In addition, the managers of Computer Operations, Computer Equipment Planning, and Software Development participated in the discussions. However direct involvement by the users must be rated as low in terms of direct participation. On the other hand, through the DSR Review Committee and from input furnished by the ongoing contacts with the directors of Systems and Programming, user information was fed into the plan. The eight-page long-range planning document included the following points:

1. A set of assumptions and considerations. The assumptions included not only the major hardware changes planned over the five-year period but major applications to be implemented. The elimination of certain computer equipment and facilities was considered, as was the possibility of third-party leasing.
2. A communications network and hardware configuration map.
3. Communication applications and types of lines.
4. General equipment conversion plans.
5. System core maps.
6. A list of the applications involved and the various software applications to be implemented over the next five years.
7. Critical time scheduling. A list of application projects and software support projects, by name, including the "go/no-go date" and the "end date" of the projects.
8. A list of the hardware critical time schedule, giving the events, the on-order date for the particular piece of equipment, the on-site delivery date, the software installation date, and the operational date.
9. An exhibit of applications manloading, hardware project manloading, and software project manloading, listing the event and the minimum and maximum staffing in terms of the man-months involved in each year of the plan. On that exhibit the dollars involved

per man-month were summarized, and an estimated cost was developed for the manpower plan.

10. The list of applications and/or actions for potential deferment, listing the applications, the total man-months that were committed during the current year, and the man-months of potential deferral.
11. A manpower reconciliation chart, listing within the major areas the original variance, potential man-months deferred, and the net man-months available or short.
12. A consolidated schedule, listing all activities by name on a general time frame.

Five-year Plan—Reservations Data Processing

The planning effort within the Reservations Data Processing Group of the Systems and Data Services Department involves their entire management staff. By its very nature a reservations system has central site hardware requirements that are essentially static within a four- to five-year period. However there is a constant process, through system life studies, to review the performance of the reservations system and to project its ultimate capacity, and therefore its need for replacement. The first five-year plan for Reservations Data Processing commenced in late 1970, when it was decided to abandon the computer equipment of one manufacturer and install a new vendor's hardware and software.

In late 1973 intensive planning efforts again commenced with a review of the current reservations system. A proposal to upgrade the PARS system is in the process of final preparation and review by the board of directors.

This long-range planning document is in the form of a proposal to upgrade the system, and it has three major sections:

1. Text of the proposal.
2. The appropriation request summary and various working papers.
3. A set of some 25 exhibits.

The text of the proposal includes a general background on the introduction of a computer reservations system and the justification for the upgrading, outlining the present system capacity, historical patterns of growth, recent growth patterns, and a growth forecast. It also gives the details of the request, summarizing the capital expenditures that will be required. Finally, there is an economic analysis and a number of alternatives to the plan. These include doing nothing, altering the current hardware configuration, and upgrading to another computer.

The appropriation request summary and the working papers included in this long-range plan are the TWA documents that summarize the proposal, the change in operating expenditures, the cost details and cash expenditure timing, the disposal of the existing equipment, the economic justification analysis, the depreciation schedules, and the net cash flow and payback. In addition, there is a return on investment calculation.

The exhibits contained in the third section, which appear as the result of the planning effort, include the following:

- Equipment listing for the proposed upgrading.
- Expenses and support of the upgrading.
- Cash flows and supporting expenses.
- A four-year projection of expense levels.
- Various exhibits relating to the financial and economic analysis.
- Projected message rates against the projected maximum capacity of the current system.
- An exhibit showing projected contributions to profit for each of the applications within the reservation system.
- Forecasts furnished by the user departments.
- Comparison of major computer system plans and alternatives.
- Comparison of the TWA reservation system with other air carriers.
- A number of exhibits relating to statistical barometers for message rates per boarding, telephone calls, passenger name records, and so on.

Other Planning Efforts

The five-year plans developed by Commercial Data Processing and Reservations Data Processing have been extremely well received by user departments and corporate management alike. Another document has been published from time to time, however, to discuss "potential future data processing applications." To develop this document, meetings are held with representatives from all major departments to discuss the areas in which the application of data processing techniques would be of potential value. We establish a list of applications organized by user departments and in order of magnitude (i.e., projects involving one to four years of man-effort, five to nine, and ten or more, respectively). In addition, for each application, potential benefits are categorized in the following areas:

1. Cost reduction or cost avoidance.
2. Critical operational needs, that is, tangible needs for which no savings can be identified at this time.

3. Those required to maintain our competitive position.
4. Those that will produce incremental revenue.

The first general document was published in 1972 and another in 1974.

A DIRECTION FOR THE FUTURE

In January 1974 a planning and control staff was organized within Systems and Data Services reporting directly to the vice president. It was organized to serve the line departments of Commercial Data Processing, Reservations Data Processing, and Operations Research. Its responsibilities include training, data center security, the operation of the project management office, computer equipment planning, computer equipment sales, and long-range planning. The approach to long-range planning for Systems and Data Services by the planning and control group has not yet been established, but it will surely complement the five-year planning efforts by Commercial Data Processing and Reservations Data Processing, using the data gathered and published in the document describing potential future data processing applications.

15 MORRIS F. COLLEN, M.D.

The Permanente Medical Group and Kaiser Foundation Research Institute

The Kaiser-Permanente Medical care program has been providing comprehensive medical and hospital services to its members since 1942. Its fundamental principles of operation include group practice, prepayment for services, integrated medical facilities, voluntary enrollment, and comprehensive benefits including preventive health care. The three major parts of the program are the health plan, the hospital organization, and the medical group.

The Kaiser Foundation Health Plan, a nonprofit, tax-exempt corporation, arranges for medical and hospital services for voluntary subscribers and their dependents on a prepayment basis. The membership of the Kaiser Foundation Health Plan in the San Francisco Bay Area currently numbers more than one million.

The Kaiser Foundation Hospitals, a nonprofit and charitable tax-exempt corporation, currently owns and operates in the San Francisco Bay Area 11 community hospital facilities containing 2100 beds. These hospitals have a representative range from 318 to fewer than 100 beds, and they function with a rather traditional professional organizational structure. Kaiser Hospitals sponsors activities in charity, education, and research, and supports a variety of educational programs including approved internships and residencies, a nursing school, and continuing staff training.

The Permanente Medical Group is a partnership comprised of more than 1000 full-time physicians representing all major and most minor specialties. The group is organized as a hospital-based, specialty group practice, and is functionally structured along the traditional lines of teaching hospital departments. Many Permanente physicians have appointments to the teaching staffs of the Stanford Medical School in Palo Alto and the University of California's Medical Schools in San Francisco and Davis, and its School of Public Health in Berkeley. By contract with the Kaiser Foundation Health Plan, the Medical Group furnishes the professional care to plan members in the 11 Kaiser hospitals and 15 outpatient medical office facilities in northern California.

Permanente Services, Inc., a subsidiary of the Kaiser-Permanente medical care entities, performs centralized business and administrative services and has its own computer center with information, statistical, systems, and procedures divisions.

Kaiser Foundation Research Institute, a division of Kaiser Foundation Hospitals, conducts and supports medical research. Medical Methods Research is a department of the Kaiser Foundation Research Institute and the Permanente Medical Group which investigates improved methods of providing medical care and conducts health services research.

HISTORICAL EVOLUTION OF COMPUTER SYSTEMS

Kaiser-Permanente in northern California does not have a medical information system master plan, nor a formal long-range plan for computer systems. Year-to-year planning and budgeting activities have been based on management's decisions relative to its objectives, priorities, and available funding, year to year. Two computer centers, one for administrative and business functions and one for medical functions, evolved separately over the past 10 years to permit each to achieve its individual potential, even though it was recognized that this would generate some increased operational costs. Year-to-year planning and operating activities of the administrative and business computer system within Permanente Services, Inc., are determined by management in accordance with its short-term objectives and priorities. In the past Medical Methods Research departmental planning and operating activities have been considerably influenced on a year-to-year basis by the Department of Health, Education, and Welfare through several grants and contracts directed toward implementing a prototype medical information system, as described below. It is anticipated that these two computer centers eventually will be integrated.

In 1953 a separate division of administrative and business functions was organized in Permanente Services to provide centralized regional support for all northern California Kaiser-Permanente medical centers, including computer services.

In 1964 the first medical computer application was initiated when data processing was added to the automatic multiphasic health checkup. An experimental pilot medical information system based on a large centralized computer system was initiated in 1965 under grants from HEW. The following description of the Kaiser-Permanente medical information system refers to the operational status of the pilot system in 1973. The project had as its primary objective the development and demonstration of a pilot medical information system for collection, storage, retrieval, and communication of a broad spectrum of inpatient and outpatient medical data.

Among the specific objectives of the pilot system were the following:

1. Development of a central integrated data base with a computer medical record for each Kaiser Health Plan patient.
2. Development of medical application subsystems, including outpatient, multiphasic testing, clinical laboratory, pharmacy, essential medical data retrieval, hospital information, admissions, and census systems.
3. Development of statistical retrieval programs to scan the data base for health services and epidemiological research.
4. Achievement of high system reliability, development of procedures to protect the privacy and confidentiality of medical data, and minimization of error production by strict quality control.

The central processor used for this medical information system in 1973 was an IBM 370/155 with 2 million bytes of memory. Its subsystems are briefly described as follows.

Data Base

The data base was perhaps the most successfully completed and innovative component of this pilot medical information system. The design of the system was based on the premise that the patient computer medical record would be the basic source of medical information. Each computer record contained a continuous integrated record of all patient visits to certain services at Kaiser facilities. Procedures were implemented for creation of backup tapes, which could be used to restore the data base in case of system failure, and to ensure the security and accuracy of the data. At its peak the data base contained 800 million bytes of data on direct access disk storage, consisting of identification and administrative and medical data on 1.5 million patients, including 3.3 million visits.

Outpatient Subsystem

Medical data were collected from every outpatient clinic in one facility and from medical clinics for multiphasic follow-up visits in five other facilities. Each patient visit was recorded on a data entry "encounter" form with checklists of diagnoses, physical examination findings, drug names, and procedures appropriate to the particular clinic. Clinic receptionists filled in patient identification and visit data, while medical data were entered by the physicians themselves. Originally data entry forms were optically read, but because of high error rates, later forms were entered via interactive typewriters. More than 1.8 million outpatient clinic visits had been recorded by September 1973.

Multiphasic Testing Subsystem

A third system provided on-line data collection for multiphasic testing clinics at three Kaiser facilities. The first application implemented, the multiphasic testing system, incorporated many kinds of medical data, including history, laboratory tests, blood pressure, spirometry, anthropometry, ECG and X-ray diagnoses. Input documents were either mark-sensed or punched cards. Summary reports of test results were generated from data base records either on-line or in batch mode. A set of requests to consider further medical action, called "advice rules," were printed on the report whenever certain patterns of abnormalities were present. About 370,000 multiphasic visits were stored.

Clinical Laboratory Subsystem

The clinical laboratory system was designed to collect laboratory test data and to generate appropriate interim and final reports, while updating the computer medical record in real time, to give medical personnel immediate access, via remote terminals, to test results. All chemistry, hematology, and urine data were collected. Data entry was performed by laboratory technicians using punched cards, typewriter keyboard, and matrix keyboard. Routine reports were printed on a line printer for both inpatients and outpatients, and more than 200,000 laboratory visits were stored.

Pharmacy Subsystem

All prescriptions filled at one Kaiser outpatient pharmacy were recorded by the medical information system. Pharmacists entered the data in real time into the patients' computer medical records, using interactive typewriter terminals in the pharmacy. The computer responded by printing medication labels. For prescription refills, the entire label could be generated merely by entering the old prescription number and refill code. About 1.5 million prescriptions were stored.

Essential Medical Data Retrieval Subsystem

Retrieval programs were designed to permit the user either to retrieve specific types of data or general data summaries from a patient's record, or to "browse" through the record. Inquiries could be made in real time by authorized users on interactive typewriters or visual display terminals. A terminal was installed in the hospital emergency room, where this system was felt to have its greatest potential value. It was used routinely for several months by physicians and nurses until the project funding was discontinued.

Hospital Information Subsystem

The hospital information system was designed to permit direct communication between hospital personnel and the patient's computer medical record. The original hardware configuration consisted of 24 Sanders visual display terminals controlled by two small processors linked to the central computer. Each terminal consisted of a display screen, keyboard, light pen, badge reader, and low-speed printer. Terminals were deployed throughout patient care areas of the hospital—in nursing stations, intensive care unit, nursery, emergency room, and admitting department. The system was to be used by medical personnel to enter data on hospital inpatients, including diagnoses, physical findings, drug orders and administrations, and test orders, and to retrieve any medical data stored in a patient's computer record. Our experience with this prototype system soon revealed that full-scale hospital operation was not a realistic goal because of frequent hardware and software failures, and inadequate system size. System operation was then restricted to a single pilot service (pediatrics), where many of the above-mentioned functions were successfully tested. The system never became operational because the funding grant was terminated.

Hospital Admission/Census Subsystem

The final system provided daily testing of admissions, discharges, and bed census by patient department and by physician. The bed location of any hospital patient could be quickly determined by means of the visual display terminals at any of the nursing station locations.

This was the status of the pilot medical information system in the fall of 1973, when government research support funds were terminated. Consequently our computer medical applications are now in transition, and we are exploring the capabilities of a system of distributed smaller dedicated computers for each subsystem module; the multiphasic subsystem is already operational on a dedicated minicomputer.

ADMINISTRATIVE DATA PROCESSING

The present administrative computer facilitity, which is under the direction of Douglass Williams, supports a library of more than 600 programs operating in a multiprogrammed batch processing mode and an on-line communications network of CRT terminals and printers that connect the medical centers and the administrative offices to a membership data base.

Administrative data processing at Kaiser-Permanente is significantly influenced by the unique organizational structure of the prepaid group practice form of medical care delivery. Rather than the usual emphasis on hospital patient billing, we have developed a membership system that maintains a basic administrative record for each individual, linked to a family account. A majority of family accounts are associated with employee benefit programs, and hence the billing of prepaid dues is affected through a cycle billing system to approximately 2500 employer groups. A separate billing subsystem for individual family accounts completes the process through which some 80 percent of the total revenues (prepayment) are collected. The remaining 20 percent of revenue comes from a separate Medicare reimbursement system coupled with a patient billing system for the collection of private patient charges, third-party payments, and supplemental charges.

The membership system also provides the basis for a comprehensive series of statistical reporting systems covering both inpatient and outpatient services. Reports comparing the distribution of the membership population to medical center service areas with corresponding utilization statistics supply both current information and trend patterns for future planning of facilities and staffing.

Administrative programs in the areas of payroll, personnel, general accounting, property accounting, pharmacy operations, purchasing, and stores inventory are also specific to the Kaiser-Permanente form of organization. Studies have been initiated for patient registration and outpatient appointment scheduling.

DEFINITION OF A MEDICAL INFORMATION SYSTEM

The implementation of computer systems for nonadministrative areas of hospital care has been very difficult. The reasons for this are the extraordinary requirements for long-term commitments of substantial amounts of money and for large numbers of scarce medical and engineering technical specialists, in addition to severe requirements for size, speed, and reliability of hardware, and the difficulties in defining and standardizing the medical care process. It is therefore essential to determine carefully the definitions, objectives, and requirements for such a technologically complex system.

A medical information system as herein defined is one that utilizes electronic data processing and communications equipment to provide on-line processing with real-time responses for patient data within the medical centers, including both inpatient and outpatient services. A hospital computer system (HCS) is a subcomponent of a medical information system that handles the inpatient medical data. A hospital administrative information system is a subcomponent of a medical information system that handles the administrative and business functions, such as admission procedures, bed census, menu planning, and patient schedules for departmental services (e.g., medicine, surgery, etc.).

REQUIREMENTS FOR A MEDICAL INFORMATION SYSTEM

Analyses of our medical program show that 80 percent of physician services are for outpatient care and only 20 percent for hospital care. In the outpatient department, the Medical Service comprises about one-fourth of our total physician staff. The single most frequent request for a Medical Service appointment is for a health checkup as part of our preventive health services program. Accordingly, although we believe that the impact of computer technology on our medical practice in both outpatient and hospital care will increase over time, the greatest immediate effect of computers in our program is in the use of automated multiphasic health testing programs for periodic health examinations to ambulatory patients.

The general functional requirements of a medical information system are as follows:

1. Individual patient data must be communicated on a 24-hour basis between the professionals providing medical care (doctors, nurses, technicians, etc.) and the patient's computer medical record (medical data base).
2. A medical data base that can provide information for clinical services, as well as for research, must be established. The data base is an essential internal component of a medical information system in that it is the repository for all patient-related data. Its data base management system must supply a continuing integrated record of each patient's encounters with the health care delivery system, and it must control the flow of patient data between the data base, the various subsystems, and input/output terminals at various locations.
3. Scheduling files must be set up and information for scheduling of patients, personnel, and medical care services must be communicated.
4. A data base for administrative and business functions must be established.
5. Data necessary for projection of health care needs and planning for medical and hospital services must be supplied.
6. Other general medical information system requirements, such as reliability, security of patient records, and data quality control, must be included. A medical information system must perform with close to 100 percent reliability. The same regulations governing release, privacy, and confidentiality of patient records in the hospital chart room must apply to computer medical records. Quality control refers to the set of procedures that ensure the accuracy and validity of data collected, stored, and retrieved by the medical information system.

The functional requirements of some of the medical information system subsystem components are as follows:

1. *Hospital administrative subsystem.* Handle administrative and business functions, including admissions, bed census, menu planning, patient scheduling, and billing.

2. *Outpatient subsystem.* Handle medical data from outpatient facilities, including diagnoses, physical examinations, histories, and drugs prescribed.
3. *Hospital computer subsystem.* Handle inpatient medical data, including orders for laboratory, X-ray, and ECG tests, drug orders, diagnoses, and so on, through input/output terminals at nurses' stations.
4. *Clinical laboratory subsystem.* Handle clinical laboratory data through a terminal system in the laboratory. Print test reports, work lists, tube labels, and similar material. Bacteriology and blood bank data may be subcomponents of the laboratory system.
5. *Pharmacy subsystem.* Relay drug orders to the pharmacist for inpatients and print prescription labels for drugs dispensed for outpatients. Provide inventory control, drug interaction data, and patient drug sensitivity data.
6. *Multiphasic testing subsystem.* Collect data from automated multiphasic health testing facility (laboratory results, ECG, X-ray, history, etc.).

PLANNING AND IMPLEMENTING A MEDICAL INFORMATION SYSTEM

Time Planning Requirements

The planning schedule for a medical information system must fit into the planning schedules for the medical organization as a whole. For example, a five-year schedule for the completion of a medical information system should not be projected at a hospital that uses only one-, two-, or three-year budgets—it will be very difficult to convince the board of such an institution to embark on a five-year program. Instead, the medical information system project can be divided into smaller modules, such as the clinical laboratory or the admission and bed census, which can be completed and whose cost can be justified on a one- or two-year basis.

The hospital computer system and the integrated medical data base are the costliest items and the most difficult to justify at current hardware and software prices. Even if their implementation is not approved at the onset, the medical information system project leader must plan ahead conceptually for a data management integrating subsystem, to ensure the eventual capability to generate integrated medical reports.

In any case, implementing several medical information system modules will take several years; and it is prudent to establish attainable objectives with realistic timetables. Therefore a medical information system is always installed in a modular fashion. Hospital business functions, hospital admission and bed census, clinical laboratory, or pharmacy services are usually initiated first; then other subsystem components are added. This requirement for an integrated, modular implementation results in a long lead time in achieving an operationally integrated medical information system.

Each modular subsystem requires a time plan schedule that can accomplish the following:

1. Define precise objectives of the total medical information system.
2. Conduct functional analyses of information load (volume and characteristics) and personnel information handling (output specifications and time responses).
3. Determine subsystem configuration.
4. Establish subsystem priorities and set timetables for implementation of each module.
5. Select project team leaders and project teams.
6. Obtain management approval for the selected configuration and implementation schedule and secure funding commitments.
7. Order equipment.
8. Write and test programs.
9. Prepare the facility for equipment installation.
10. Install, test, and debug equipment and programs.
11. Prepare users' manuals and train personnel.
12. Conduct pilot operational test.
13. Implement manual backup mode.
14. Implement operational subsystem.
15. Evaluate performance.
16. Revise, modify, and improve, as needed.

Often there is great value in implementing a manual backup mode of operation before proceeding with the implementation of the automated operating mode. This practice tends to separate systems benefits from computer benefits and thoroughly trains users in the backup mode that must be used when the computer systems go down.

Time schedule plans should be furnished for both management and the project staff, in sufficient detail for each subsystem component to permit all to check progress against projected dates and to allow review of accomplishments at critical points, to be certain that the system will achieve its desired objectives and will meet schedule, functional, and performance specifications.

Personnel Requirements

Commercially packaged turnkey systems are available for some medical information system modules, such as automated multiphasic health testing, clinical laboratory, and ECG. Since such systems do not exist for an integrated, comprehensive medical information system, however, one must consider the current status of medical information system to be essentially developmental.

A medical center or hospital of sufficient size (300 beds or more) to justify spending the money for its own independent medical information system should develop an in-house staff rather than depend on outside consultants or contractors. Consultant-designed or off-the-shelf turnkey systems often can be installed faster (saving perhaps 6 to 12 months of implementation time), but they are less flexible and more costly to change than systems developed in house, since consultant contracts are more rigidly defined at first and later involve further expenditures for changes as new requirements develop. For the development and implementation of a medical information system, in addition to medical and data processing personnel, the following qualified specialists are necessary:

1. *Project chief.* A "biomedical-engineer" (person with training in medicine and in engineering, biophysics, or computers), to be responsible for the medical information system project. Because of the great difficulties associated with interdisciplinary communications between physicians and engineers, at least one key person must have adequate expertise in both technologies. It is advisable to support the project chief with several physicians who also have some background in the physical sciences and devote at least part of their time to the project.
2. *Systems supervisor.* Preferably a medical administrator familiar with the needs of the medical facility.
3. *Computer center manager.* A computer scientist having adequate training in the biological sciences to be able to communicate freely with physicians; this person is responsible for design and implementation of the hardware and software for the central computer and its satellite processors and terminals.
4. *Information engineer.* One qualified in information science to develop and monitor the procedures for quality control of the medical information processing.
5. *Medical system analysts.* Persons trained in analysis of medical subsystems to define the needs and problems and to recommend alternative

solutions. Good medical systems analysts are required if the medical information system is to be used for innovative approaches rather than for mechanization of existing manual methods. To facilitate interdisciplinary communication and maximize the user acceptance, it is necessary to orient physicians, nurses, laboratory technologists, and other personnel in methods in systems analysis.

6. *Applications programmers.* To write computer programs for the medical functions. It is desirable to train a pharmacist, a laboratory technician, a nurse, and a physician to function as a programmer for their particular applications function, to facilitate communications with other programmers not trained in the biological sciences.
7. *Systems programmers.* To design and implement the complex data base management and control system to store, retrieve, and process patient data for the various medical application modules. The systems programmers are also responsible for installing and monitoring the vendor's computer operating system software.
8. *Equipment engineers.* To work out problems of interfacing hardware from different manufacturers and maintaining the terminal equipment. Although the manufacturer usually maintains the major components of data processing equipment, it is necessary to have a resident maintenance engineer trained on the selected terminal equipment.
9. *Orientation and training personnel.* To develop standard operating procedure manuals and to orient and train medical information system users in system operation. Successful achievement of objectives requires use of middle management hospital personnel in planning and implementing medical information system subsystem components. To obtain user compliance for data input terminals as an operational part of a hospital service, be it a nursing station, laboratory, or pharmacy, the planning and the implementation of the terminal systems must evolve as an integral part of that hospital department's development. To develop data outputs with content and format of high utility to physicians requires careful planning. Regular meetings, followed by intradepartmental orientation sessions, must be held between the project chief and representatives of the departments affected.

DISCUSSION OF SPECIAL PROBLEMS AND OPPORTUNITIES

Studies have been conducted to determine the reasons for the failure of efforts to implement medical information systems (as herein defined) within the United States. The results point to the following as the primary causes:

1. *A suboptimal mix of medical and computer specialists was the most common cause of failure.* Usually the project staff consisted of (*a*) well-motivated medical personnel who had little experience with computers, and (*b*) computer and systems experts with little experience in medical applications. The extreme difficulty of communicating the highly technical and complex aspects of these two disciplines between the practitioners of each resulted in the computer staff usually underestimating the vast medical needs. Thus they planned a system adequate perhaps for the hospital administrative subsystem but totally insufficient for the medical functional requirements. By the time the medical staff became aware of the deficiencies of the system, the investment in time and money had already been so heavy that the project had to be either terminated or severely reorganized.
2. *Inadequate commitment of capital for long-term investment was the second most frequent cause of failure.* Most organizations grossly underestimated the large amounts of money and time involved in implementing a medical information system. Many projects were terminated after three to five years because several million dollars had been spent and the medical information system was still far from being completed.
3. *A suboptimized systems approach was frequent.* Several medical information system projects failed because they had successfully implemented one or more subsystem components for the administrative, laboratory, bed census, patient scheduling, or pharmacy units and now desired to integrate them all into a medical information system. At this point they discovered serious incompatibilities between the various modules which would require major reprogramming, at prohibitive cost, to achieve an integrated patient file. When this was learned, the projects usually continued the individual subsystem modules as independent computerized units.
4. *Inadequate management organization was an occasional cause of failure.* Several projects, initiated in smaller hospitals having inexperienced medical management, were terminated after one or two medical information system subsystem modules, usually administrative-business types of applications had been established.

Since there is as yet no completely successful total medical information system, we can only suggest factors that, if recognized, may help hospital management avoid failure for the reasons just listed and may perhaps ensure success in the future:

1. *Optimal mix of medical and computer personnel is essential.* All projects that appear to be moving steadily toward the successful implementation of a total medical information system have a large in-house staff of medical, systems, and computer personnel.
2. *Large investments of capital for long-term commitments are required.* The hospital management must recognize that the more complex the technology, the greater will be the lead time from outset of planning to completion of system. They must be prepared to commit several million dollars for three to five years before an operational system is likely to emerge.
3. *An integrated, modular systems approach is fundamental.* It is absolutely essential to plan from the beginning to integrate the various operational modules into the eventual total medical information system. The best way to ensure compatibility of all modules, with or without small dedicated computers, is to have one common central data base file containing an integrated, continuing computer record for all data from each individual patient for every hospitalization and for every outpatient visit. Small collections of patient data for subsystem components on dedicated minicomputers for the laboratory, blood bank, or hospital admissions and discharges, will never satisfy medical service requirements.

   A complete medical information system will require many years to implement; the technological system is so large and complex that a complete MIS cannot be implemented at any one point in time. Accordingly, a medical information system can be successfully installed only in a modular fashion. As noted previously, hospital business functions, hospital admission and bed census, clinical laboratory, or pharmacy services are usually initiated first; then other subsystem components are added. This requirement for modular implementation results in a long lead time in achieving an operationally complete medical information system.
4. *A fairly large hospital (or group of hospitals) is required,* with effective organization and management by technically sophisticated personnel who can make reliable decisions based on consideration of technological alternatives. Management needs to understand enough about computers to avoid accepting a faulty proposal and to be able to decide when a system is good enough—and then agree to it. Large technological systems tend to commit an organization to a relatively fixed goal for a number of years. Since a total medical information

system does not yet exist, great uncertainties result in large, unanticipated costs in time and manpower. Flexibility in committing capital and other resources is required to meet the inevitable deficiencies not foreseen in early planning of a large project conducted over a long period of time. Since an investment in medical information system is usually a very heavy one, good technical judgment is an imperative.

IV

Information Services Planning in the Public Sector

Part IV examines five governmental agencies or organizations, two at the federal level (the Board of Governors of the Federal Reserve System and the U.S. Army Materiel Command), two at the state level (the government of the State of California and the University of California), and one at the local level (the Los Angeles City Unified School District). Not surprisingly, the information systems activities in support of these organizations differ widely, ranging from the highly structured to the quite diffuse. For most of them, the ability to do long-range planning is closely linked to the planning patterns and organizational stability of the parent organization. As has been pointed out before, it is quite difficult to undertake planning for information services for organizations that do not themselves undertake long-range planning.

PUBLIC SECTOR MIS PLANNING

The Board of Governors of the Federal Reserve System is responsible for the regulation of the country's monetary system and financial institutions.

The board consists of seven members, each appointed for a 14-year term, who oversee the functioning of the system, supported by a staff of approximately 1500 people, working within 13 divisions or offices. The Division of Data Processing is one of these divisions, having an annual budget of some $7 million.

Long-range planning within the division was started in 1969, using a five-year planning horizon. For the first two years, however, most of the attention was directed at "relatively short-term technical studies of equipment [and software. The plans] were addressed primarily to achieving much-needed current improvements and to the expansions needed to meet the backlog of unsatisfied demands from the user community." Since 1971, however, the planning horizon and the scope of the investigation has expanded considerably.

Although the Data Processing Division has been active in its planning efforts, the other divisions have not. Even the board itself has only undertaken planning in a very general way. An Advanced Planning Committee was established at board level and, by means of a Delphi approach, developed several possible scenarios for the future. Unfortunately, none was specific enough to be of much use in connection with information systems planning, and "this lack of substantive long-range objectives and plans from the board, coupled with the continuing emphasis of the user community on highly demanding short-range needs and the dominant research character of the majority of user requirements, have all inhibited the progress of long-range planning by the division." In addition, the plans for specific projects are frequently developed "in an unrestrained fashion, . . . [lacking] the necessary tradeoff analyses, cost-return studies, and statements of objectives and goals." Recently, however, "the impact of a much more restricted budget has brought home the realization that longer term planning is a necessity."

The division planning staff consists of five senior professionals. The head of the staff reports directly to the division director. The staff has three interrelated areas of responsibility: long-range planning, including planning for user requirements and assessment of the emerging technology; division study projects; and activities of the Federal Reserve Board and/or System. User inputs to this planning effort are obtained through the Data Processing Advisory Group, composed of representatives from all the user divisions and from the Division of Data Processing.

The long-range plan itself is "a strategic, integrated, comprehensive management plan that attempts to project the environment, needs, opportunities, and constraints expected to prevail at the board over the next five years. . . . Basically, the long-range plan deals with the futurity of current decisions."

Planning begins in January of each year, and the long-range plan, completed by midyear, serves as input to the annual plan that is completed by year end. There are six major steps in the process; the first step—the development of division planning assumptions and guidelines—is "top down" and the balance are "bottom up." The resultant long-range plan contains several sections: an introduction, a management summary, a detailed description of specific plans and milestones within the five-year horizon, a description of the planning process itself, and a section containing planning documentation.

The U.S. Army Materiel Command is responsible for the research, development, procurement, distribution, and maintenance of all the army's weaponry and other equipment, spending more than $8 billion annually in pursuit of this mission. The MIS activity needed to support this effort is correspondingly quite extensive, employing more than 4000 data processing professionals and having an annual operating budget of $130 million (plus $10 million to $20 million for capital expenditures).

The planning process for the Command is guided by the Automatic Data Processing (ADP) and Management Information Systems Plan. This comprehensive planning document (reproduced in Appendix C) was prepared in 1971 and has been updated and extended every year since. The plan covers objectives that are of major interest to the Command as well as those primarily of interest to the MIS group. "Though these objectives cover a five-year planning horizon, they are broken into discrete increments for the immediate fiscal year to permit more careful monitoring of progress." The major goals of the Command are prepared by October of each year and are translated into specific ADP objectives by March of the following year. These updated objectives then serve as the basis for the new five-year plan that goes into effect on the following July.

The budget for MIS has a two-year horizon, with the first year being highly detailed and the second, more general. The planning for this budget proceeds in parallel with the planning for the five-year plan, however beginning slightly ahead of the latter to permit inclusion in the President's budget submission to Congress in January. This requirement of having the annual budget precede, rather than follow, the development of the long-range plan may appear to be somewhat inconsistent, but since the major program objectives "are forecast for five years and do not change that rapidly, it has not resulted in a significant problem."

The active participation of field organizations and user groups is sought in preparing both the budget and the five-year plan. Business data processing chiefs, engineering and scientific computing chiefs, and those concerned with computer networks meet at least twice a year to discuss ADP trends and other matters. Also, a Command-level systems advisory group evaluates overall systems development activity and resolves priority conflicts among users.

The Los Angeles City Unified School District is the second largest school district in the country, serving almost three-quarters of a million students and having an annual budget slightly in excess of $1 billion. The district is governed by a central board of education but is organized into 12 decentralized areas, each having its own area superintendent.

Until 1972 information services were similarly decentralized; there were services "for educational activities, for evaluation and measurement, and for general business operations [provided] by three separate data processing organizations which often duplicated functions. On July 1, 1972, the board of education consolidated all data processing organizations and the Management Information Division resulted from this merger."

At the time the division was created, the board also formed an "Information Systems Planning Section, which had overall responsibility for planning for the division, with particular emphasis on long-range planning." This section is headed by a supervisor who reports directly to the head of the Management Information Division. In addition, there are two senior data systems analysts, six data systems analysts, a data base administrator, and a research assistant. This group has responsibility for equipment evaluation and selection, for all matters relating to data bases, and for the development of new systems requirements, as well as for long-range planning.

All new major systems projects are reviewed by a Management Information Committee, consisting of a broad representation of top management of the district. "This committee, serving in an advisory capacity, approves or disapproves all new systems, the annual plan, and the long-range plan. In addition, steering committees have been established for important projects . . . [consisting of] division or department heads who are concerned with the particular project under development."

Within the district, "long-range planning is defined as anticipating the needs of the organization so that they can be dealt with in an orderly and meaningful way. . . . The long-range plan currently under development in the Management Information Division covers two to five years." The plan has a four-step development process. First, individual meetings are held with various levels of management throughout the district, to determine attitudes toward present systems and requirements for future systems.

Next, data obtained from these meetings are analyzed and translated into specific hardware and software requirements. These requirements are then compared to available resources within the division, both existing and anticipated, with necessary tradeoffs being made and priorities and schedules being set. Finally, the long-range plan is compiled and passed up the chain of command for review and approval. It is estimated that the preparation of the plan involves about 12 man-months of work each year.

The State of California, with its annual budget of $10.3 billion, would be the tenth largest government in the world if it were not a part of the United States. Its activities are spread out among some 80 state departments and agencies, many of them highly autonomous. These "individual organizations have the responsibility for the design, development, and implementation of their own information processing systems." Thus, with each agency developing its own systems, central control becomes quite difficult; and so, since 1966, the Legislature has required that "No expenditures for EDP activities . . . should be certified unless a feasibility study has been conducted . . . and an implementation plan has been developed by the department and approved by the Department of Finance." In other words, it was the intention of the legislature that all projects be reviewed and authorized by an independent body having no vested interest in the project in question.

Within the State of California, "there is no overall approach to planning; it is done on a project-by-project basis. This is due to the nature of state government. . . . This type of volatile environment virtually precludes strategic long-range EDP planning." Yet although overall planning is not achievable, individual project planning is, and a list of eight standards or objectives has been established against which all projects are measured. In addition, the state has a set of guidelines to be used in the preparation of the required feasibility study-implementation plan report. In this way long-range planning is approached through a review strategy.

The University of California is composed of nine campuses located throughout the state and having a combined enrollment in excess of 110,000 students. Although the university is headed by a president and governed by a board of regents, each campus has a chancellor who is given wide discretion in the discharge of his responsibilities. Each chancellor has authority over the computing activities on his campus, and there has been a considerable proliferation of equipment. A 1973 survey revealed that there were nearly 300 computers on the nine campuses, ranging from small minicomputers to huge IBM 360/91's. These computers provide instructional, research, and administrative services to their respective campuses, and this range of activities further complicates the problem of control and coordination.

In 1968, after two major studies had been conducted on computer utilization, a coordinator of computer activities was appointed and given responsibility for long-range planning for computing. This official, working with the directors of the various campus computing centers, prepared a document entitled "Long-range Planning—Instruction and Research Computing." Submitted to the university president in 1972, the plan was rejected "because it was not felt to be sufficiently definitive to warrent adoption." This is not surprising, since "the document was quite innocuous and recommended very few alternations of existing practices."

In 1973 the president appointed a "computer task force to recommend an approach to 'the organization and configuration of the university's computing resources (both equipment and personnel) to meet the university's needs.' " The final report contained four recommendations, chief among which were the establishment of a computer policy board and the appointment of an executive director of computing. Both of these actions have been taken, but "it remains to be seen whether this new approach will permit the university to come to grips with [the underlying problems]." As of this time, "no long-range plan has been adopted."

On the administrative side, some progress has been made. In 1971 the university-wide Information Systems Council was formed, charged with promoting intercampus cooperation on administrative information systems matters. In addition, the university-wide Hospital Systems Council and Library Automation Program were also established, with similar coordination responsibilities among their respective constituencies.

CONCLUDING REMARKS

As was pointed out earlier, the ability to do planning for information services is partially a function of the planning maturity of the parent organization. The following chapters demonstrate, however, that the public sector presents some unique problems in this regard. The MIS organizations represented here have responded to this challenge in a variety of ways, and it is informative to study their responses.

16 CHARLES L. HAMPTON

Board of Governors, Federal Reserve System

The Federal Reserve System was created by the Federal Reserve Act, which became law on December 23, 1913. The statute provides for a Board of Governors in Washington, the 12 Federal Reserve Banks and their 24 branches, the Federal Open Market Committee, the Federal Advisory Council, and the member banks.

The basic function of the System is to make possible a flow of credit and money that will foster orderly economic growth, production, and employment and will facilitate a stable dollar and a long-run balance in our international payments. Essential to the accomplishment of this objective is the function of collecting and interpreting information bearing on economic and credit conditions. The Division of Data Processing of the Board of Governors supports the implementation of this objective.

The Board of Governors comprises seven members, each appointed by the President and confirmed by the Senate for a term of 14 years. It is an independent agency of the federal government, reporting directly to Congress. Its funds are derived from semiannual assessments of the Federal Reserve Banks. The Federal Reserve System is supported by interest earned on discounts and open market operations by the System in carrying out its functions as an agency of the federal government. In 1973 it had a total operating cost of $495 million; but it returned $4.341

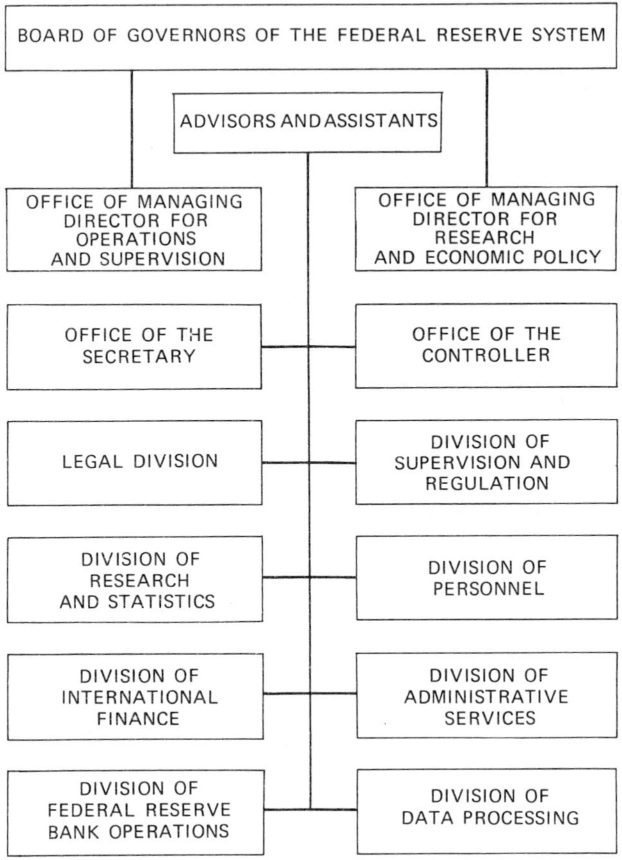

Figure 1 The Federal Reserve System.

billion to the U.S. Treasury after expenses and the legally required return to member banks (based on their participation in the capital stock of the local district banks).

The Division of Data Processing is one of 13 divisions and offices comprising the staff of the Board of Governors. The total staff of the board numbers 1486, of which Data Processing accounts for 258, or 17.4 percent. The major line divisions are Research and Statistics, International Finance, Supervision and Regulation, and Bank Operations. Figure 1 is an organization chart delineating the board's structure. Support of current economic policy and research emanating from the divisions of Research and Statistics and International Finance accounts for the majority of Data Processing's work load. This is followed by supervision and regulation of member banks and holding companies by the Division of Supervision and Regulation. The Division of Bank Operations, responsible for operational overview of the district banks and branch offices, constitutes the third main source of requirements; all other divisions and offices contribute to the rather minimal administrative data processing requirements of the board.

The Board of Governors of the Federal Reserve System established an Advanced Planning Committee in mid-1969. As its first objective, the committee decided to formulate its "best current judgment" of the likely social, political, and economic environment of the United States 20 years hence. This forecasting effort was designed to shed some light on the context in which current and future board decisions are to be made, and to help clarify the role of the System in a changing environment. Three stages of this work were conceived; Stage I has been completed and critiqued, and Stages II and III are still evolving. Significant benefits are accruing to this effort in areas of policy formulation and evaluation; but the accumulation of data forecasts that could contribute materially to operational issues, particularly those of Data Processing, have not followed. The heavy research emphasis of the user community is not conducive to longer range planning, and along with an annual budgetary commitment cycle for all programs of the board, this stance tends to contravene the longer term systems and applications planning by the Division of Data Processing for addressing the user requirements.

DIVISION OF DATA PROCESSING

Background

The Division of Data Processing, in its present context as a central service organization to the Board of Governors, was restructured in 1969 and has grown from a base of 169 employees to the present authorized level of 258 professional and support personnel. Budget growth has increased from $2.3 million in 1969 to $6.9 million in 1974. Major computer equipment has grown from an IBM 360/50 in 1969, through a 360/65 and a 370/165, to the IBM 370/168 installed in April 1974.

The most critical resource constraint has been the applications analyst-programmer staff. User community requirements have consistently exceeded the manpower available and, as such, is indicative of the need for both improvement in productivity and for extended planning horizons in user applications areas. Figure 2 charts the growth of de-

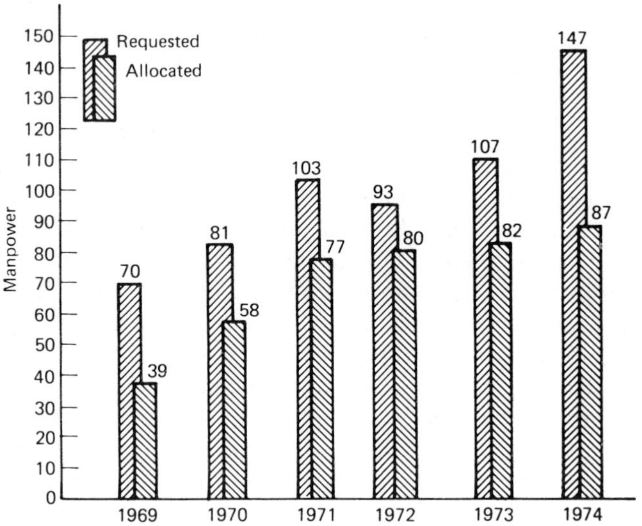

Figure 2 Growth in analyst-programmer requirements and staffing.

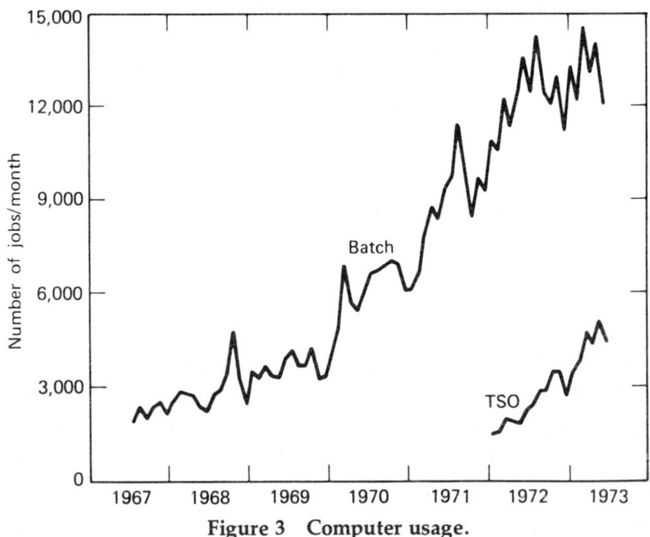

Figure 3 Computer usage.

mand and allocated resources for the past five years. It is noteworthy that after significant growth in both demand and available resources between 1969 and 1971, available resources have increased only very slowly since 1971, whereas demand has accelerated. In addition to the increased qualitative work by the board staff, this growth also reflects the carryover from one year to the next of project requirements not met;

and to these conditions must be added the growing base work load of maintenance and modifications to existing systems.

In the area of data center or computer operations, comparable growth has been experienced. However, significant cost-performance improvements have been realized and the cost per job has actually decreased. Growth in the number of jobs and cost-performance figures are given in Figure 3 and Table 1, respectively.

Table 1 Data Center Trend of Jobs and Costs

Year	Number of Jobs	Total Cost	Cost per Job
1970	73,239	$1,105,112	$15.09
1971	105,988	1,322,192	12.47
1972	155,540	1,487,715	9.56
1973	196,206	1,493,824	7.61
1974 (est.)	217,780	$1,365,036 [a]	$ 6.27

[a] Reduction due to purchased components and amortized cost.

As presently organizated the Division of Data Processing has three main line functions and two staff functions. The line functions are the Applications Branch, responsible for all systems design and programming of user requirements; the Data Systems Branch, providing supporting data base design, data administration, data editing and maintenance, and data production; and the Information Services Branch, containing computer operations, systems programming, and graphic communication services. The staff functions are planning and resource management (administration). The organization chart appears in Figure 4.

The present computer configuration is an IBM 370/168. In addition to a large number of CRT and hardcopy terminals, several interactive graphic terminals are in use, supporting program development, certain interactive applications, and on-line edit, update, and inquiry programs. Three card-reader, line-printer RJE (remote job entry) terminals serve remote office areas of the board. In addition to an IBM 2968 tape-to-tape communication link with each Federal Reserve Bank, a store and forward message-switching computer connects each bank and the board. Direct computer-to-computer communication is being implemented.

User application requirements extend over a wide range of end uses and complexity. However research projects constitute more than 60 percent of our development work and are most indicative of the type of development projects at the board. Research involves various forecasting and econometric models, as well as time series and statistical analyses of economic and financial data.

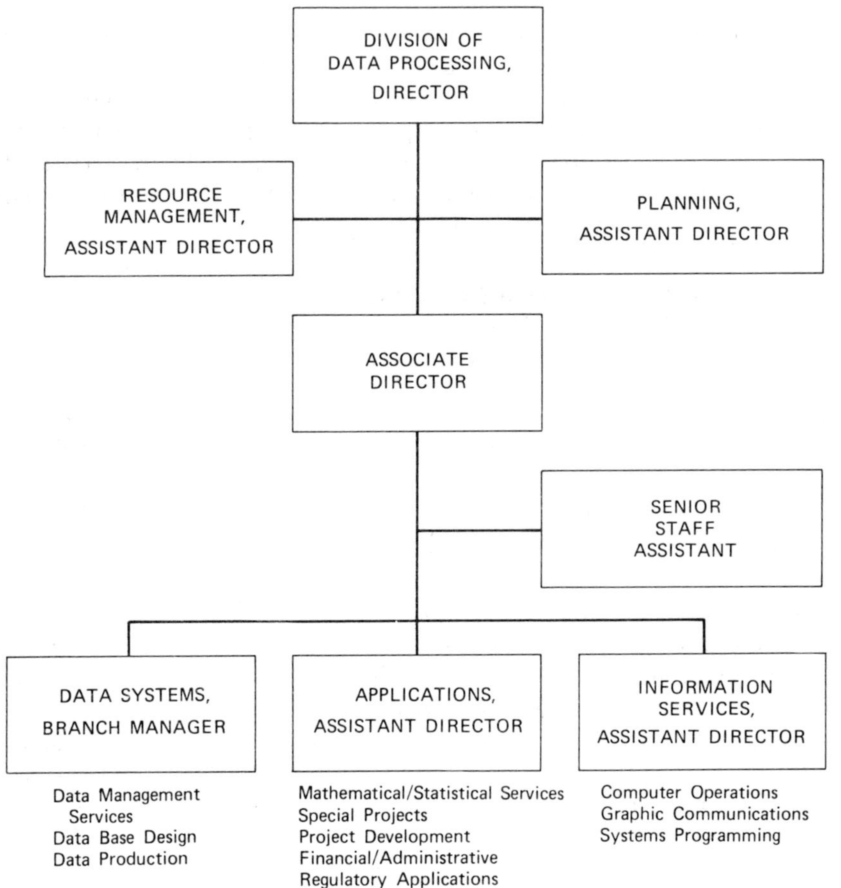

Figure 4 Organization chart, Division of Data Processing.

To effect greater coordination of communication, planning, and resource allocation, the board has established a user's group, the Data Processing Advisory Group, composed of representatives of each user division and Data Processing. This group is becoming increasingly active in considering issues of common interest, in developing longer range planning requirements, and in screening for the board the new application development and analyst-programmer resource allocation decisions that arise at budget time.

Division Objectives

The Data Processing Division conducts programs in direct support of the Board of Governors and makes certain services available to the Federal Reserve System. These objectives and functions are summarized in

Table 2. Board requirements for system design, programming, computing facilities, data communications, graphic design and automation, and data editing support are developed jointly by the division and users throughout the board.

Table 2 Objectives and Functions of the Division of Data Processing

Objectives

1. To respond to management-approved user requests for data processing services efficiently and in a timely manner.
2. To lead in the development and application of advanced data processing and information systems technology in support of the Federal Reserve System and the economic/financial community.
3. To plan, develop, implement, and maintain cost-effective information systems and data processing services that effectively meet user requirements. To provide information from established data files to all levels of the Federal Reserve Board and the Federal Reserve System.

Functions

1. Supports Federal Reserve Board objectives and goals through the planning, development, operation, and maintenance of information processing systems.
2. Provides information systems, mathematical analysis, computer programming, equipment operation, data reports, graphic communications, advanced systems planning, management systems, and communications network services to the Federal Reserve Board, Federal Reserve System banks, and approved external organizations.
3. Develops, collects, and processes statistical information on banking developments and on the condition of Federal Reserve Banks and member banks.
4. Maintains a constant awareness of technological advances in all areas of responsibility; adapts, modifies or develops, and applies such advanced techniques in the performance of assigned responsibilities.
5. Participates in and supports board committee activities as required.

The board's statement of program structure and objectives establishes the top level set of objectives underlying the following, more definitive objectives:

1. Formulation of monetary policy.
2. Supervision and regulation of financial institutions.
3. Financial services for the System, the government, and the public.
4. System policy direction and board support.

These board objectives translate into information needs, as follows:

1. Statistical data, research and analysis, and bank regulation.
   - Data collection, editing, and publication
   - Data storage and organization
   - Data manipulation and analysis
   - Data presentation
   - Sharing resources with the Federal Reserve System, the government, and the public
2. Management information.
   - Board internal management information systems
   - System-wide operational information systems

Specific division objectives emanating from the preceding goals and established for the planning horizon of five years are as follows:

1. Maintain and improve the quality and timeliness in handling the large flow of statistical information in the banking and economic communities through
   - Greater use of automated techniques
   - Upgrading of current data collection systems
   - Use of Federal Reserve System communications facilities
   - Potential major reform of present commercial bank data flows.
2. Provide a more effective computing environment by increasing direct interaction between the user, his data, and his analysis through
   - Reasonable computer response time
   - Development of generalized data bases and data libraries
   - Use of terminals, including graphics, in an interactive or conversational mode
   - Development and use of user-oriented languages, applications, and other user software interface aids
   - Expanded use and increased productivity of visual presentation methods, including automated charting.
3. Develop more meaningful information systems for use by management for direction of both Board and System operations.
4. Foster and support cooperative efforts to develop more efficient System-wide data processing and data communications services.

5. Concentrate on the development of generalized capabilities to
   - Serve a broad range of users in the research and managment areas
   - Provide more responsive and efficient data processing services
   - Facilitate appropriate levels of integration of information systems with generalized data bases.
6. Improve utilization of data processing resources by
   - Increasing productivity
   - Developing more effective methods of providing services
   - Eliminating unnecessary service requirements
   - Developing new measures of performance.

Planning History

Before 1969, data processing at the Board of Governors was slowly evolving as an extension of specific user organization; it was primarily a passive, dependent function that did not initiate any significant independent efforts such as long-range planning. During the 1960s, an early IBM 650 installation was replaced by an IBM 1410. In 1969 the installation of an IBM 360/50, along with the appearance of the first operating systems, a growing professional data processing staff, and the beginning of long-range planning, were indications of the advent of a more structured, independent service organization. A small, highly competent staff of experienced technical data processing personnel was assembled and officially recognized as a planning staff reporting to the division director. Their objectives and functions are outlined in Table 3.

Long-range planning was considered important, but initial attention and major effort was directed at relatively short-term technical studies of equipment evaluation and selection, operating system software, facility planning, computer graphics, time-sharing systems, technical operating systems, and econometric-statistical software packages. Until 1971, the long-range plans published annually were addressed primarily to achieving much-needed current improvements and to the expansions needed to meet the backlog of unsatisfied demands from the user community.

Since 1971, the long-range planning effort has grown in several directions: it has extended its horizon in projecting both the changing nature of requirements and the level of demand; it has involved the user community in such projections by co-sponsored studies, surveys, consulting assistance, and development projects of multiyear spans; and it has included projections of hardware technology, operating systems, data organization and storage, and data communications.

Table 3 Objectives and Functions of the Planning Staff

Objectives

1. To conduct studies and to contribute to the state of the art in information and computer sciences in support of the functions of the Federal Reserve System.
2. To develop long-range plans for the division.
3. To provide to the division and to the board expertise in computer hardware, software technology, data communications, information systems, and management science.

Functions

1. Develops and maintains a long-range plan for the division with close coordination with the operating organizations. Helps develop division objectives and specific goals.
2. Prepares long-range and advanced planning studies on topics relating to board requirements.
3. Provides analysis of major new technologies (including hardware and software) or major new information systems and their applicability to the division's goals.
4. Maintains state-of-the-art information, develops technology forecasts, and provides advice and consultation to the division, to board members, and to user divisions on the subject of information and computer sciences technology and data communications networks. Prepares technical input for and coordinates with other planning groups within the Federal Reserve System.
5. Represents the division or the board on necessary committees both within the System and without.
6. Performs research in the area of computer sciences and data communications technology.
7. Reviews and recommends action on Federal Reserve System data processing budgets and proposals for new data processing and data communications equipment.
8. Develops with users and the line organization long-range requirements for future information systems.
9. Performs special studies as assigned by the director.

Most other board divisions do not overtly undertake long-range planning operations, although coincident with the Division of Data Processing effort, an Advanced Planning Committee was established at the board level, consisting of the executive director, a staff aide, and the directors of the board's divisions. A part-time planning consultant was employed to aid this committee. This effort has been primarily a Delphi approach to developing possible scenarios of economic and financial developments and alternative policy actions to deal with them. This is certainly a stimulating and useful exercise, but it has not been extended to the consideration of implementation techniques and the concomitant analytical techniques, data requirements, and information processing technology needed if the data processing planning horizons are to be extended.

This lack of substantive long-range objectives and plans from the board, coupled with the continuing emphasis of the user community on highly demanding short-range needs and the dominant research character of the majority of user requirements, have all inhibited the progress of long-range planning by the Division of Data Processing.

Another major weakness of the planning effort has been the tendency to develop plans in an unrestrained fashion. Thus in spite of very adequate supportive studies and strong advocacy arguments, there is frequent omission of the necessary tradeoff analyses, cost-return studies, and statements of objectives and goals in a manner permitting translation to annual operating plans and specific development projects.

The successes that have occurred have been primarily in such areas as scalar resource projections, equipment configurations, operating system development, macro language capabilities, data communications, graphic automation and display, data base administration approaches, and both integrated information systems and generalized application program development. The latter area probably offers the most promise for truly involving the user community in projecting their longer term requirements and in taking an active role in long-range system development.

In the past three years the impact of a much more restricted budget has brought home the realization that longer term planning is a necessity if expensive and much needed developments are to be properly balanced against ongoing short-term requirements. The Chairman of the Federal Reserve Board has been a strong advocate of zero-base budgeting in which all ongoing projects and activities are considered and assigned priorities along with new requirements in the effort to fit only the most critical ones into the budget. This emphasis is beginning to have a salutory effect on the planning activity throughout the board. It is expected to result in the ability to produce a more complete and comprehensive long-range plan for Data Processing.

Planning Responsibilities

The planning staff is composed of five senior professionals and a secretary. The head of the staff is an assistant director of the division and reports to the director. The staff divides its efforts into three major areas, all related to some degree. The long-range planning activity, composed of three major subsections, occupies approximately one-third of the staff's time. Division study projects, which also contribute in part to preparation of the long-range plan, utilize another third of the staff's resources, and board and/or System activities take up the balance of the time. The major sections and the subelements of each are outlined below:

1. Long-range planning activities
   - User requirements and planning
   - Technology assessment
   - Update to long-range plan
2. Division study projects
   - Extension of the interactive environment
   - Information systems development
   - Improvements in on-line data editing
   - Other study projects
3. Board and/or system activities
   - Federal Reserve System planning support
   - National standards
   - Committee on Federal Reserve Bank Computers
   - Link project
   - Report reform project.

In addition to the contribution of the planning staff to the long-range planning effort, the senior line staff of the division participate significantly in establishing direction, in defining major areas of emphasis, and in conducting the review and approval cycles. Section chiefs are becoming more and more involved in all planning activities, particularly in supporting the planning staff in their select functional areas of expertise.

The user community has also been involved in various ways, including requirements surveys, projections of scalar growth, identification of operational improvement requirements, and definitions of selected user projects, particularly those of a multiyear scope. The users also participate in various study teams such as data base technology, terminal system requirements, and econometric-statistical macro data and language system definition and development.

Collectively, the user community is represented by the Data Processing Advisory Group, which is moving toward more active participation in such long-range problems as the review of annual operating plan requirements and the allocation of the limited analyst-programmer resources to the most critical board requirements.

THE LONG–RANGE PLAN

The long-range plan is a strategic, integrated, comprehensive management plan that attempts to project the environment, needs, opportunities, and constraints expected to prevail at the board over the next five years. It endeavors to assess the division's capabilities, strength, and weaknesses relative to that projection; it weighs assumptions regarding expected changes in the environment, the levels of demand for data processing support, the availability of resources, and the probable effects of changing technology; and it presents specific objectives, strategy alternatives, and strategic action programs designed to maximize the division's effectiveness in meeting the board's data automation requirements. It is, in short, the product of the long-range planning efforts of the division's senior management.

Long-range planning brings a perspective to the process of establishing goals and objectives that often are lost in the press of day-to-day operational considerations. This perspective helps to strike a balance between what is needed and desirable with respect to the goals and objectives of the board, the users, and those of the Division of Data Processing, versus what is achievable within the limits of available resources and applicable technology. Within this perspective, the division is viewed as an entity to ensure that collectively its goals and objectives are in consonance with those of the board and the user divisions.

Basically, the long-range plan deals with the futurity of current decisions. It examines the chain of cause-and-effect consequences over time of actual or intended decisions that management expects to make. If what is seen ahead does not appear to be desirable, the decisions can be changed. The long-range plan also considers the alternative courses of action that are open in the future and identifies management's choices, which then become the basis for current decisions. The essence of the plan is the systematic identification of opportunities and threats that lie ahead; knowledge of these contingencies, in combination with other relevant information, provides a basis for making current decisions to exploit the opportunities and avoid or counter the threats.

Since most commitments to the board for specific projects are made at budget approval time, much of the discussion in the plan is in terms of forecasts of most probable events. Exceptions include longer term plans submitted and approved by way of the overall board planning process, as well as separate issues brought to the board by the division before the normal budget approval cycle.

The plan is made up of key events that either are firm commitments by the division or can be forecast to take place within the next five years. It identifies, as much as possible, discrete tasks to be performed. Major alternatives are proposed wherever possible. In no sense, however, is the plan a substitute for careful project-level planning, which is strongly influenced in most cases by direct user involvement. Again, these plans concentrate on internal development projects.

The value of the plan is fourfold:

1. The analytical process of developing the plan enables long-range goals and objectives for the division to be set through participation by line and staff members.
2. Accomplishments to date can be assessed and next-year budget reviews can be conducted in a framework that is results oriented, even when the goals are two to five years in the future.
3. The process of developing the plan encourages other divisions to focus on long-term requirements rather than concentrating exclusively on day-to-day needs.
4. Support from the entire board for programs of the division will benefit from the availability of a long-range plan—in effect, a forecast of user services and their requirements.

The Planning Process

The long-range planning process begins with the first of the calendar year and progresses through six major phases culminating in the completion of an updated five-year plan by midyear. The six major phases in the process are as follows:

1. Development of division planning assumptions and guidelines.
2. Development of scenarios for major strategic (or functional) areas.
3. Establishment of specific objectives for major strategic areas.
4. Development of strategy alternatives.
5. Development of strategic action programs.
6. Final editing, management approval, and publication of the long-range plan.

The first phase follows a modified "top-down" approach to develop a division planning assumptions and guidelines document. This phase is initiated by an annual planning letter, prepared for the division director by the planning staff and spelling out the mechanism of the planning process. The senior managers who will be responsible for preparation of plans find suggested in this letter areas to be considered in the development of the planning assumptions and guidelines statement. The letter also solicits their comments and recommendations. Following discussions with the senior staff, the director provides the senior managers with a completed assumptions and guidelines document, which reflects his views. The document does not of itself constitute a division "grand strategy," but it gives the senior managers a common basis for planning in their respective areas of responsibility.

The remaining phases of the process are essentially "bottom up"; each senior manager develops a scenario for the strategic area for which he is responsible, establishes specific objectives, and develops strategy alternatives and strategic action programs. Review and approval of each successive phase by the senior staff, and final edit and management approval of the plan, is coordinated by the planning staff.

Inputs to the long-range plan include information from the managing directors on the board's long-range plans, board planning papers, any available statements of user divisions' long-range plans, a survey of user requirements of both using divisions and internal sections, a technological trend forecast, special staff studies, and recommendations from and coordination with users and division personnel on specific developmental proposals.

By mid-year, major studies have been completed and the new version of the long-range plan is established in sufficient detail to serve as an input to the annual operating plan. The latter effort is initiated in the second half-year and is scheduled for final approval by year end. The final quarter-year is a period of iteration between finalization of the annual operating plan and the annual operating budget. Plan and budget come together by year-end for division and board approval. Formal midyear and year-end reviews are accomplished by division management.

The planning process, in the form of models used by the planning staff and division management, is shown in Figures 5, 6, and 7.

Figure 5 is a macro model of the planning process for the board, with particular emphasis on the Division of Data Processing. Long-range plans within using divisions are at best sketchy, but there is strong evidence of movement in the direction of more coordinated and longer range planning, both at the user division level and at the board level.

Figure 6 describes the division's own planning process with respect to the phases already described, encompassing long-range planning (Figure 6a), the budgetary and operating planning cycles (Figure 6b), and

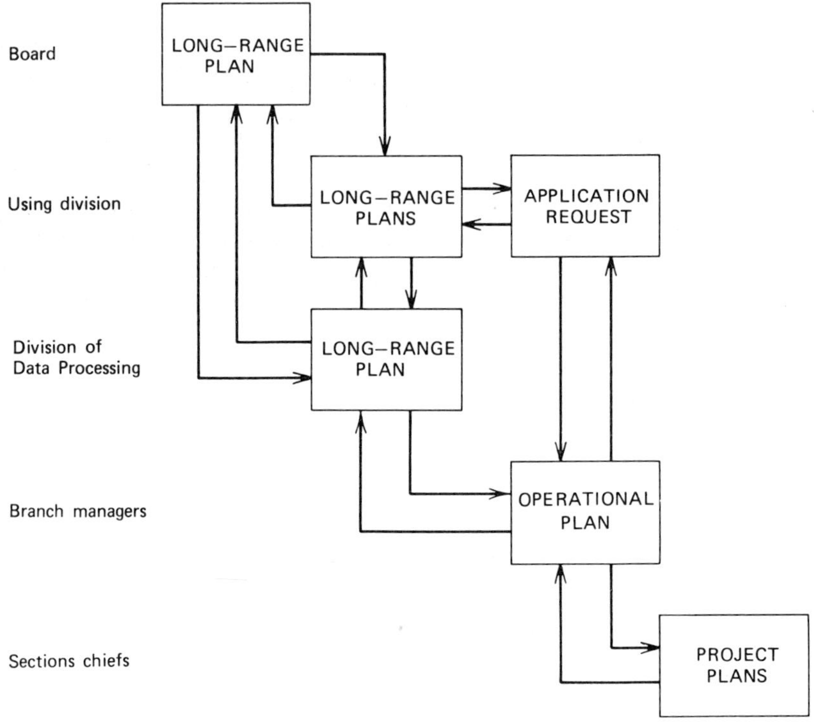

Figure 5 Model of the planning function.

the budget approval steps (Figure 6c). Figure 7 represents the flow of information and approval processes in an overall view of the planning process.

Structure of the Long-Range Plan

The structure and content of the long-range plan varies from year to year but generally includes certain major segments.

The *introduction* sets forth the background, perspective, and rationale for the division long-range plan and identifies the uses and values of the planning process and the resultant plan.

A *management summary* follows, identifying in succinct form the board's mission, program structure, and objectives, as well as general areas of need in the user community and the long-range objectives of the Division of Data Processing. Major division long-range goals are identified and related to division objectives. Major plans, issues, and

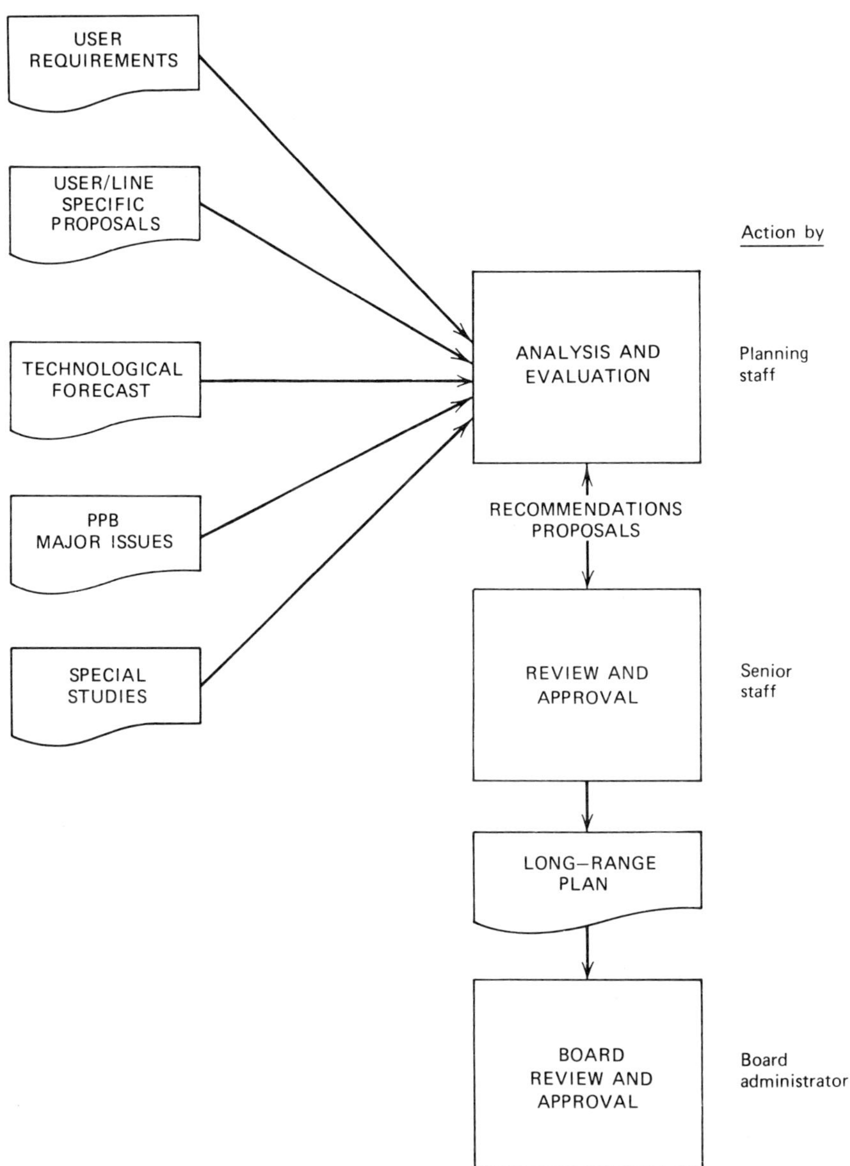

Figure 6 *a* Phase I, long-range planning cycle.

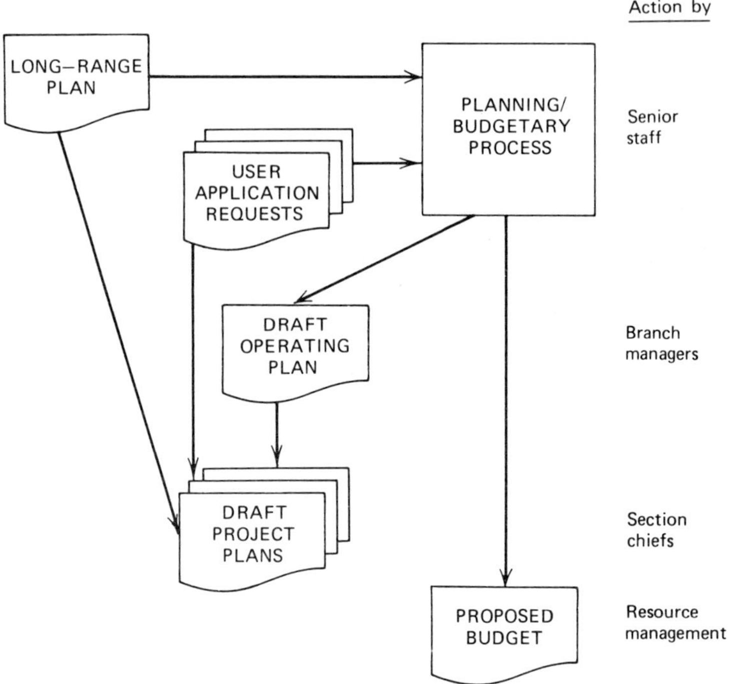

Figure 6 ***b*** **Phase II, preparation of budget, yearly operating plan, and project plans (initial).**

milestones are summarized, and a textual management summary of the long-range plan completes the section.

The *long-range plan* itself follows, giving a detailed background and description of each specific plan or issue with associated milestone for the five-year planning span. Milestone charts are included for each major and subsidiary element, and responsibility matrices identify the lead and support organizational or functional elements of the division that will be pursuing the specific plan or issue.

The fourth major section is a description of the *planning process* itself, documenting the basis and timing for the preparation of subsequent versions of the long-range plan and showing its interrelationship with the board, user community, division management, annual operating plan, and annual budget.

The last section of the plan collects the *planning documentation* and includes a detailed description of the board's program structure, major user research project descriptions, and references and extracts from related documents and supporting studies.

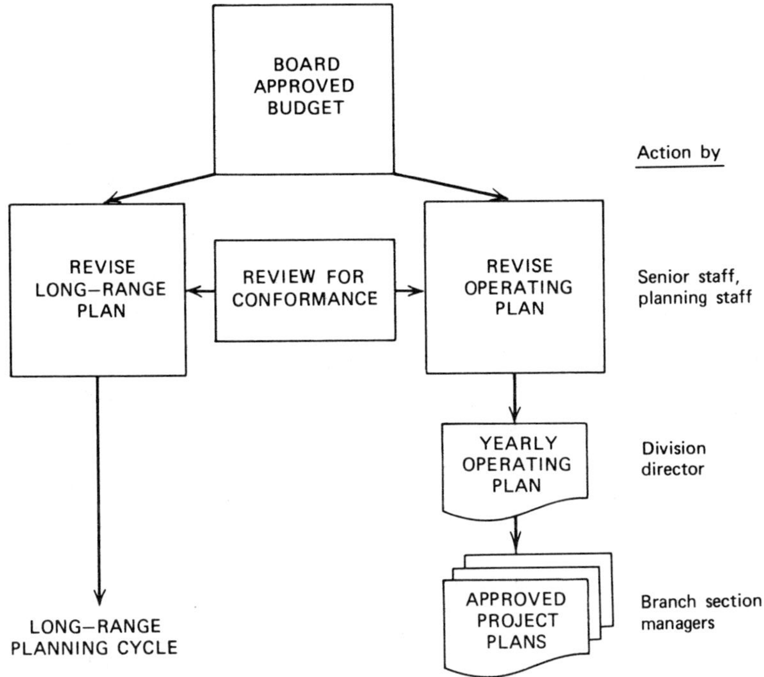

Figure 6 c Phase III, budget approval—revisions (as required) to operating plan and project plans (final).

IMPROVEMENT OPPORTUNITIES

Though the Division of Data Processing has benefited significantly from the long-range planning effort—perhaps as much as from the process as from the end product—there remain serious deficiencies in the process, the end product, and the ultimate use of the long-range plan.

Perhaps the most pervasive problem is the inadequacy of the goals and objectives derived by the board from the more global planning context of the entire Federal Reserve System. Data Processing goals, objectives, and long-range plans should be in consonance not only with those of the board and System, they should directly support specific priority issues if the value of the services provided is to be optimized within the limited resources of the division. Significant improvement opportunities are becoming possible for the division through greater involvement and participation in both the board and System planning processes. This should lead to more definitive guidance in the definition of pertinent issues, projection of requirements, and assignment of priorities of efforts for the long-range plan.

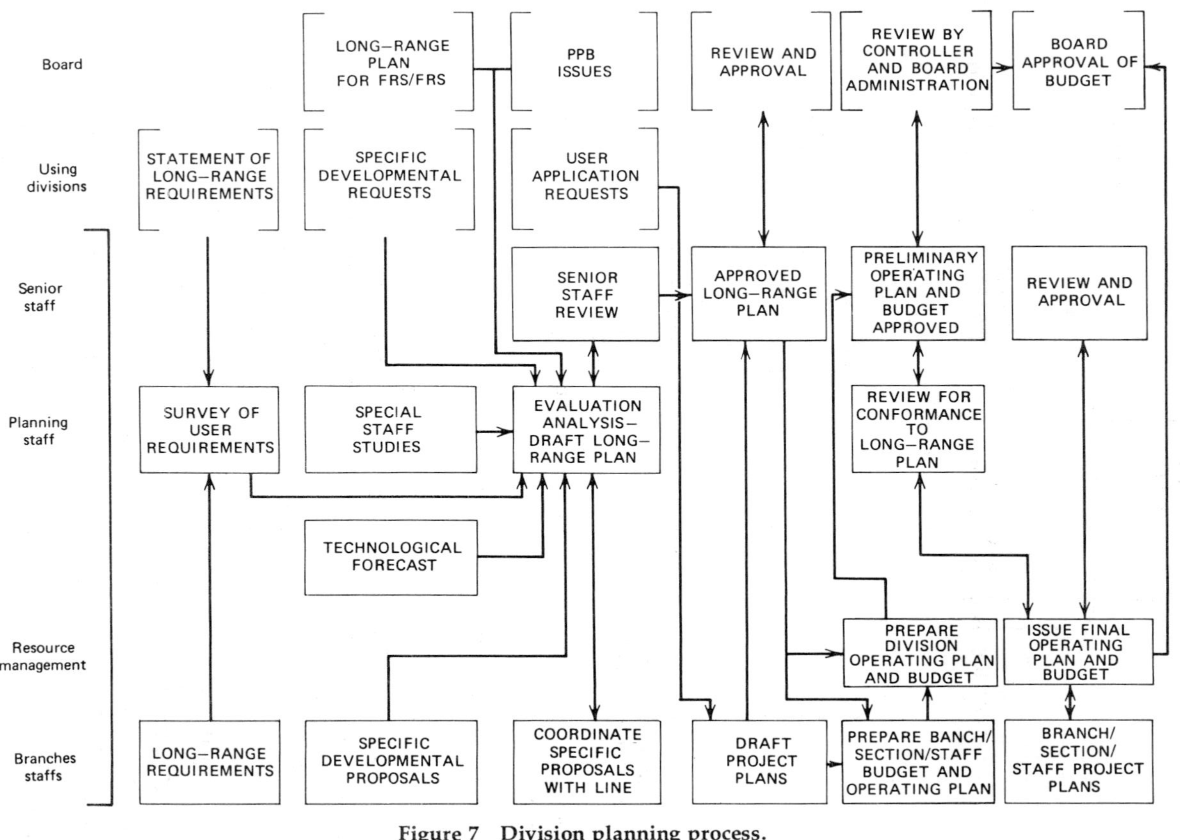

Figure 7 Division planning process.

As noted in earlier sections, since the heavy emphasis on research activities in the user community is not conducive to long-range planning, users have not been adequately involved in the development of the division long-range plan. Though user surveys have been employed and numerous personal contacts pursued, the results have not been very satisfactory for either party, nor do they reflect an overall picture of the user community needs and appropriate priorities. The rather recent implementation of the Data Processing Advisory Group, with representation from the entire user community, offers major improvement opportunities for greater structured interaction in the planning process.

Within the framework of the present plan, a need is evident to incorporate expanded analyses of alternatives, of tradeoffs, and of developmental and operational costs, and for better measures of value and return on investment.

Although the present treatment of hardware requirements, projections, and technological considerations is adequate, more attention must be directed to the division's most important resource—its people. Training needs and programs have been addressed, but the relative strengths and weaknesses of the staff have not been consciously analyzed and included within the long-range planning context. Also, specific consideration of the potential impact of changes in personnel or the constraints imposed on other plans by this dimension have not been included. Productivity improvements, which have become of paramount importance in certain functional areas, must therefore assume a larger role in future long-range planning efforts.

Because of the sequential nature of the long-range plan, operating plan, and annual budget efforts, treatment of the financial aspects of longer range issues has been inadequate. Greater consideration must be given to the growth in costs; the interrelationships of System, board, and division budgets; the impact of a growing system maintenance obligation; and the implications of the financial dimensions of each of the major long-term issues and projects. It is equally important, however, in a long-range planning context, not to stifle innovation or discard opportunities too early in the planning process because of their financial implications. In this context, the development costs of potentially attractive long-range projects should be estimated, the operating costs projected, an evaluation of risk devised, and a substantive evaluation of potential net benefits made. This work should be done early enough to permit incorporation of the results into the initial planning effort, to facilitate the subsequent development of an annual operating plan that is within budget constraints, yet gives the assurance that the best alternatives have been selected.

17 JOHN C. GILBERT

U.S. Army Materiel Command

The U.S. Army Materiel Command (AMC) was formed in 1962 as an amalgamation of the various Army Technical Services, including some dating back to George Washington's time, such as the Ordnance Corps and the Quartermaster Corps. The basic premise in the formation of the Command was to unify and standardize development of the army's materiel. The missions include technical intelligence, research, development, and procurement of army weapons and their distribution, maintenance, and finally demilitarization prior to disposal.

The Army Materiel Command operates 78 major installations and approximately 122 activities. It consists of six major commodity commands: the Tank-Automotive Command, the Armaments Command, the Aviation Systems Command, the Troop Support Command, the Missile Command, and the Electronics Command. In addition, it includes a Test and Evaluation Command that incorporates such far-flung activities as White Sands Missile Range in New Mexico and Aberdeen Proving Ground in Maryland. AMC includes a number of independent laboratories such as the Ballistics Research Laboratory at Aberdeen Proving Ground and the Materials Research Laboratory in Watertown, Massachusetts. It also inherited a complex of approximately 33 depots, which were eventually reduced to a dozen major depots and a half-dozen minor ones.

The Army Materiel Command spends approximately $8 billion annually in the accomplishments of its missions. It employs between 125,000 and 135,000 people, and it processes approximately 3 million requisitions for army equipment and spare parts per year. It is because of this volume, of course, that computers play such an important role in the business of the Command. It is important to realize that in 1965—only three years after the Command was formed—it had to mobilize to provide equipment for the Vietnam war. In 1968, at the height of the war, the Command was spending approximately $15 billion for army equipment; and only since 1968 has it contracted to the dimensions just given.

INFORMATION SYSTEMS BACKGROUND

Computers are used extensively in AMC in a variety of ways, including the scientific and engineering activities of the laboratories and the business activities of the commands, depots, and other installations. The annual expenditure for ADP is approximately $130 million, with an additional capital expenditure ranging between $10 million and $20 million per year. Of the $130 million, approximately $35 million is spent for scientific and engineering computing support. Computers are operated at approximately 80 locations, of which 30 would be classified as major computing installations, that is, they have equipment equal to or larger than IBM 360/40's or CDC 3300's. AMC spends between 1.5 and 2.0 percent of its gross budget on computing. It employs approximately 4000 ADP professionals, which is approximately 3 percent of the Command work force.

AMC has standardized two of its major business data processing systems using multifunctional integrated data bases, one in the commodity commands and the other in the depots. Both were developed by independent central systems design agencies that report to the director of Management Information Systems at AMC headquarters. In addition, the Test and Evaluation Command has standardized its ADP systems, without, however, the use of an integrated data base.

INFORMATION SYSTEMS OBJECTIVES

The planning horizon for the Command is five years. It is oriented toward one of the major AMC goals, the implementation of the Five-Year Automatic Data Processing and Management Information Systems Plan (reproduced in Appendix C.) This plan ensures that a totally integrated, responsive, and economic management system is achieved. The significant objectives have been categorized into two groups: major (i.e., of Command interest) and minor (i.e., of primary interest to the director of Management Information Systems). Though these objectives cover a five-year planning horizon, they are broken into discrete increments for the immediate fiscal year to permit more careful monitoring of progress. The five-year plan is updated and extended each year and comprises one of the major long-range planning documents of the Command.

The planning process in AMC begins in October with the statement of the Command's major goals. By March of the following year, these are translated into more specific objectives. Thus the Command's major goals for fiscal year 1974 were developed in October of 1972, and the ADP program objectives for July 1973–July 1974 were developed by March of 1973.

When the Army Materiel Command was formed, two basic objectives were seen as vital to obtain the unification of the Command: that the commodity commands be standardized organizationally, and that the systems they operated also be standardized. Hence these major Command goals have been incorporated into the ADP program as objectives every year. Since this standardization has now been largely accomplished, however, the standardization of ADP systems was not included as a program objective in the stated goals for fiscal year 1975. Subsequent developments in the ADP arena will have the goal of making more effective utilization of Command resources in the performance of its assigned missions.

INFORMATION SYSTEMS PLANNING RESPONSIBILITIES

The AMC long-range ADP plan consists of a set of documents based on continuing technological forecasting and systems reviews conducted by the staff of the Headquarters Directorate for Management Information Systems. Taken together, these documents comprise the AMC five-year program. (Volume 1 of this program, containing the ADP & MIS Plan, is reproduced in Appendix C.) The program also contains the budget, which is prepared in July of one fiscal year for the following fiscal year. Though prepared by the Headquarters Management Information Systems staff, the document is based on a continuing dialogue with the field level activities. Cost-benefit studies covering the anticipated life of the major standard systems are prepared annually; and again the preparation, accomplished by the headquarters MIS staff, is based largely on inputs from the field central systems design agencies and coordinated with functional users. Finally, the central systems design agencies responsible for the commodity command and depot standard systems do detailed work load forecasting for the next two-year period.

Priorities for this work load are developed with functional user groups on a continuing basis and are reviewed twice annually by a Command-level systems advisory group, which has ultimate responsibility for assuring that the level of activity devoted to systems development is appropriate. This group also resolves priority conflicts among functional users which would lead to the need for resource reallocations within the central systems design agencies.

Several organizations affect the documents described. The business data processing chiefs throughout the Command meet twice a year with the leaders of the headquarters MIS staff to exchange information on the current status of, and anticipated future activities in, the ADP area. From time to time they form working groups to study and make recommendations concerning specific problem areas that have been identified either by headquarters or by the organization of ADP chiefs. A group of scientific and engineering computing chiefs, organized similarly, also meets semiannually. Finally, the Computer Network Steering Committee, consisting of laboratory directors and the chiefs of some of the major scientific computing activities, meets to advise the deputy for Laboratories, the director for Research and Development, and the director for Management Information Systems on policy issues concerning the formation of a computer network and the use of scientific computers within the Command.

Since most of the planning documents are prepared by the headquarters MIS group, it is helpful to understand how the group is organized. It consists of a directorate with three subordinate divisions. The Systems Operations Division is primarily responsible for representing the business data processing community to the director and ensuring that directorate policies are conveyed and implemented in the business data processing community. To accomplish this, the division is organized into three branches. Two of the branches perform similar functions but simply share the work load by serving different activities within the AMC complex. For instance, one of them has the primary responsibility for the commodity command standard system, whereas the other is responsible for the depot standard system, the two largest efforts within the Command. The function of the third branch, the ADP Evaluation Branch, is to provide teams to perform management reviews of the data processing installations within AMC.

The Scientific and Management Information Division performs two distinctly different functions. First, it represents the scientific and engineering computing needs to the director and conveys to the scientific and engineering computing community the directorate policies. In addition, it is responsible for the development of information systems for strategic decision making and management control within the Command. Management information tends to draw much of its data from the business data processing systems, but it was decided to place the responsibility in a different element, to give the director the benefit of the interaction between the two divisions. To this end the divisions are organized into three branches: the Scientific Branch, the Management Information Branch, and a Reports Management Branch (included because of the strong relationship between reports management and management information).

The third division, Resources, ensures that personnel, money, and equipment are in balance and are available to support the ADP community as needed. It is organized as a separate division to give the director the visibility of the interaction between the user and his needs and the resources required to accomplish these needs. It is similarly organized into three branches, two of which share the work load of monitoring the individual data processing installations in a manner analogous to the way the Systems Operations Division is subdivided into two branches to spread the work load. The third branch, a planning branch, is the integrator of the planning effort. It carries the additional responsibility for establishing policy for the ADP career programs within AMC.

INFORMATION SYSTEMS PLANNING PROCESS

Technological forecasting is accomplished by the headquarters MIS staff. Active liaison with professional groups and manufacturers is maintained in all areas where technological breakthroughs that would affect the shape of computing within the Command are anticipated.

For example, satellite communications is being investigated with two commercial companies to determine the feasibility of this technological innovation to support the scientific and engineering computing network and to form service centers to provide business data processing support. Similarly, the development of very large storage is constantly being surveyed as a possible mechanism for keeping engineering drawings in a digital format.

The role of the AMC five-year program and its timetable have already been discussed. Budget planning occurs slightly out of sequence, preceding the development of program objectives, because the budget must be submitted to Congress in January to become effective in the fiscal year beginning in July. Therefore, preparation must be completed by the preceding September to allow time for submission through the various echelons of the army and Department of Defense before being incorporated into the President's budget. This appears to be inconsistent, but since program objectives are forecast for five years and do not change that rapidly, it has not resulted in a significant problem.

Though budgets are forecast for two years in advance, primary attention is devoted to the next fiscal year. The year of execution is actively monitored because, in general, changes that occur in the year of execution frequently affect the succeeding fiscal year. The budget is prepared by the headquarters MIS staff; but as with the preparation of the five-year program, field-level data processing installations also actively participate.

A recently installed automated system permits real-time updating of the budget data base. Individual changes are made for each installation as they occur, and these changes are automatically summarized. The central systems design agencies annually estimate their work load in great detail for the next two years. The estimates are coordinated with those of the functional users of the standard systems, and appropriate priorities are negotiated between the central systems design agency and the user groups. Finally, the Command-level systems advisory group, chaired by the director of Management Information Systems, reviews the estimates.

This information is reviewed six months later by each of the central systems design agencies; and, where changes have occurred, the same coordination is again achieved. This is necessary because there is a high degree of change in the individual tasks within the central systems design agencies. Finally, cost-benefit studies are prepared for the major standard systems. Ultimate responsibility for this task is borne by the headquarters MIS staff, but a number of other organizations contribute to it. Anticipated benefits developed by the central systems design agencies are discussed with the functional users and, when agreement is obtained, are incorporated into the benefits document. Cost data come from the budget, and both costs and benefits are extended throughout the anticipated life of the system. During the systems development period, and before the commitment to install, several alternatives —including the status quo—are analyzed within the framework of these cost-benefit studies.

IMPROVEMENT OPPORTUNITIES

Two significant areas need improvement in the planning process in the Army Materiel Command. First, career planning must be greatly strengthened. The Command has been contracting at a rapid rate since

1968, and this has inhibited progress in this area since career opportunities have been greatly restricted. However it appears that a period of stability is approaching, and it is to the benefit of the Command to be able to identify potential executives and managers and to ensure their development and availability to fill key positions when they are needed. A model that anticipates the retirement of the existing work force is needed so that new blood can be brought into the Command and trained appropriately.

Another area calling for further improvement is the development of the cost-benefit studies to ensure that future systems development activities can be focused in high-payoff areas. The commitment to the major standard systems that was discussed earlier was not preceded by cost-benefit studies because the decision was seen as being vital to the unification of the Command. With these goals accomplished, candidates for future standardization must be picked in a more rigorous manner. Progress has been made in this area within the last three years. Heretofore, benefits tended to focus on the elimination of personnel. Recently developed, techniques, however, focus on the other effects of systems. For instance, the Delphi technique for providing expert forecasts for uncertain futures has been used to estimate changing logistics requirements. Results with using this technique are quite encouraging, and it may have some promise in areas that are even harder to quantify, such as the value of management information.

18 THOMAS E. REECE

Los Angeles City Unified School District

The Los Angeles City Unified School District is the second largest school district in the country. It covers 710 square miles and operates the schools in seven other cities, including Cudahy, Gardena, Huntington Park, Lomita, Maywood, San Fernando, and Vernon. Portions of 18 more cities fall within the district's boundaries and use its services. The district contains 662 elementary, secondary, physically handicapped, and adult schools. More than 60,000 employees served 726,803 students in the 1973–1974 school year. The district also operates 80 centers that provide day care and extended day care for children of working parents. The student population is larger than the total population of at least seven of the nation's states.

The district has a central governing board of education and central offices, but is itself decentralized; there are 12 largely autonomous areas, each having its own area superintendent and staff to provide services to the schools in that area.

The board of education is responsible for making policy for the school district as a whole, and its seven members are elected at large for staggered four-year terms. The budget administered by the board for 1973–1974 amounted to approximately $1.004 billion, not including funds received from the federal government and other sources.

It costs the district an average of $1021.19 per pupil to provide a variety of regular educational and other services to students from kindergarten through the twelfth grade. The total tax rate for 1973–1974 is $4.9746 per $100 of assessed valuation, including all general purpose and special fund taxes. Approximately 23.9 percent of the district's income comes from the state, approximately 35.0 percent from federal and other sources, and the remainder from local property taxes.

HISTORY OF DATA PROCESSING

Tabulating equipment was introduced in the 1930s to assist with student testing and evaluation projects, and use of this equipment was expanded in the 1950s to furnish services such as payroll, stock accounting, and job accounting in the Controlling Division.

The district's first computer, installed in 1961 largely for processing the payroll, was replaced in 1968 by an IBM 360/50. Later in 1968 the Data Processing Branch was established under the Controlling Division to expand data processing services to other divisions in the school district. Considerable growth resulted from this impetus, and new systems were developed for the Business, Budget, Personnel, and Personnel Commission divisions and for the Division of Secondary Education.

Although much progress was made, no structure was available to give top management the opportunity to evaluate the success or failure of projects; and the branch was hindered by lack of a long-range plan having the support and commitment of top management and the board of education. Data processing services were provided for educational activities, for evaluation and measurement, and for general business operations by three separate data processing organizations, which often duplicated functions.

On July 1, 1972, the board of education consolidated all data processing organizations and the Management Information Division resulted from this merger. The division was given the responsibility of setting a new direction for data processing in the district, aimed at supplying greatly expanded services to schools and increased support and coordination of administrative programs. The division has three major branches and one section, as indicated in Figure 1.

- *The Educational Systems and Programming Branch* is in charge of the design, development, and programming of the district's educational information processing systems and for providing in-service education for computer-related educational programs.

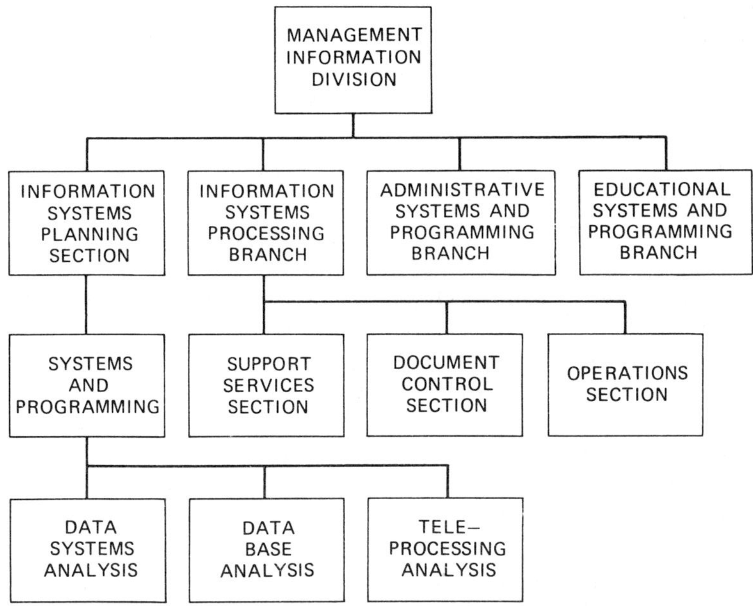

Figure 1 Organization chart, Los Angeles Unified School District Management Information Division, 1973–1974.

- *The Administrative Systems and Programming Branch* has responsibility for the design, development, and programming of the district's information processing services for administrative and business purposes. This includes installing, testing, modifying, and maintaining computer-based administrative systems and programming.
- *The Information Systems Processing Branch* operates the district's computers and related data processing equipment. This branch receives, schedules, controls, routes, and distributes data processing products.
- *The Information Systems Planning Section* is responsible for long-range general and technical planning of information systems processing services.

INFORMATION SYSTEMS OBJECTIVES

In July 1972 controller William Barbour presented a report to the board of education recommending the establishment of the Management Information Division and listing a number of objectives to be accomplished by the new division. These objectives are paraphrased as follows:

1. To change the direction of data processing in the Los Angeles Unified School District, placing greater emphasis on providing schools with services to reduce administrative record keeping and the clerical work load borne by teachers; this will give them more time to devote to the instructional program.
2. To provide increased educational opportunities to schools by furnishing computerized learning systems, with the aid of time-sharing and teleprocessing, thereby giving schools the opportunity of improving productivity.
3. To assist the district in its efforts to plan, manage, control, and operate through the development of improved budgeting, accounting, position control, personnel, and payroll systems designed to yield more accurate, timely, and meaningful information.
4. To provide schools on all levels with a variety of automated support services, including test scoring and analysis, attendance accounting, supply ordering, accounting of school funds, student scheduling, report cards, and student data banks.
5. To give the district a modern, on-line teleprocessing network supported by an upward-expandable current-generation computing system that would make available to the district the latest technological improvements in data processing.
6. To strengthen the internal organization of the division by supplying support services in areas such as documentation, library services, technical writing, forms design, and quality control, to improve the efficiency of the division and to ensure that management and schools have more accurate and timely reporting.[1]

INFORMATION SYSTEMS PLANNING HISTORY

Before the establishment of the Management Information Division in July 1972, planning activities were fragmented and carried on independently by each of the three existing organizations. The person in charge of each branch was responsible for all operations including long- and short-range planning; as a consequence, coordination between the three groups was limited. This resulted in duplication of effort and some rivalry among the branches. Resources for long-range planning activities were not fully utilized.

The reorganization of all data processing activities in the district, following the establishment of the Management Information Division, re-

[1]*Educational Support: Computers and Information Processing,* presented to Los Angeles Board of Education, July 1, 1972, pp. 9–11.

sulted in the creation of the Information Systems Planning Section, which had overall responsibility for planning for the division, with particular emphasis on long-range planning. This section reviews all requests for new systems to evaluate their feasibility with respect to existing personnel and equipment, practicality, and cost; it also makes recommendations to the Management Information Committee with respect to development of the system. The Planning Section is also responsible for systems research, development of plans for a data base management system and teleprocessing network, modeling and simulation work, and plans for the procurement of a new computing system.

INFORMATION SYSTEMS PLANNING SECTION

The Information Systems Planning Section is headed by a supervisor who reports directly to the assistant superintendent in charge of the Management Information Division. In addition to the supervisor, the planning section has two senior data systems analysts, who serve as project leaders, six data systems analysts, one data base administrator, and one research assistant.

All plans for major new projects are reviewed by the Management Information Committee, whose members are the associate deputy superintendent, the budget director, the controller, the business manager, the assistant superintendent in charge of the Personnel Division, a principal from each of the three levels of the school district, and the assistant superintendent in charge of the Management Information Division. This committee, serving in an advisory capacity, approves or disapproves all new systems, the annual plan, and the long-range plan.

In addition, steering committees have been established for important projects such as the development of a new budget-accounting system, a new payroll personnel system, and an automated student scheduling system. The members of these steering committees are the division or department heads who are concerned with the particular project under development.

The planning section has been assigned the responsibility for the following functions:

1. The evaluation of the information processing requirements in district operations.
2. The definition of problems, the development of guidelines, and the determination of parameters for system and programming studies.
3. The development of recommendations regarding the needs,

priorities, and other matters associated with long-range studies.
4. The preparation of reports and other materials related to long-range planning.
5. The control of the content, logical structure, physical organization, and security of data bases used in information processing systems.
6. The evaluation of telecommunications and other information processing the preparation of benchmarks and other related material.
7. The plans needed for the acquisition of a new computer system, including the preparation of benchmarks and other related material.

INFORMATION SYSTEMS PLANNING PROCESS

Long-range planning is defined as anticipating the needs of the organization so that they can be dealt with in an orderly and meaningful way. Usually a long-range plan is developed for periods ranging from one to five years. The long-range plan currently under development in the Management Information Division covers two to five years. Recognizing that a long-range plan is never static but is subject to modification due to external influences, the plan should allow for orderly changes when necessary. Changes to the plan include task redefinition, updating, status controls, rescheduling, revision of estimates originally made, and reallocating resources. A formal structure to handle these changes must be established in an organization if the plan is to be effective.

The following sequence of events describes the methodology used by the division in developing its long-range plan.

1. *Individual meetings with top-level management, middle management, and other levels of the school district.* Participants discuss the services currently provided, the services requested for the future, and the priorities of these requested services. The meetings are initially held with the division head, and the purposes and intent of the project are described. The assistance of the division head is solicited to gain his support and approval of meetings to be held with his department heads.
2. *Analysis of data.* The data obtained from the meetings are analyzed, and the needs of various users in the district are detailed in terms of software development and the need for computer terminals. The communications requirements to support the specified terminals are developed. Results, where appropriate, are communicated to the users, and the concurrence of their management is obtained.
3. *Resource allocation and scheduling.* The required software development

costs and the acquisition of terminals and communications equipment are compared to the available and projected resources of the division. Resources are allocated, tentative schedules determined, and total costs estimated. A basic plan is derived for the division, and possible variations are indicated.

4. *Presentation of long-range plan.* The completed plan document is first presented to Management Information Division management for their comments or revisions. It then goes to the Management Information Committee for review. Thereafter it is presented to the superintendent of schools for his approval or revisions. Finally, the support and financial commitment of the board of education are requested.

The foregoing are the four major facets in the preparation of the long-range plan. It is estimated that one man-year of work is involved in the preparation of the plan. A projected table of contents for our long-range plan is shown in Table 1.

Table 1 Projected Table of Contents for Long-Range Plan

Executive Summary

I. Introduction
  - A. Historical background
  - B. Objectives
  - C. Description of approach

II. Description of Available Computer Hardware Configuration and Major Software Systems

III. Data Processing Needs of the District
  - A. Software development
    1. New administrative systems and programs
    2. New educational systems and programs
    3. New analytic modeling efforts
    4. Maintenance and modification of existing programs
    5. Conversion of programs
    6. Manpower requirement estimates for one- to five-year period
  - B. Terminals
    1. Requirements for types, speeds, and numbers in various locations
    2. Estimated costs
  - C. Communications
    1. Network configuration (modems, multiplexers, and lines)
    2. Estimated costs

Table 1 *(continued)*

IV. Matching of Resources and Needs
- A. Projected division budget
- B. District priorities
- C. Time phasing of projects
- D. Costs
- E. Strategic considerations

V. Primary Plan and Variations
- A. Schedule of projects
- B. Deployment of teleprocessing network
- C. Loading of the machine
- D. Checkpoint milestones

VI. Future Requirements
- A. Personnel
- B. Equipment
- C. Facilities
- D. Education and training
- E. Budget
- F. Organization

VII. Updating and Revision of the Long-Range Plan

VIII. Recommendations

IMPROVEMENT OPPORTUNITIES

The several improvement opportunities present in the planning process include greater user involvement, better resources estimation, and the provision for increased flexibility.

1. *Greater user involvement.* User involvement plays a major role in any information systems planning process. Frequent contact with users regarding their problems and aspirations is imperative. The ability to translate user needs into meaningful and operationally feasible projects is another necessary ingredient to the planning process.
2. *Better resource estimation.* Resource estimation is an important part of planning. Clearly, very wonderful plans can easily be made. But if they are not realistically achievable, the information systems organization will not be able to deliver and will lose credibility.
3. *Increased flexibility.* Flexibility is an essential part of the planning pro-

cess. Viable variations must be allowed for in the plan's structure. Needs change, estimates contain errors, and new circumstances develop. Planners, explicitly or implicitly, must develop a rich enough program to accommodate changes without undue loss in efficiency.

19 KENT H. GOULD

State of California

The government of the State of California employs more than 150,000 people and has a budget in excess of $10.3 billion. It conducts a myriad of activities relative to the health, welfare, and lives of its citizens. Probably the most significant and unique characteristic of California state government is that its budget makes it the tenth largest government in the world. The breadth and character of governmental activities in a state environment influence information processing in a way that makes the variety of applications almost endless. It would be safe to say that almost every major application conducted in computing today, except for those relating to high technology research or defense, are undertaken by California state government. The sheer volume of data required to operate a government the size of California's strongly influences the scope of data processing activities within the state.

California state government is separated into some 80 departments or agencies and includes the executive branch, the state college system, the university system, the courts, and the legislature. Within the executive branch there are numerous constitutional officers who are independently elected and have prescribed constitutional and statutory powers.

In general, the operational planning activities of California state government are involved in the budget development process. The budget in California is prepared annually, beginning approximately one year ahead of its submission to the legislature. Broad guidelines are issued by the Budget Division of the Department of Finance, which is the primary budget planning agency within the state. These guidelines go to all agencies, which submit budget data for incorporation into "the Governor's Budget" which is presented to the legislature early in January. Each agency specifies its budgetary support requirements for information processing activities, describing in broad terms the planned application of resources. California's budget may best be described as a broad, program-oriented budget document giving specific emphasis to problem areas. Continuing program support is also covered in the document.

INFORMATION SYSTEMS BACKGROUND

Computing activities in California government began in 1957 with the limited application of electronic accounting machines for the resolution of record-keeping problems. Today, of the 80-odd organizations in state government, almost every one uses computing, some to a very minor degree, others to the maximum extent. There are currently 19 computer installations to the executive branch. Every campus of the University of California and of the state college system has computer installations. However the EDP budget levels for each organization are not clearly visible, and this poses a significant problem for the state. Through research, we have been able to establish the historical budget and expenditure levels for data processing from 1962 forward (Table 1).

There are several types of organizational structures within California

Table 1 EDP Costs, State of California

Year	Personnel	Equipment	Other [b]	Total
1962	$ 6,553,000 [a]	$ 4,370,000	$1,456,000	$12,379,000
1963	7,956,000 [a]	5,304,000	1,768,000	15,028,000
1964	9,225,000 [a]	6,150,000	2,050,000	17,425,000
1965	9,975,000 [a]	6,650,000	2,218,000	18,843,000
1966	16,000,000 [a]	8,000,000 [a]	2,666,000	26,666,000
1967	22,000,000	10,998,000 [a]	3,666,000	36,664,000
1968	27,130,000	12,946,000 [a]	3,079,000	43,155,000
1969	30,300,000	16,650,000 [a]	6,623,000	53,573,000
1970	43,725,000 [a]	21,862,500 [a]	7,287,500	72,875,000
1971	48,213,000 [a]	24,106,500	8,035,500	80,355,000

[a] Estimates.

[b] Excludes the University of California.

state government. It is important to understand these structures because they affect the EDP planning functions in different ways.

In California state government, there are three broad classes of organizational entities. First, there are those which serve the public directly and have no control relationship or direct interface relationship in terms of serving other units of government. Second, there are the organizations that have both a direct public service relationship and a control relationship with other state governmental entities. Last, there are those whose sole purpose is to serve the operation of government, as opposed to serving the public directly. The latter organizations (e.g., the Department of Finance) generally are called control agencies.

INFORMATION SYSTEMS PLANNING

Let us briefly discuss the way in which information systems activities are planned and initiated, as well as the various kinds of controls that exist within state government in terms of those agencies and EDP activities. Individual organizations have the responsibility for the design, development, and implementation of their own information processing systems. There are legal and policy restraints, management guidelines, and standard practices relative to the development of information systems. Furthermore, these practices relate to the authorization for information systems use and to their operation. Individual organizations determine the way in which information processing facilities will serve the implementation of programs, both in the long-range strategic and short-range operational senses. Thus the information processing system is a genuine product of the program it must support.

In 1966 the legislature began to notice a tremendous proliferation in the number of computing systems. A July 1971 inventory indicated that there were 41 computers in the executive branch and 43 computers in the state college system. As of July 1970 there were 117 computers in the University of California, and today that number exceeds 260. A review of several studies dating back to 1966 revealed that every time an investigation was conducted on computing in California state government, it was paralleled by a marked *increase* in the number of computers—not a decrease, which might normally be expected in the light of such scrutiny! It is not surprising that the legislature displayed a certain degree of dissatisfaction with the way in which the control agencies, as originally established, were meeting their call for control. Therefore in July 1971 a new organization was constituted and the old organization was abolished. The purpose and mission of the new organization, however, are virtually identical to those of the body it replaced.

As noted previously, individual organizations define their information systems needs, propose them, go through an approval cycle, and undertake the implementation if the projects are approved. Thus although we have individual organizations defining their information system processing needs, we have other organizations sitting in review to pass on the adequacy of the approach selected. There is an obvious need for a baseline or guideline against which information system development proposals can be evaluated. This baseline was incorporated into the Budget Act of Fiscal Year 1966 and has been incorporated into every subsequent budget act. The requirement disallows the approval of expenditures for additions, improvements, or expansion in excess of $10,000 unless the director of Finance certifies that the criteria specified in the report of the Committee on Conference have been met. A portion of these procedures, quoted below, is of particular interest.

New Project Authorization

No expenditures for EDP activities subject to Section 4 of the Budget Act should be certified unless a feasibility study has been conducted justifying such expenditures, including need, objectives, constraints, alternatives, costs, and benefits, and an implementation plan has been developed by the department and approved by the Department of Finance. The implementation plan shall include an organizational plan; a time schedule; authorizations required; statutory or administrative changes required, if any; a description of the impact on existing operations; an explanation of the consequences of a failure to take the proposed actions; an explanation of the sources of funds; and an estimate of total resources required including a statement of existing resources and resources required. The Department of Finance will review the feasibility study and implementation plans to determine the systems' relationships with other systems or other levels of government, the feasibility of immediate or future integration with other systems outside the department, and the credibility of the department's cost and benefit estimates.

Progress Reporting

During the implementation of an approved project, the [implementing] department shall provide quarterly reports to the Department of Finance and the Joint Legislative Budget Committee that relates progress to the implementation plan. The Department of Finance shall monitor the project to determine if it is being conducted in accordance with approved plans, policies, standards, procedures, and budgets.

Continued Implementation Funding Review

When requesting funds for the continuance of a program approved for development and started in a prior year, the [implementing] department will provide Finance with a statement of the current scope and objectives of the program, task and cost schedules for the remainder of the program, and a report on the status of the program. Finance will then determine whether the scope and objectives of the program have changed since its approval; determine if the requested appropriation is what was projected for the budget year when the program was approved; determine whether the program is progressing according to the approved schedule; and determine, if any of the above conditions are not met, whether the program should be subjected to reevaluation in accordance with the procedures set forth above for a new program.

Continued Operation of an Implemented System

When requesting funds for the continued operations of a system or program implemented in a prior year, the [implementing] department will describe the technical objectives of the program and present current and projected work load data. Finance will then determine if work load estimates are reasonable; determine if requested funds are consistent with work load estimates; and evaluate the effectiveness of the program if such an evaluation has not been performed in the preceding two years.

It is necessary to establish here that the process of determining feasibility (i.e., whether a project should be done, and how it should be done if justified) should be carried out by the using organization and attested to or signed off by the using department head. The process of developing the analysis of feasibility and the implementation plan should be jointly conducted by the data processing arm and the using department, giving greatest emphasis to the participation of the using department.

Organizations in California state government used to decide what they wanted to do and how they wanted to do it without really conducting a feasibility study. Then they set about putting together a document that outlined and justified their approach. This is clearly improper, for the feasibility study report should cover all the avenues explored, all the alternatives considered, the reasons for selection, and the methodology by which successful implementation will be achieved.

The concept now employed calls for an independent body, having no vested interest, to do the review and authorization. This procedure would be equally well suited to an organization whose long-range objectives are in a state of change. In the case of a General Motors, a Procter & Gamble, or a multifacility manufacturer, review and authorization might well be the responsibility of a corporate steering committee for EDP applications. These functions might also reside in a branch of corporate finance; it is probably not desirable, however, to have the financial arm perform these duties. Instead, representatives of the point of strongest control, reporting to the highest level within the company or corporate entity, should review and authorize. If the entity is governmental, controls should be established as close to the chief executive as possible. There should be sufficient statutory authority to back up the actions of the control agency.

The proposal can be as simple and limited as a three-page report on the selection of a piece of software, or as complex as a thousand-page plan to outline a five-year criminal justice information system. The guidelines for the preparation of a feasibility study and implementation plan should emphasize that the document should be no more complex than the problem to be analyzed and reported on. Certainly the level of effort expended on the feasibility study should be commensurate with doing a good job, not merely a predefined level of effort associated with the preparation of a report.

Though it may not be possible to embark on long-range or even intermediate-range planning for the use of information system technology in state government, there is a method by which the conservation of resources and the application of new information system technology can be accomplished simultaneously. California has utilized this methodology for the past six years. Since 1966, the concept of individual project authorization has been rigorously enforced. This specific approach for evaluating state projects may not be ideal for every situation, but it does provide a baseline against which to measure all proposed projects. The following eight standards were established by the legislature toward this end:

1. That the goal of consolidation and optimum utilization of electronic data processing equipment be pursued whenever possible.
2. That there be maximum practical integration of electronic data processing systems.
3. That service centers be established, as required, to provide data processing services to units of state government not included in consolidation plans.
4. That the goal of any consolidation be to create functional information systems that are designed to process and provide information related to broad areas of subject matter.
5. That the ultimate goal of the state's information systems be to provide the most effective means of data storage, retrieval, and exchange between units and agencies of state and local governments.
6. That such goals as one-time collection of data, minimum duplication of records, and maximum availability of information at lowest overall cost, will not jeopardize or comprise the confidentiality of information as provided by statute or the protection of the right of individual privacy as established by law.

7. That there be adherence to proper standards to ensure appropriate compatibility of systems and interchange of data and information.
8. That proper management controls be instituted to ensure the most efficient, effective, and economical use of the state's resources.

Given this broad set of objectives, it is possible, and indeed necessary, to establish a procedure requiring that every expenditure for the addition, improvement, or expansion of any aspect of information systems processing be measured in terms of its feasibility and that its careful implementation be monitored against a detailed implementation plan. The 13 components of the feasibility study as presently constituted are outlined in the following section.

GUIDELINES FOR PREPARATION OF A FEASIBILITY STUDY REPORT AND IMPLEMENTATION PLAN

Problem Definition Portion

Identification of Needs

1. Explain why action must be taken.
2. Identify the needs with sufficient clarity to provide understanding.
3. Quantify the needs wherever possible.
4. If the need arises as a result of legislative or executive action, identify the specific statute or directive that brings about this need.

Statement of Objectives

1. Describe what is to be achieved.
2. Wherever possible, quantify the objective.
3. Describe the objective in a results-oriented manner.

Constraints. Identify the situations, statutes, or policy decisions that cannot be changed and yet that introduce constraints on the alternatives that would otherwise be possible.

Consequences of Failure to Act

1. Explain what will happen if no action is taken.
2. Be specific, and quantify costs wherever possible.

Solution Analysis Portion

Alternatives. Within this area of the report the submitter should present all the possible alternatives considered as a part of the feasibility study. It is essential that the submitter make a full and complete presentation of alternative solutions to meet the needs discussed under "Indentification of Needs." Furthermore, an often overlooked but equally important area is the discussion of the possible alternative methods for implementing the recommended solution.

Cost and Benefits

1. Identify the costs of each alternative, including the present method. Costs for each resource (manpower, equipment, supplies, and services) must be identified.
2. Identify both quantitatively and qualitatively any benefits to be derived, including savings to be achieved. If monetary savings are to be realized, project the respective costs and savings until the breakeven point is reached, or for at least a two-year period, whichever is greater.
3. Identify the costs associated with the development and implementation of an alternative and the costs associated with the continuing operation after implementation.
4. Provide detailed information supporting all identified costs and savings; indicate how any cost savings will be applied.

Organizational Plan

1. What are the staffing requirements for each alternative?
2. Highlight any *significant* variances that each alternative may introduce.
3. Indicate how the project will be motivated for progress and revision of plans.

Implementation Schedule

1. Identify the specific tasks to be accomplished for each alternative.
2. Identify the responsibility for task performance.
3. Indicate the proposed manpower allocation by task.
4. Identify any significant milestones or decision points.

Authorizations Required

1. What specific authorizations must be obtained for each alternative?

   A. Authorization required from another agency within the executive branch
   B. Authorizations required from local or federal agencies outside the state government
   C. Other authorizations required

2. Explain the steps that have been taken to obtain authorizations required and results, if any.

Required Statutory Administrative Changes

1. Identify specific statutes or directives that must be changed to implement each alternative.
2. If other governmental entities must also make changes, include the data on that aspect.

Impact on Existing Operations

1. What is the anticipated effect on the current operations of the department if the alternative is implemented?
2. If an alternative entails the diverting of manpower or other resources from other projects, indicate the effect of such a diversion on the departmental program.
3. Identify programs delayed, canceled, or in other ways affected.

Sources of Funds

1. Identify the sources for any funds.
2. How could each alternative be financed?
3. If conditional funding has been approved, indicate how this has been communicated.

Estimation of Total Resources Requirement

1. For each alternative, identify the following resource requirements necessary to carry out the alternative:

   A. Personnel
   B. Equipment

C. Services
D. Other

2. Estimate these requirements for each of the following periods:

    A. Development
    B. Conversion/start-up
    C. Annual production
    D. Maintenance

3. Indicate levels of effort over time and total requirements. If manpower or other resources are to be diverted from other tasks, identify the diversion.

LONG–RANGE PLANNING FOR EDP IN STATE GOVERNMENT

The state government does not sit down and say, "We will allocate a certain percentage of our revenues to EDP technology." Rather, EDP technology is viewed primarily as a means by which the masses of data and the problems created by the sheer size of state government can be made more manageable. There is no overall approach to planning; it is done on a project-by-project basis. This is due to the nature of state government. For example, the following are illustrations of some recent projects and of the scope, cost, and rapidity with which they came about.

In 1970 the likelihood of a personal withholding tax in the State of California was quite remote, given the many public and private statements of the executive branch. Yet within one year's time, the decision was made to establish such a withholding tax and to have it operating by the following year. Implementation required the expenditure of more than $4 million by the Franchise Tax Board; the entire sum was expended in less than 18 months, and the program was successfully implemented.

Another example concerns the recent decision of the Department of Motor Vehicles to stagger automotive registrations over the course of the year. This project, which will be implemented over an 18-months period and at a cost exceeding $4 million, involves $50 million in revenues.

This type of volatile environment virtually precludes strategic long-range EDP planning. The government cannot select its marketplace; its marketplace is already there, and the recurring demands of the citizenry create the problem.

The inescapable conclusion is that long-range strategic planning is simply not possible within state government. Many, many hours would be wasted creating a plan that was necessarily so flexible and general that it contained few specific features. Therefore its cost and benefits, the return on investment, and the responsibility for its implementation could not be meaningfully established. To be of any value, EDP resources, and the strategic planning for their use, must be viewed in the context of a particular agency, charged with a specific area or segment of government. Only in this more focused way can any benefit be derived from planning.

SUMMARY

It is extremely difficult, if not impossible, to develop a long-range strategy for information systems technology within state government. The problem is not the technology; the problem is that the programs of the executive branch are subject to the whims of the legislative branch, and the power struggles that go on in this environment create one impasse after another. State governments do not have the stability found in private corporations. Whereas it is most unusual for a private corporation to decide to become involved in a given sector or to undertake a given program—and then cancel this involvement—state governments frequently do just that.

However it is important to note that some effort can be undertaken relative to the review aspects of long-range strategy. If every information system plan is reviewed to assess its contribution to an individual organization or to a group of organizations, and if it undergoes a superagency review at the cabinet level, then both the particular EDP application and the approach being employed can be evaluated. And until there is a change in the governmental environment, this aspect of planning is probably all that is possible.

20 WARD C. SANGREN

University of California

Computing services are an integral and essential part of the instructional, research, and administrative programs of the University of California. This chapter presents an overview of computing and computing planning at the university.

The University of California was established by the state legislature on March 23, 1868, as a public trust, to be administered by a corporation known as "The Regents of the University." By the fall quarter of 1973, the university had expanded to nine campuses having an enrollment of 113,270 students (80,478 undergraduates and 32,792 graduates). The faculty and staff number 52,630, exclusive of the Energy Research and Development Agency laboratories in Berkeley, Livermore, and Los Alamos. Enrollment is projected to reach 125,700 by 1980.

In early 1974, after much study and review, a new management structure for the university's computing was proposed. The anticipated management structure will require a number of evolutionary steps. Two major steps, which have already been implemented, are the establishment of a university-wide computer policy board and the appointment of an executive director of computing. (Dr. Melvin P. Peisakoff, formerly corporate director, Computing Requirements and Planning, Rockwell International Corporation, was appointed as executive director in April 1974.)

Though the university does not yet have an accepted long-range plan for computing, it is expected that a long-range plan will be developed during 1975. Furthermore, it is likely that this plan will be influenced greatly by the recently completed Computer Task Force Report and by the personality of Dr. Peisakoff.

To show the widespread and varied applications of computing within the university, three major aspects are discussed: (1) financial, (2) instruction and research, and (3) administrative, hospitals, and libraries. Following these sections is a short history of the university's computing planning activities.

FINANCIAL

Computers have been in use at the university for about 25 years. During this period instructional and research computing has developed primarily in a decentralized manner and administrative computing in a separate and centralized manner. This development has been suitable for the time period in question; but it has been concluded that this approach will not be adequate for future computing.

During the last eight years, several studies concerned with the utilization of computing resources were performed. Even though none of the computing plans resulting from these studies were ever fully implemented, each contained valuable recommendations.

It is convenient, in discussing computers at the university, to use the following four categories. (For a summary of computers presently installed, see Figure 1.)

1. *Adminstrative data processing centers.* There are four computers located in two administrative data processing centers. One center is located in the office of the president at Berkeley, and the other is on the Los Angeles campus. These two centers are under the control of the university director of information systems and have the mission of providing computing in support of the university's administrative needs.
2. *Campus computing centers.* There are 33 computers distributed among the 9 campus computing centers, which provide general computing service in support of the research and instructional needs of the campus. Limited administrative data processing support is also supplied.
3. *Specialized and dedicated computers.* The remaining campus computers fall into this category; the majority are small computers used by departments in support of research projects. Also included in this category, however, are a few large dedicated computers, such as those at the hospitals and the Center for Health Sciences at UCLA.

4. *Energy Research and Development Agency (ERDA).* Computers in this category are controlled by and used in support of the programs assigned to the respective ERDA laboratories located at Berkeley, Livermore, and Los Alamos. Faculty having federal contracts and grants make use of these facilities (primarily the Berkeley laboratory) to accomplish some of their computing needs.

Control of the computing facilities is vested with the chancellor of each campus and the directors of the ERDA laboratories. Because of their special objectives, no further comment will be made concerning computing at the ERDA laboratories. Each campus has assigned the responsibility for the operation of the campus computing centers to a computing center director. The center director at most campuses reports to a vice chancellor. Campus computing centers operate as service enterprises and charge for services. The specialized computers are, for the most part, under the control of their respective departments and do not charge for service.

The office of the president exercises general supervision over the university's computing activities. Before the appointment of the executive director of computing in 1974, the president had assigned to the vice president, administration, most general supervisory and review responsibilities in computing. The director of information systems heads the university's administrative data processing efforts and in that capacity continues to report to the vice president, administration. The activities of the coordinator of computer activities, who reported to this vice president, were assigned in 1974 to the executive director of computing.

The expenditures for the university (excluding the ERDA laboratories, but including the hospitals) associated with computing services over the past three fiscal years has remained essentially constant at about $19 million per year. Furthermore, the expenditures for administrative computer services (including hospitals) is slightly under $5 million, and the expenditures for instructional use of computers (IUC) at campus computing centers has been slightly under $3 million for each of the last three years. The sources of these funds have similarly remained nearly constant: about 44 percent federal, 35 percent state, and 21 percent university and others.

The financial concern with computing has centered mainly on the campus computing centers, which are operated as service enterprises and thus do not have the predetermined income enjoyed by the other categories of computing (e.g., administrative). During the fiscal year 1972–1973, for the first time in five years, the net operating revenue for the nine campus computing centers resulted in a small positive balance.

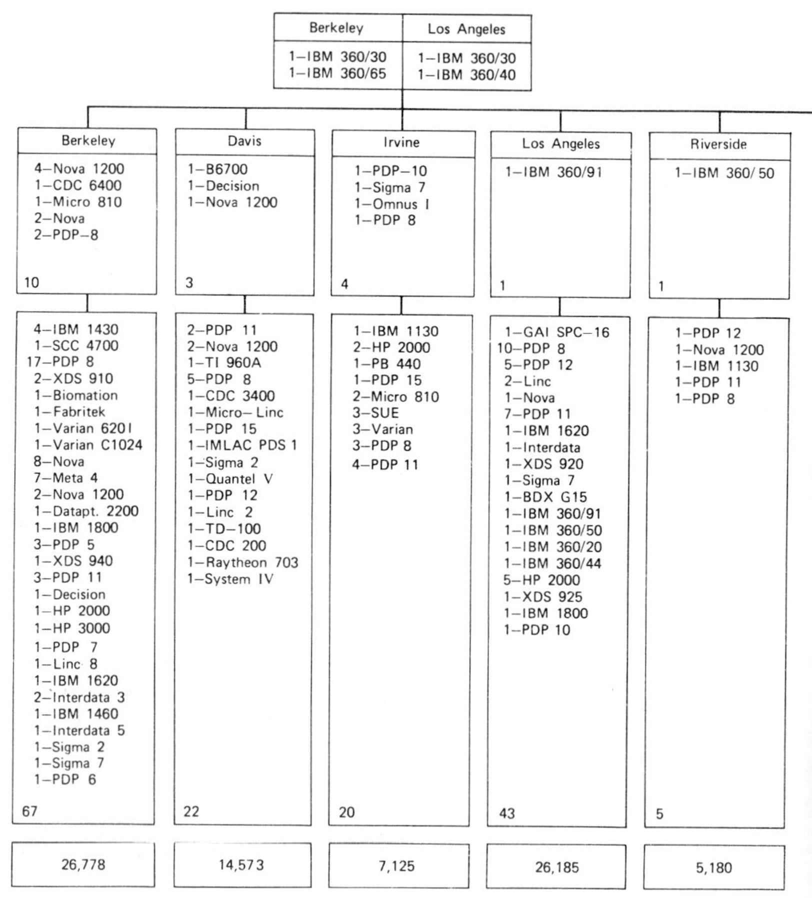

Figure 1 Computer activities within the University of California, fiscal year 1972–1973.

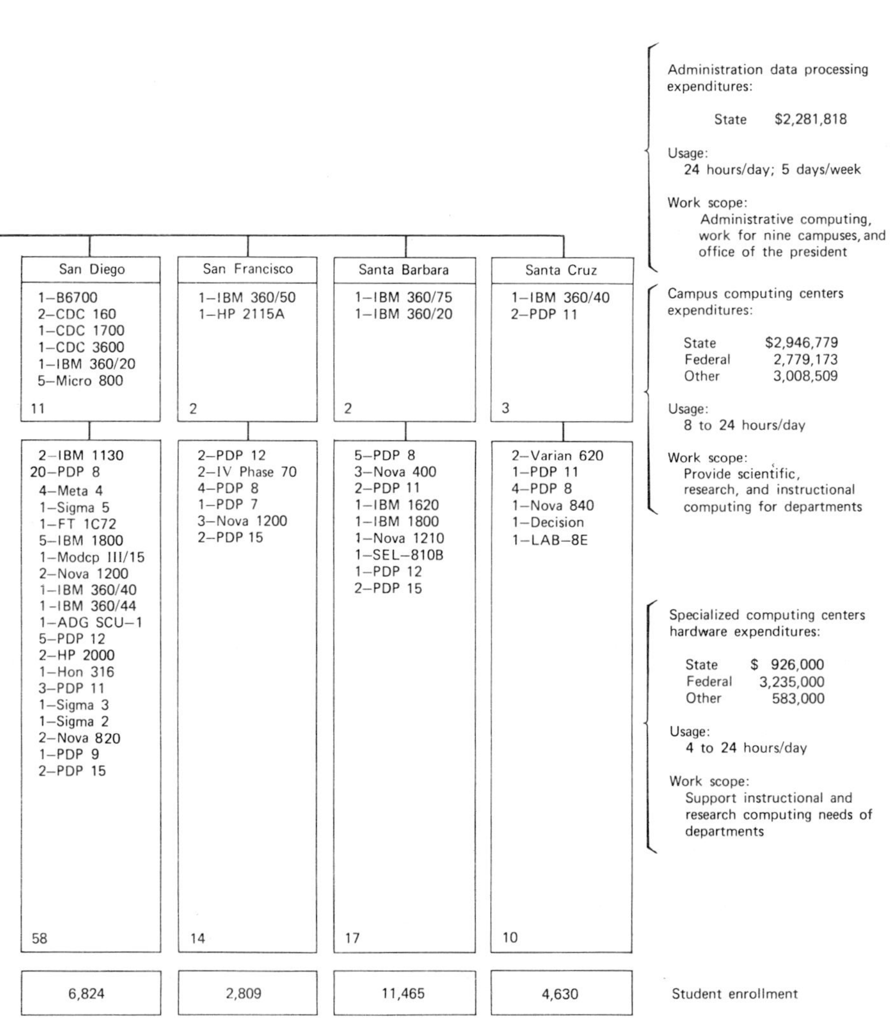

San Diego
1–B6700
2–CDC 160
1–CDC 1700
1–CDC 3600
1–IBM 360/20
5–Micro 800
11
2–IBM 1130
20–PDP 8
4–Meta 4
1–Sigma 5
1–FT 1C72
5–IBM 1800
1–Modcp III/15
2–Nova 1200
1–IBM 360/40
1–IBM 360/44
1–ADG SCU–1
5–PDP 12
2–HP 2000
1–Hon 316
3–PDP 11
1–Sigma 3
1–Sigma 2
2–Nova 820
1–PDP 9
2–PDP 15
58
6,824
San Francisco
1–IBM 360/50
1–HP 2115A
2
2–PDP 12
2–IV Phase 70
4–PDP 8
1–PDP 7
3–Nova 1200
2–PDP 15
14
2,809
Santa Barbara
1–IBM 360/75
1–IBM 360/20
2
5–PDP 8
3–Nova 400
2–PDP 11
1–IBM 1620
1–IBM 1800
1–Nova 1210
1–SEL–810B
1–PDP 12
2–PDP 15
17
11,465
Santa Cruz
1–IBM 360/40
2–PDP 11
3
2–Varian 620
1–PDP 11
4–PDP 8
1–Nova 840
1–Decision
1–LAB–8E
10
4,630
Administration data processing expenditures:
State $2,281,818
Usage:
24 hours/day; 5 days/week
Work scope:
Administrative computing, work for nine campuses, and office of the president
Campus computing centers expenditures:
State $2,946,779
Federal 2,779,173
Other 3,008,509
Usage:
8 to 24 hours/day
Work scope:
Provide scientific, research, and instructional computing for departments
Specialized computing centers hardware expenditures:
State $ 926,000
Federal 3,235,000
Other 583,000
Usage:
4 to 24 hours/day
Work scope:
Support instructional and research computing needs of departments
Student enrollment

Figure 1 *(Continued)*

This is in strong contrast to the previous three years, when the consolidated deficits averaged about $800,000 per year (see Figure 2). It would be erroneous to interpret this as an indication that the financial problems that have confronted the computing centers over the past several years are over. The most difficult situations exist at the larger centers of Berkeley, Los Angeles, and San Diego, which have accumulated significant deficits. It is worth noting that if the funds requested from the legislature for instructional computing had been granted, the deficit situation would not have occurred. Although sufficient time was available on the computers for use by students, it could not be used for these instructional purposes without funding. Because all the campus computing centers obtain some funding from federal contracts and grants, they are subject to the restrictions given in Bureau of the Budget Bulletin A-21, which specifies that no nongovernment user may be charged a cheaper rate than a government user. Thus all computer time used at a center must be funded.

INSTRUCTION AND RESEARCH

The impact of computing on society and on higher education has become enormous, and any modern university education must include some work with computers. The quantity and nature of computer in-

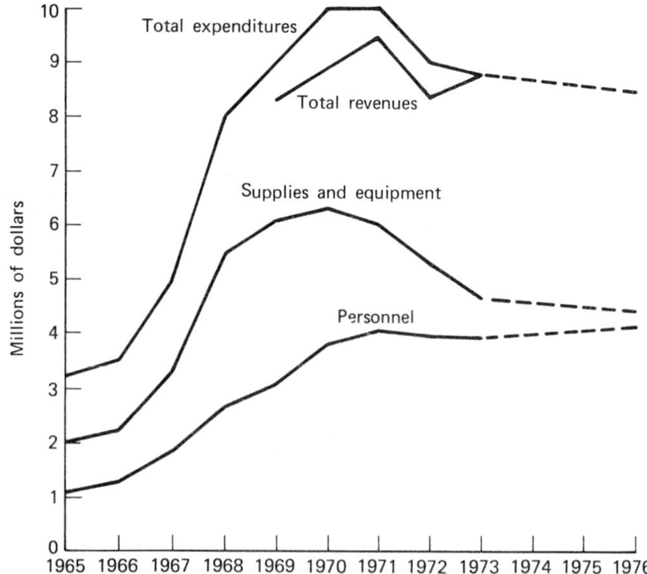

Figure 2 Computer Center expenditures for the nine campuses of the University of California.

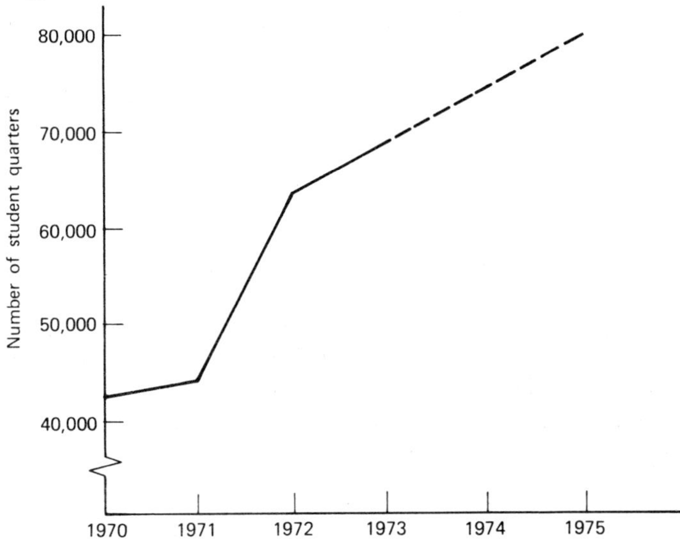

Figure 3 Growth in student demand for computing.

struction required by a student depends on his field and level of advancement. It is convenient to divide the instructional use of computers into three categories: elementary, intermediate, and advanced.

An elementary-level student needs to be exposed to computer programming and introduced to the impact of computers on society. The typical cost per year for such a student is $13, representing the amount associated with a single quarter-long course. The intermediate level is for students who need to learn problem-solving techniques involving computers in particular academic and professional disciplines such as engineering, science, and business. An average expenditure of $75 per year is required in this case, representing three quarters at $25 each. A small group of graduates and advanced undergraduate students require an advanced level of IUC with an expenditure of about $118 per quarter or $354 per year. These students make heavy use of computing because they are involved in the computer sciences or in research projects requiring extensive computations.

Because IUC funds have been steady and limited, the number of students in each of these three levels of use has been very much restricted. The immediate needs, as determined by surveys, indicate that about twice as many students require each level of computing services. At present, of the students who have any exposure to IUC, 60 percent are in the elementary level, 30 percent are at the intermediate level, and 10 percent are at the advanced level. Figure 3 depicts the growing number of student quarters involving computing.

Table 1 Instructional Use of Computers

Period	Budget Allocation	Amount Expended at all Campus Computing Centers
1968–1969	$ 941,400	$2,241,510
1969–1970	1,041,802	2,614,048
1970–1971	1,156,330	2,854,233
1971–1972	1,156,330	2,834,919
1972–1973	1,156,330	2,880,225

Table 1 shows the budget allocation and the total amount expended by campus computing centers for IUC. Although the needs, both met and unmet, have increased, the budget allocation has remained constant at approximately $1.16 million for the last three years. The amount expended for IUC has similarly remained at about $2.85 million. The differences between the budget allocations and the actual expenditures have been made up by other funds from federal, state, and vendor sources. Unfortunately the two principal sources of extramural funds, IBM and the National Science Foundation, are no longer available. Not only are there serious problems in obtaining funds to meet existing demands for computer services, there is an equally serious difficulty because many of these services are outmoded and inadequate.

The university has been particularly fortunate in the past in obtaining research funds (primarily federal) to support research computing. Considerable credit must be associated with the many illustrious faculty members who have justified their research computing. Because these funds are part of research contracts and grants, and are not in the budget process, they are financially self-determining.

ADMINISTRATIVE, HOSPITALS, AND LIBRARIES

Administrative

As was noted earlier, the administrative data processing services for the university are centralized in the Information Systems Division (ISD) under the office of the president. The computing support is provided by two centers, one at Berkeley and one at Los Angeles. These centers report to the director of ISD who reports to the vice president, administration.

In January 1971 the university-wide Information Systems Council was formed. It was assigned the following objectives:

To encourage campus participation in systems developments throughout the University to assure that responsive uniform systems are developed, to provide effective coordination and communications within and among campuses and units of the Office of the President in administrative information systems matters, to aid in the elimination of duplicative or redundant efforts, to recommend priorities for the use of the University's administrative data processing resources, to determine the impact of proposals for new or revised systems upon other systems or applications and assure smooth interfaces, and to make possible the maximum utilization of any proposed system by other campuses by involving all potential users in the design.

These objectives remain applicable, and their attainment is closely monitored and controlled by the office of the president.

The activities of ISD can be separated into two portions: data processing operations and systems development. The data processing operations have experienced an ever-increasing work load because of the demand for more data and the increased use of both old and new systems. Additionally, there is a pressing backlog of needs for new and replacement administrative systems. Present progress in developing these new systems is limited by the funding. In particular, a heavy initial investment is now needed to move ahead with important segments of a new university financial system.

Hospitals

Computers have become a major resource for modern hospital management, especially in large hospitals with a high volume of ambulatory and inpatient care activity. In the university setting, computerized census, billing, and accounts receivable systems are critical to successful financial management. These systems require six to eight hours of dedicated computer time every night to record all the patient care activities of the day and to maintain current financial balances of each patient's account.

The billing systems are the biggest single users of computers within the hospitals. In addition, computers are used for financial management, for data collection, and for reporting to meet governmental reporting requirements, as well as for internal management purposes. Recording of clinical laboratory test results, pharmacy inventory control, patient registration verification, and instrument monitoring are other areas in which the computer is contributing to efficient hospital administration and patient care.

Hospital computer operations are financed entirely by patient income and amount to no more than 3 percent of the total operating costs at each university hospital, including ongoing systems design efforts. Under the university's hospital systems development policy, a university-wide Hospital Systems Council has been established to ensure that systems ideas and developments are shared to the maximum feasible extent, recognizing the differences in each hospital's operating circumstances. Since hospital computer operations are financed from patient income, adoption of any system by one hospital, either new or adapted from another institution, must be cost justified as a matter of good hospital management.

Libraries

In 1972 the library automation programs of the university were reorganized into the university-wide library automation program (ULAP). ULAP was established as a separate center within the Institute of Library Research (ILR). Though ULAP shares the institute's facilities, its director reports directly to the university's vice president, academic affairs. The director of ULAP works closely with the Library Council on all automated library systems.

Among the projects being developed in association with ULAP are a Bibliographic Center, a UC Union List of Serials, a UC Union Catalog, and a Center for Information Services.

PLANNING HISTORY

It is informative to review the main university planning efforts during the last eight years. In 1966–1967 two studies concerned with the proper utilization of computing resources were performed; one with external consultants,[1] and one with university personnel.[2] A primary result of these studies was the establishment in late 1968 of the Office of the Coordinator of Computer Activities. It was anticipated that an essential task for this office would be long-range planning for computing. In 1969–1970, the following four actions were taken by the coordinator's office to help form the basis for a long-range plan.

1. An *ad hoc* committee composed of highly qualified campus and laboratory computing managers who had wide computing experience and background was established to advise and assist the computer

[1]*University of California Computer Study Phase I Report,* Management Analysis Center, Inc., October 31, 1966.

[2]*A Review and Reconsideration of "University of California Computer Study Phase I Report,"* Fred M. Tonge, December 1967.

coordinator in the development of a long-range plan for research and instructional computing.

2. In early 1969, with the aid of this committee, a lengthy questionnaire was sent to each of the nine campuses requesting information about the five-year needs for instructional and research computing of each campus. The responses were informative; and after difficult correlation and interpretation, they proved helpful in overall university planning.
3. A rotating committee consisting of computing center directors and representatives of the office of the vice president, business and finance, completed visits to each campus computing center to review in detail the justifications of the existing research and instructional computing facilities and the existing and future plans for computing at the campuses.
4. A lengthy report entitled "Computing Activities—University of California," dated April 27, 1970, reviewed the development and present status of the university's computing activities at each campus and provided a frame of reference for the formulation of plans for meeting the future research and instructional computing needs of the university.

This long report on computing activities was used to prepare a document entitled "Long-range Planning—Instruction and Research Computing," which appeared in revised form in January 1972 after review by the vice presidents and chancellors of the nine campuses. The plan, containing the suggestions of these officials, was submitted to the president. However the plan was not accepted because it was not felt to be sufficiently definitive to warrant adoption. In retrospect, the document was quite innocuous and recommended very few alterations of existing practices. It is thus not surprising that it had received the tentative approval of all the affected groups before reaching the president's office.

In 1970 the state legislature asked the university to report on its long-range planning and future needs for computers. A report submitted in October 1970 summarized the university's computer position at that time. It was noted that the university did not anticipate any expansion of its general purpose hardware until a long-range plan had been completed. Since no long-range plan has been adopted yet, no significant expansion of large general-purpose computer hardware has taken place.

Much effort is still being expended in long-range computer planning. A major concern in the 1970–1973 period has been the difficult financial condition of the nine campus computing centers. As discussed earlier, these financial difficulties arose primarily because of reduced federal and vendor support, coupled with failure of the state to increase its support for instructional use of computing. Another concern in planning has been the belief of many, both within the university and outside it, that increased central control or consolidation of computing would be more efficient and economical. In addition, the planning has been concerned with technical computing advances, particularly the centralizing features of communication networks and the decentralizing aspects of minicomputers.

Early in 1972, and at a special meeting in May 1972, the Council of Chancellors discussed fundamental issues concerning computer operations. In particular, this led to the support for a study of networking for the university. This interest had been stimulated by the favorable experiences of the Santa Barbara, Los Angeles, and San Diego campuses in using the computer network supported by the Advanced Research Projects Agency (ARPANET) and the less favorable experience of operating a small experimental data switching network in 1971. With financial assistance from the National Science Foundation, and the backing of the chancellors, a report entitled "A Study of the Impact of Networking on University Computing" was prepared by May 1973. Concurrently, the Academic Council was asked to prepare a position paper on the educational policy aspects of computers. This report underlined the essential and integral way that computing enters into instruction. The report further pointed out the increasingly complex problems involved in devising and implementing a rational plan for the variety of uses of computers at a multicampus university.

In June 1973 president Charles Hitch appointed a computer task force to recommend an approach to "the organization and configuration of the university's computing resources (both equipment and personnel) to meet the university's needs with optimal use of present and future facilities, staff, and operating funds, and plans and policies necessary for implementation." In September 1973 the task force submitted its report, which was accepted, and its recommendations are being implemented.

The text of this report now forms the foundation of the university's computing plans. The main points are as follows:

1. Assumptions
   - A. The totality of computing is considered.
   - B. The computing situation is uncomfortable, particularly for the instructional use of computers.
   - C. Technology is ahead of management experience.
   - D. The technical changes are producing centralization (e.g., networks) and decentralization (e.g., minicomputers) trends that

challenge the financial and technical independence of campus computing centers.

E. Governmental and commercial practices have major impact on operations.

F. An evolutionary approach to computing is essential.

G. Management of computing resources is the key issue.

2. Analysis

A. Any significant new machines or systems must be treated as investments.

B. The university will require one or more additional large computers in the next two to five years.

C. The personnel and software costs are increasingly the major computing costs.

D. New machine(s) and services should be linked in a network. Experiments in networking and network management should be developed.

E. Development of strong computer management is crucial.

F. Small special purpose machines may be acquired for particular operating units under consistent university-wide policies.

G. The primary objective of any computing policy or plan is to furnish support to the academic and administrative programs of the university.

3. Recommendations

A. The next large-scale augmentation of the university's computing capability must be considered as a system-wide capability.

B. A computer policy board should be established, consisting of a senior representative from each of the nine campuses, ERDA laboratories, and the office of the president.

C. An executive director of computing, responsible to the president, should be appointed.

D. The computer policy board should develop computer policies for approval by the president. In this policy role the board must deal with such problems as computer fiscal arrangements, major changes in hardware and software, networking, optimum configuration of computing resources, and any computer decision of system-wide concern.

With the adoption of this report, computing at the University of California has entered a new era. The Computer Policy Board has been formed and an executive director of computing has been appointed. However all the underlying problems still exist, and it remains to be seen whether this new approach will permit the university to come to grips with them. The demand for computing services is steadily increasing, and budgets are stable, even decreasing (especially if adjusted for inflation); thus the problems are not easy to solve. And until solutions become more apparent, the role of long-range planning for computing within the university will be informal at best.

A

IBM Information Systems Planning Requirements

TABLE OF CONTENTS

Table of Contents

List of Forms

LIST OF FORMS

1.0 INTRODUCTION

It is intended that DP Group, and its divisions, review and update Information Systems Plans according to the following schedule:

Month	Action
February	Divisions submit to Group Director of Information Systems Control and Planning, Divisional Information Systems Plans which have been assessed and signed-off by the submitting organization.
March	Group-wide assessments and divisional feedback. Preparation and review of the DP Group Information Systems Plan. Publication of a fully-assessed DP Group Information Systems Plan.
September	Divisions review Divisional Information Systems Plans and obtain approval by the appropriate division management.
October	Divisions submit Information Systems resource summaries, and any significant deltas, to Group Director of Information Systems Control and Planning.
November	DP Group Management and Staff review Information Systems resource summaries and any significant deltas.

The requirements for preparation of the Divisional Information Systems Plans are the elements essential to the planning process. The sections should be provided in the sequence as shown and should convey the essence of the planning requirements logically and objectively in concise language.

2.0 KEY PLANNING

Key Planning elements are Environment, Goals, Objectives, Strategies, and Organization.

2.1 Environment

Environment factors are those affecting the developments and operation of information systems. Among the factors to be considered in the planning process are:

1. Assumptions which have significant impact on future operations.

2. Assessment of control adequacy of the division's current systems.

3. Business control exposures that must be addressed.

4. Trends of users' needs and systems required to meet these needs. Consider the division environment, objectives, strategies, the effect of transaction volume, unique data processing needs, technological changes and trends, etc.

5. Information Systems organizational strengths, and current projected deficiencies that must be addressed.

6. IBM policy or product mission changes affecting the division's systems needs.

7. Significant interdivisional dependencies required.

8. Legislative, policy, or product mission changes affecting the division's information systems needs.

This statement of environmental analysis provides a rationale for the goals, objectives and strategies to follow.

2.2 Goals

Goals are the levels or statements, concerning information systems, that express where we want to be, although we may not necessarily know how to get there, or whether the levels are altogether attainable. Goals are something we plan toward.

2.3 Objectives

Objectives are the levels or statements, concerning information systems, that express what we believe we can achieve. It is implied that we know how to get there. The main difference between objectives and goals is that a credible plan of action exists for achieving the objectives.

Objectives should, as a minimum, meet requirements for information needs in the business and functional areas. Objectives should be in synchronization with the overall Corporate and divisional objectives.

Furthermore, objectives should be stated so that some manner of measuring accomplishment of these objectives is available.

2.4 Strategies

Strategies are the broad courses of action which have been selected to accomplish the information systems objectives. Included may be an overview of current efforts, statements of the direction chosen for long range development of these systems, and the guiding principles or systems philosophy utilized in the strategies selected.

Key risks in the strategy, including potential exposure and probability of occurrance, should be described briefly. Include, also, assumptions that relate directly to the strategies established and are key to achieving success.

Information systems strategies should relate to the objectives and strategies for the division and should address both Business Support strategies and Dat Processing Excellence strategies.

2.4.1 Business Support Strategies

Business Support strategies should directly relate to the two or more major functions of a division. The nine possible functions are Engineering, Administration, Finance, Manufacturing, Marketing, Personnel, Planning, Services, and Information Systems.

2.4.2 Data Processing Excellence Strategies

Data Processing Excellence strategies should stress the following:

1. Personnel Oriented Excellence - Education, recruitment, organization, and management development.

2. Equipment Oriented Excellence - Effective equipment selection and utilization, equipment and communications consolidation, and establishment of information systems centers.

3. Technique Oriented Excellence - Development and application of advanced techniques.

4. Project Control Excellence - Development and application of project controls, including value analysis.

2.5 Organization

Include in the Organization section a statement as to how the Divisional Information Systems function will be structured over the planning years to deal with the following information systems areas:

1. Information Systems Planning Control, and Measurements.

2. Systems Development.

3. Standards and Data Management.

4. Operations and Maintenance.

5. Recruitment and Education.

Describe current strengths and current or projected deficiencies. Show how these deficiencies are being or will be addressed.

Strategies addressing these deficiencies should be included as part of the Data Processing Excellence strategies indicated in Section 2.4.2.

2.6 OTHER CONSIDERATIONS

Other significant considerations, which are not specifically included in the detailed instructions, should be described in Section 3.

3.0 RESOURCE SUMMARY (SCHEDULE I)

3.1 Description

The RESOURCE SUMMARY (SCHEDULE I) is the Division Resource Summary for the planning years. Each Division is responsible for ensuring that the resources shown are the total Information Systems resources planned for the years indicated.

Information Systems resources are defined as all resources which are used to support internal IBM activities for the collection, organization, control, and display of data necessary to:

1. Measure, plan, operate, and control the business and/or facilitate decision-making.
2. Support design automation, process automation and other product information systems.
3. Support scientific computation and the application of computer-assisted instruction to IBM employees.
4. Support IBM personnel or IBM-funded projects.

3.2 Submission

Schedule I is to be submitted at planning time. It should be reviewed quarterly. A revised Schedule I is to be submitted if resources for 1970, 1971, or 1972 are expected to deviate from the previous plan by ±5%.

3.2.1 Schedule I - Divisional Total

Submit a Divisional Total Schedule I.

3.2.2 Schedule I By Location

A separate Schedule I is to be submitted for each geographic location in the Division.

3.2.3 Schedule I By I/S Category

A separate Schedule I is to be submitted for each I/S category in the Division.

I/S Categories are defined as follows:

1. Administrative

   Includes general and administrative functions: manufacturing material control; management science activities; such as CTS and MIS; and developments of systems support packages for internal use.

2. Technical and Scientific

   Includes the activity and support of engineers and scientists; design automation; engineering release and control.

3. Manufacturing Process Support

   Includes the development of process control; data acquisition and sensor base systems; systems which perform tests on manufactured products.

3.3 Preparation

The following items should be addressed:

3.3.1 Heading

1. Actual resources for the year 1969.
2. Committed resources for the years 1970, 1971, and 1972.
3. Outlook, or tentative resources, for the year 1977.

3.3.2 Line Items

Item I. EXPENDITURES ($000)

Expenditures are subdivided as follows:

Item I.A. I/S GROSS

The accumulation of resources for I/S services to be performed for a particular reporting entity regardless of who is the intended recipient of the service.

Item I.B.1 I/S Charges In

I/S Charges In are the resources associated with I/S services performed by another reporting entity which have been billed to this reporting entity.

Item I.B.2 I/S Charges Out

I/S Charges Out are the resources associated with I/S services performed by this reporting entity and billed to another I/S entity.

Item I.C. I/S NET

The total sum planned to be expended in the years indicated for all Information Systems items. Include all expenses associated with Line Items II, IV, V, and other items, such as communications.

Expenditures for Product Programs are to include only the PID publication costs.

I/S Net is obtained by subtracting the I/S Charges Out from the Adjusted I/S Gross and is intended to represent the resources required to support the true mission of the reporting entity.

(Definition of Adjusted I/S Gross: This is the sum of I/S Gross plus I/S Charges In.)

Item I.C.1 Development

The net sum planned to be expended in the years indicated for all Information Systems Development. Included are Key Project Development and Other Development, as defined in Section 4.

Item I.C.2 Operational & Maintenance, and Systems Support

The net sum planned to be expended in the years indicated for all Information Systems Operations, Maintenance, and Systems Support as defined in Section 4.

The sum of Items I.C.1 and I.C.2 should equal Item I.C. for each year indicated.

Item II. DP EQUIPMENT EXPENDITURES ($000) BUSINESS (10, 11, 14, 15, 16, 17, 18)

The yearly expenditures for DP equipment used in functions 10, 11, 14, 15, 16, 17, and 18, as defined for internal IBM use in the DP Branch Office Manual, Customer Master Record section. For further details see DP Group Staff Letter, Finance - Information Systems No. 3.

Item III. DP EQUIPMENT EXPENDITURES ($000)

The yearly expenditures for all DP equipment used, as defined in the DP Branch Office Manual, Customer Master Record section.

Functions are defined as follows:

Function	Definition
10	Research
11	Administrative
14	Scientific Computing
15	Computation Cost Center (Internal use, servicing on a charge basis several departments and/or divisions).
16	Management Services and Sciences
17	Technology Development
18	Internal Application Programming

For further details see DP Group Staff Letter, Finance - Information Systems No. 3.

Item IV. MANPOWER (as of 12/31)

Year-end Information Systems IBM headcount for the years indicated. Enter as whole units. The sum of Items IV.A.1, IV.A.2, IV.B., plus DP Equipment Operators, Keypunch, Secretaries, and Clerks should equal Item IV.

Item IV.A. Systems Analysts, Programmers and Other Professionals

Year-end headcount of all Systems Analysts, Programmers, and Other Professionals who are primarily associated with Information Systems activities, including those involving physical planning, equipment control, project control, etc. Do not include non-professionals engaged in these activities.

Item IV.A.1 Development

Year-end headcount of all Systems Analysts, Programmers, and Other Professionals who are associated with Information Systems Key Development and Other Development, as defined in Section 4.

Item IV.A.2 Operational, and Maintenance and Systems Support

Year-end headcount of all other Systems Analysts, Programmers, and other Professionals.

Item IV.B. Managers

Year-end headcount of all managers within the Divisions who are primarily associated with Information Systems activities.

Item V. SUBCONTRACTORS

IBM or non-IBM resources from outside the division. Include temporary or supplemental IBM employees. Show as man-years of effort; not headcount. (Where another IBM organization will be supplying resources to the reporting division, written confirmation of such support should be available between the supporting and supported organizations.)

3.3.3 Footing

Make appropriate entries.

3.4 ANALYSIS OF CHANGES

3.4.1 PLAN-TO-PLAN CHANGES

Include an explanation of significant changes which have occured since submission of the last Information Systems Plan. State whether the significant changes are due to better reporting, broadening of the reporting base, or additional product missions, etc.

A significant change is defined as:

1. ±10% difference in any resource of Schedule I.

2. ±10% difference in the manpower of any project in Schedule I.

3. ±60 days difference in any date of Schedule II.

3.4.2 YEAR-TO-YEAR CHANGES

This Section applies to the years 1969, 1970, 1971 and 1972 only.

Include in this an explanation of changes in resources from year to year, if these changes are not consistent with the growth pattern of the Division.

4.0 PROJECT SUMMARY (SCHEDULE II)

4.1 Description

The PROJECT SUMMARY (SCHEDULE II) is the Division Project Summary for the planning years. Each division is responsible for ensuring that the projects shown include all Information Systems projects planned for the years indicated.

Information Systems efforts are defined in Section 3.1.

Project Numbering is defined in Section 5.2.

4.2 Submission

Schedule II is to be submitted at planning time. It should be reviewed quarterly. A revised Schedule II is to be submitted whenever a project is approved, initiated, or terminated, or modified in terms of scope, equipment, resources (±10%) or schedule (± 60 days).

4.3 Project Classifications

Major classfications are DEVELOPMENT and OPERATIONS. Development is broken into Key Projects and Other Development. Operations includes Scientific Computing, Maintenance/Enhancements, Systems Support and Training. Each project on SCHEDULE II should appear under a classification heading. See Section 4.7 for example.

This guideline defines these project classifications and further prescribes the reporting procedure to be used.

This reporting procedure permits those levels of activity which are of relatively minor significance (as outlined in the definitions) to be combined and reported under one project number. The divisional and location control functions, however, will still have the responsibility of tracking these projects at the necessary level of detail.

4.4 Development Classfications

4.4.1 Key Project Development

This classification consists of those activites necessary to determine, develop, and implement the significant design, structure, and operating elements of an Information System.

4.0 Project Summary (Schedule II)

Included are those efforts involved in the study, design, programming, testing, and installation phases of an I/S project. Included in installation activities are all efforts necessary to install the system on an operational basis including, for example, training, file conversion, user documentation, parallel operations, and bridging.

Key Project Development consists of all development efforts which exhibit any of the following characteristics:

- Require $200,000 or more in any year including subcontract.
- Extend longer than two years.
- Have significant inter-divisional implications.
- Have significant multi-location implications.
- Effect other Key Projects.
- Are noteworthy because their timely completion is necessary to prevent a control exposure.

Include all requested Schedule II information. Furthermore, provide a full line of information for each Subsystem and Application Project Number.

4.4.2 Other Development

Those development efforts which do not have any of the above defined characteristics of Key Project Development can be combined by location and reported under one project number as an "Aggregate Project". The project description should provide visibility of the significant elements of the aggregate by giving: a brief description of each, their inter-relationships, and dependencies, if any.

The narrative portion of the project description should begin with the statement...This development project is an aggregate of __X__ and includes __Y__ separately defined efforts of which the significant ones are described below... Where 'X' is a description of the function and 'Y' is the number of identifiable projects included in the aggregate.

Only Title, System Project Number, and Resources for Previous Years, 1970, 1971, and 1972 are required.

4.5 Operations Classifications

Only Title, System Project Number, and Resources for Previous Years, 1970, 1971, and 1972 are required. Operations includes Scientific Computing, Maintenance/Enhancements, Systems Support, and Training.

4.5.1 Scientific Computing

Scientific Computing consists of those programming and analysis efforts for application of the computer to engineering and/or scientific problems, except when those efforts have the characteristics of a Development Project.

4.5.2 Maintenance/Enhancements

This classification consists of those activities necessary to provide continued operational support of the business. Included in this classification are those efforts which are necessary to keep an existing system running or make adjustments necessitated by policy, organization, and statutory changes. The classification also includes those activities performed to fine tune existing systems to user needs including systems conversions or configuration changes. Also included in this classification are small scale user support activities such as the preparation of a specialized report for a particular function. Those activities which result in significant redesign or restructuring of the existing system are part of the Development categories.

4.5.3 Systems Support

This classification includes those professional resources necessary to install, use, maintain/enhance, and manage System Control Programming. Included in the classification would be, for example, OS release maintenance, bridging to utilize new access methods, and machine utilization analysis.

Continuous activities necessary to support Information Systems which do not fall under other defined activities are also reported under this category.

4.5.4 Training

Training consists of two separate activities.

1. Those resources engaged in giving the training; instructors, test time, and teaching materials.

2. Those resources engaged in receiving the training.

4.6 Preparation

The following items should be addressed:

4.6.1 Heading

DIVISION: Division Title, spelled out.

4.6.2 Line Items

PROJECT TITLE

The common term or Acronym commonly used to identify the project.

PROJECT NUMBER

Same as described in Section 8.2.

SCHEDULE; PHASE DATES 1-4

The four digit month-year date in which the project completed a phase, or is scheduled to complete a phase.

PHASE
- I Study/Feasibility/Proposal-Complete
- II General Design-Complete
- III Detail Design, Programming, Testing-Complete
- IV Complete Install

RESOURCES: MAN-YEARS

For each detail entry, enter the man-years of Systems Analysts, Programmers, and other Professionals resources.

PREV. YEARS (Previous Years)

Enter the man-years devoted to the project in all previous years. Round to the nearest whole number.

TOTALS

Total man-years for the years indicated.

4.6.3 Footing

Make appropriate entries.

5.0 PROJECT PLANS

This section provides instructions for the uniform preparation and organization of the project plans for each project listed in Schedule II.

5.1 Purpose

Project Plans provide a formal means for communicating general information about a project. They are an essential vehicle for further understanding the application of information systems effort in the IBM Company, and provide an initial source of project information to facilitate further research.

5.2 Preparation

The following items should be addressed. Any item not applicable should be marked N/A.

DIVISION: Division Title, spelled out

LOCATION: Location of this project

PROJECT NUMBER

The terms "project", "application", and "system" have various meanings among the divisions. In order to establish a consistency of terms, the following definitions are to be used for classification:

Division: (Position 1) - Division code referred to as follows:

0. Group Staff Services
1. Systems Development Division
2. Systems Manufacturing Division (Manufacturing)
3. Components Division
4. Data Processing Division
5. Field Engineering Division
6. Information Systems Control and Planning

7. Product Test

8. Systems Manufacturing Division (Distribution)

9. General System Division

System: (Positions 2 and 3) - A set of related subsystems linked together by the common tasks that they support. This is the highest level of the hierarchy.

Subsystem; (Positions 4 and 5) - a set of related applications or modules that form a complete integrated information handling unit. This unit begins with the generation of data and ends with the delivery of information to users.

Application: (or module) (Positions 6 and 7) - The smallest series of related programs or program segments that act as a separate integrated unit for the complete processing of data from raw input to finished output.

Every project may not necessarily have to be organized into subsystems and/or applications. The above hierarchy provides the capability to identify resources for subordinate and related efforts in the project system.

Projects should be specified on SCHEDULE II with separate line entries down to the lowest applicable levels of the system hierarchy.

Application of this coding is:

01 00 00 System

01 01 00 Subsystem

01 01 01 Application

01 01 02 Application

02 00 00 System

The combination of division code (Position 1), system code (Positions 2 and 3), subsystem code (Positions 4 and 5), and application code (Positions 6 and 7) forms a unique identification for any and all projects.

System numbers 80-99 are reserved for Corporate-wide activities and will be assigned by Corporate.

LINE ITEMS

a. TITLE: Same as on Schedule II. (See Section 4.6.2)

b. PROJECT DESCRIPTION

A brief statement including the project objectives, major processes being improved, and problems being solved.

c. ORGANIZATIONAL DEPENDENCIES

(User and Inter-Divisional) In the course of project development activities, a variety of inter-organizational dependencies could be required. These dependencies range from inputs or supporting information required from other divisions to outputs to be supplied to them.

These dependencies, including products that may be required by the supporting or supported divisions to complete the data processing cycle, should be described.

Where the success of a project is also dependent upon dedicated user resources, such a dependency should be described.

Where an application in another division is required, its dependency (i.e. the application, or its target date, etc.) should be identified.

Prose statements, not detailed listings, are desired.

d. EQUIPMENT REQUIREMENTS

Equipment required for the operation of the system being developed, i.e. computer, input-output equipment, remote terminals, etc.

Complete at the highest applicable level of project hierarchy. If the equipment is not totally dedicated to the project, estimate the percent usage of main frame time by the project.

---

e. DPD STANDARDS DEVIATIONS

List any deviations from the Corporate Instructions and Guidelines as outlined in the Corporate Data Processing Systems Manual.

f. MAJOR FILES

Name of file, file size (number of logical records), and estimated transactions per year.

g. COMMUNICATIONS REQUIREMENTS

Volume (characters) per time frequency of data which will be transmitted from one location to another over leased communication lines. Specify desired response time.

h. CAPABILITY/LIMITING FACTORS

Expressions of the upper capability range of the project in terms of peak volume during the life of the system once it becomes operational.

i. CONVERSION PLANS

Comments and provisions on how the conversion to the system will be effected.

j. CONTINGENCY PLANS

Provisions that have been made to minimize exposure and the impact of schedule slippages.

Provisions that have been made for equipment backups.

Unusual resources requirements or technical breakthroughs.

k. ECONOMIC CONSIDERATIONS (Must be completed)

Cost effectiveness in terms of estimated investment costs (non-recurring), savings, and benefits expected from the project.

l. INTANGIBLES

Values, efficiencies, or benefits not expressed in item k.

m. WHOM TO CALL - The name and location of the person to be contacted for additional information regarding this project.

n. CLASSIFICATION

The status of the project, classified as follows:

Key Project Development

Other Development

Scientific Computing

Systems Support

Maintenance/Enhancements

Training

o. DEVELOPMENT LOCATIONS

The 3-character location identifiers defined in the Corporate Data Processing Systems Manual, Part III-Data Management.

p. INSTALLATION LOCATIONS

The 3-character location identifiers defined in the Corporate Data Processing Systems Manual Part III-Data Management.

HEADING & FOOTING: Make appropriate entries.

5.3 Project Plan Working Forms

The Project Plan Working forms can be used for writing up the Project Plans. (The forms can be used as a master for preparing additional copies as required.) For final preparation all line items which are not applicable (N/A) should be entirely omitted.

PROJECT PLAN WORKING FORM

IBM - DP GROUP
INFORMATION SYSTEMS PLAN
DIVISION: ______________________
LOCATION: ______________________

Project No. ________
Issued: 02-15-71

PROJECT PLAN

a. TITLE

b. PROJECT DESCRIPTION

c. ORGANIZATIONAL DEPENDENCIES

5-6

PROJECT PLAN WORKING FORM

IBM - DP GROUP
INFORMATION SYSTEMS PLAN
DIVISION: ______________________________
LOCATION: ______________________________

Project No. ________
Issued: 02-15-71

d. EQUIPMENT REQUIREMENTS

e. DPS STANDARDS DEVIATIONS

f. MAJOR FILES

5-7

PROJECT PLAN WORKING FORM

IBM - DP GROUP — Project No. ________
INFORMATION SYSTEMS PLAN — Issued: 02-15-71
DIVISION: ________________________
LOCATION: ________________________

g. COMMUNICATONS REQUIREMENTS

h. CAPABILITY/LIMITING FACTORS

i. CONVERSION PLANS

j. CONTINGENCY PLANS

PROJECT PLAN WORKING FORM

IBM - DP GROUP
INFORMATION SYSTEMS PLAN
DIVISION: ______________________
LOCATION: ______________________

Project No. ________
Issued: 02-15-71

k. ECONOMIC CONSIDERATIONS

l. INTANGIBLES

m. WHOM TO CALL

n. STATUS

5-9

PROJECT PLAN WORKING FORM

IBM - DP GROUP — Project No. ________

INFORMATION SYSTEMS PLAN — Issued: 02-15-71

DIVISION: ____________________

LOCATION: ____________________

o. DEVELOPMENT LOCATIONS

p. INSTALLATION LOCATIONS

PREPARED BY: ____________________

DATE PREPARED: ____________________

DATE REVISED: ____________________

5-10

6.0 TESTING THE PLAN

6.1 Purpose

The purpose of this section is to provide the preparer of the Plan with a basic set of tests to interrelate the various elements of the Plan with Divisional, Group, and Corporate plans.

6.2 Instructions and Guidelines

6.2.1 Test 1 Are DP Group Missions and Objectives Met?

Test the DP Group mission and objectives against the DP Group Plan, with added emphasis on the Information Systems section. This test will be performed by DP Group Information Systems Plans and Audits, and Corporate.

6.2.2 Test 2 Are Divisional Missions and Objectives Met?

Test the Divisional Information Systems Plan against the Divisional Program of the DP Group Plan. Both Divisional Information Systems and Divisional Finance parties should participate in an iterative process until agreement is achieved.

Compare the projects identified on the Divisional Project Summary (Schedule II) against the Divisional Program of the DP Group Plan to ensure that objectives and strategies are being addressed. Establish priorities for the projects.

6.2.3 Test 3 Are Resources in Line with Workload?

Compare the Divisional Project Summary (Schedule II) against the Divisional Resource Summary (Schedule I).

For a division, the total available man-years of systems analysts, programmers, and other professionals (calculated from Items IV.A, IV.B, and V of Schedule I) should equal the total man-years required on Schedule II.

6.0 Results of Testing the Plan

An example best illustrates the test:

	1969		1970		1971		1972	
Schedule I	IBM	Sub-Contr.	IBM	Sub-Contr.	IBM	Sub-Contr.	IBM	Sub-Contr.
Systems Analysts & Programmers	50	5	66	6	60	5	60	0
Computed Available Man Years			58		63		60	
Total Available Man Years			64		68		60	
Schedule II Man Years Required			85		70		65	
% Variance			33%		2%		8%	

Schedule I reflects year-end manpower inventory for the category labeled "IBM." This must be converted to man years to be consistent with other factors involved with this test.

To convert, add the year being converted to the previous year (i.e. 1970 shows 66, previous year shows 50). Divide by two, and add any subcontract man years.

This yields the total man years available for the year being converted.

Total Available =

1/2 (converted year + previous year) + subcontracts.

The balance of the illustration is self-explanatory. If the percent variance is greater than 8%, either rework the schedules or submit an explanation of the variance with the plan.

6.2.4 Test 4 Does A Project Plan Exist For Each Project?

Check the Project Plans against the Schedule II project listing. There should be a Project Plan for each project reported.

6.2.5 Test 5 Do DP Equipment Expenditures Tie In with DP Equipment Plan?

Equipment expenditures on Schedule I (Items II and III) should be reconciled to the latest DP Equipment Plans submitted in accordance with DP Group Finance Letters Number 1 and 2.

6.2.6 Test 6 Are Project Plans Adequately Supported by DP Equipment Plan?

Test Schedule II and the Project Plans against the DP Equipment Plan to ensure that project requirements for equipment are well stated and have been approved and ordered.

7.0 TYPING INSTRUCTIONS

GENERAL:

Use typewriters with SELECTRIC COURIER - 10 PITCH. You may use 10 Pitch MTST and CTS/ATS terminals.

Number all pages sequentially on the line beneath the words "IBM CONFIDENTIAL", centered at bottom of page.

SCHEDULES:

Type directly on the appropriate Schedule I or II form.

TEXT:

Type all headings and footings as shown on forms. Use plain white typing bond, do not type on the lined Working Form. For Project Plans omit all line items which are not applicable (N/A) and close up the space between the items.

Type in the allotted space and maintain margins established by the heading. (6-1/2" width by 7" depth.)

Use block form; do not indent at the start of a paragraph.

Use double spacing between paragraph headings and paragraphs.

Single space elsewhere.

8.0 REPRODUCTION INSTRUCTIONS

GENERAL

Each division is responsible for the quality of its reproduced material. Use a suitable printing process to obtain clear copies.

Order 25 printed copies, printed on both sides, with margins maintained for binding. Collate copies and distribute according to distribution instructions.

SCHEDULES

Photo-reduce copies to 70% and print on 8-1/2" x 11" paper.

TEXT

Make copies at 100% and print on 8-1/2" x 11" paper.

9.0 DISTRIBUTION INSTRUCTIONS

In order that we may expedite the plan review process, it is requested that each divisional IS director or manager supply one copy of his divisional Information Systems Plan to the following:

(OMITTED)

DIVISION: ____________
LOCATION: ____________
I/S CATEGORY: ____________

DP GROUP
INFORMATION SYSTEMS PLAN
SCHEDULE I - RESOURCE SUMMARY

Issued: 02-15-71

ITEM	DESCRIPTION	ACTUAL	COMMITTED			OUTLOOK
		1969	1970	1971	1972	1977
I.	EXPENDITURES ($000)					
	A. I/S Gross	____	____	____	____	____
	B. Apportionments					
	1. Charges In	____	____	____	____	____
	2. Charges Out	____	____	____	____	____
	C. I/S Net	____	____	____	____	____
	1. Development & Studies	____	____	____	____	____
	2. Operational & Maintenance	____	____	____	____	____
II.	DP EQUIPMENT EXPENDITURES ($000) BUSINESS (10, 11, 14, 15, 16, 17, 18)	____	____	____	____	____
III.	DP EQUIPMENT EXPENDITURES ($000) TOTAL	____	____	____	____	____
IV.	MANPOWER (as of 12/31)	____	____	____	____	____
	A. System Analysts, Programmers and other Professionals: 1. Development	____	____	____	____	____
	2. Operational & Maintenance	____	____	____	____	____
	B. Managers	____	____	____	____	____
V.	SUBCONTRACTORS Analysts, Programmers, Other Professionals	____	____	____	____	____

PREPARED BY: ____________
DATE PREPARED: ____________
APPROVED BY: ____________
DATE APPROVED: ____________
DATE REVISED: ____________

CONTROLLER'S SIGNATURE: ____________

IBM Confidential

DP GROUP
INFORMATION SYSTEMS PLAN
SCHEDULE II - PROJECT SUMMARY

Issued: 02-15-71

DIVISION: DIVISION TITLE SPELLED OUT
LOCATION: GEOGRAPHIC LOCATION

PROJECT		SCHEDULE				RESOURCES - MAN YEARS									
TITLE	NUMBER	PH.1	PH.2	PH.3	PH.4	PREV YRS.	1970	1971	1972	1973	1974	1975	1976	1977
xxxxxxxxxxxxxxxxxxxxxxxx	nnnnnnn	mmyy	mmyy	mmyy	mmyy	nnnn	nnnn	nnnn	nnnn	nnnn	nnnn	nnnn	nnnn	nnnn
KEY PROJECT														
SING I	0010000	1068	0270	0372	0672	17	46	46	32					
BLIP (4A)	0020000	0169	0269	0771	0974	5	9	10	10	12	12			
OTHER DEVELOPMENT														
ACCOUNTING	0010101					55	12	8	10					
MANUFACTURING	0020100					39	10	6	10					
LOCATION SUPPORT	0020101					10	6	6	4					
MAINTENANCE/ENHANCEMENTS														
ACCOUNTING	0030100					5	4	4	5					
PERSONNEL/PAYROLL	0040100					10	10	8	9					
PLANNING SYSTEMS	0050100					25	25	15	15					
SYSTEMS SUPPORT	0060100					36	18	18	18					
TRAINING	0070000						6	6	6					
TOTALS							146	127	119					

PREPARED BY: John Henry
DATE PREPARED: 01/31/71
APPROVED BY: Al Jones
DATE APPROVED: 02/01/71
DATE REVISED: ________

IBM Confidential

SAMPLE

DP GROUP
INFORMATION SYSTEMS PLAN
SCHEDULE II - PROJECT SUMMARY

Issued: 02-15-71

DIVISION: ____________________

LOCATION: ____________________

PROJECT		SCHEDULE				RESOURCES - MAN YEARS								
TITLE	NUMBER	PH.1	PH.2	PH.3	PH.4	PREV YRS.	1970	1971	1972	1973	1974	1975	1976	1977
xxxxxxxxxxxxxxxxxxxxxxxx	nnnnnnn	mmyy	mmyy	mmyy	mmyy	nnnn	nnnn	nnnn	nnnn	nnnn	nnnn	nnnn	nnnn	nnnn
TOTALS														

PREPARED BY: ____________

DATE PREPARED: ____________

APPROVED BY: ____________

DATE APPROVED: ____________

DATE REVISED: ____________

IBM Confidential

B

Mobil Oil Corporation Planning Documents

MS PLANNING CYCLE

1975 MS OBJECTIVES

A. I FINANCIAL DATA - COSTS BY BUDGET CATEGORY

($000)

		Actual 1974	Plan 1975	FORECAST 1976	1977	1980	% Change 1975-1980
01	Personnel						
02	Equipment						
03	Outside						
04	Other						
05	Total Expense						
06	Inter-Division Charges Received						
06M	Inter-CSMSD Charges Received						
07	Total Expense Before Revenue						
08	Inter-Division Revenue						
08M	Inter-CSMSD Revenue						
09	External Revenue						
10	Total Revenue						
11	Net MS Cost						

Percent Change Over Prior Year

Memo Item

Actual or Effective Salary Inflation Rate

Source of Salary Inflation Rate

Dept/Division ____________ Date Completed or Latest Update ______

1975 MS OBJECTIVES
FORM AI

MS PLANNING CYCLE

1975 MS OBJECTIVES

A. 2 FINANCIAL DATA - INTER-DIVISION CHARGES DETAIL

	Actual 1974	Plan 1975	FORECAST 1976	1977	1980
06 Charges Received From					
NAD					
ID					
CORPORATE (non-CSMSD)					
CHEMICAL					
MRDC					
METS					
TOTAL (line 6, Form A. I)					
06M Charges Received From					
CTD					
MSP					
CTMS					
TOTAL (line 6M, Form A. I)					
08 Charges Issued To					
NAD					
ID					
CORPORATE (non-CSMSD)					
CHEMICAL					
MRDC					
METS					
TOTAL (line 8, Form A. I)					
08M Charges Issued To					
MSP					
CTD					
CTMS					
P&A					
TOTAL (line 08M, Form A. I)					

Dept/Division ____________ Date Completed or Latest Update ________

1975 MS OBJECTIVES
FORM B3

MS PLANNING CYCLE

1975 MS OBJECTIVES

A. 2 FINANCIAL DATA - INTER-DIVISION CHARGES DETAIL

($000)	Actual 1974	Plan 1975	FORECAST 1976	1977	1980
06 Charges Received From					
NAD					
ID					
CORPORATE (non-CSMSD)					
CHEMICAL					
MRDC					
METS					
TOTAL (line 6, Form A. 1)					
06M Charges Received From					
CTD					
MSP					
CTMS					
TOTAL (line 6M, Form A. 1)					
08 Charges Issued To					
NAD					
ID					
CORPORATE (non-CSMSD)					
CHEMICAL					
MRDC					
METS					
TOTAL (line 8, Form A. 1)					
08M Charges Issued To					
MSP					
CTD					
CTMS					
P&A					
TOTAL (line 08M, Form A. 1)					

Dept/Division ____________ Date Completed or Latest Update ________

1975 MS OBJECTIVES
FORM A.2

MS PLANNING CYCLE

1975 MS OBJECTIVES

A. 3 FINANCIAL DATA - EXPENSE ALLOCATION/RECOVERY ANALYSIS

($000)	Actual 1974	Plan 1975	FORECAST 1976	1977	1980
01 Total Expense (line 05, Form A. 1)					
02 Cost of Corporate and Internal Services (C+D, +E pro rata)					
03 Cost of Client Services (A + B, +E pro rata)					
04 Recovery, non-CSMSD (A only)					
05 Net cost of Client Services (03 minus 04)					

Dept/Division ____________ Date Completed or Latest Update ________

1975 MS OBJECTIVES
FORM A3

MS PLANNING CYCLF

1975 MS OBJECTIVES

B. I PERSONNEL DATA - HEADCOUNT

	Actual 1974	Plan 1975	FORECAST 1976	1977	1980
01 Management/Supervisor	____	____	____	____	____
02 Professional	____	____	____	____	____
03 Operations	____	____	____	____	____
04 Service & Support	____	____	____	____	____
05 Meth. & Proc. Analyst	____	____	____	____	____
06 TOTAL PERSONNEL	====	====	====	====	====
Change from Prior Year		____	____	____	____
Percent Change over Prior Year		____	____	____	____

Dept/Division ________________ Date Completed or Latest Update ________

1975 MS OBJECTIVES
FORM BI

MS PLANNING CYCLE

1975 MS OBJECTIVES

B. 2 PERSONNEL DATA - PERSONNEL COST DETAIL

($000)

	Actual 1974	Plan 1975	FORECAST 1976	1977	1980
01 Salaries & Wages	____	____	____	____	____
02 Burden	____	____	____	____	____
03 Personnel Expenses	____	____	____	____	____
04 Total Personnel Cost (Line 0l, Form A. l)	====	====	====	====	====

Dept/Division ________________ Date Completed or Latest Update ________

1975 MS OBJECTIVES
FORM B2

MS PLANNING CYCLE

1975 MS OBJECTIVES

B.3 STAFF ALLOCATION

	Actual 1974	Plan 1975	FORECAST 1976	1977	1980
01 Client Services - Direct (A)					
02 Client Services - Indirect (B)					
03 Corporate Services (C)					
04 CSMSD Services (D)					
05 Internal Activities (E)					
06 TOTAL HEADCOUNT					

Dept/Division ________________ Date Completed or Latest Update ____________

1975 MS OBJECTIVES
FORM B3

MS PLANNING CYCLE

1975 MS OBJECTIVES

C.1 EQUIPMENT DATA - COMPUTERS BY SIZE

	Actual 1974	Plan 1975	FORECAST 1976	1977	1980
01 Small (General Purpose)					
02 Small (Dedicated)					
03 Medium					
04 Large					
05 TOTAL COMPUTERS					
Net Change from Prior Year					

Dept/Division ______________ Date Completed or Latest Update ________

1975 MS OBJECTIVES
FORM C1

MS PLANNING CYCLE

1975 MS OBJECTIVES

C.2 EQUIPMENT DATA - COMPUTERS BY USE

	Actual 1974	Plan 1975	FORECAST 1976	1977	1980
01 GENERAL PURPOSE TOTAL					
02 PROCESS CONTROL TOTAL					
Lab Automation					
Refinery Control					
Oil Field Control					
Pipeline Control					
Other Process Control					
03 SPECIAL PURPOSE TOTAL					
Scientific Computing					
Credit Card					
Marketing Operations					
Message Switching					
Other					
04 TOTAL COMPUTERS (Line 05, Form C.1)					

Dept/Division ____________ Date Completed or Latest Update ________

1975 MS OBJECTIVES
FORM C2

MS PLANNING CYCLE

1975 MS OBJECTIVES

D.1 WORKLOAD DATA - COST ALLOCATION BY FUNCTION

($000)

	Actual 1974	Plan 1975	FORECAST 1976	1977	1980
01 Accounting & Financial					
02 Marketing					
03 Credit Card					
04 Exploration & Producing					
05 Manufacturing					
06 S, D&T					
07 R, D&E					
08 Employee Relations					
09 Other					
10 Total Net Cost (Line 11, Form A.1)					

Dept/Division ____________ Date Completed or Latest Update ________

1975 MS OBJECTIVES
FORM D1

MS PLANNING CYCLE

1975 MS OBJECTIVES

D. 2 WORKLOAD DATA -- COST BY ACTIVITY

($000)	Actual 1974	Plan 1975	FORECAST 1976	1977	1980
MS Application Efforts for Clients					
01 Production/Maintenance					
a. Maintenance					
b. Production					
Total	___	___	___	___	___
02 Enhancement/Development					
a. Enhancement					
b. Development					
Total	___	___	___	___	___
MS Efforts for MS Function					
03 Applications for MS/Other Efforts					
a. Applications for MS					
b. Other Efforts					
Total	___	___	___	___	___
04 Total Net Cost (Add 01, 02, 03)	___	___	___	___	___

Dept/Division ________________ Date Completed or Latest Update ______________

1975 MS OBJECTIVES
FORM D2

MS PLANNING CYCLE

1975 MS OBJECTIVES

CTD COMPUTER SERVICES

($000)

E#I MSP AND CTD—CLIENT DIRECT CHARGES

			Estimated actual	Profit plan	FORECAST		
			1974	1975	1976	1977	1980
01 Production/maintenance	Maintenance	Computer					
		Keypunch					
	Production	Computer					
		Keypunch					
02 Enhancement/development	Enhancement	Computer					
		Keypunch					
	Development	Computer					
		Keypunch					
03 Other		Computer					
		Keypunch					
04 CTD total		Computer					
		Keypunch					

MSP ANALYST SERVICES

05 Production/maintenance	Maintenance	Computer					
		Keypunch					
	Production	Computer					
		Keypunch					
06 Enhancement/development	Enhancement	Computer					
		Keypunch					
	Development	Computer					
		Keypunch					
07 Other		Computer					
		Keypunch					
08 MSP total		Computer					
		Keypunch					

09 Client total							

Department/division ______________________ Date completed or latest update _____1975 MS objectives Form #1

C

U.S. Army Materiel Command ADP and MIS Plan

AUTOMATIC DATA PROCESSING
AND
MANAGEMENT INFORMATION
SYSTEMS PLAN

VOLUME 1
CONCEPTS AND POLICIES

CONTENTS

CHAPTER 1

BACKGROUND

1-1. <u>Introduction</u>. a. The U.S. Army Materiel Command (AMC) Automatic Data Processing/Management Information System (ADP/MIS) Plan encompasses the entire spectrum of the AMC information and data systems and supporting business and scientific data processing activities. This Plan's primary objective is to continually improve command support for the Army logistic system. For business and information systems, this objective will be achieved principally through standardization of programs and supporting equipment. For scientific and engineering (S&E) systems, this objective will be achieved by providing for a much greater exchange of information within the AMC S&E data processing support community.

b. This Plan consists of two segments--Volume 1 contains the concepts and policies; and Volume 2, The AMC Five-Year ADP Program, contains implementation details, schedules, and resources.

c. The portion of this Plan which deals primarily with business data processing, evolves from and is responsive to the long-standing objectives of AMC to standardize operations at the commodity commands and depots.

d. S&E data processing activities were at one time governed by policies and guidelines which were geared primarily to business applications. Some of these policies and guidelines were not appropriate for application to S&E computing; therefore, this Plan will address the S&E automatic data processing (ADP) separately wherever this is appropriate.

1-2. <u>Purpose</u>. This Plan establishes the basic ADP guidance necessary for the orderly achievement of the AMC mission, including standardization of ADP systems and equipment. The Plan will be updated annually to reflect the changing conditions and will provide the basis for progress reporting and selected budgeting actions; however, it does not, in itself, authorize resources.

1-3. Scope. The AMC ADP/MIS Plan applies to all AMC information systems both manual and automated, as well as all AMC data processing resources, exclusive of computers which are an integral part of a weapon system and computers used to control a process or RD&E (research, development, and engineering) special purpose equipment.

Note. With prior approval of the Director of Management Information Systems, Headquarters, AMC, non-ADPE (automatic data processing equipment) systems which include computer elements will be acquired in accordance with paragraph 4-5, AR 18-2.

1-4. Abbreviations and acronymns. For the purpose of this Plan, the following abbreviations and acronymns apply:

ADP-----------automatic data processing
ADPE----------automatic data processing equipment
AMC-----------U. S. Army Materiel Command
AMC ALMSA-----AMC Automated Logistics Management Systems Agency
AMCCDO--------USAMC Catalog Data Office
AMC DED-------AMC Data Element Dictionary
AMC LSSA------AMC Logistic Systems Support Agency
AMC-WEP-------U.S. Army Materiel Command War Emergency Plan (U)
ANSI COBOL----American National Standard Institute Common Business Oriented Language
AUTODIN-------Automatic Digital Network
AVSCOM--------United States Army Aviation Systems Command

CAD-E---------Computer-Aided Design and Engineering
CAM/NC--------Computer-Aided Manufacturing/Numerical Control
CCIC----------Computer-Controlled Information Center
CCMIS---------Commodity Command Management Information System
CCSS----------Commodity Command Standard System
CDC-----------Control Data Corporation
CIDS----------Chemical Information and Data System
COBOL---------common business oriented language
COMSEC--------communications security
CONUS---------continental United States
CPU-----------central processing unit
CSDA----------Central Systems Design Agency

DA------------Department of the Army
DEPMIS--------Depot Management Information System
DFSR----------Detailed Functional System Requirement
DMIS----------Director of Management Information Systems
DOD-----------Department of Defense
DPI-----------data processing installation
DPTFD---------Director of Personnel, Training, and Force Development

EDSR----------Engineering Data Storage and Retrieval

FORTRAN-------Formula Translation
FORTRAN IV----Formula Translation, Fourth Generation

GFSR----------General Functional System Requirement
GSA-----------General Services Administration

IBM-----------International Business Machines
IL------------International Logistics

LABMIS--------Laboratory Management Information System

MILSTRIP------Military Standard Requisitioning and Issue Procedures
MISD----------Management Information System Directorate
MRO-----------materiel release order

NICP----------national inventory control point

OSD-----------Office, Secretary of Defense

PEMA----------procurement of equipment and missiles, Army
PPBMIS--------Planning, Programing, and Budgeting Management Information System
PPC-----------production planning and control
PROMIS--------Project Management Information System

RD&E-----------research, development, and engineering
RIN------------report identification number

S&E------------scientific and engineering
SAG------------Systems Advisory Group
SDI------------Selective Dissemination of Information
SPEED----------System-wide Project for Electronic Equipment at Depots
SPEEDEX--------SPEED Extended
STINFO---------Scientific and Technical Information

TACOM----------United States Army Tank-Automotive Command
TDP------------technical data package
TDY------------temporary duty
TEAMUP---------Test, Evaluation, Analysis, and Management Uniformity Plan
TECOM----------United States Army Test and Evaluation Command
TISA-----------Technical Information Support Activity
TRMS-----------Test Resource Management System

USAAA----------United States Army Audit Agency
USAILC---------United States Army International Logistics Center
USALDC---------United States Army Logistic Data Center
USALMC---------United States Army Logistic Management Center
USAMETA--------United States Army Management Engineering Training Agency
USAMIDA--------United States Army Major Item Data Agency

WSMR-----------White Sands Missile Range

CHAPTER 2

ENVIRONMENT

2-1. AMC environment. a. U.S. Army force structure. Progressive reductions in the active U.S. Army force structure will occur during the next few years. Concurrent with these reductions, the reserve force structure will become more viable for use in emergency situations. Increased emphasis will be placed on achieving and maintaining a high-level readiness posture and quick-reaction capability in response to conventional or nuclear warfare situations. Units in the force structure will require materiel support for a high degree of unit mobility, in using the most technical and complex advanced equipment. The active forces outside of the United States geographical areas will be reduced and greater reliance will be placed on rapid deployment of CONUS (continental United States) forces when the situation requires. Materiel systems in support of these rapid-force deployments will require extensive planning and automation to assure positive and timely reaction.

b. AMC force structure. Concurrent with the overall reduction in the U.S. Army forces, AMC will be progressively required to phase down both civilian and military manpower. Closures, consolidations, manpower reductions, and reserve actions will reduce the number of AMC installations and activities. Particular emphasis will be placed on centralization of common functions related to materiel management, administrative overhead, and related automated data processing (ADP) support. Manpower reductions throughout AMC will require effective designation of workload priorities and a greater reliance on automated systems. Decreases in ADP manpower and resources will be minimized by the ever-increasing dependence on ADP support by the functional users to support expanded mission responsibilities and to compensate for known and anticipated functional manpower reductions.

c. Materiel systems automation requirements. New concepts and essential improvements in materiel acquisition and logistics support management and operations will require increased ADP support. Priorities and emphasis on quick-reaction capability will require automated systems with expanded data bases to ascertain logistics support status. Improved supply activity processing for timely and expeditious supply actions will be dependent upon new automated systems support. Increased utilization of automated supply data bases to formulate analytical studies on alternative courses of action for logistics support will require new systems development efforts and will increase ADP operations. A higher degree of interface with other DOD (Department of Defense) activities to implement standard systems for materiel management and logistics support operations will require the progressive revision of AMC automated systems.

d. Supply-related considerations.

(1) Materiel support to friendly foreign governments is expected to remain at a high level and, in all probability, will increase during the next 5 years. In order for AMC to respond to present and anticipated increased supply activity in the area of International Logistics (IL), a joint ADP systems developmental effort has been initiated by the IL Center (ILC) and the central systems design agency (CSDA) (i.e., AMC ALMSA) for ultimate use by the ILC and the various commodity commands.

(2) The number of items managed by AMC will be reduced. Also, many items in which Army has an interest will be transferred to a DOD supply activity. These AMC-item reductions should reduce support requirements in AMC ADP operations regarding items of supply management, procurement, and related areas.

(3) Intermediate logistics support will expand AMC interests in retail-type supply operations. New automated systems for more extensive AMC management control of inventory movement from supply sources into the hands of users will require added systems development and ADP operations to process increased detail activity and maintain expanded data bases.

e. AMC systems levels--business applications.

(1) Resources management. Progressive centralization of AMC administration and management and the consolidation of ADP data bases will centralize and/or reduce ADP support operations. It is anticipated that ADP support operations will decline, even though substantial ADP systems revisions and design of new applications will be required to implement (and interface) Army- and DOD-wide standard systems.

(a) Financial management will require increased emphasis on comprehensive data collection and detailed cost accounting, reporting, and analysis which will be reflected in the financial management ADP supporting systems. These requirements will be offset to some degree by the reduction in the strength of the Army and the decrease in the number and variety of authorized items in the Army supply system.

(b) Management information systems will continue to grow during the next 5 years as management data requirements are identified and new applications developed. Simulation models for management use will increase to provide users with various analyses of alternatives for assisting the management decision processes.

(c) Personnel systems reductions in the volume of detailed transactions processed and the consolidation of multiple data bases will reduce ADP support operations. Integration and interfacing of AMC with Army- and DOD-wide automated standard systems with systems revisions and design of new applications will require extensive systems development and conversion.

(2) Logistics support. New concepts in supply support criteria and operating procedures will require automated systems which are more responsive to time requirements and provide in-depth management control of assets from supply source to user or consumer.

(a) Stock control systems will require more intensive coverage of inventory status and control of inventory movement. This will require increased ADP systems development and ADP support to maintain expanded coverage of data bases.

(b) International logistics will centralize operations, and systems improvements will reduce workloads at NICP's (national inventory control points).

(c) Maintenance production planning and control (PPC) will increase automated systems for recording depot maintenance capability and capacity, detailed activity, and maintain expanded data bases for recording in-process status.

(3) Transportation. More complete item movement control will be required. The volume of transactions will increase to maintain expanded data bases recording more detailed movement status.

(4) Materiel acquisition.

(a) The procurement and production activity will increase by more detailed accounting of in-process activity status.

(b) Use of direct delivery from manufacturers to users will require expansion of existing or the development of new ADP systems and processing operations in order to provide effective management control.

(c) Analytical models for the acquisition process will require development to assist in decision-making and analysis of results.

(5) Supply management. Many factors, such as the rapid changes in force structure, expanded mission responsibilities, and reductions in AMC manpower and resources will support the increasing employment of current methodology and the development of new techniques regarding the use of computer simulation models in such areas as forecasting supply performance, readiness postures for potential contingencies, and simulated distribution patterns. These simulation models will utilize data and information from expanded data bases such as consumption factors and new innovations in transportation such as the C5-A Program and thus will avoid the development and employment of alternatives which subsequently prove infeasible. Further, this use of the expanded data bases in conjunction with the simulation models will enhance in-depth analysis and detailed determinations by supply managers of economical asset requirements and ultimate distribution.

f. Scientific and engineering (S&E).

(1) Considerable emphasis will be placed on the use of computer simulation prior to prototype construction. This will generate an increased workload in S&E data processing. As RD&E (research, development, and engineering) programs continue to increase in complexity there will be a much greater demand for conversational computing by the scientific community. As equipment becomes more complex, testing will also increase in complexity which will result in greater volumes of test data, as well as greater complexity in the test data itself. The computer will be called upon to solve both the data gathering and the data processing problems introduced by this greater volume and sophistication.

(2) One of the most important areas of emphasis will be in the interactive use of the computer for both design and engineering applications. The AMC Computer-Aided Design and Engineering (CAD-E) Five-Year Program addresses functional requirements in this area in detail.

2-2. ADP environment. a. Technological forecast.

(1) General.

(a) The next decade is not expected to produce any startling new developments in ADP technology; however, breakthroughs in technology are exceptionally difficult to predict. The most significant aspect which can be anticipated is greatly increased central processor speeds and faster peripheral devices.

(b) The transition to "fourth generation" computers will be evolutionary rather than revolutionary. During the next 5 years there will be more extensive use of minicomputers either in lieu of large computers or in combination with large computers. The major advances in this decade will be in peripheral devices based on the exploitation and improvement of existing technology. Expanded use of improved memory devices such as high-speed tape drives, magnetic drums, and disk storage will be used. Greatly improved look-ahead software will move information stored on the comparatively slow aforementioned memory devices, to high-speed memory prior to the time a computer program requires the information. This will have the effect of making the mass memory devices act like a part of main memory to the user. In combination, improved hardware and software will significantly increase the amount of on-line information directly accessible to functional users.

(c) Major advances will occur in communication. Use of remote terminals located at great distances from the computer, supporting functional users, will increase substantially, as will the use of direct communication between computers. Because of increased processing speeds coupled with communication advances, improved software, and lower lease costs, the ADP product cost should go down substantially. Greater use of special purpose hardware in lieu of general purpose computers can be anticipated, which will result in greatly improved flexibility at lower costs.

(2) Effect on AMC. The effect of advances in technology on AMC during the next decade will be primarily in the area of cost effectiveness. There is no compelling technological reason at this time to consider replacement of equipment selected for standard systems during the next 5 years; however, there will be an increasing use of minicomputers for a variety of applications including the scientific and engineering network. Modifications and augmentation of faster peripheral devices to include core storage, thereby increasing the use of the central processing unit (CPU) with a corresponding increase in data throughput, will thereby improve the cost effectiveness and efficiency of operations.

b. ADPE acquisition.

(1) ADPE acquisition is based on the policy of having compatible ADPE at all installations with similar data processing requirements which will permit the use of standard systems and programs.

(2) Makes and models of third-generation ADPE, approved for standard AMC systems, are identified within the discussion of major system levels in chapter 6. The approved equipment will replace a mixture of makes and models of second-generation computers now in use throughout AMC.

(3) Third-generation ADPE has the following advantages over the presently installed second-generation equipment:

(a) Greater throughput per dollar of cost.

(b) Reduced number of main frames.

(c) Multiprograming capability.

(d) Modular design which permits future expansion without significant reprograming.

(e) Improved manufacturer-furnished software which reduces the workload for programing.

(4) The ADPE costs are generally based on the assumption that third-generation ADPE will be leased with the option to purchase. Purchase is programed within limitations of funds expected to be available.

(5) ADPE acquisition provides for AMC to have a computerized data base by the end of Fiscal Year 1976. Remote terminals will be used to provide ADP capability to insta lations with a workload too small to justify a separate computer.

(6) Some ADPE replacement in the 1976-1978 time frame will be desirable in order to take advantage of new capabilities which will then be available. However, this will be accomplished on a cost/effectiveness basis rather than for the sake of technology.

(7) ADPE operations at AMC arsenals, laboratories, and other activities offer the least opportunity for standardization and consequently are scheduled for actions on an individual basis.

2-3. Key features. a. General.

(1) Standard ADP management procedures. These procedures assure commonality of the ADP effort and include the data element documentation, programing standards, and centralized ADP management control.

(2) Data Element Dictionary. The AMC Data Element Dictionary (DED) establishes a single authorized definition for any data element and the unique mnemonic for that element. Employment of standard data elements is mandatory to assure command-wide system standardization. Responsibility for approval and establishment of data elements is centralized at AMC ALMSA.

(3) Equipment and modular flexibility.

(a) In today's environment, three significant problems are associated with machine independence and modular flexibility, as follows:

1. Limited commonality between a vendor's various equipment families, and no commonality between vendors results in total ADPE dependence.

2. The equipment modularity problem exists today in that it is not possible to add or remove various devices without major reprograming.

3. The variety of programing languages that have been employed offers little possibility for interchange between families.

(b) Satisfactory resolution of the above-mentioned problems within the limits of this ADP/MIS Plan will be progressively accomplished throughout AMC by assuring that all AMC ADPE procurement specifications have established mandatory requirements, applicable to all vendors, which will eliminate problems resulting from lack of modularity and flexibility. Further, by utilization of American National Standard Institute Common Business Oriented Language (ANSI COBOL) or FORTRAN IV (Formula Translation, Fourth Generation) System, the problems related to language incompatibility between computers will be resolved. Consequently, it will be possible to modify main frames to increase or decrease the speed and capacity of the equipment without adverse reaction to on-going systems.

(4) <u>**Data** transmission</u>.

(a) The manual delivery system between activities will be replaced by a direct communication link between the local communication center and the data processing activity.

(b) On-line remote devices are planned at selected activities on an installation. These remote devices will include a mix of input/output devices, dependent upon the type of data required and the urgency involved.

(c) Plans also include the establishment of a Computer-Controlled Information Center (CCIC) in Headquarters, AMC. By using secure remote terminal devices, the problem-solving and selective-inquiry capabilities will be provided to management and action officer levels.

b. Business systems.

(1) Integrated data base. The integrated data base concept is fundamental to the standard systems. It is a combination of key files which can be accessed in a single cycle to process data for a variety of functional managers.

(2) On-time data accessibility. Selected data base files are accessible to functional managers at all times and rapid retrieval techniques provide selected logistical management data in various data element combinations.

c. S&E systems.

(1) S&E ADP systems will provide the capability and capacity to accommodate an increasing volume of complex S&E workloads. Emphasis will be on the use of standard languages and improved documentation rather than standard hardware which will facilitate the exchange of computer programs and subprograms among scientific and engineering activities within AMC and with other elements of Army, other military services, and Government agencies.

(2) An S&E program index will be established to facilitate exchange of computer programs.

(3) A network of S&E computers will be established to provide access to many different types of computers for scientists, engineers, and functional managers within AMC, wherever cost effectiveness can be demonstrated. This will help to balance the S&E ADP workload and reduce the problems associated with nonstandard equipment.

2-4. Assumptions. a. That the Department of the Army/AMC system evaluation test of the on-going prototype system at the United States Army Aviation Systems Command (AVSCOM) will result in Department of the Army approval to extend the standard system to all commodity commands.

b. That closures, consolidations, manpower reductions, and resource restrictions within AMC, coupled with expanded mission responsibilities, will require effective designation of ADP workload priorities and an increased dependence on automated systems by the functional users. Consequently, there will be increasing emphasis on centralization of common functions with a corresponding increase in requirements for ADP support.

c. That the requirement for expanded and improved management systems and scientific computer support by higher echelons will continue. The growth of these requirements will be limited only by the availability of resources to plan, program, install, and operate such systems, and the availability of computer processing time.

d. That DA/OSD directives for installation of new policies, procedures, or concepts that require increased ADP resources will not be accompanied by the authority for additional equipment, personnel, and facilities.

CHAPTER 3

SYSTEM CLASSIFICATIONS

3-1. System levels. a. The AMC major subordinate commands and operating elements which perform essentially the same functions and have generally the same missions, have been grouped into system levels. This grouping makes it possible to define common business systems and to establish priorities for incorporation into the standardization program. The most significant of these levels are identified below:

SYSTEM LEVELS	STANDARD SYSTEM DESIGNATION	CSDA
Commodity commands/NICP's	CCSS*	AMC ALMSA
Depots	SPEEDEX	AMC LSSA
Test activities	TEAMUP	TECOM

*Previously referred to as AMC Logistics Program--Hardcore Automated (ALPHA) and command follow-on applications.

b. While considerable scientific and engineering (S&E) automatic data processing (ADP) support is required at these levels, unique aspects of S&E applications preclude their standardization within the framework of the CCSS. Other levels for which varying degrees of common system standardization can be achieved are data banks, laboratories, arsenals, and other AMC subordinate activities. It is anticipated that as certain standard business ADP applications developed by the Central System Design Agency (CSDA) become operational, these applications will be modified as necessary to satisfy the requirements of these AMC activities.

3-2. System structure. a. The identification and control of ADP systems is of major importance in a complex environment such as the total AMC mission. Classification by mission is necessary to monitor and control the design, development, and operation of

ADP systems by accumulating cost and status information and related management details. These categories have been established in Volume 2, AMCR 18-5, and are defined as follows:

(1) Module. A major division of the Headquarters, AMC, representing a mission for which information and data systems are collectively designed and related tasks defined. Each module is assigned a single numeric code.

(2) Cell. A primary subdivision of the Headquarters, AMC, mission representing a function which is susceptible to separate identification for system design and related tasks. Each cell is assigned a single alphabetic code.

(3) Subcell. A secondary subdivision of the Headquarters, AMC, mission representing a subfunction which is susceptible to more finite identification for system design, with generally identified inputs, processes, outputs, and related tasks. Each subcell is assigned a two-digit numeric code.

b. An example of the AMC major function breakouts identified as missions, divided into cells and displays representative of AMC logistic assignments, is as follows:

RESOURCES MANAGEMENT
- Financial Management
- ADP Systems Management
- Personnel, Training, and Manpower Management
- Command Management

SCIENTIFIC AND MATERIEL DEVELOPMENT
- Scientific and Technical Information (STINFO)
- Scientific and Engineering

ITEM DATA CONTROL
- Technical and Logistics Data and Information (TLDI)
- Equipment Control
- Cataloging
- Quality Assurance

LOGISTICS SUPPORT
- Stock Control
- International Logistics
- Maintenance
- Provisioning
- Transportation

MATERIEL ACQUISITION
- Procurement and Production
- Research, Development, and Engineering (RD&E)
- Supply Management

3-3. System implementation. System implementation is accomplished in three major phases. These phases apply to each organizational level of the AMC complex and permit an orderly progression from the documentation of specifications for ADPE through the operational implementation of standard business systems.

a. Phase I. Preparation and submission of General Functional System Requirements (GFSR's), selection of the ADPE, and the installation of prototype equipment at the AMC designated test center.

b. Phase II. Designing, developing, operational or prototype testing, and installing the initial standard systems. This phase will consist of those systems and subsystems which are vital to the accomplishment of the prime missions and functions of the commodity commands, depots, or other AMC subordinate activities and, simultaneously, afford the greatest benefits for the expenditure of resources with corresponding improvement of mission efficiency and responsiveness. Following the successful operational demonstration of the Phase II systems, approval by the Senior Army Policy Official and completion of the individual Department of the Army readiness reviews, the standard equipment and Phase II systems will be installed at the participating installations.

c. Phase III. Designing, developing, operational testing, and installing standard systems not included in Phase II will be extended to the remaining functions; these Phase II systems will be the basis for integration and development of the Phase III systems. The Phase III effort may be segmented into subphases depending upon priority requirements and availability of resources. Those ADPE applications not incorporated into the standard systems developed under the Phase II or Phase III efforts or those ADPE systems considered as unique to a given installation will, on a progressive basis, be reprogramed to use the standard ADPE selected in Phase I.

CHAPTER 4

RESPONSIBILITIES

4-1. Command staff. The Director of Management Information Systems (DMIS) is responsible for staff guidance and central system control and coordination of the AMC ADP/MIS Plan. Directors and staff office chiefs are responsible for the identification and definition of the functional system requirements, policies, and standard functional procedures within their assigned areas. Responsibilities for the development of General Functional System Requirements (GFSR's) are provided in AR 18-1.

4-2. Systems Advisory Group (SAG). The Assistant Deputy for Logistics Support; the Assistant Deputy for Materiel Acquisition; the Deputy Comptroller; and the Deputy Director of Personnel, Training, and Force Development form the AMC SAG under the chairmanship of the DMIS. The SAG is responsible for resolving and analyzing system development problems and, in addition, the group is responsible for resolving priority conflicts in system development to assure timely implementation of valid system requirements.

4-3. Central system design. System design responsibility is centralized by system level at a CSDA (Central Systems Design Agency) to facilitate and expedite development and maintenance of standard systems for the entire AMC complex, and the CSDA will recommend to Headquarters, AMC, approval or disapproval of appropriate GFSR's and DFSR's (Detailed Functional System Requirements) prepared by other AMC activities. Further, the CSDA may, as directed by Headquarters, AMC, develop and implement certain GFSR's and DFSR's and will serve as the proponent for selected AMC-wide standard systems. The CSDA's are:

a. The AMC Automated Logistics Management Systems Agency (AMC ALMSA) at St. Louis, Missouri--responsible for designing and developing standard commodity command systems.

b. The AMC Logistic Systems Support Agency (AMC LSSA) at Chambersburg, Pennsylvania--responsible for designing and developing standard depot systems, depot and administrative data banks, and for providing management information system support to Headquarters, AMC. Principal support in this area is through the Planning, Programing, and Budgeting Management Information System (PPBMIS).

c. Headquarters, United States Army Test and Evaluation Command (TECOM), Aberdeen, Maryland--responsible for developing the standard test activity system of the AMC Five-Year ADP Program.

4-4. Software and ADP technology. AMC ALMSA is the CSDA assigned the responsibility for developing technique-oriented software for AMC-wide implementation and is also responsible for full exploitation of new ADP-related technology for the entire command. AMC LSSA and other AMC system developing agencies and activities will depend upon AMC ALMSA for software design to the maximum extent practicable.

4-5. Operations. Responsibility for the operational use of the centrally designed and programed system is retained at the resident activity utilizing these systems. Technical assistance in installing new systems will be provided by the applicable CSDA. If the standard system becomes inoperative due to a malfunction other than equipment input/output deficiencies, that activity will contact the appropriate CSDA for permission to implement interim changes required to correct the malfunction until such time as the CSDA provides a permanent solution. The resident activity will, immediately after implementing the change, submit a copy of the change to the CSDA.

CHAPTER 5

POLICIES AND GUIDELINES

5-1. Policies. Policies of the Commanding General, AMC, pertaining to the ADP/MIS Plan include:

a. Continued emphasis on system standardization. Development of the standard systems and support of these efforts has priority second only to support of the Department of Defense (DOD) or Department of the Army (DA) directed projects and unforecasted contingencies.

b. Development of systems and acquisition of equipment. The development of systems and the acquisition of equipment will be subject to economic analysis and cost benefit analysis based on parameters given below; any deviation must be directed by the Commanding General, AMC, as recommended by the Director, Management Information Systems (DMIS).

(1) The acquisition of specially designed peripheral devices which are unique unto themselves and which cannot be economically utilized elsewhere in the AMC complex must be amortized over a period not to exceed 3 years. Standard peripheral devices will be amortized in accordance with regulatory guidance in effect at the time of acquisition.

(2) The developmental cost including the cost of design, testing, and implementation of a system will be equally prorated over the life of the system. Any major change during the life of the system will result in a re-analysis based upon the cost of the change and the remaining life of the system.

c. Interface with the United States Army Audit Agency (USAAA). Close coordination with the USAAA will be maintained to insure that all systems developed comply with regulatory requirements and provide an audit trail for managerial purposes which is acceptable to the USAAA.

d. AMC staff direction and coordination. Directorates in Headquarters, AMC, will provide direction, guidance, and coordination in the system design effort and will be prepared to support this effort on a cost-effective basis.

e. Liaison with elements of the Army and other services. The CSDA's (Central Systems Design Agencies) will maintain liaison, on a continuing basis, with appropriate Army system development agencies and other military services or Government agencies to insure adequate exchange of information; to reduce duplicate efforts in ADP (automatic data processing) system design; and to take full advantage of ADP advancement, techniques, and innovations developed outside the AMC complex.

f. Contractual support. Use of contractual services will be kept to an absolute minimum and used only for temporary overloads or specialized requirements for projects requiring skills not available in-house, except when the contractual method is clearly cost-justified on a continuing basis, such as a contract with a university for scientific and engineering ADP support.

g. Training. Commanders at all echelons will assure that adequate training is provided to all levels of ADP personnel and to all levels of functional personnel. ADP training will include COBOL (common business oriented language); FORTRAN (Formula Translation) System; Advanced ADP Techniques; Software Programing; and other appropriate ADP training. Functional training will be provided at all AMC subordinate activities and will include the training of selected functional area specialists, middle level managers, and top level managers in the use of on-going systems and appropriate standard systems emanating from the various CSDA's.

h. Temporary duty (TDY) requirements. Directorates in Headquarters, AMC, and/or the various AMC subordinate activities will designate representatives for TDY assignment at appropriate CSDA's to assist in the design of the standard ADP systems or the development of functional specifications and functional acceptances. The utilization of TDY personnel will be limited to the minimum required to insure necessary representation by AMC components in the development of standard systems and subsequent conversion functions.

i. Purchase action. The policy of exercising a lease with purchase option will be continued subject to the availability of procurement of equipment and missiles, Army (PEMA) funds.

j. Programing languages. All business application programs will be written in American National Standard Institute Common Business Oriented Language (ANSI COBOL). All scientific application programs will be written in Formula Translation, Fourth Generation (FORTRAN IV) System or an equivalent higher-level language. Any deviations must have Headquarters, AMC, approval prior to implementation.

k. GFSR development. GFSR's (General Functional System Requirements) for future AMC-wide standard systems will be sponsored by the DMIS (Director of Management Information Systems) and the appropriate CSDA with the functional proponent. The development of all GFSR's will be in accordance with AR 18-1 and developmental effort should not exceed a 12-consecutive-month period, unless specifically authorized by the DMIS, Headquarters, AMC.

l. System development. System development will not be undertaken when it is estimated that system development time prior to installation at the prototype site will exceed 12 months. Those systems requiring greater than 12 months for development, which can be installed in a manner that will enable them to be cost-effective on an incremental basis, may be authorized for development providing each increment can be developed within a 12-month period.

m. System measurement. ADPE hardware or software measurement systems will be installed at all AMC installations using standard equipment. Summary results will be forwarded to the DMIS, Headquarters, AMC, on a scheduled basis.

n. Site preparation. Site preparation for ADPE will be limited to minimum essential facilities. ADPE operations and the Record Communications Center will be collocated whenever feasible.

o. System maintenance. The system design and computer programing activity at the data processing installation level will be restricted to the maintenance of locally developed systems, interim maintenance (with prior approval) of standard systems, generation of reports from the standard operating systems, bridging between standard and unique systems, recoding unique systems to accommodate changes in ADPE, and the design and programing of new or revised unique systems as approved by Headquarters, AMC.

p. Contingency planning. Each data processing installation (DPI) will submit a plan to Headquarters, AMC, for approval. This plan will depict the proposed actions required by that DPI to provide necessary ADPE capability in the event of a national emergency resulting in an increased workload. This plan will be submitted by the DPI when ADP equals 16 hours daily.

q. Regulatory restrictions. AMC ADP installations at all levels will maintain continuity of operation plans in accordance with the guidance provided by Appendix VIII to U.S. Army Materiel Command War Emergency Plan (U) (AMC-WEP); and by AR 18-7. These plans will be reviewed and revised as required but not less frequently than annually.

5-2. Guidelines. a. Headquarters, AMC, will have a computerized data base utilizing third-generation ADPE by the end of FY 76. Maximum use will be made of remote units and satelliting of small activities upon larger installations for ADP support and services.

b. Headquarters, AMC, will have the capability of accessing data of selected installations and activities through an integrated network of data bank and command echelon computers by the end of FY 76. Existing common-use facilities will be used for transmitting data between installations. Point-to-point dedicated circuits will be acquired only after determination of a valid requirement by Headquarters, AMC.

c. The General Services Administration (GSA), the DOD, and the DA established policies regarding acquisition of ADPE have resulted in a lengthening of the leadtime for procurement of ADPE. This necessitates the requirement for early identification of ADP applications. In this connection, the following general guidance is provided:

(1) Acquisition of multiple computer configurations will require a 4-year leadtime.

(2) Single computer acquisition will require a 3-year leadtime.

(3) Computer augmentations will require a minimum of 6 months for minor changes and major computer augmentations will require 18 months.

d. Documentation for scientific and engineering (S&E) computer programs will be standardized to facilitate exchange of programs between activities and reduce requirements for reprograming.

e. Maximum use will be made of direct interfaces and sensors for data collection between S&E equipment and the computer. Intermediate outputs, which are manipulated by human beings before being input to the computer, are to be discouraged. Maximum use of analog to digital conversion equipment will be made. Semiautomated or automated equipment for analysis of optical data which are ultimately analyzed on a digital computer, will be used wherever it can be shown to be cost-effective or essential to the RD&E (research, development, and engineering) mission.

f. Use of precision-plotting devices for generating graphic displays evolving from computer outputs will be used wherever they are cost-effective or essential to the RD&E mission.

g. Time-sharing to support conversational computing on S&E problems is encouraged wherever it can be cost-justified, or if it is essential to the accomplishment of the RD&E mission.

h. All commanders of AMC elements which have an ADP mission must include security considerations in the planning for DPI sites, even though the information processed is unclassified. Under these conditions, concern is expressed for the dollar value of the equipment as well as for the need for protection of the information processed. Classified operations require additional physical security measures and the transmission of classified data between computer and remote sites must be considered. Existing directives and regulations provide guidelines for the security measures applicable to ADP operations. Of primary importance is the need for pre-planning of a variety of security requirements prior to constructing sites, moving or modifying existing sites, and purchasing equipment. Coordination will be affected with the following activities which are responsible for the indicated areas of security applications:

(1) Security Support Agency--Physical security.

(2) AMC Installations and Services Agency--

(a) Site preparation.

(b) COMSEC (communications security) requirements for cryptographic applications.

(c) Tempest applications for all areas using information processing equipment for classified data.

(3) Functional Managers--Identification of classified data.

CHAPTER 6

MAJOR SYSTEMS (BY LEVEL)

6-1. Commodity Command Standard Systems (CCSS). a. Introduction. The total CCSS is a network of interrelated logistics functions standardized to the maximum practical degree across commodity groupings and weapon systems. These logistics functions, supported by standardized ADP (automatic data processing) systems and equipment, provide advanced techniques for control accounting and requisition processing, weapon system stratification, and integrated decision-making.

b. Concept. The CCSS provides for processing a combination of key computerized files which can be accessed in a single cycle to process data supporting a variety of functional managers.

c. Key features.

(1) Improved design features include extended flexibility with regard to processes of the CCSS that will be operational during multidaily processing. This capability ranges from processing multiple cycles to satisfy MILSTRIP (Military Standard Requisitioning and Issue Procedures) requirements including depot receipts and adjustments, to scaled-down cycles to process only high-priority requisitions.

(2) The CCSS Remote Inquiry System, using the integrated data base, will provide the capability for functional users, using remote display terminals, to inquire and obtain current updated information from the computerized files. This responsive information retrieval approach will upgrade the logistics data handling techniques as well as significantly reduce the printed report outputs.

(3) An additional use of remote display terminals is "decision reentry" to correct computer input conditions which were rejected. This will open the field of complete man-machine dialogue and lead to further development of this technique with the attendant benefit of bypassing intermediate data handlers.

(4) The system features maximum use of micromation techniques for producing computer-output products. Utilization of micromation will dramatically reduce the computer throughput time required to produce voluminous print products and will provide improved accessibility of information to functional users on a timely basis.

d. System development plan. The System is being implemented in three phases as follows:

(1) Phase I. Consists of the selection of the IBM 360 equipment configuration, the installation of the test-bed configuration at the CSDA (Central Systems Design Agency), and the installation of the prototype configuration at the United States Army Aviation Systems Command (AVSCOM) which has been accomplished.

(2) Phase II. Provides for the implementation of the initial standard systems necessary for inventory management and related supporting activities. It is planned that implementation of this phase at each command will be in three equal increments or steps covering a 6-month period. These steps generally consist of, but are not limited to, the following subsystems:

(a) Step 1--Cataloging, Provisioning, and Budgeting Stratification Subsystems.

(b) Step 2--Maintenance Subsystem including Overhaul Consumption, Parts Explosion, and Primary Financial Subsystems.

(c) Step 3--Multidaily Processing for Procurement and Production, Supply Management, Stock Control Subsystems; and the remainder of the Financial Subsystems.

(3) Phase III. Includes the refinement of selected Phase II applications and the development and subsequent implementation of those subsystems not included in Phase II.

6-2. Depot systems. a. Introduction.

(1) The total AMC depot complex is responsible for the receipt; delivery; storage; inventory; and depot level overhaul/repair of equipment, managed by AMC national inventory control points (NICP's); and selected items of other Government activities. The

standardization of depot operating systems supporting these functions are an integral part of the total AMC ADP/MIS Plan.

(2) Major AMC depots are currently operating standard ADPE (automatic data processing equipment) and are using standard programs and procedures which are centrally maintained by the AMC Logistic Systems Support Agency (AMC LSSA), Chambersburg, Pennsylvania. This major standardization effort is referred to as "Project SPEED" (System-wide Project for Electronic Equipment at Depots).

(3) Events, such as new computer applications and the continued increase in requirements for computer support by depots and headquarters activities, have overtaken the original SPEED concept, thus requiring an upgrading of ADPE. This requirement with attendant new ADP applications and computer support requirements, resulted in the establishment of Project SPEEDEX (SPEED Extended).

b. <u>Concepts</u>.

(1) SPEEDEX incorporates many new depot management techniques as well as enlarges on the concepts that were introduced under Project SPEED.

(2) The SPEEDEX systems, using Control Data Corporation (CDC) 3300 equipment configuration, provides increased ADPE capability and will permit reduction in local or unique applications from the nonstandard ADPE to the SPEEDEX configuration.

(3) The SPEEDEX systems will provide the capability for total utilization of remote computer input/output devices physically located in the appropriate functional areas and will substantially reduce requirements for card processing. Further, this concept of automated support will be progressively expanded during the next 5 years to the point that the SPEEDEX systems will satisfy the requirements of depot complexing.

c. <u>Key features</u>.

(1) The SPEEDEX System provides the capability to accelerate processing of high-priority materiel release orders (MRO's) by the use of remote devices such as visual

terminals, card readers, card punches, and printers located in functional areas. Use of these techniques provides immediate access to computer-stored data.

(2) The SPEEDEX Hardcore System covers the most significant functions of depot operations; i.e., storage, management, location and inventory, MRO processing, transportation planning, ammunition supply, and surveillance. The remaining primary depot operations which will be part of the SPEEDEX Hardcore or Follow-on Systems are Financial Management, Installation Management, Quality Assurance, Maintenance Production Planning and Control, Personnel Training, and Manpower Management Systems.

d. System development plan. The SPEEDEX System is being implemented in three phases as follows:

(1) Phase I. Consists of the selection of the CDC 3300 equipment configuration, the installation of the test bed and prototype, and the installation at other participating depots which is proceeding on schedule.

(2) Phase II. Provides for the implementation of the initial standard systems necessary for depot operations and related supporting activities. These Phase II standard systems are referred to as "Hardcore Systems."

(3) Phase III. Includes the refinement of selected Phase II applications and the development and subsequent implementation of those subsystems not included in Phase II; these latter subsystems are referred to as "Follow-on Systems."

Implementation of the SPEEDEX Hardcore Systems has been initiated. SPEEDEX Follow-on Systems will be implemented on a scheduled basis starting in FY 72.

6-3. Technical data centers. a. Introduction. A technical data center is a facility established under a major subordinate command which has the responsibility for command management and control of technical and logistical data on commodities for which that command is assigned management responsibility. The technical data centers will use a computerized system for identification, storage, and retrieval of engineering data to support key engineering and logistic functions. The technical data center concept is composed of the Technical Data and Configuration Management System and the Technical Data Retrieval System.

(1) The Technical Data and Configuration Management System. This system is intended to stabilize the design of configuration of the major end items. It is supported by a large data base containing engineering records such as the latest applicable drawings, specifications, and data concerning the peculiarity or commonality of use of any piece, part, or assembly making up the major end item.

(2) The Technical Data Retrieval System. This system permits the interrogation of a micromated file of the drawings and specification data extracted from the technical data and configuration management data base. The most important use of this system is the automated selection and duplication of the specifications and drawings needed to assemble a technical data package (TDP) in support of procurement.

b. Concepts.

(1) Technical data supports the requirements of many functions, including procurement; research, development, and engineering; configuration management; in-house manufacturing; testing and supply; and maintenance and initial provisioning.

(2) The Technical Data and Configuration Management System contains a massive data base of technical data in digital form that can be manipulated in normal digital computer processing. In addition to control of configuration changes, a major use of this system is the preparation of technical data package lists for procurement of Army supply items.

(3) The Technical Data Retrieval System uses index data from the technical data package list to locate and select copies of specifications and graphic data contained in the data base. These copies, when assembled, make up the TDP.

c. Key features.

(1) The technical data centers provide automated assistance in the preparation of TDP's.

(2) These centers will provide quick response for review of drawings and technical data by engineers.

(3) To reduce duplication of data, the CCSS data base will be used wherever possible.

d. Developmental responsibility. The developmental responsibility for the Technical Data Center Systems is assigned to the AMC Automated Logistics Management Systems Agency (AMC ALMSA), St. Louis, Missouri.

e. Implementation plan. The United States Army Tank-Automotive Command (TACOM), Warren, Michigan, has been designated a test-bed site for evaluating the technical data center concept. The purpose of the test is to collect data and to document actual cost savings and other benefits prior to proceeding with the AMC standard system and committing additional resources at other commodity commands.

6-4. Data Bank System. a. Introduction.

(1) An AMC data bank is a formally designated activity with the primary mission of centrally gathering, processing, evaluating, and storing data in order to provide selected and summarized information in specified areas. A data bank consists of a management element with associated functional system analysts or functional area specialists and a data processing element with supporting ADPE, computer systems analysts, programers, and machine operators.

(2) Currently there are six data banks (e below) in the AMC complex which were established to satisfy specific information requirements and to facilitate system planning and control. The present missions of data banks may not substantially change during FY 72-76, but the range of information will increase significantly as the standard systems for the commodity commands, depots, and other AMC activities are implemented. A long-range objective is to increase the performance capability of data banks and reduce the number of data banks where practicable.

b. Concepts.

(1) Within the AMC complex, there are essentially two types of data banks--those that are administrative in nature in that they exist primarily for the purpose of providing management information to satisfy managerial requirements, and those that are operational in nature and provide a data repository in support of a functional mission. Some data banks will necessarily assume both administrative and operational characteristics.

(2) AMC data banks, under the supervision of Headquarters, AMC, will be responsive to AMC's overall objectives; the functional directors' requirements; and information requirements of higher authorities and, further, will anticipate and be responsive to DOD, DA, and AMC trends and requirements and the continuing standardization of systems and ADPE.

(3) AMC data banks will not duplicate information at the same level of detail stored elsewhere and will not perform functions duplicated elsewhere unless it can be fully substantiated that mission performance will be jeopardized by elimination of such duplication.

(4) The evaluation of AMC data bank management will be significantly influenced by the following factors:

(a) The long-range implications of central standard systems at the commodity commands, depots, and other AMC activities.

(b) The requirements of DOD, DA, other military services, and AMC lateral commands and the relationships with other data banks.

(c) The sources of information needed, the activities to which service is provided, and the ability to accept interrogation from any level.

(d) The continuing need for improved economy and effectiveness.

(e) The standardization of data bank operations and the elimination of duplicate information processing.

(5) The ultimate concept for the administrative-type AMC data bank design is to create sufficient data bank capability, in conjunction with sophisticated ADP systems AMC-wide, to provide for remote retrieval of necessary data from the source, on an "as required" basis to provide the desired management information. In this environment, there would be no necessity for a data repository type data bank as the data would be "in motion" and present in the data bank only during the management information production operation.

c. Key features. Data banks will continue to increase their capability to respond to information and reporting requirements of AMC by incorporating the following features:

(1) Standard AMC management procedures.

(2) Organizational structures standardized to the maximum extent and installation of similar or compatible ADPE.

(3) A completely integrated data base with the capability for providing timely management information.

(4) Development of automated inquiry/reply systems which will interact with data sources, user activities, higher headquarters, and other data banks.

d. Developmental responsibility. Each AMC data bank under the overall supervision of Headquarters, AMC, is responsible for the development, programing, and implementation of their individual systems and operation; system standardization will be achieved wherever possible.

e. System development plan. Current plans call for the installation of third-generation ADPE at the various AMC operational data banks listed below. Determinations concerning equipment requirements or data bank locations for FY 75 and beyond have not been finalized.

United States Army Major Item Data Agency (USAMIDA)
United States Army Logistics Data Center (USALDC)
United States Army International Logistics Center (USAILC)
USAMC Catalog Data Office (AMCCDO)
*AMC Logistic Systems Support Agency (AMC LSSA)

*Depot Data Center and Administrative Data Center.

6-5. Test, Evaluation, Analysis, and Management Uniformity Plan (TEAMUP). a. Introduction.

(1) TEAMUP encompasses the entire ADP program, both business and scientific, for the United States Army Test and Evaluation Command (TECOM). Due to the unique nature of the mission of TECOM, with respect to the seven other major subordinate commands of AMC which are responsible for commodity management, it was decided that a separate program should be established for TECOM. The major objectives of TEAMUP are to provide standard programs for the business data processing of TECOM, at each of their activities which comprise TECOM, and to satisfy the scientific and engineering (S&E) ADP requirements at each of these activities. Except at White Sands Missile Range (WSMR), the S&E ADP is to be done on the same hardware as the business data processing. Separate equipment will be used for S&E ADP at WSMR.

(2) TEAMUP is being implemented in four separate parts as follows:

(a) Part A. Provides for S&E computation and standard business management systems at the larger TECOM installations and activities.

(b) Part B. This segment is no longer applicable due to a mission transfer from TECOM.

(c) Part C. Provides for real-time missile performance monitoring and control and for S&E computation in support of missile test and evaluation at WSMR.

(d) Part D. Provides terminal support through communication lines to Aberdeen Proving Ground, WSMR, and Deseret Test Center for implementation of applicable standard Part A business systems and local S&E requirements of the appropriate TECOM test boards and activities.

b. Concepts.

(1) Implement standard business systems on standard ADPE at TECOM installations and activities.

(2) Extend the appropriate standard business systems of Part A to the test boards and activities through remote terminals which tie into the Part A computers. These same terminals will also be used in satisfying local S&E requirements of these test boards and activities. A detailed description of the remote terminal network is contained in Volume 2, The AMC Five-Year ADP Program.

(3) Part C implements the use of real-time control of missile test missions. The two controlling computer configurations will operate in a multiprograming/multiprocessing mode and will be supported by backup computers. These backup computer configurations will also support batch-processing of S&E data. A separate computer will be used independently for processing classified work.

c. Key features.

(1) The standard business data processing subsystems of TEAMUP (Part A) are integrated through the cost accounting subsystem.

(2) A standard system for management of test resources is provided.

(3) Extensive use of remote processing will be made to provide third-generation computer capability throughout TECOM and to better utilize the computers.

(4) Part C will substantially increase the mission capability of WSMR to allow up to six simultaneous tests to be conducted. Current capabilities allow only up to three simultaneous tests.

(5) Part C provides the increased capability required for competent analysis of test data.

d. Developmental responsibility. The developmental responsibility for the entire TEAMUP program is assigned to Headquarters, TECOM; however, resources of the various TECOM installations will be used in development of the Part A subsystems. All of Part C is being developed at WSMR.

e. Implementation plan.

(1) Following implementation of the Part A prototype at the appropriate TECOM installations, the remaining business applications will be developed and implemented.

(2) The two computers designated for batch-processing configuration have been installed and are currently operational at WSMR for TEAMUP (Part C). The separate configuration for classified batch-processing is scheduled to be installed early in FY 72 and the real-time configuration consisting of two multiple processing UNIVAC 1108's is scheduled for installation in mid-FY 72 and is scheduled to be fully operational approximately 1 year later. Installation of equipment for TEAMUP (Part D) should be completed within approximately 1 year of full implementation of TEAMUP (Part A) prototype throughout TECOM. Full implementation of all subsystems under Part D should be completed approximately 1 year later.

6-6. Scientific and Engineering Systems. a. Introduction.

(1) S&E ADP appears in all of the major system levels, including commodity commands, test activities, laboratories, depots, and arsenals. Two general types of S&E ADP can be distinguished. One is in support of research, development, and engineering (RD&E) for Army materiel. The other is operations research/management science-type support; e.g., simulation analysis to evaluate programs for management. Primary emphasis within AMC is support of the RD&E mission; however, full support for the operations research/management science-type application will be provided.

(2) In order to distinguish S&E applications from business applications and management information systems, AMC has adopted the following definition: "An Automatic Data Processing (ADP) application will be classified as a scientific and engineering (S&E) application if it is accomplished by or in direct support of a scientist or engineer in carrying out his prescribed mission, function, or project; i.e., the immediate user of the computer output is a scientist or an engineer. All other applications will be classified as either business or management information systems." Under this definition, an information system which provides scientific information directly to a using scientist is a scientific application, even though it has most of the characteristics that are normally associated with business data processing. An example is the Chemical Information and Data System (CIDS). On the other hand, a financial management system for RD&E funds is classified as a business system since it is not used directly by scientists or engineers, but is instead used by management.

(3) In general, S&E ADP is characterized by inputs and outputs which are relatively small compared to the amount of actual computing. Many more mathematical computations are carried out on the input in scientific data processing than on equivalent amounts of input in business data processing. These characteristics are not universally true and should be regarded only as guidelines.

(4) Within the S&E level there are several major subprograms designed to accomplish a specific purpose. Additional details regarding some of the more significant of these subprograms such as the Computer-Aided Design and Engineering (CAD-E) Program; the Computer-Aided Manufacturing/Numerical Control (CAM/NC) Program; the Scientific and Technical Information (STINFO) Program; and the program to develop an S&E computer network, are provided as conceptual approaches in the text given below. These subprograms and many other large programs such as TEAMUP are all interrelated to some extent and are considered a part of the overall S&E level.

b. Concepts.

(1) The major purpose of the S&E level is to provide ADP support to the S&E community within AMC in the most efficient and effective way possible. It is recognized that the computer is used as a direct tool, including interactive computing by the

scientist or engineer, in S&E work to a much greater extent than in business applications. The goal is not to maximize the use of a particular computer since this would make it impossible to provide effective support to the S&E community. The goal is to provide the required support in the most cost-effective way. This involves some trade-offs between more efficient use of a particular computer main frame and S&E user requirements.

(2) In business applications, once a program is developed it is normally used over-and-over again in a production environment. In S&E applications, a program is normally developed for a specific end and is run a relatively few times in a production environment. The majority of time is spent in computer program development; therefore, a major emphasis within this level will be to find ways of reducing the problems associated with development of S&E computer programs. One means of doing this is to make it easier for scientists and engineers throughout AMC to exchange computer programs with each other. This can only be realized through use of a standard programing language and emphasis on program documentation.

(3) In many cases, S&E applications will share the same computer main frame with business applications; however, a single policy cannot be established in this area. In some cases it is more cost-effective to have separate computers for business and S&E applications.

(4) In many applications the scientist or engineer must carry out extensive mathematical computations as part of his work. He must make decisions on "what to compute next" based on the results of previous computations, and the complexity of the logic involved in these decisions is such that this logic is not easily programable. In such applications, interactive computing by the scientist or engineer is usually not cost-effective, since the user has direct access to a computer through a remote terminal. He calls for required computations and the results of these computations are returned to him within minutes. Typically, the computer will respond to any one request from the user within five seconds. Interactive computing will be fully supported within AMC; however, it must be recognized that from a strictly ADP point of view, interactive computing is costly and is frequently very inefficient with respect to use

of computer resources. Therefore, interactive computing should not be used as a substitute for remote batch-processing which is generally much less expensive.

(5) The CAD-E Program will effectively use ADPE at the various design and engineering activities. This program will intensify the application of automated and computer-aided techniques to the conceptualization design, simulation, testing, and documentation of military equipment and weapon systems as part of the materiel acquisition process within AMC. Implementation of this program will permit evaluation of a wider range of concept and design alternatives prior to final commitment of expensive engineering and testing resources. An extensive 5-year program to improve the CAD-E Program in AMC has been developed and is currently being implemented.

(6) The CAM/NC Program will provide improved support for in-house manufacturing requiring production of small lots of materiel which cannot be obtained economically from commercial sources. This production generally requires the use of Government-owned, numerically controlled machine tools which are controlled by individually programed servomechanisms to carry out certain machining activities. On a limited basis, Government-owned, numerically controlled machine tools will use a general purpose computer for control of multiple machine tools; the computer can then control the scheduling of the various machine tools connected to it and can substantially improve utilization of resources.

(7) The STINFO Program is not in itself a system but encompasses a number of separate and independent systems, including the Engineering Data Storage and Retrieval (EDSR) System, CIDS, Selective Dissemination of Information (SDI), and Technical Information Support Activities (TISA's). STINFO includes those management and support functions involved in the manipulation of scientific and technical data and information of primary interest to the scientific community. Such data and information are generally recorded in technical reports and published in journals or technical papers. The primary purpose of this program is to enable the scientist or engineer to rapidly access data he needs to accomplish his immediate objective.

(8) Development of a network of S&E computers is currently under study. From a management point of view, the basic purpose of this network is to minimize the number of computer main frames which must be installed. This network which provides scientists

and engineers with remote terminal access to computers with a much greater capability than could otherwise be justified, applies a load-sharing concept whereby ADP programs and data are shifted among computer main frames to take advantage of reserve capacity when one computer is overloaded.

c. Key features. Emphasis is on providing effective support to the S&E user. Use of standard program languages supported by standard program documentation and indexed program bibliographies will be utilized.

d. Developmental responsibility. Responsibility for development of S&E computer programs rests with each individual S&E activity. Requirements are specified by the S&E community, and application programs are frequently written by the using scientist or engineer.

e. Implementation plan. Computer hardware for S&E support is currently undergoing a substantial upgrading to third-generation equipment throughout AMC. Currently approved equipment includes the following computers: IBM 360, CDC 6500 and 6600, and UNIVAC 1108.

CHAPTER 7

MULTILEVEL MANAGEMENT INFORMATION SYSTEMS

7-1. Introduction. This chapter pertains to management information systems for internal management within AMC. In the AMC context, "management information system" refers to an information system either manual or automated which provides data and information to middle and top managers to evaluate progress against plans and programs identifying potential problem areas and allocating or reallocating resources to resolve potential problems.

7-2. Concepts. a. The primary characteristics of AMC management information systems, designed for management control, will aid the manager in making decisions, generate management action, predict potential problem areas of plans and programs, and provide feedback from the manager to the subordinate activities submitting information.

b. AMC management information systems are being developed to support managerial and operational requirements of Headquarters, AMC, and subordinate activities.

c. Management information systems to support Headquarters, AMC, are:

Planning, Programing, and Budgeting Management Information System (PPBMIS)--for functional management.

Project Management Information System (PROMIS)--serves end item oriented management.

c. Management information systems to support major subordinate activities, are:

Commodity Command Management Information System (CCMIS).
Depot Management Information System (DEPMIS).
Laboratory Management Information System (LABMIS).

e. These management information systems do not duplicate data which are contained in the business ADP (automatic data processing) systems within AMC but rather they use summary data forwarded to the various data banks from appropriate management information systems. A long-range goal is that all recurring reports to Headquarters, AMC, and higher authority will be prepared from the summary information contained in the AMC data banks.

7-3. Key features. a. The primary purpose of AMC management information systems is to aid management in making decisions and to generate management action.

b. Each management information system emphasizes prediction of potential problems so that top management can initiate policy or reallocate resources required to resolve the problem.

c. All AMC management information systems provide feedback information to submitting activities so they are afforded visibility on management action resulting from data they submit.

7-4. Planning, Programing, and Budgeting Management Information System (PPBMIS).
a. Concepts.

(1) The PPBMIS objective is to satisfy the requirements of the directors in Headquarters, AMC, for management information. It is closely tied to the formal planning, program, and budgeting system. As part of the PPBMIS, each director formulates program objectives for the next fiscal year. These program objectives must be formulated in such a way that progress in achieving the objectives can be measured quantitatively. A typical program objective would establish quarterly targets for obligation of PEMA (procurement of equipment and missiles, Army) funds by each of the major subordinate elements of AMC. Progress in achieving established objectives is reported using standard performance indicators.

(2) Participating activities submit a monthly report containing performance for the preceding month, and the forecasted performance for the next 60 to 90 days for

each standard performance indicator which applies to a program objective. The complete set of standard performance indicators is assembled at a central point and graphic displays showing each of the standard performance indicators are displayed on microfilm. On a monthly basis, copies of this microfilm are distributed simultaneously to all Headquarters, AMC, directors and to each reporting element.

b. Developmental responsibility. The PPBMIS has been developed by the AMC Logistic Systems Support Agency (AMC LSSA) under the direction of the Management Information Systems Directorate (MISD), Headquarters, AMC.

c. Implementation plan. The PPBMIS was implemented in September 1970 and is currently operational. The System will be expanded and refined as time and resources permit.

7-5. Commodity Command Management Information System (CCMIS). a. Concepts.

(1) The purpose of the CCMIS is to provide managers within the commodity commands of AMC with an improved capability to assess the status, effectiveness, and efficiency of operations on a timely basis and to provide the management information required from commodity commands by higher authority. The standard performance indicators, contained in the previously described PPBMIS, form a subset of the CCMIS standard performance indicators. The standard performance indicators are related to specific management functions and decisions which must be made by managers within the commodity commands.

(2) The CCMIS data will be accessible through an information retrieval system which will provide information to managers at the commodity commands via remote terminals.

b. Developmental responsibility. The General Functional System Requirement (GFSR) for the CCMIS is being developed through the coordinated participation of all commodity commands in a steering group under the chairmanship of a representative from the MISD, Headquarters, AMC. Detailed system design and computer program development will be the responsibility of the AMC Automated Logistics Management Systems Agency (AMC ALMSA).

c. Implementation plan. Full implementation of a standard CCMIS cannot occur prior to full implementation of the Commodity Command Standard System (CCSS). However, in support of immediate requirements, an interim CCMIS will be implemented during the next fiscal year.

7-6. Depot Management Information System (DEPMIS). a. Concept. The purpose of DEPMIS is to provide the depot commander and his staff with summary information for direction and control of depot activities. The concept is completely analogous to the CCMIS.

b. Developmental responsibility. The GFSR for the DEPMIS is being developed through the coordinated participation of all depots in a steering group under the chairmanship of a representative from the MISD, Headquarters, AMC. Detailed system design and computer program development will be the responsibility of the AMC LSSA.

c. Implementation plan. Full implementation of the DEPMIS cannot occur until full implementation of SPEEDEX (System-wide Project for Electronic Equipment at Depots, Extended). Installation of DEPMIS in pilot functional areas will occur in the depots by the end of FY 72. Additional areas will be installed as time and resources permit and in accordance with progress in implementation of the full SPEEDEX System.

7-7. Laboratory Management Information System (LABMIS). a. Concepts.

(1) The purpose of the LABMIS is to provide a standard management information system for use by all laboratories in local control of progress of the total technical, cost, and schedule efforts, and the allocation of personnel and technical facilities in meeting laboratory mission objectives.

(2) The LABMIS will provide a reporting vehicle to the Deputy for Laboratories, AMC. Capability will exist to incorporate selected data into the AMC PPBMIS.

(3) The essential features of the LABMIS are now in operation in the Test Resource Management System (TRMS) which is a major subsystem of TEAMUP (Test, Evaluation, Analysis, and Management Uniformity Plan) (Part A), at Headquarters, TECOM (United States Army Test and Evaluation Command).

b. Developmental responsibility. A Headquarters, AMC, working group composed of representatives from each AMC laboratory; the commodity command laboratories; Deputy for Laboratories, AMC; Director of Research, Development, and Engineering; and Director of Management Information Systems will be convened to begin this effort. Further developmental responsibility will be assigned after that time.

c. Implementation plan. Because considerable planning remains, no implementation plan can be provided at this time.

7-8. Project Management Information System (PROMIS). a. Concept. PROMIS consists of two parts--

(1) PROMIS I. A reporting system designed to provide Headquarters, AMC, and project managers with information on cost schedules and technical performance from the research and development phase through initial production of selected weapons and critical end items of equipment. Also provides flexibility to accommodate information requirements related to multiple end items in different life-cycle phases.

(2) PROMIS II.

(a) Supports the project manager in arriving at more timely management decisions by using computer modeling techniques for system planning and management control. When implemented, the project planning model will evaluate trade-offs of various decisions to resolve problems identified by the management control models.

(b) Establishes a library of simulation models that will provide a means by which the AMC project managers can apply the most effective mathematical and analytical techniques to their problems of assessing and making judgements in the areas of risk and uncertainty involved in the development and acquisition of weapons and critical end items of equipment.

b. Developmental responsibility. The PROMIS concept for both phases I and II was designed by the United States Army Management Engineering Training Agency (USAMETA) under the direction of the MISD, Headquarters, AMC. Computer programing required to support PROMIS will be the responsibility of the AMC ALMSA.

c. Implementation plan. PROMIS Phase I was implemented in February 1970 and is now in use on all AMC projects. PROMIS Phase II will be implemented on two pilot projects during FY 72. Full implementation of PROMIS on all projects must await installation of equipment for the CCSS at all commodity commands. PROMIS Phase II should be fully implemented within 6 months following the installation of standard equipment for the CCSS at the last commodity command.

CHAPTER 8

REPORTS MANAGEMENT

8-1. Introduction. The control of AMC automated reports and ADP (automatic data processing) products is a Department of the Army delegated mission responsibility of the AMC reports management function. This control is accomplished through interfacing with AMC standard and nonstandard management information systems and the administrative and functional operations of all AMC data processing activities. All formal recurring and one-time reports, both manual and automated, and all AMC-generated output products are closely controlled by Headquarters, AMC.

8-2. Concept. The primary objective of reports management is to provide cost-effective and qualitative-computerized data to AMC managers on a timely basis as a management tool for effective decision-making and to eliminate reports which are of marginal value or are not proven as cost-effective.

8-3. Key features. a. Establishes control over AMC-generated ADP output products by assigning report identification numbers (RIN's) to all ADP output products as required by Chapter 8, AR 335-15.

b. Provides for direct use of the AMC Data Element Dictionary (AMC DED) in applying standard data element codes and terminology to all new reporting requirements.

c. Provides interfacing with AMC standard and nonstandard management information systems to identify existing controllable reports which are prepared as management information system output products.

d. Establishes standard procedures for costing ADP output products on a command-wide basis.

e. Provides for approval, control, and cyclic review of AMC-generated automated reports and ADP output products, to provide managers with qualitative but economic management data.

f. Makes provisions for the systematic conversion of manual-type report preparation systems to a standardized computer-based reporting system.

8-4. System development plan. To carry out the reports management objectives and take maximum advantage of ADP technology and available capabilities in support of attainment of these objectives, Headquarters, AMC, has initiated a three-phase program as follows:

a. Phase I. Current effort is concentrated on reductions in existing reports through the medium of in-depth reviews to eliminate marginal value and nonessential reporting requirements. All major reviews thereto are expected to be completed by March 1972.

b. Phase II. A broader evaluation of remaining valid report preparation cost-effectiveness by feeder input elements and consolidation elements throughout the command. In this effort, consideration will be given not only to increasing the degree of automation at source data and collection locations, but also the most efficient methods of highlighting and displaying exception performance and planning information for managers on an "as needed" rather than on a "high frequency" recurring basis.

c. Phase III. The performance of in-depth reviews of valid reporting requirements in terms of data element usage densities through the capability of automated data element identification, analysis of demand, and stratification for appropriate summarization at successive levels of managerial usage. Through application of ADP techniques, it is expected that much of the current redundancy in related reports will be identified and subsequently eliminated. Therefore, substantially fewer ADP output report products will satisfy a larger field of manager users who formerly specified requirements for a variety of unique data element conbinations.

CHAPTER 9

DATA COMMUNICATION

9-1. Introduction. This portion of the AMC ADP/MIS Plan describes the development of long-range conceptual and operational approaches to communications which will be responsive to rapidly changing data transmission technology and to the increasing sophistication of Automatic Data Processing (ADP) Systems. The Plan is predicated on the fact that during the next 5 years, there will be significant technological advances in the data communication. For example--faster computers with greater storage capacities, versatile remote terminal facilities, and communication networks with greater capacity, will be available. Channels of planning and coordination have been established with the communications-electronics component of the Directorate for Installations and Services. While the long-range planning is accomplished by the staff elements, implementation is accomplished by the Installation and Services Agency at Rock Island, and the ADP Laboratory Division of AMC ALMSA (AMC Automated Logistics Management Systems Agency), which undertakes the development of the various ADP and communications projects. This group draws upon other command resources, as necessary, for assistance and expertise in both the ADP and communications areas.

9-2. Concept. The interrelationship of the AMC management information systems and the supporting communications services is categorized into four developmental phases described below. Implementation of each phase will coincide with the implementation of the various standard ADP programs.

9-3. Key features. a. Remote terminals located in the functional areas and connected to the central processor will result in accelerated processing and immediate access to computer-stored data.

b. Rapid transmission of data between AMC installations will eliminate unnecessary duplication of data and will increase overall efficiency of operations.

c. Management information systems, utilizing dedicated circuits between essential installations, will provide responsive near real-time data exchange.

d. By using versatile remote terminals in large capacity, high-speed computer configurations placed in a central location, will provide ADP service to a multitude of AMC activities at scattered geographical locations.

9-4. System development plan. The interrelationship of AMC management information systems and the supporting communication services are being implemented in four distinct and successive developmental phases, as follows:

a. Phase I--Operational environment.

(1) AUTODIN (Automatic Digital Network) capabilities have not been fully exploited by AMC, particularly in the area of transmission of logistics data. In this connection, a working group composed of representatives from the Installation and Services Agency at Rock Island, and the ADP Laboratory Division of AMC ALMSA, is developing practical procedures which will allow an IBM 360/30 terminal to process data in such a way as to transmit and receive data in a magnetic-tape-to-magnetic-tape mode.

(2) In a related effort, procedures are being developed to permit the transmission and receiving of data through the use of a disk interface (shared disk) between a depot or a commodity command standard system ADPE configuration and an IBM 360/30 AUTODIN terminal.

b. Phase II--Remote processing applications. The concept of using centralized ADP facilities to support ADP requirements of widely dispersed AMC activities is being tested in this phase by satelliting the Sierra Army Depot on the Letterkenny Army Depot for ADP support. This concept of centralized ADP support will be progressively expanded during successive phases of this plan.

c. <u>Phase III--Use of AUTODIN for high-volume traffic</u>.

(1) The data communication portion of this plan will require increased and extensive use of AUTODIN facilities and the full utilization of the Defense Communications System. The full utilization of AUTODIN by ADP facilities and activities has never been realized because of the limitations imposed on high-volume traffic loads by the message-switching mode of operation. The transmission is in 80-card column format and is restricted to 500 cards per transmission to include a header and trailer card. Circuit switching eliminates much of the format and message size restrictions which have precluded effective usage by data processing activities in the past.

(2) New techniques are under continued development and refinement to assure the full utilization of the AUTODIN circuit-switching capability. This will, for the first time in the AMC complex, afford full use of AUTODIN by high-volume subscribers with extensive requirements for variable length record transmissions.

c. <u>Phase IV--Communications in support of management information systems</u>. Implementation of this phase may require the use of dedicated circuits between selected activities for transmission and receipt of data concerning management information systems; however, applications requiring dedicated circuits must be fully substantiated and will not be accomplished without prior approval of Headquarters, AMC.

CHAPTER 10

TRAINING

10-1. Introduction. The United States Army Logistics Management Center (USALMC) has been designated by the Director of Personnel, Training, and Force Development (DPTFD) as the "Executive Agent" for monitoring the progress of the Training Program for the AMC ADP/MIS Plan. All training requirements associated with this Plan will be directed to the DPTFD for consideration. The DPTFD, in response to the DMIS (Director of Management Information Systems) guidance, provides the necessary administration and control over the Training Program for the AMC ADP/MIS Plan.

10-2. Concepts. The Training Program for the AMC ADP/MIS Plan consists of the following two major areas of training:

a. First--training of functional personnel in the specific techniques and procedures to be used in the implementation and operation of the AMC standard systems.

b. Second--providing technical training to ADP personnel who will implement, operate, and maintain the standard ADP programs, systems, and equipment. The area of ADP training consists of two subdivisions--that of retraining ADP journeymen to use the standard systems and the training of ADP interns.

10-3. Key features. a. In order to facilitate the training of 22,000 functional personnel in the required time frame and still insure a high quality training program, USALMC has developed and successfully employed the "multimedia technique." This technique consists of the use of instructors from the local installation who will manage and present to the 22,000 personnel, a training package that consists of prepared video lectures, programed instruction text, computer-assisted simulations, and automated student tests that are reinforced by lecture conferences. Use of the multimedia technique in lieu of conventional teaching methods will result in a significant reduction in training cost over a 5-year implementation period.

b. The United States Army Management Engineering Training Agency (USAMETA), is responsible for providing and insuring the formal ADP classroom training for the 3,000 ADP personnel to be retrained and the newly recruited ADP interns.

10-4. Training plan. a. General. The USALMC will be responsible for providing the functional training and USAMETA will be responsible for the ADP training. Training materials will be prepared at the USALMC and the USAMETA from information provided by the central system design agencies. USAMETA will also use information provided by the appropriate computer manufacturers. Methods of instruction that will be used are lectures, conferences, practical exercises, simulations, programed instructions, television, films, and instant feedback techniques.

b. Functional training. Instructors for functional training will be selected from personnel assigned to the activity implementing the standard system. Courses for instructors will be conducted at the USALMC for functional areas. When these instructors have completed their training they will conduct courses for appropriate personnel of their home activity using the multimedia technique.

c. ADP technical training. The USAMETA will prepare and conduct training courses for the ADP technical areas required by the activity implementing standard systems. These courses will be presented to appropriate ADP personnel at the implementing activity through the use of formal classroom training conducted by USAMETA's instructors. ADPE (automatic data processing equipment) manufacturers will augment the USAMETA training program and, where appropriate, will provide specialized training pertinent to the equipment available at the activity.

d. ADP Intern Program. This Program consists of 6 months of formalized training under the supervision of the USAMETA. During this period, 16 weeks of classroom training and 10 weeks of on-the-job training (OJT) is provided. Following the initial 6-months' syllabus, interns are assigned to central system design agencies and selected ADP activities of AMC for 12 additional months of OJT. Approximately 72 ADP interns will be trained annually to maintain an adequate source of manpower to meet immediate and future requirements.

D

Xerox Corporation Information Systems Long-Range Plan

Attached is a revised set of planning guidelines and formats for the preparation of the 1974 Long-Range Systems Plan. You should have received a preliminary package via Corporate Planning and your Group Planning Office some weeks ago.

This final guideline set includes a shortened planning horizon—to 1980—thus agreeing with the corporate revenue/profit forms. In the interest of reducing the bulk (and expense) of the plan preparation, we have significantly reduced the extent of the instructions.

If this plan is to show an improvement over the 1973 submission, several key weaknesses in last year's plan must be addressed:

- The Volume I narrative should be expressed, wherever possible, in terms of objectives and strategies that achieve quantifiable improvements in our operations. The guidelines suggest ways in which to express these objectives.
- The focus on computer-based systems should be *balanced* with a strategy that applies to the overall administrative costs of each operation. Essentially, the plan should address the impact that the long-range strategy will have on our growing clerical costs.

The timetable that has been established for this year's cycle in terms of a functional review is as follows:

Draft:	4/26/74
Feedback:	5/15/74
Final:	6/1/74

We will be contacting you to establish a convenient time for a presentation of your plan to the Information Systems Director and interested members of your group and corporate staff.

7.4 INFORMATION SYSTEMS

7.4.0 Introduction

These instructions have been prepared to promote a discussion of the role information systems and telecommunications managers must play in achieving corporatewide goals. The guideline structure will highlight the attention that is to be focused on the administrative efficiency and cost effectiveness of the people and resources used to administer our business.

This Information Systems Long-Range Plan must concentrate on identifying the elements of our administrative costs and resulting:

Payoff in operations
Administrative productivity improvement
Systems productivity improvement

7.4.1 Format Guidelines—Information Systems

Volume I

The following schedules represent data requirements to be included in Volume I of the Long-Range Plan submission, summarized at the group/division level. They are designed for completion by systems, programming, telecommunications, and data processing functions within the corporation. To facilitate consolidation and analysis, it is important to adhere to the formats in the guide.

1. Prepare a group/division narrative which addresses the following topics:

Mission Statements

Quantify the potential in performance improvement in terms of:

Increased calls/day
Lower cost/sale
Lower cost/drawing
Fewer days of stock holding
Lower cost/page of text composition
Fewer return calls/tech rep

Approach and Tactics

The following subjects are to be reviewed to provide the full management narrative:

a. *General Administrative Efficiency*—the productivity of the office environment, in terms of costs over the period.
b. *Investment in Information Tools per Worker*—to include telephones, copiers or copy volume, telecopiers, terminals, paging systems, programmable calculators, microfilm viewers, closed circuit TV systems, drafting aids, mechanized filing systems, electronic status keeping, etc.
c. *Persons Engaged in Data Handling*—non-I/S personnel sitting at terminals (financial planners using APL, engineers using BASIC, stockroom clerks at DE devices), and those involved in transaction batching, control, transmittal, processing, drafting, typesetting, error correction.
d. *Internal Productivity*—the levels of output per man-month in the internal information systems function (project control techniques, working hours, mechanized tools, language schemes).
e. *Standardization of Business System Solutions*—the tactic for insuring the widest possible utilization of successful software, procedural logic, or hardware tools for all the appropriate applications in each area of responsibility.
f. *Audits*—the status of all *operational* audit action items dealing with the *functions* served by information systems.
g. *Effectiveness of the Base of Existing, Installed, Computer-Based Systems.*

2. Complete the Long-Range Systems Plan Summary, specifying headcount, expense, and capital requirements of the group/division to support the organization throughout the plan period (Form 741-1).

3. Summarize the telecommunications staff and major operational headcount, expense and capital requirements of the responsible organization to support the plan. Assume centralized accountability for circuitry and equipment required for major intercity telecommunications networks (Form 742-1).
4. All amounts should be stated in U.S. dollars at exchange rates used in the latest approved Operating Plan.
5. Use constant dollars for all revenue and expense elements throughout the plan period.
6. All 1974/1975 data should be based upon the latest available outlook. Specify the month's outlook which has been used.
7. Assume current organization and accounting practices as a base, commenting on the potential impact of any changes that might be accommodated during the plan period.
8. The plan period commences in 1974 and extends through 1980.

Volume II

The following schedules represent data requirements to be included as backup for the Volume I Long-Range Plan submission. They are designed for completion by all systems, programming, and data processing functions within the corporation and provide the detail to support the summary information above to be included in Volume I.

1. Prepare an expense projection schedule which identifies both the gross (hard dollar) and transfer expense (if any) incurred by the organization to support that organization's systems, programming, data processing, or telecommunications activities (Form 741-2).
   - All "other" labor expense should include shift and overtime premiums, payroll costs, and, where applicable, profit sharing expense.
   - All equipment expenses should include intercompany markup for the organization incurring the expense.
   - Local telephone and network circuitry expense categories are defined as follows:

     Local Telephone—Cost of telephone instruments, switchboards, and lines (excluding intercity lines). Also included are local message unit calls and all taxes related to the foregoing.

     Voice Circuitry—All long distance toll and private intercity line services used primarily for voice communication including: WATS, INWATS, FX, tielines, etc.

Data Circuitry—All costs for record and data communications including terminal equipment, circuits, and modems.

- Exclude labor cost of switchboard operations unless such cost is applied to long distance network administration.

2. Prepare a manpower projection schedule (Form 741-3).
   - Use December headcount figures for each year.
   - Confidential employees should be counted as exempt, hourly employees as non-exempt, where appropriate.
   - Do not include contract employees.
3. Prepare a development projects/feasibility study schedule for each project/study (Form 741-4).
   - Use one page per development project/study throughout the plan period.
   - Specify whether the project/study has been approved by management with funding and estimated target dates established.
   - Provide a system organization code which most nearly describes the nature of the project/study.

	Code
Sales	1
Service	2
Distribution	3
Procurement	4
Manufacturing operations	5
Engineering	6
Research	7
Administrative/other	8
Finance	9
Product planning	10

On this form, include a brief paragraph discussing the following topics:

General Overview

Specific Feateres/Benefits

Primary System Interfaces/Organizations Impacted

Key Dates (Feasibility Study, Proposal, and Implementation)

- Expenses should be stated in terms of transfer cost where such costs exist; if such costs are not charged because of current accounting policy a proration of direct (gross) costs should be made and allocated to each project/study.

- Not more than 10% of the group/division's development projects should be classified as "other"; the remainder should be supported by separate forms.

4. Prepare a maintenance schedule (Form 741-5).
   - Summarize all maintenance effort by systems organization code.
   - Expenses should be treated as described above for development projects/feasibility studies and include data center, programming, management sciences, telecommunications, and systems costs where applicable.

5. Prepare a data center or telecommunications equipment schedule (Form 741-6).
   - Describe each major hardware component, providing costs which include depreciation, maintenance, use charges, rental/lease charges, and intercompany markup, as applicable.
   - Provide a narrative describing the reason for the changes in cost throughout the plan period.

INFORMATION SYSTEMS
RESOURCE SUMMARY
1974 LONG RANGE PLAN

DECEMBER MANPOWER REQUIREMENTS	1973	1974	1975	1976	1977	1978	1979	1980
Exempt (1)	$	$	$	$	$	$	$	$
Non-Exempt								
Total	$	$	$	$	$	$	$	$
EXPENSE REQUIREMENTS ($000)	1973	1974	1975	1976	1977	1978	1979	1980
Labor	$	$	$	$	$	$	$	$
Hardware (2)								
Supplies								
Travel								
Other								
Total	$	$	$	$	$	$	$	$
CAPITAL REQUIREMENTS - APPROVAL BASIS ($000)	1973	1974	1975	1976	1977	1978	1979	1980
Buildings	$	$	$	$	$	$	$	$
Computers (3)								
Office Furniture & Expenses								
Other								
Total	$	$	$	$	$	$	$	$

Note 1 - Exempt includes confidential, non-exempt includes hourly.
Note 2 - Hardware includes rental/lease costs, maintenance, depreciation and intercompany markup, where applicable. Other includes transfer expense, if any, for support provided by other Groups/Divisions.
Note 3 - Computers excludes intercompany markup.

FORM 741-1

TELECOMMUNICATIONS
RESOURCE SUMMARY
1974 LONG RANGE PLAN

DECEMBER MANPOWER REQUIREMENTS	1973	1974	1975	1976	1977	1978	1979	1980
Exempt (1)	$	$	$	$	$	$	$	$
Non-Exempt								
Total	$	$	$	$	$	$	$	$
EXPENSE REQUIREMENTS ($000)	1973	1974	1975	1976	1977	1978	1979	1980
Labor	$	$	$	$	$	$	$	$
Hardware (2)								
Supplies								
Travel								
Other								
Total	$	$	$	$	$	$	$	$
CAPITAL REQUIREMENTS - APPROVAL BASIS ($000)	1973	1974	1975	1976	1977	1978	1979	1980
Buildings	$	$	$	$	$	$	$	$
Computers (3)								
Office Furniture & Expenses								
Other								
Total	$	$	$	$	$	$	$	$

Note 1 - Exempt includes confidential, non-exempt includes hourly.
Note 2 - Hardware includes rental/lease costs, maintenance, depreciation and intercompany markup, where applicable. Other includes transfer expense, if any, for support provided by other Groups/Divisions.
Note 3 - Computers excludes intercompany markup.

FORM 742-1

XEROX LONG RANGE PLAN - Volume II

INFORMATION SYSTEMS

EXPENSE PROJECTIONS ($000)

Group/Division	Organization							Comments
Expense Category	1974	1975	1976	1977	1978	1979	1980	
Labor								
Exempt								
Non-Exempt								
Other								
Total								
Equipment								
Sigma/530, etc.								
Other								
Total								
Other								
Supplies								
Travel								
Other								
Total								
Transfers								
Data Center								
Prog/Mgt. Sciences								
Telecommunications								
Systems								
Other								
Total								
TOTAL NET								

FORM 741-2

XEROX LONG RANGE PLAN - Volume II

INFORMATION SYSTEMS

MANPOWER PROJECTIONS

Group/Division	Organization														Comments
	1974		1975		1976		1977		1978		1979		1980		
Function	E	N/E	E	N/E	E	N/E	E	N/E	E	N/E	E	N/E	E	N/E	
Programming															
(including Mgt. Science)															
Systems Analyst															
Data Center															
Operations															
Other															
Total															
Other *															
TOTAL															

* Identify Manmonths acquired from Information Services Division

FORM 741-3

XEROX LONG RANGE PLAN - Volume II

INFORMATION SYSTEMS

DEVELOPMENT PROJECTS/FEASIBILITY STUDIES

Group/Division	Organization		Date
Project Title	Sys. Org. Code	Base Case ☐ Strategy Case ☐	
		Management Approval Yes ☐ No ☐	

Resources:	1974	1975	1976	1977	1978	1979	1980
Manpower							
Expense ($000)							
Systems							
Programming							
Data Center							
Total							

FORM 741-4

XEROX LONG RANGE PLAN - Volume II
INFORMATION SYSTEMS
MAINTENANCE SUPPORT ($000)

Group/Division	Organization	Date

Manpower by System Org. Code

	1974	1975	1976	1977	1978	1979	1980
1.							
2.							
3.							
4.							
5.							
6.							
7.							
8.							
9.							
10.							
TOTAL							

Expense by System Org. Code

	1974	1975	1976	1977	1978	1979	1980
1.							
2.							
3.							
4.							
5.							
6.							
7.							
8.							
9.							
10.							
TOTAL							

FORM 741-5

XEROX LONG RANGE PLAN - Volume II

INFORMATION SYSTEMS

DATA CENTER EXPENSES ($000)

Group/Division			Organization					Comments
Major Component	1974	1975	1976	1977	1978	1979	1980	
A.								
Explanation of Changes:								
B.								
Explanation of Changes:								
C.								
Explanation of Changes:								
D.								
Explanation of Changes:								
E.								
Explantion of Changes:								
TOTAL EXPENSE								

FORM 741-6

E

Survey Questionnaire Forms

INITIAL QUESTIONNAIRE ON LONG–RANGE PLANNING FOR INFORMATION SYSTEMS

As part of the Conference on Long-Range Planning for Information Systems, the sponsors would like to develop a list of common planning pitfalls which participants have found from experience should be avoided if the planning process is to be most effective.

The first four pages of the questionnaire ask some general questions about your company or organization, the EDP function, and its information systems long-range plan (LRP). The remaining pages of the questionnaire list potential pitfalls and ask for an indication of those pitfalls which your company or organization has experienced, as well as an estimate of the degree of impact these have had on successfully developing a realistic plan. Space is also provided for describing other pitfalls not already listed.

Please return the completed questionnaire before March 25, 1974. The the replies can be tabulated in time for discussion at the conference. They should be returned to:

Dr. Ephraim R. McLean
Center for Information Studies
Graduate School of Management
University of California
Los Angeles, California 90024

Your individual responses will be considered confidential and will not be quoted without express permission. A summary of the results of the survey will be distributed at the conference and should be helpful in structuring our discussion.

A. COMPANY INFORMATION

1. Company Name: ______________________________

2. Company Revenues: ______________________________

3. Total Number of Employees: ______________________________

4. Company Organization:

	PHYSICALLY	FUNCTIONALLY
Centralized		
Decentralized		

5. Number of Independent EDP Organizations in Company: ______________

6. Total EDP Budget: ______________________________

7. Total Number of EDP–Related Employees: ______________________

B. EDP INFORMATION

1. EDP Organization:

	COMPUTER OPERATIONS	SYSTEMS DEVELOPMENT
Physically Centralized		
Functionally Centralized		
Physically Decentralized		
Functionally Decentralized		

2. Number of Independent EDP Organizations Covered by LRP: ______________

3. EDP Budget Covered by LRP: ______________________________

4. Number of EDP–Related Employees Covered by LRP: ______________

5. Number of Employees Covered by LRP In:

______ Systems Design and Programming

______ Methods and Procedures

______ Management Science/ Operations Research

______ Other (Specify)

____

____

______ Telecommunications

______ Information Systems Planning

______ Education and Training

______ Computer Operations

C. INFORMATION SYSTEMS LRP DATA

1. LRP Planning horizon: ____________________ (YEARS)

2. Elapsed Time Required to Develop LRP: ____________________ (MONTHS)

3. Effort Required to Develop LRP: ____________________ (MAN–MONTHS)

4. Length of LRP Document: ____________________ (PAGES)

5. LRP Update Frequency: ____________________

6. Executive Responsible for LRP: ____________________

7. Highest Level of LRP Approval: ____________________

8. Degree of Satisfaction With LRP:

	HIGH	MEDIUM	LOW
Top Management			
Information Systems Management			
User Management			

9. Year First LRP Was Developed: ____________________

10. Annual Operating Plan Separate From LRP: Yes ________ No ________

11. Planning Methodology Used:

_____ Bottom-up, i.e., based on ideas generated during user interviews

_____ Top-down, i.e., based on financial analysis of the company or organization and its environment

_____ Combination of both

12. LRP Modeled After Corporate Plan: Yes ________ No ________ No Corporate Plan ____________

13. Degree of Participation in Developing LRP:

	HIGH	MEDIUM	LOW	NONE
Top Management				
Corporate (Non-EDP) Planners				
Users				
Information Systems Executive				
Systems Development Group				
Computer Operations Group				
Information Systems Planning Staff				
Vendors				
Consultants				

14. Items included in your information systems LRP:

	INCLUDED IN OUR LRP	NOT INCLUDED BUT SHOULD BE	DON'T BELIEVE SHOULD BE INCLUDED
Statement of objectives			
Projection of possible future EDP environment			
Projection of possible future user environment			
Projection of possible future industry environment			
Summary of strengths & weaknesses of EDP staff			
Evaluation of past performance vs. plan by EDP			
Alternate strategy definition/evaluation			
Financial plan			
Hardware plan			
Facilities plan			
Personnel plan			
Education plan			
Organization plan			
System development plan			
Recommended implementation plan			
Other (Specify:)			

15. Items included in the system development plan subset of your information systems LRP:

	INCLUDED IN OUR LRP	NOT INCLUDED BUT SHOULD BE	DON'T BELIEVE SHOULD BE INCLUDED
Specific project descriptions			
Specific project development cost estimates			
Specific project operating cost estimates			
Specific project benefits estimate			
Specific project ROI estimate			
Specific project risk evaluation			
Project priority ranking			
Development timetable for project portfolio			
Other (Specify:)			

16. Please weight (5 = most important, 1 = least important) each purpose you had in mind when undertaking your information systems LRP effort and then weight the degree of attainment to date (5 = outstanding relative to expectation, 1 = poor relative to expectation) in carrying out the LRP effort.

PURPOSE	INITIALLY DESIRED	ACTUALLY ATTAINED
Identifying new applications		
Improving communications with users		
Improving communications with top management		
Forecasting resource requirements more accurately		
Identifying internal improvement opportunities		
Improving short-term decision making		
Improving the allocation of personnel resources		
Securing budget increases		
Improving morale and sense of purpose		
Increasing ROI of new applications		
Decreasing costs of computer operations		
Decreasing "fire fighting"		
Increasing user cooperation		
Increasing employee productivity		
Increasing top management support		
Canceling marginal projects		
Increasing visibility of EDP in the company		
Increasing understanding of the company		
Other (Specify)		

D. PITFALLS OF LONG–RANGE PLANNING

The following pages provide a checklist of potential pitfalls in launching conducting, and using the long-range plan. Please check (√) the appropriate columns to indicate whether this potential pitfall, in fact, did initially or does now have an effect on your planning effort.

POTENTIAL PITFALLS	Effect of This When You *INITIATED* Planning Effort				Effect of This *NOW* in Your Planning Effort			
	None	Minor	Major	Extreme	None	Minor	Major	Extreme
PITFALLS IN LAUNCHING THE PLANNING EFFORT								
1. Not being in sufficient control of systems development and computer operations performance to have credibility with users								
2. Ignoring the people and politics side of planning								
3. Failing to get top management support for the planning effort								
4. Not having a clear-cut corporate plan to guide the information systems planning effort								
5. Not viewing planning as a learning process for users and information services								
6. Underestimating the need for a clear, concise, formal planning procedure								
7. Deciding on too long a planning horizon								
8. Deciding on too short a planning horizon								
9. Failing to anticipate likely changes in EDP technology which might affect the LRP								
10. Delegating the planning responsibility to an individual without sufficient experience, influence, or time to do a thorough job								
11. Being unable to obtain sufficiently qualified personnel to do a proper job								
12. Not allowing enough time to do a substantive effort								
13. Not having free communication and commitment to change throughout the company/organization								
14. Not investing sufficient "front-end" time to ensure that all the planning tasks and individual responsibilities are well understood								
15. Other (Specify) ______________								
PITFALLS IN DEVELOPING THE LRP								
16. Not performing a top-down analysis to identify high profit leverage areas prior to interviewing users								
17. Not performing a bottom-up analysis to identify opportunities								
18. Relying exclusively on user "wish lists" for application ideas								
19. Ignoring overall company and user business goals								
20. Neglecting to assess realistically internal weaknesses of the EDP group in determining capabilities to carry out the recommended strategy								

POTENTIAL PITFALLS	Effect of This When You *INITIATED* Planning Effort				Effect of This *NOW* in Your Planning Effort			
	None	Minor	Major	Extreme	None	Minor	Major	Extreme
21. Not securing the minimum data required to make the results credible and useful								
22. Failing to consider and explicitly evaluate alternate strategies in order to give top management a meaningful choice								
23. Failing to involve users and top management a meaningful choice								
24. Requiring too much formality so as to restrain creativity on the part of the planners and users in defining information requirements								
25. Overoptimism on the part of the planner								
26. Failing to translate goals and strategies into a tactical action plan								
27. Failing to review the LRP with all managers concerned so as to obtain support and cooperation for its implementation								
28. Other (Specify:) ______________________________								
PITFALLS IN USING THE LRP								
29. Ignoring the plan once it has been developed								
30. Not using the plan as a standard for measuring managerial performance								
31. Neglecting to adjust the plan to reflect major environmental changes								
32. Consistently making intuitive decisions which conflict with the approved strategy								
33. Other (Specify:) ______________________________								

34. What is the largest single factor standing in the way of better information systems planning in your organization?

FOLLOW–UP QUESTIONNAIRE ON PLANNING FOR INFORMATION SYSTEMS

During the analysis of the data provided in the initial questionnaires to us, it became apparent that a few important areas had been overlooked in the questionnaire and that a greater depth of detail was needed in some other areas. In order to gather this missing data, we are asking you to respond to this follow-up questionnaire. A copy of your original questionnaire has been enclosed in case you want to review how you answered some related questions earlier. We will collect the completed follow-up questionnaires at lunch time on Thursday. The results from this follow-up questionnaire will be merged with the results from the initial questionnaire and a summary of the combined results will be mailed to you after the conference. Thank you for your cooperation.

1. Company/organization name: ______________________________

2. Please check below the appropriate degree of benefits quantification that is currently provided for major systems development projects.

LEVEL OF BENEFITS QUANTIFICATION	LONG-RANGE MIS PLAN		PROJECT FEASIBILITY STUDY		SHOULD NOT BE INCLUDED IN EITHER
	INCLUDED	NOT INCLUDED BUT SHOULD BE	INCLUDED	NOT INCLUDED BUT SHOULD BE	
A dollar range of tangible benefits is given					
Quantitative description of tangible benefits, e.g., 10% inventory reduction, but this is not translated into dollar impact					
Qualitative benefits description only, e.g., better management information					
No benefits specification					
Other (Specify): ____________					

3. Indicate the host organization's degree of sophistication in the areas of business planning, capital allocation, and objective setting by checking (✓) the most appropriate statement in each category.

CATEGORY	√	DEGREE OF SOPHISTICATION
LONG-RANGE BUSINESS PLANNING	____	No formal long-range business planning
	____	Mostly financial and headcount projections
	____	More tactical than strategic
	____	Clearly strategic in nature
CAPITAL ALLOCATION	____	No formal capital allocation criteria
	____	Formal document stating purpose and level of investment but no financial measure of attractiveness such as ROI, present value, payback period, etc.
	____	Rigorous financial analysis for all major expenditures but no post-audit
	____	Rigorous financial analysis with post-audit of results
OBJECTIVE SETTING	____	No formal setting of individual objectives
	____	Only generalized individual objectives are set
	____	Highly targeted individual objectives are set but no formal follow-up or appraisal of results
	____	Highly targeted individual objectives with strong follow-up
	____	Highly targeted individual objectives with strong follow-up directly affecting compensation

4. Indicate the MIS group's stage of maturity in the areas of computer operations, systems development, user involvement, feasibility assessment, communications, and tactical planning by checking (✓) the most appropriate statement(s) in each category.

CATEGORY	✓	STAGE OF "MATURITY"
COMPUTER OPERATIONS	____	Users are dissatisfied with the timeliness and accuracy of computer operations
	____	Users are generally satisfied with timeliness and accuracy of computer operations but no formal production statistics such as turnaround time, percent of reruns, etc., are communicated to them
	____	Production control has been formalized, production objectives are set, and performance versus plan is communicated to users on a regular basis
SYSTEMS DEVELOPMENT	____	No formal standard for systems development exists
	____	Users have little confidence in the MIS group's ability to deliver major systems on time, within budget, and meeting specifications
	____	Users are very confident of the MIS group's ability to consistently deliver major systems approximately on time, within budget, and meeting specifications
USER INVOLVEMENT	____	Users are rarely involved in the systems development process
	____	Users are involved only as much as necessary to define the system specifications and to implement it
	____	Users are actively involved in all phases of the systems development process and often manage the project team
FEASIBILITY ASSESSMENT	____	No formal standard for assessing the feasibility of proposed major systems development projects exists
	____	Feasibility assessments are well defined and required for all proposed major systems development projects but no post-implementation audit is performed
	____	Feasibility assessments are well defined and required for all proposed major systems development projects and followed up by post-implementation audits
COMMUNICATIONS	____	Communications with users are adequate
	____	Communications with users need improving
	____	Communications with top management are adequate
	____	Communications with top management need improving
	____	Communications within the MIS group are adequate
	____	Communications within the MIS group need improving
TACTICAL PLANNING	____	No tactical plan is documented
	____	A comprehensive, documented annual operating plan exists with quantitative performance targets for the MIS group as a whole
	____	A comprehensive, documented annual operating plan exists with quantitative performance targets for each manager
	____	Tactical planning consists largely of budgets and headcount forecasts
	____	Tactical planning consists of budgets, headcount forecasts, and hardware schedules

5. Please check below the initial and current degree of participation in developing the LRP as well as degree of satisfaction with the LRP by various groups.

Initial Effort				DEGREE OF PARTICIPATION IN DEVELOPING LRP	Current Effort			
High	Med	Low	None		High	Med	Low	None
				Top Management				
				Corporate (Non-EDP) Planners				
				Users				
				Information Systems Executive				
				Systems Development Group				
				Computer Operations Group				
				Information Systems Planning Staff				
				Vendors				
				Consultants				

Initial Effort				DEGREE OF SATISFACTION WITH LRP	Current Effort			
High	Med	Low	None		High	Med	Low	None
				Top Management				
				Information Systems Management				
				User Management				

6. Please check below the degree of emphasis on possible long-range planning steps both in your initial LRP effort and in your current effort.

Initial Effort						Current Effort				
High	Med	Low	None, But Should Be Some	Should Not Be Any	DEGREE OF EMPHASIS ON	High	Med	Low	None, But Should Be Some	Should Not Be Any
					Defining the planning process itself					
					Launching the formal planning effort					
					Agreeing on MIS group objectives					
					Identifying highest potential areas in host organization for use of computers					
					Identifying likely longer term structure and management style of the host organization					
					Identifying likely longer-term MIS needs of the host organization					
					Defining longer-term MIS system architecture					
					Analyzing applications in use by competition or similar organizations					
					Documenting assumptions regarding future computer technology trends					
					Identifying potential projects among current user groups					
					Identifying potential projects among non-user groups across the organization					
					Identifying potential projects among non-user groups in higher management					
					Evaluating internal MIS group improvement needs					
					Defining criteria for evaluating and ranking potential projects					
					Evaluating potential projects					
					Ranking potential projects					
					Identifying strategic alternatives					
					Forecasting resource needs for each strategy					
					Evaluating strategy alternatives					
					Selecting most appropriate strategy alternative					
					Translating selected strategy into action plans					
					Translating strategy into short-term middle management performance milestones					

7. Please indicate below what percent of the total planning effort is currently expended by the MIS group during each major step listed below.

STEP DESCRIPTION	PERCENT OF TOTAL MIS EFFORT
Planning the LRP effort	
Analyzing the environment external to the MIS group	
Documenting long-term user MIS needs	
Defining the long-term MIS system architecture	
Assessing the current capabilities of the MIS group	
Compiling the ranked list of potential systems development projects	
Identifying and evaluating strategy alternatives	
Gaining management approval/support for implementing LRP	
Translating strategy into action plans	
Other (Specify): ____________________	
TOTAL MIS GROUP EFFORT	100%

8. Please check the appropriate columns to indicate which potential pitfalls in using the LRP did initially, or do now, have an effect on your planning effort.

POTENTIAL PITFALLS	Effect of This When You *INITIATED* Planning Effort				Effect of This *NOW* in Your Planning Effort			
	None	Minor	Major	Extreme	None	Minor	Major	Extreme
PITFALLS IN USING THE LRP Plan is good communication vehicle but not fundamental direction setter								
Plan is not translated into shorter term performance milestones for MIS middle management								
Higher level management requests cause changes in direction not anticipated in plan								
Unanticipated budget cuts or reallocations require shifts in direction of effort								
Changes in host organization structure or management results in redirection of effort								
Unanticipated changes in host organization's environment (e.g., government regulation, energy crisis) create short-term demands on MIS staff								
Unanticipated changes in computer software or hardware technology cause need for fundamental rethinking of long-term direction								
MIS group cannot deliver applications as scheduled and users become disenchanted								
Lack of user commitment to, and cooperation with, plan results in continuing short-term shifts in direction								
Changes in design scope of scheduled projects negates value of plan								

About the Contributors

Roger W. Barbey is manager of Information Systems Development of the Pacific Gas and Electric Company, San Francisco. He previously served as civil engineer in the engineering function and in an administrative capacity in the materials function. He holds an engineering degree from Yale University.

Morris F. Collen has been director of the Department of Medical Methods Research of the Permanente Medical Group and the Kaiser Foundation Research Institute in Oakland, California, since 1961. Dr. Collen received his BEE and MD degrees from the University of Minnesota and became a certified specialist in internal medicine and a member of the American College of Physicians. He has served as chief of Medical Service and medical director of the Kaiser Foundation Hospital and as chairman of the Executive Committee of the Permanente Medical Group. He has published more than 100 articles and five books. He has served as a consultant to the U.S. Department of Health, Education, and Welfare and other governmental agencies, and to the World Health Organization. He is a member of the Institute of Medicine of the National Academy of Sciences.

Anthony J. Craine, director of Management Services, CIBA–GEIGY Corporation, Ardsley, New York, joined the Geigy headquarters in

Switzerland as international head of Management Services. While there, he was a member of the team responsible for coordinating the merger of Geigy and CIBA corporations. In 1970 he returned to the United States as director of Corporate Planning and was named director of Management Services in 1971.

Mr. Craine studied at Columbia, Northwestern, St. John's (Minnesota), and New York universities, and was a Fulbright Scholar at the University of Cologne, Germany. He has published papers and has lectured in the United States and in Europe on the major aspects of data processing and management sciences.

John R. Frey, Director of Computer Services, Consumers Power Company, Jackson, Michigan, served in various engineering and planning capacities within the company before assuming responsibility for computer operations and application development. He has a degree in electrical engineering from the University of Michigan.

Jack B. Gearhart, vice president and director, Management Systems, TRW Systems Group, Redondo Beach, California, is responsible for policy and organization planning, management systems and information systems development, training systems implementation, and business data processing. He is a member of AIAA, NCMA, and ADPA, as well as numerous civic and social organizations. He received BS and MS degrees in aeronautical engineering from Iowa State University and an MS in engineering from UCLA.

Alan H. Gepfert is manager of the Management Sciences Programs Department, Mobil Oil Corporation, New York City. A former management consultant with McKinsey & Company, Inc., he has also been an executive with the Chicago and North Western Railway Company, an instructor in management, and a member of the consulting group at Case Institute of Technology of Case Western Reserve University. He received a BS in engineering administration and an MS in operations research, both from Case Institute. He has had articles on finance, operations research, business logistics, and other subjects published by the *Harvard Business Review*, McGraw-Hill, McKinsey, the Institute of Management Sciences, Railway Systems and Management Association, and others, and has been consulting economic editor for *Modern Railroads* magazine.

John C. Gilbert, director of Management Information Systems, U.S. Army Materiel Command, Alexandria, Virginia, is responsible for computing and management information systems in all the Army Materiel Command's installations. Formerly he was director of the U.S. Army Management Systems Support Agency, which provided data processing support for the Secretary of the Army and the Army Chief of Staff. He studied at Virginia Polytechnic Institute and American University, majoring in mathematics.

F. A. Gitzendanner is manager, Information Systems Development, Information Services and Management Sciences Department, Standard Oil Company (Indiana), Chicago. Following engineering and sales work and Army service in World War II, he joined Standard Oil (Indiana) in the Engineering Research Department. Initially directing work in the engineering economics area, in 1953 he established a technical computing and operations research division in the Research and Development Department of Amoco Oil Company, one of Standard's subsidiaries. When commercial data processing, technical computing, and operations research in Amoco Oil became centralized in 1966, he transferred to the new Information Services and Management Sciences Department as head of technical computing and operations research. He became department manager in 1968. In 1971 he became manager, Information Systems Development, in the further centralized Information Services and Management Sciences Department in the parent company, responsible for systems development for the parent and the five affiliates headquartered in Chicago.

Kent H. Gould, as chief of EDP Control and Development for the State of California under the Reagan administration, was responsible for planning and monitoring the implementation of the state's EDP consolidation plan. This also included implementing the legislative requirements for security and privacy in state EDP installations. Before that he had been director of Management Information Services for the Larwin Group; western regional manager of technical services for Boole & Babbage; and manager, Services and Systems, Manufacturing Engineering, McDonnell Douglas Corporation. Mr. Gould has also been a consultant to the U.S. General Accounting Office as well as to several branches of California state and local government. He is currently manager of Management Information Services, National Semiconductor, Hong Kong.

He received his BA in international relations and foreign economics at the University of Southern California and has done postgraduate work toward an MBA at the University of California, Berkeley. He is a professional member of the Association for Computing Machinery, Data Processing Management Association (Certified), and Association for Systems Management, as well as other professional and technical societies in the United States and in Asia.

Charles L. Hampton is director, Division of Data Processing, Board of Governors, Federal Reserve System, Washington, D.C. He was formerly manager, Computing Sciences Division, Aerojet-General Corporation, Azusa, California. He holds degrees in electrical engineering and in economics from the University of Illinois and from Claremont Graduate School, respectively.

Ephraim R. McLean is Associate Professor of Information Systems, Graduate School of Management, University of California, Los Angeles. He was the founding chairman of the Computers and Information Systems Curriculum Committee within GSM and more recently was the director of the Graduate School of Management Center for Information Studies. Before joining the UCLA faculty, he obtained his SM and PhD degrees from the Sloan School of Management at the Massachusetts Institute of Technology. Before that, he was employed for seven years by the Procter & Gamble Company in manufacturing management and systems analysis work. His undergraduate degree was in mechanical engineering from Cornell University. In addition to co-authoring this book, he has written a number of articles for academic and professional journals and has consulted for organizations in both the public and private sectors.

Eldon G. Nicholson is director, Systems and Data Services Planning and Control for Trans World Airlines, Inc., Kansas City, Missouri. In addition to his present responsibilities of equipment planning, budgeting, project management, security, and training, he has been a manager for TWA in the areas of computer operations and systems and programming. He has taught data processing for the University of Kansas Extension Center and has lectured for the American Management Association. He received his BS in business administration from the University of Kansas.

Thomas E. Reece started his career with the Los Angeles City Unified School District in 1941 as a teacher and subsequently served as an elementary school principal, an administrative assistant in the Division of Elementary Education, and an area superintendent. He received his BA in education from the University of California, Berkeley, and his EdD from UCLA. In addition to his educational career, he has had several years of engineering experience and is presently in charge of the Management Information Division, Los Angeles City Unified School District.

Carl H. Reynolds graduated from Harvard in 1945 with a bachelor's degree in physics. Following service in the U.S. Marine Corps Reserve, he joined the staff of the Woodshole Oceanographic Institution in 1946. He attended Brown University and received his master's degree in physics in 1949. After a year at the Naval Ordnance Laboratory in Washington, D.C., he became an applied mathematician at Goodyear Aircraft in Akron, Ohio, where in 1952 he was named manager of the Analog Computer Laboratory. Mr Reynolds joined IBM in Boston in 1954 and held various positions in sales, engineering, and development programming from then until 1966. From 1962 to 1966 he was manager of Systems Programming for the Systems Development Division of IBM. Between 1966 and 1970 he was associated with several small software firms, and in 1971 he was appointed corporate staff director of Computing and Data Processing for Hughes Aircraft Company, Fullerton, California.

Ward C. Sangren, coordinator of computer activities, University of California, formerly held the following positions (listed in reverse sequence): vice president and member of the board of directors, Computer Applications, Inc.; chief of mathematics and computing, General Atomic Division of General Dynamics; chief of mathematics and computing, Curtiss-Wright Research Division; assistant chief of mathematics panel, Oak Ridge National Laboratory; Assistant Professor of Mathematics, Miami University (Ohio). He received a BA from Princeton in mathematics and physics and MA and PhD degrees from the University of Michigan. Dr. Sangren recently left the University of California to undertake similar responsibilities for the State of Oregon.

John V. Soden, co-author of this book, is a partner in the New York office of McKinsey & Company, Inc. His management consulting experience has included a broad range of management concerns, with particular emphasis on information services management. Prior to joining McKinsey, Dr. Soden consulted with the RAND Corporation, a number of high-technology manufacturers, and a proprietary software firm.

Dr. Soden holds a PhD in operations research from Cornell University, as well as BS and MS degrees in engineering from North Carolina State University. His articles have appeared in *Cahiers du Centre d'Etudes de Recherche Operationelle, Corporate Financing, Data Base, Data Management, Harvard Business Review, Management Science,* and *Operations Research*. He is a frequent speaker at national professional society meetings.

George A. Steiner is Professor of Management and Public Policy in the Graduate School of Management, UCLA. He is also the director of the Center for Research and Dialogue on Business in Society. He has had long experience in planning as a practitioner, both in business and government. He has written many books and articles on planning and on the interrelationships between business and society. He received his PhD in economics from the University of Illinois and was awarded an honorary LittD from Temple University for his business publications.

P. Duane Walker is senior vice president, Humana, Inc., Louisville, Kentucky, an investor-owned company that owns and operates more than 60 acute care hospitals. He was previously manager of Business Systems Planning, and manager of Information Systems Planning and Architecture, for the IBM Corporation; manager, Management Advisory Services for Price Waterhouse and Company; and consultant on the controller's staff at Westinghouse Electric. He received his BS in mathematics at Pennsylvania State University and an MBA in management and marketing from New York University.

Laurence S. Weinstein is corporate systems controller, Xerox Corporation, Stamford, Connecticut. He also served as Information Systems Manager, Xerox Education Group, and Controller, Information Services Division. Prior to this he held systems engineering and marketing positions with the IBM Corporation and was application development manager for their Advanced Administrative System Project. He holds BS and MS degrees from the Massachusetts Institute of Technology.

Index

Numbers in *italics* indicate charts, tables, etc.